P0 73615

11-29-00

**True Security**

The Institution for Social and Policy Studies
at Yale University

The Yale ISPS Series

# TRUE SECURITY

Rethinking American Social Insurance

**MICHAEL J. GRAETZ**

**JERRY L. MASHAW**

YALE UNIVERSITY PRESS NEW HAVEN & LONDON

Set in Adobe Garamond type by dix!, Syracuse, New York.

Printed in the United States of America.

Library of Congress Cataloging-in-Publication Data

Graetz, Michael J.

　　True security : rethinking American social insurance / Michael J. Graetz and Jerry L. Mashaw.

　　　　　p.　　cm. — (The Yale ISPS series)

　　Includes bibliographical references and index.

　　ISBN 0-300-08150-2 (cloth : alk. paper). — ISBN 0-300-08194-4 (pbk. : alk. paper)

　　1. Social security—United States.　I. Mashaw, Jerry L.　II. Title. III. Series.

HD7125.G69　2000

368.4'3'00973—dc21　　　　　　　　　　　　　　　　　　　99-30910

　　　　　　　　　　　　　　　　　　　　　　　　　　　　　　　　　　CIP

A catalogue record for this book is available from the British Library.

10　9　8　7　6　5　4　3　2　1

*For our children and grandchildren:*
*Casey, Dylan, Jake G., Jake M., Jay, Lilly, Lisa, Lucas, Mark, Mary, Paige,*
*Samantha, Sydney*

# Contents

# Acknowledgments

*True Security* is one product of a long collaboration—a collaboration whose boundaries are barely discernible. We first taught a seminar on distributional issues in law a quarter century ago at the University of Virginia. The time boundary stretches at least that far. Since then our personal and intellectual friendship has survived vast spatial separations and many twists and turns in our individual interests. Reunited at Yale in the 1980s, we began to explore a series of discrete policy domains—health care, pensions, federal-state roles and relationships, and finally the whole of social insurance—in a series of year-long seminars on the design of public institutions. This book tells something of what we have learned over that extended intellectual journey and argues for what we have come to believe about the design of effective and durable social insurance programs in the United States.

Our debts to the students, colleagues, and academic institutions that have supported, informed, and criticized this joint enterprise can be only partially acknowledged and never repaid. We have been blessed with students of high intellect and endless curiosity; with colleagues (both at Yale and elsewhere in the academic and policy community) who combine enormous learning with generous critical instincts; and with academic homes where the pursuit of knowledge for its own sake, wherever it leads, is the defining institutional ethic. From among the many who may have contributed to our understanding, a few demand special mention because of their direct contributions to this book.

Several of our colleagues at Yale offered helpful comments on various drafts, including Bruce Ackerman, Anne Alstott, Bob Ellickson, Alvin Klevorick, John Langbein, Ted Marmor, and Kathleen Sullivan. We also received useful guidance from workshops and seminars at Harvard University's John F. Kennedy School, the Brookings Institution, the National Academy of Social Insurance, and the Robert Wood Johnson Health Policy Seminar at Yale. Jacob Hacker, David Halperin, and Bob Myers all read the entire manuscript, saved us from errors, and offered extremely helpful suggestions. Dallas Salisbury of the Employee Benefit Research Institute and Eugene Steuerle of the Urban Institute were extremely generous in providing data. Figure 12.2 is reproduced with permission of Greenwood Publishing Group, Inc., Westport, CT.

Many students have assisted us in large and small ways. They include Elbert Lin, Kevin Cremin, Kristin Madison, Josh Galper, Sachin Pandya, Noah Messing, and Eileen Chung. Zoë Neuberger prepared the figures and tables—a crucial task that she carried off with great dedication, care, and unflappable good humor. This thank you is inadequate to express our gratitude to her.

Gene Coakley and Laura Orr of the Yale Law Library were, as always, tireless in answering our inquiries and locating books and other resources for us. Our dean, Tony Kronman, was generous in his financial support for our research, and a grant from the Institute for Social and Policy Studies at Yale facilitated publications. Special thanks also to John Covell at the Yale University Press for his support and enthusiasm.

Marcia Mayfield and Patricia Page typed and retyped and typed again the many versions of this manuscript. They can hardly contain their joy at its completion.

Finally, thanks to the *Annie M.,* who avoided leading us to where the fish were, thereby facilitating many long and fruitful conversations on Long Island Sound about the content of the pages that follow.

## Prologue  Of Fables, Fears, and Fundamentals

Recall our childhood friends the Three Little Pigs, children sent out by their mother to seek their fortunes. Each meets a man who, simply for their asking, offers them building materials for a house—the first, straw; the second, twigs; and the third, bricks. Potential calamity soon comes calling in the form of a large-lunged wolf bent on huffing and puffing their newly built houses to the ground and eating the pigs. The wolf easily blows down the straw house and has only a bit more trouble with the one built of sticks; but the third pig, who had made his house windproof by building it of bricks, ultimately triumphs by enticing the wolf down his chimney into a pot of boiling water.

In the way that we tell this story to our children and grandchildren—a way no doubt influenced by an upbeat Disney cartoon version—the practical third pig not only saves himself but also provides refuge for his two siblings, who have managed to escape the wolf. The original version is harsher. The little pigs left home not because "the time had come to go," but rather because their mother "had not enough to keep them." [1] The wolf devours the first two little pigs, and in a macabre but perfectly retributive finale, the third pig "lives happily ever after" only after eating the boiled wolf for dinner. Virtually nothing is said about the first two pigs—but wolves, it turns out, are more than a residential threat. The third pig goes apple-picking and to a fair with the wolf following; this pig ultimately escapes only by rolling home in a butter churn fortuitously found nearby.

As with all fairy tales, there is a morality lesson here, but there are many interpretations as well as many versions. One interpreter is particularly sympathetic to the second pig; he regards him as having the sad luck to be "alone, small in a world filled with predators and not especially bright or industrious, just a Joe SixPack adrift on a sea of fate without a paddle or enough sense to keep afloat."[2] A modern "politically correct" version has the wolf die from a heart attack from all his huffing and puffing coupled with a lifetime of eating food high in cholesterol.[3]

Walt Disney, who told the most influential American version, uses the story as a paean to cleverness, hard work, and personal responsibility. Disney depicted the first two pigs as foolish and lazy, wanting only to sing and play all day. He even named them "Fiddler" and "Fifer," in sharp contrast to their hardworking brother, "Practical."[4] But in Roald Dahl's version, the third pig is too clever by half and ends up as a pigskin purse for Little Red Riding Hood.[5] *Having* a brick house is good wolf protection. Yet *building* a brick house may take too long, leaving the industrious, but too fastidious, builder without shelter when the wolf happens by.

We view these tales as a complex meditation on the question of true security, and as a strong suggestion that no single strategy for achieving it is foolproof. Pigs who seek opportunity in the world can come to grief, but stay-at-homes may find that personal resources are too meager to provide for their families. We all sometimes benefit from the generosity of strangers, but how much their kindness adds to our security depends on what we do with what we are given. When planning our lives to maximize our own security, the long view may be prudent—or a formula for disaster. Individual responsibility is crucial, but it will not guard us against all hazards.

## THE HOUSE THAT ROOSEVELT BUILT

When the Disney cartoon was released in 1933, the Big Bad Wolf was widely taken as a metaphor for the Depression. The finale, with all three pigs merrily singing "Who's Afraid of the Big Bad Wolf," was viewed as an appropriate and uplifting response to those hard times, a "national rallying cry." [6]

While the Disney cartoon was providing homiletic encouragement to a frightened populace, Franklin Roosevelt was trying to shape his own response to the Depression. He had no intention of rewarding laziness or inventing incentives for indolence, but he recognized that in modern America true family security was both an individual and societal responsibility. President Roosevelt's Committee on Economic Security (CES) produced a comprehensive blueprint for building a program of social insurance in the United States, a program that was designed to keep at bay the wolves of cyclical and structural unemployment, along with those who appeared in the form of the absence, premature death, illness, disability, or old age of the family's breadwinner.[7] Congress failed to deliver the full brick house Roosevelt desired, but he did obtain enactment of the Social Security Act. That statute provided immediate aid to the elderly poor and to poor dependent children and their adult caretakers. It also began the program of retirement pensions that is now virtually synonymous with "Social Security."

Congress enacted major amendments to the Social Security Act in 1939, adding spousal benefits for retirees and survivors' benefits for the dependents of deceased contributors. Simultaneous or near simultaneous action put in place a variety of jobs programs, of which the Works Progress Administration (WPA) is the best known, and prodded all states to enact unemployment insurance programs. Disability insurance was added in the late 1950s. Universal national health insurance, which the CES also endorsed, has never become law, but health coverage for the elderly (Medicare) and the poor (Medicaid) was enacted in the 1960s. In 1970 the Supplemental Security Income (SSI) program replaced earlier programs of federal support for state aid to poor persons who are also blind, aged, or disabled.

Elsewhere in the industrialized world, social insurance has for nearly a century guarded against a similar group of risks to family income. As in the United States, illness, disability, unemployment, old age, childhood poverty, and death of the family breadwinner are the usual "wolf-at-the-door" threats to family well-being that are covered.

Anybody's list of the most successful laws ever enacted by Congress surely would include both Social Security and Medicare. For decades, Social Security has been known as the third rail of American politics; any politician who tries to "reform" it courts grave political danger. Medicaid, which provides health insurance for the poor, enjoys almost as much public support—as do unemployment insurance and disability insurance. Together these programs provide a crucial, but still incomplete, system of "social insurance," one that guards against many of the basic risks to family economic security. American social insurance thus represents one of the greatest triumphs of twentieth-century domestic public policy.

## CONTEMPORARY CONCERNS

Today the edifice of social insurance begun in the 1930s faces huffing and puffing from many critics, who are prompted principally by a vision of future financial difficulties. The aging of the baby-boom generation, along with increasing life expectancies, means that both Social Security and Medicare must increase their funding, reduce their benefits, or perhaps both. If recent trends persist and the fastest growing segment of the American population continues to be those over age eighty, these financial problems will only get worse. Medicaid has become the eight-hundred-pound gorilla of state budgetary politics—causing financial stress for state budgets and crowding out opportunities for other innovations. "Entitlement" is rapidly becoming a political epithet, notwithstanding the popularity of these entitlement programs and the impossibility of assuring financial security without a legally enforceable promise to pay.

Influential economists have argued that, despite their popularity, social insurance programs are costly to the nation's economy. They believe that the Social Security and Medicare programs contribute to the nation's low rate of savings and, thus, are a drag on economic growth. Whatever the truth of that charge, the growth of payroll taxes to finance Social Security and Medicare has been stunning—quadrupling from 10 percent of total budget receipts in the 1950s to 40 percent in the 1990s. Middle-income workers now routinely pay more in wage taxes than in income taxes. And many argue that workers are not getting their "money's worth" from their contributions to Social Security pensions because, on average, they might make more money investing their payroll taxes in the stock market. By contrast, others complain that cutbacks in programs for the poor have destroyed the safety net for the most economically disadvantaged American families. To listen to the critics, our social insurance protections today have become simultaneously inadequate and unaffordable.

Ideological opponents of social insurance programs view this atmosphere of complaint and disappointment as an opportunity to undo the nation's longstanding approach to social insurance. They delight in characterizing Social Security as a Ponzi scheme, while knowing full well that, whatever its financial stresses, the government's taxing power makes such a label absurd.[8]

Behind the hyperbole, however, lie genuine problems and a real danger that the long-term political support for social insurance programs could come unglued. America's young people—Generation X—are said to doubt that they will ever see their promised retirement benefits. Polls reveal unprecedented levels of skepticism. The favorite (and inaccurate) story is that more young people believe in space aliens than that they will receive a Social Security pension.[9] Upper-income citizens are simultaneously observing that they could achieve far greater personal financial returns from private investments than from Social Security. This threatens a political "revolt of the haves" like those that spurred popular anti-tax measures such as Proposition 13 in California.[10]

These concerns about personal stakes in social insurance arrangements play into the hands of those who believe that America's current constellation of programs is simply unsustainable and must be scrapped. A chorus of critics have taken up the mantra that anything social insurance can do well, individual savings and private insurance markets can do better.

Financial and political stresses on social insurance programs are not unique to America. Europe and Japan, for example, face far worse demographic prospects: their populations are older and aging faster than ours. Because of the greater robustness of their social insurance arrangements, they also already impose much higher payroll taxes than we do, leaving them much less room to maneuver. Hence both here and abroad a political battle is looming over the future shape of social insurance arrangements.

But the debate is seldom described or carried on in those terms. Discussions are instead "crisis" driven and programmatically and institutionally fragmented. Rather than asking how much and what forms of social insurance protection Americans need and can afford, policymakers lurch from one financial crisis to another. Fearing the political fallout from reshaping popular policies, they put this or that program's future into the hands of an advisory board here, a bipartisan commission there. These politically insulated, ad hoc groups often devise a temporary fix for financial troubles in one or another program and then disappear until a financial crisis emerges somewhere else. This process cannot address fundamental issues of programmatic goals or institutional means. We seem never to have a national conversation about social insurance as a whole.

Indeed, while various social insurance *programs* often engage our attention, "social insurance" is not really a familiar term to most Americans. We tend to talk about "Social Security" or "Medicare," about "workers' compensation" or "unemployment compensation," about "welfare" or the "Earned Income Tax Credit"—the programmatic embodiments of various social insurance approaches. Public concern and debate are limited to particular programs—and are usually occasioned by claims of scandal or the projection of future financial calamity. Policy wonks write jargon-filled essays about "entitlements" financing and about choices between "universal" and "means-tested" programs. But these limited exceptions tend to prove the rule: policy debates about social insurance are fragmented into program-by-program controversies that seldom engage the fundamental question of how to provide Americans with effective and affordable social insurance protections.

This incomplete approach is a big mistake. We would think it foolish for a private household to debate whether it could afford a new winter coat for Grandma without considering whether the children needed new shoes or the furnace was about to expire. Nor would it make much sense for a family to fret about the emptiness of Dad's coin purse when Mom's wallet was stuffed with cash. But in the world of social insurance, we often fall into that sort of thinking.

For example, many have called attention to the shocking childhood poverty statistics—approximately one in four American children between birth and six years old live in poverty. But this depressing tale is seldom connected to other stories that help to explain it: the irrelevance of Social Security survivors' insurance to the single, divorced, or never-married parent households that account for a substantial percentage of childhood poverty; the increasing numbers of contingent, low-wage workers cut off from employer-based social insurance benefits; the precipitous decline in the real coverage of unemployment insurance; and the always spotty public and private protections against workers' loss of earnings through illness and disability.

More examples could be given, but the point is clear enough: a careful, thoughtful, and detailed examination of particular programs and particular problems is necessary. But it has been a long time—about seven decades—since Americans have considered broadly what types of social insurance they want and how much they want to pay for those protections.[11] There is a critical need to expand the conversation to try to make sense of our social insurance arrangements and to ask how existing programs relate to the overall purpose of cushioning economic risks in a capitalist society. What combination of individual and collective action will produce the true security that we all want?

## THE COMPLEX WORLD OF SOCIAL INSURANCE

In order to pursue that question, we must do more than look at interconnections among social insurance programs. We must carefully and consciously distinguish between the goals of social insurance and the programs or techniques that promote income security. For much that is social insurance in the panoply of American income security programs is hardly recognized as such.

The popularity and success of big programs like Social Security pensions and Medicare induce a sort of historical amnesia. Unless a program is structured like one of these, with wage tax "contributions," "trust funds," specific benefit packages, federal administration, and all the rest, we do not think of it as social insurance. We tend to forget that, like the Three Little Pigs, the 1930s architects of America's income protection programs used the materials that came to hand. They used general resources and benefits limited to the most needy to deal with the pressing problems of poverty in old age and to rescue the states' collapsing "mothers' pension" programs. They engaged in massive public jobs creation, and they stimulated state unemployment insurance coverage by an almost comical federal tax scheme that imposed a tax that was never meant to be collected.

In later years, strategies shifted. Pension and health insurance coverage was stimulated by massive tax subsidies to employment-based plans and individual retirement savings. Disability coverage was begun through a grant-in-aid program that was partially financed and wholly administered at the state level and limited to needy beneficiaries. But that program was then federalized and became a supplement to the federal disability insurance program put in place in the mid-1950s. A decade later, health insurance for the elderly (Medicare) was added.

But even Medicare flaunts the conventional "social insurance" model. Hospital payments are financed by a payroll tax, but physicians' services are covered by voluntary premiums subsidized by a massive infusion of general revenues. Health care coverage and pension savings for active workers have been subsidized by "tax expenditures" (the failure to tax earnings received in the form of health insurance coverage or employer contributions to a pension plan). And income support for poor working families has also migrated to the tax code in the form of the Earned Income Tax Credit.

We ignore this history of multiple programs and the heterogeneous techniques that they embody at our peril, for by failing to recognize and assess the full range of social insurance coverage now in place, we miss opportunities for making our arrangements more effective. Similarly, some of what we do recognize as social insurance could be abandoned or radically reshaped while maintaining—indeed, improving—current commitments. Conflating the defense of Social Security or Medicare with the defense of the idea of social insurance limits our possibilities.

### THE BASIC PLOT LINE

The chapters that follow will reveal that there is some substance to claims that American social insurance provision is simultaneously inadequate and unaffordable. But ultimately we will show that such claims are overblown. Like Marc Anthony, we come to praise social insurance, not to disparage it. Yet Anthony's oration hardly ignored Caesar's faults. We must rethink social insurance in order to get a clearer vision of its appropriate goals; to appreciate how well those goals are currently being met; and to explore and evaluate alternative techniques for providing a truly adequate and affordable social insurance system—the true security that all Americans crave.

Telling our full tale will obviously take us down many highways and byways, but we should always keep our destination in view. We seek to convince you of a few straightforward propositions. First, social insurance is a crucial underpinning of a vibrant market economy. For a host of reasons, the citizens of developed nations properly demand and institute social insurance programs to buffer the inherent risks of working and living in a market economy.

Second, these risks to family economic security have much in common.

We live almost exclusively by current labor income or from savings out of past labor income. And like pigs rendered insecure by predators, our basic economic insecurities lie in some incapacity to provide for ourselves by participating in the labor market. These incapacities include youth and advanced age, as well as the involuntary unemployment, illness, disability, or death of a family breadwinner. The incidence and importance of these risks changes throughout the life cycle of each individual. Moreover, once we know something about our individual genetic endowments, family circumstances, and the like, these risks vary dramatically across individuals of the same age.

But before we know who we are, what sort of families we are born into, and something about our likely economic fates, we all face similar risks. And given uncertainty about the future, "individual economic security" is always to some degree problematic. It is this vision of our common fates—the intuition that undergirds the common sentiment "There, but for the grace of God, go I"—that provides the most important moral foundation for universalistic social insurance provision. However different our personal histories, we also share a common humanity that binds us together in a common enterprise.

Third, the essential commonality of the risks that social insurance addresses does not demand or even imply that they can all be addressed in the same fashion. Collective provision for economic security always threatens to undermine rather than support individual effort and responsibility. But this so-called moral hazard—the idea that when you are protected against the consequences of a risk you will behave cavalierly toward incurring it—varies enormously with the types of economic risks in question. People cannot age more rapidly to collect a retirement pension, nor will income supports for children limit their labor force participation. Substituting government payments for the earned income of prime-age, able-bodied workers, by contrast, is fraught with the potential for reducing work effort.

Moreover, moral hazard aside, techniques must fit the realities of risks and of family or individual circumstances. Requiring everyone to save for their old age may protect against an impoverished retirement, but it will have no effect on childhood poverty and only limited efficacy when careers are interrupted or cut short by death, disability, or unemployment. Subsidizing wages may protect against inadequate income for children whose parents earn low wages, but those subsidies will not be enough to cushion the shock of a major medical expense.

These considerations lead to a straightforward conclusion: Pursuit of a simple social insurance goal—family economic security in the face of common circumstances that prevent or interrupt labor force participation—must be carried on through complex and heterogeneous means.

Fourth, and here we become truly argumentative, the necessity for heterogeneous approaches does not justify the particular set of programs that now deliver social insurance to American families. For reasons of history, politics, inertia, and simple error, we have constructed a social insurance regime that is riddled with gaps, overlaps, inefficiencies, and inequities. That is how programs come to be simultaneously inadequate and unaffordable. We will argue in considerable detail that much of American social insurance provision is badly designed.

The presenting symptoms of malaise in our social insurance arrangements are different at different stages of the life cycle. For those out of the workforce because of their youth, it is the extraordinarily high rate of poverty. For those in their prime working years, it is largely gaps and maldistribution of coverage. For the aged, it is a combination of projected fiscal strain and limitations on existing protections.

The underlying design flaws are also heterogeneous. Effective transfer programs to combat childhood poverty have foundered on an inability to construct means to support family income that coincide with widely held and sensible beliefs concerning parental responsibility. Protections for prime-age workers suffer from misplaced reliance on the financial capacities of states and on tax-subsidized employer-based benefit packages. Retirement programs have depended too heavily both on tax-subsidy approaches and on retirement income benefits tied exclusively to the performance of labor markets. And for every stage of the life cycle, we believe that health care insurance has taken on unnecessary and complex tasks, utilized profligate financing arrangements, and failed in its core goal of protecting economic security when families incur high medical costs.

Our fundamental claim is that America can do much better without necessarily spending much, or perhaps any, more. But, effective system redesign demands that we be clear about our goals, realistic about the efficacy of different techniques, and attentive to behavioral and fiscal constraints. Even then there is no guarantee that the political will can be mustered to accomplish necessary reforms. While we are attentive to the structural features that make programs politically attractive and durable, we do not attempt to solve strategic political problems here. We take our task to be the elaboration of a morally attractive, intellectually coherent, and fiscally feasible approach to social insurance. That task is a necessary condition for useful political action.

In Part 1, we explain the rationale for social insurance in a market economy and argue for a particular conception of what counts as "social insurance." We then explore in Part 2 the risks to family income experienced by persons at different stages in the life cycle and the degree to which existing programs provide appropriate insurance against those risks. In Part 3 we begin by stepping back to make more explicit the normative and factual presuppositions that will have often been implicit in the discussion and to summarize the issues that now face American social insurance. Those understandings then guide our policy proposals in Chapters 9 through 13. We conclude in Part 4 by describing the institutional implications of our proposed approach and our understanding of the "politics" of institutional design. The epilogue provides a revised understanding of the allegory of the Three Little Pigs.

# Part One  Understanding Social Insurance

# Chapter 1  The Foundations of

# Social Insurance

Think about three pigs who are not simply fungible porkers, but who have instead lived complex and different lives. Bob Pig, for example, has a game leg and never did very well in school. Bob's labor force participation has been sporadic, and his best years have been spent at a large package-delivery company, where he has a thirty-hour-per-week job with no benefits. Bob built his house of straw because straw was the only building material he could afford.

Betsy Pig did better in school and landed a pretty good job with an accounting firm. Betsy, however, had two kids who took her out of the labor market for a while. On her return, she needed a job that provided flexible hours, good benefits, and a dependable paycheck. She managed to work this out with her employer and settled into a job with a steady, but unremarkable, living wage. A stick house Betsy could afford; bricks were out of the question.

Bartholomew Pig had well-to-do parents, went to the Harvard Business School, became an investment banker, and never married. Bartholomew could afford a brick house with ease—perhaps in a gated community.

## THE NATURAL EVOLUTION OF PRIVATE INSURANCE MARKETS

In this revisionist story of the Three Little Pigs, they— like the population as a whole—have heterogeneous circumstances and life histories. They have at least one thing in common, however. Each faces a threat from wolves and would be well advised to carry some wolf insurance. How can they achieve a reasonable level of security from this threat? Will private markets permit them to do it on their own? And on terms that they will individually and collectively find acceptable?

A number of factors may limit the private market's ability to provide reliable and affordable wolf insurance.[1] The likelihood of huffing and puffing lobos may be so difficult to predict that insurance company actuaries cannot make reliable estimates about exposure, even over large groups. Or, in insurance parlance, risks may "covary." That is, rather than Bob's risk being independent of Betsy's and Bartholomew's, wolves may show up in packs that threaten all policyholders at once. If these risks cannot somehow be diversified, private insurance may be impossible to organize.

If pigs have much better information about their risks of wolf depredation than do insurance companies, the market will be characterized by an insurance demon called "adverse selection," the tendency of those at high risk to be overrepresented in the insurance pool. If insurance companies charge premiums based on average risks, they will go broke because most of their clients will in fact be porkers at high risk. And if they assume that all buyers are in the high-risk category, their premiums will be very steep—pricing the moderate and low-risk pigs, and perhaps many high-risk pigs as well, out of the market.

Finally, many insurance markets are characterized by high "moral hazard." A pig who has insurance may change her behavior to increase the risk. With good wolf insurance, Betsy might settle for a straw house, and the whole pig community might be more likely to disband the wolf patrol. These sorts of effects are almost always present to some degree, but in certain forms of insurance they are so prevalent that private insurance is precluded.

Uncertainty, covariance of risks, adverse selection, and moral hazard are the common causes of insurance "market failure." The effects of such a failure will vary from the absence of insurance for certain kinds of risks, to high prices and limited coverage for others. Private insurers have developed many clever strategies for combating insurance market failure, but such strategies do not always work.[2]

Moreover, the mere existence of insurance does not mean that it will be available on terms or at prices that are satisfactory. The natural dynamics of private insurance markets segments risks in ways that society may well find unattractive. A private insurer cannot insure Bob, Betsy, and Bartholomew at the same rate. If a company is so foolish as to attempt to do so, it will find competitors offering both Bartholomew and Betsy lower rates because they pose lower risks. (Betsy's house was once blown down, but not every wolf will have lungs that strong.) It is the nature of private insurance to segment the market into homogeneous risks. Indeed, private insurers compete with each other as much by their creativity in segmenting markets and charging differential rates (sometimes called "underwriting") as by their service and other attributes of an insurance package.

For many purposes this market segmentation is sensible, efficient, and desirable. To the extent that high insurance premiums require changes in behavior, such as horrible drivers driving less or not at all, society is better off. And unlike pigs with wolves at the door, many risks are sufficiently minor or unlikely that not everyone would care to insure against them, or at least to be insured to the same extent. But there are a wide range of circumstances in which mandatory insurance, and subsidizing bad risks with the premiums of good risks (or from other revenue sources), also make perfect sense. Indeed, for one reason or another we "socialize" most insurance markets to some degree. Private insurance contributes to true security, but it is not likely to provide the type, level, and scope of security that any society desires. In particular, when the risk to be insured against is being out of the labor force—for a short or long period of time—private insurance coverage has proved to be spotty and incomplete.

## THE MANY REASONS FOR SOCIAL INSURANCE

### Market Failure

If the wolf insurance market is characterized by one or more of the features that cause private insurance markets to fail, but the pig community wants wolf insurance, it may find that public action can remedy the market failure. Governments have the power to tax and to regulate; private insurance companies do not. Therein lies a world of difference.

For highly uncertain risks the government can pay compensation when the risks materialize and can impose taxes to pay the costs after they are known. This sort of after-the-fact assessment is not unknown in the history of private insurance—it was the standard technique of the early English burial societies and is a hallmark of the Lloyd's of London approach to reinsurance contracts. But private attempts to use assessments in insurance contracts covering large groups have generally failed.

The taxing (and borrowing) power of government is also critical to the solution of the problem of covarying risks. A widespread and prolonged wolf infestation can wipe out private insurers; governments are more permanent. They can borrow to meet current emergencies on the credible commitment to tax later to retire their debts. Private insurers cannot conscript either new investors or new policyholders.

Regulation is the critical device for combating adverse selection and moral hazard. Indeed, in the face of a government mandate that everyone be insured, adverse selection simply disappears. Moral hazard is not so easily solved, even with the power of government, but that power sometimes helps. For example, while the pig community may not wish to ban straw houses when providing wolf insurance, it can limit its exposure by requiring wolf alarms, zoning high-risk dwellings out of forests, and increasing the effectiveness of the wolf police.

Combating market failures in private insurance markets clearly provides a fundamental basis for collective action to support or create insurance against important community risks. But social insurance also emerges where some forms of private insurance would be available. Here the approach is not necessarily to create a market, but to change its character in order to pursue broader social goals or to implement basic social values.

### Solidarity

A society made up of Bob, Betsy, and Bartholomew might well decide out of simple moral sentiment to treat wolf insurance as a collective good. As pigs facing ever-present wolf threats, they may view themselves as all in the same boat. It may simply be unacceptable for Bob, who needs wolf insurance most and can afford it least, to go uncovered.

This desire to treat everyone alike, although they are demonstrably different, is sometimes explained by a "social contract" metaphor. If we think of the pigs as making their social contract about how their society is to be organized before their lives begin, they would have little or no information about what their lives would in fact be like. Given little information about where they would start or end up in the income distribution, it may seem in everyone's interest to agree to the collective provision of affordable wolf insurance in order that they all have reasonable protection against foreseeable risks. And, of course, much of the information they do have now, such as Bob's game leg and Bartholomew's plentiful family resources, may seem a morally arbitrary basis upon which to decide whether each should be left to his or her own devices in the labor and insurance markets.

### Obligation

Pigs with lower rates on their wolf insurance might also feel that they have some obligation to assist those in riskier circumstances because their behavior, or some aspect of social organization that benefits them, actually increases those risks. Sensible wolves will not waste their time huffing and puffing at Bartholomew's brick house. They will pass on to Betsy's, or better yet, Bob's, as likely candidates for producing a porcine meal. Bartholomew's choice is not irrelevant to Bob or Betsy's risks.

In addition, the institutions of private property and free markets that produce Bartholomew's wealth, and thereby give him the freedom to build a brick house, also affect Betsy's and Bob's situations. If Bartholomew's actions, and the institutions that produce his good fortune, increase the premiums Bob and Betsy face by increasing their risks, they all may feel that he has some special obligation to contribute to their purchase of protection.

### Self-Regard

Bartholomew may also find that it is in his personal interest to help Bob and Betsy insure. After all, in Walt Disney's story of the Three Little Pigs, the pig with the brick house ended up with two—perhaps long-term—guests. Bartholomew may well believe that he will be unable to refuse Bob and Betsy's request for refuge. And he may prefer to contribute to their insurance premiums so that they can live independently, rather than risk having them camp out for months or years in his guest rooms.

### Paternalism

This self-regarding motivation is closely connected to various forms of paternalism. Pigs with low risks may think that those with higher risks should make some provision for a time when the wolf is at the door. But given the latter's low incomes and high private insurance rates, they are unlikely to do so. And given the natural piggy tendency not to value things they can't afford, Bob and Betsy are likely to underestimate the risk of carnivorous windbags as well. Even if they could afford some insurance, they might not buy any.

If Bartholomew wants the Bob and Betsy pigs of the world to have insurance and to make a contribution toward their own protection, his best recourse may be to participate with them in a community-wide social insurance pool. With social insurance Bob and Betsy will be able to get back on their feet, *and* they will make some contribution to their own protection. Without it, Bartholomew must witness his fellows' suffering and perhaps provide them with a humiliating handout—or he may find himself stuck with tax bills for a public shelter for pigs whose houses have been blown away.

### Social Harmony and Productivity

Finally, the availability of insurance to protect against known risks may be an important determinant of the overall stability and productivity of society. Everybody is better off if Bob and Betsy devote their talents to tasks other than worrying about wolves; engaging in armed self-defense, which may put others at risk; or agitating for wolf extermination or anti-wolf zoning regulation. At some level of insecurity Bob and Betsy will simply be unwilling to support a system that makes Bartholomew fat, happy, and safe while they are lean, surly, and anxious.

In short, a guarantee of insurance against certain risks may not only free up human resources, it may also avoid various sorts of regulation—or even more fundamental changes in a society's political or economic organization—that would stifle social productivity in general. It is frequently said that social insurance began as a crucial part of capitalism's answer to Karl Marx. Marx famously believed that the insecurity characteristic of capitalist means of production—including its tendency toward subsistence wages and the inevitability of workers' losses of income through industrial accident, unemployment, and redundancy due to old age—would render capitalist society unstable and unsustainable. In the end, Marx thought workers would be forced to seize the means of production in order to stabilize incomes and achieve reasonable levels of economic security.

But, so the conventional story goes, Germany's "Iron Chancellor," Otto von Bismarck, was too shrewd. By instituting workers' compensation, and then additional programs of social insurance and labor market protection, Bismarck and his counterparts in other European societies interrupted their capitalist economies' march off the precipice. Cushioned by protections against illness, old age, injury, and unemployment, a regulated but relatively free market in labor became bearable for workers. The upside of the market looked far more promising once a floor on the downside had been provided. Chancellor Bismarck pioneered social insurance to combat socialism and the rise of labor parties not because he was a notorious softie. Rather, he recognized that in a very real sense the true security of the nation depended upon adequate social insurance for its families.

We view all of these bases for social insurance as perfectly sensible—at least in principle. To be sure, paternalism can get out of hand, and solidarity may be a treacherous foundation for long-term commitments in a changing world. Too much focus on security can stifle productivity, thereby undermining market capitalism rather than sustaining it. And market failure justifies state intervention only if "government failure" is not the predictable outcome. But the possibility of excess should not blind us to the collective good sense of social insurance provision. Our contention here is just this: the many good reasons for social insurance overdetermine its existence. The primacy of individual and family responsibility for economic well-being notwithstanding, sensible argument in any society must be about "how" and "how much" social insurance to provide, not about "whether to have any."

Given the multiple motivations for particular security arrangements, we will not spend much energy attempting to unravel the "true" bases of existing programs. Nor will we justify our proposed reforms by tediously exploring just how they relate to the goals of correcting market failure by producing social solidarity, achieving an appropriate counterweight to individual myopia, assuring widespread (if not universal) individual contributions to social insurance protections, or undergirding and sustaining a market economy. These are judgments to be made in context and, even then, are highly contestable. But the particular conclusions to be found in these pages proceed from our fundamental understanding of the core functions of social insurance.

For example, we embrace the American commitment to providing social insurance against the risk of impoverishment in old age. But, while familiar, this stance toward collective rather than family responsibility is hardly the result of some invariant "natural law." At an earlier time in American history, and currently in other cultures, the presumption was and is that adult children bear responsibility for the support of their aged parents.

We accept the good sense of some form of social provision against the risk of an impoverished old age not because such a provision is universally available, but because it conforms to our understanding of the role of social insurance in cushioning the common risks to income security in a market economy. Those risks demonstrably include removal from the labor market because of old age, combined with widespread inability to acquire, or inattention to acquiring, adequate individual wealth to live on in retirement.

Our understanding of the role of social insurance in ameliorating the effects of age-induced lack of labor income, however, also leads us in a direction contrary to the current social consensus. Americans seem reasonably content to pay taxes to support their and other people's parents, but bridle at paying for the support of other people's children. We agree that parents have primary responsibility for support of their children, but we believe that social insurance has a larger role here than is reflected in current American social insurance practices. Children, after all, face a common risk—that they will simultaneously lack labor income of their own and fail to have parents capable of supporting them. As we explain in more detail in later chapters, youthful poverty risks parallel the risks of destitution in old age. We propose, therefore, a much more active role for social insurance in protecting children's income security than that which is now embodied in U.S. social programs targeted at children or families with children.

Our conception of the role of social insurance also commits us to an understanding of effective action that does not shrink from requiring universal participation in programs. Social insurance entails both substantial redistribution of income across the life cycle of individuals and more modest, but still substantial, redistributions across families. As our discussion of health insurance and old-age pensions in the private sector will demonstrate, voluntarism—even highly subsidized voluntarism—will not produce true security. Moreover, putting the young and the old or the rich and the poor in separate insurance pools, as private markets would, will often produce coverage only for low-risk populations. Its dominant effect will be limited to forcing the affluent to spread their income prudently over their own life cycle. True security for all Americans demands that most social insurance programs treat everyone as sharing the same risk characteristics. This means that programs will skew benefits toward those who are able only to pay lower "premiums."

Rugged individualism and social insurance are not comfortable bedfellows, and we will not pretend that struggles between liberty and security, or individual and collective responsibility, are not at stake. Our task, therefore, is to convince you that our vision of social insurance puts these competing values into an appropriate balance. Individual or family responsibility for economic security is and must remain the primary organizing principle in a market economy. But no society can have the cake of true security and eat from the full larder of pure individual responsibility at the same time.

It is also our view, following Bismarck, that too much can be made of this competition between the demands of the market and the demands of security. A mix of individual and collective responsibility is the only realistic approach. Every step away from individual responsibility is not a step away from the true path of either liberty or economic productivity. High levels of economic insecurity do not make people free. And voters will not long support a system of economic organization that relies wholly on free markets and a "Devil-take-the-hindmost" approach to those who lose out in the free-for-all of labor market competition. Social insurance protections and individual responsibility must live together in some fashion for capitalist societies to survive and prosper.

## THE COMPLEX AND CONTESTED WORLD OF SOCIAL INSURANCE

We cannot, therefore, charge ahead to consider current and possible social insurance arrangements before pausing to examine some more basic questions. What kinds of risks require public rather than private insurance? And what sorts of public actions fit within the general framework of social insurance? Life is full of risks, and there are hundreds of ways to try to protect against them. Which risks are important enough to justify public concern? Where do we draw the line between private and public responsibility? How is social insurance different from social policy in general?

Viewed historically, answers to these questions are not too difficult to provide. Social insurance in the United States is a twentieth-century creation, largely a product of the Great Depression. Before that, economic security was mostly a family responsibility. Children worked beside their parents on the farm or in the family's business after school. Family members who became too old to work were supposed to be cared for by the next generation; the pastoral image was Grandpa at the fireside waiting to greet his hardworking children and grandchildren as they returned from the fields. (Grandmas never retired from housework and other chores.) Family members who became disabled were cared for within the family. Private philanthropy provided some assistance.

Employment-based protections were spotty. The clergy were often cared for by their churches or synagogues. But few private employers took responsibility for the economic security of their workers until workers' compensation legislation made them responsible for injuries on the job. The employer-based pension and health insurance systems that are commonplace today had not yet come into being.

Government generally took responsibility only for its military and civilian employees, who were protected by federal or state pensions and health and disability insurance. A number of states did provide cash assistance for widows and orphans. A few large employers had introduced some pension benefits. Anyone else without an income was supported by relatives or was relegated to the "poorhouse."

The industrialization and urbanization of late-nineteenth- and early-twentieth-century America radically changed the reality of family-based security arrangements long before the Great Depression of the 1930s forced collective attention to the problems that Progressive reformers had documented and decried. But political action was generally postponed until suddenly nearly everyone's family income was viewed as at risk. When the Depression hit, the wolves the reformers had warned us about were clearly at the door—and no entity other than the national government had the capacity to respond.

President Roosevelt's 1935 Committee on Economic Security proposed a comprehensive scheme of social insurance to provide protections against what were then perceived to be life's major threats to family income—loss of parental support, old age, death of the family breadwinner, disability, illness, and unemployment. But that scheme was never completed. Over the years, Americans—benefited and burdened by the New Deal legacy—have continued to add and subtract, modify and reaffirm a vision that has been all but lost behind the details of and political struggles surrounding particular programs.

Indeed, once history and individual programs are left behind, getting a handle on the domain of social insurance is not easy. Social insurance has no "essence." It is defined concretely for any society by the complex interaction of collective purposes and acceptable political techniques. It changes over both time and space as a result of political struggle concerning both ends and means. And historical baggage and political conflict aside, many crucial conceptual boundaries of social insurance are blurry at best. To define social insurance is thus to argue for a particular conception of it. That is not only the particular task of Chapter 2, but also the burden of the remainder of this book.

# Chapter 2 The Social Insurance Contract

"Private insurance" is usually thought of as a contract to pool common risks so that statistically predictable economic losses will be experienced as small subtractions from all insured persons' wealth rather than as calamities for a few. "Social insurance" also pools risks. But social insurance is dependent on government action, directed at a particular class of risks and designed to pursue societal purposes that could not or would not be achieved through individual contracting in private insurance markets.

Social insurance is not merely a variation on private insurance. It is a different product—a social rather than an individual (or group) contract. But the relationship between the two forms of insurance is not just metaphorical. Private insurance and social insurance arrangements must address some common questions: What risks or "events" will be insurable? What level of protection against those risks is to be provided? Who is to be covered? How is coverage to be paid for? And how can insurance protection be structured to limit undesirable behavioral adaptations that might increase costs, undermine other goals, or both?

## RISKS COVERED BY THE SOCIAL
## INSURANCE CONTRACT

In a market economy, income is obtained in two ways: by providing labor, and by supplying capital. Most who have capital income have it because of savings from labor income. A few "propertied" families aside, the critical risks to an individual or family lie in not having the types of capacities to earn income that the market values. In short, the distinctive risk that social insurance addresses is the risk of inadequate labor income.

This unitary risk emerges in many forms and in varying intensities. For some, loss of access to labor income may be complete and permanent, such as when death or total and permanent disability strikes. Others may lose labor income only episodically, temporarily, or partially as in the case of unemployment or less severe illnesses or injuries. For yet others, the risk occurs as part of the normal progress of the life cycle. Both youth and old age tend to put one out of the labor market.

### A Life Cycle Perspective on Risks

Indeed, risks to labor income change so substantially over the course of a person's life that we tend to view them as different in kind. Children are not expected to work. In early childhood they cannot, and later they are often prohibited from or limited in the amount of work they are allowed to do. Unless they inherit wealth, children have no opportunity to amass capital by saving. In childhood, therefore, the dominant threat to income security is the risk that one's parents or custodians have insufficient income and resources to provide an adequate level of support. Hence, we tend to think of the child's risk not as the risk of lacking labor income, but as the risk of being in a particular economic condition or status, *childhood poverty*.

During the working years, the focus of our concern shifts. Our anxieties typically relate to loss of income from illness or accident, loss of a job because of economic dislocation or family responsibilities, or inadequate income because of persistent low wages. These risks to workers tend to be thought of as risks of *low wages* or *loss of wage income*.

When we consider our retirement years, we tend to think in yet different terms. In some ways, retirement in old age can resemble leaving the workforce due to disability or unemployment. Decline in personal physical and mental capacities or changes in the skills the market demands surely explain much retirement behavior. And because this decline tends to happen to everyone who lives long enough, the risk of old age is similar to the risk of youth. Some retirements, of course, seem "voluntary"—the purchase of leisure time with prior work effort. And most of us hope that at least some of our retirement years will be of this sort.

Whatever the cause, we expect that virtually everyone will experience two periods out of the labor market, first as a child, then again as an elderly adult. In the latter case, we often conceive of the risk to economic well-being not as lost labor income, but as having *inadequate savings* to support us in old age. But to glimpse how similar this risk is to that of children, remember that in an earlier era we might well have characterized the risk in old age as the risk that our children would be unable to support us.

Because these risks are thought of differently—inadequate childhood resources, loss of wage income, and insufficient retirement savings—they tend to be addressed in different ways and by different programs. Moreover, as we shall see, there are many practical reasons for structuring social insurance differently when responding to risks at different stages in the life cycle. Nevertheless a fundamental unity of purpose lies behind this multiplicity of policy initiatives. The domain of social insurance includes a society's overall set of policy responses to the risks of inadequate income and resources from participation in the labor market. Social insurance, operating through direct transfers, subsidies, or regulation, alters the distributive consequences that labor markets and private insurance (or annuity) markets would otherwise produce.

### Risks and Current Realities

While generally successful, American social insurance is doing very badly in some arenas. Looking over the life cycle, our social insurance efforts provide quite well for older and retired workers, reasonably well for workers in their middle years, but, as the childhood poverty statistics suggest, very poorly for children.

Indeed, looking just at important cash (or near cash) transfer programs, as figure 2.1 shows, American social insurance has a dramatic skew toward the later years of the life cycle. It provides a relatively small amount to children, modest supports for persons ages eighteen to sixty, and substantial payments to the elderly. As figure 2.2 shows, this picture changes only slightly when in-kind transfers, particularly medical care costs and subsidies in the form of tax expenditures, are added to the mix. The dual message of these figures is clear: looking only at cash social insurance transfers

Fig. 2.1.    Life-cycle breakdown of social insurance transfers

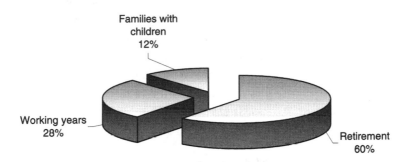

(*Source:* Authors' calculations based on FY 1996 figures contained in budgetary appendix.)

Fig. 2.2.    Life-cycle breakdown of social insurance transfers and tax expenditures

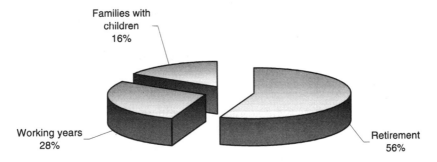

(*Source:* Authors' calculations based on FY 1996 figures contained in budgetary appendix.)

gives a very partial picture of our social insurance arrangements. But even from a comprehensive viewpoint, the system provides vastly greater support for the elderly than for any other group. As we argue later, inattention to security arrangements affecting earlier segments of the life cycle is not justified by the nature of the risks involved at those stages or the capacities of families to provide for their own security.

## TIME, CHANGE, AND SOCIAL INSURANCE

The basic categories of risks that we have identified here were clearly recognized by President Roosevelt's Committee on Economic Security. But the society and the economy have changed since the 1930s. Some changes have made old risks more pressing or highlighted new ones. Others have reduced the risks that family income will prove inadequate or have provided new techniques through which individuals or families can effectively provide for their own security. Yet others look in both directions at once. We will take up these matters in more detail later, but it is worth reflecting for a moment on how changing circumstances alter both the market risks that families face and the social insurance techniques that might be used to combat those risks. It also allows us to glimpse how the concept of an "insurable event" differs in social and private insurance.

### The Increase of Women in the Labor Force

The massive increase of women in the workforce over the last four decades, and the major impact of their earnings on family economic security, have produced perhaps the most crucial and complex effects on the contemporary consideration of what social insurance should be about. As figure 2.3 illustrates, the labor-force participation of women has more than doubled since the 1930s.

Two-earner families have higher incomes and a more diversified portfolio of workers than do single-earner families. This can translate into greater capacities to save for retirement or to ameliorate other risks to family income, such as the unemployment, illness, disability, or death of one wage earner. On the other hand, even though the *incomes* of two-

Fig. 2.3.    Female labor participation

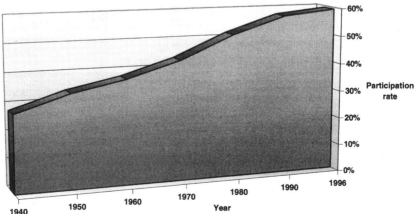

(*Source:* U.S. Historical Statistics, ser. D29-41, 58-62; *1997 Statistical Abstract,* table 630.)

earner families have increased somewhat, there has been an accompanying stagnation in each worker's *wages*. The average full-time worker in U.S. business earned $440 a week in 1996. Twenty-five years earlier, the average worker earned $517 a week in 1996 dollars. Median family income in the United States in 1996 was $42,300 (roughly the same as a decade earlier in comparable dollars). Twenty-five years earlier it was $40,100, just 5 percent less.[1]

Clearly average real wages have declined and median family income has been stagnant over recent decades. But looking at national levels of the median family income masks important differences among families, especially the large differences between one-parent and two-parent families. For example, in 1995 median family income for married-couple families was about $48,500, compared to $31,000 for single-parent families headed by a male and $20,000 for single-parent families headed by a female.[2] The very slow growth in family income in recent decades not only has reduced the "insurance effect" of having two workers when one must leave the workforce, but also has put single-earner families (particularly divorced or never-married single parents) at greater risk.

The importance of the second earner's income to the well-being of low- and middle-income families has sharply escalated the "opportunity costs" and "out-of-pocket costs" of bearing and rearing children. Among other things, the confluence of these trends has made the absence of adequate and affordable child care one of the crucial concerns of late-twentieth-century American workers—a risk that 1930s social insurance planners could hardly have anticipated. They believed that Social Security's Survivors' Insurance, buttressed by federally subsidized state programs for low-income "dependent children," would meet the income security needs of America's children. They were wrong.

## Stagnant Wages and
## Rising Returns to Capital

Other changes of similar import are not difficult to identify. The flat wages that have resulted from shifts in the labor market have perhaps been reinforced by the "globalization" of production, and surely by the slump in unionized labor. Meanwhile, in recent years returns to capital have escalated (fig. 2.4).

Conceiving of family security as turning exclusively on job holding and wage replacement makes less and less sense given these developments.

Fig. 2.4.   Returns to labor compared to returns to capital

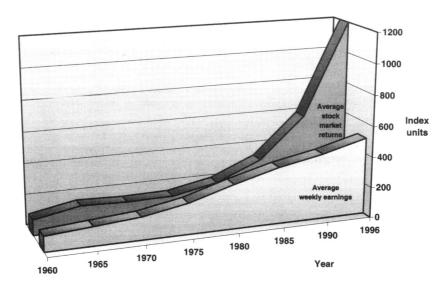

*Note:* Indexed so 1960 = 100. Stock market returns based on Standard & Poor's Common Index. (*Source: Statistical Abstract,* 1956, 1981, 1997.)

Workers increasingly need some way to supplement low wages and to connect their long-term security to the performance of both labor and capital markets. Social insurance benefits financed solely by wage taxes and calibrated to prior earnings are not necessarily effective strategies for coping with the risk and reward structures of the contemporary economy. Nor is this a necessary feature of social insurance provision. As we explain in later discussions, social insurance can offer an important vehicle for allowing all workers to share in the risks and rewards of the capital market.

### The Changing Nature of Employment

Social insurance also needs to be organized so that the dynamism of our labor markets does not undermine security arrangements tied to the financial well-being of specific firms or the continuance of specific employment relationships. America has made huge investments in tax subsidies for voluntary, employment-based health insurance coverage, disability payments, and retirement pensions. In the era of the "family wage" and expectation of long-continued employment relationships, organizing so-

Fig. 2.5.    Median number of years with current employer for male workers

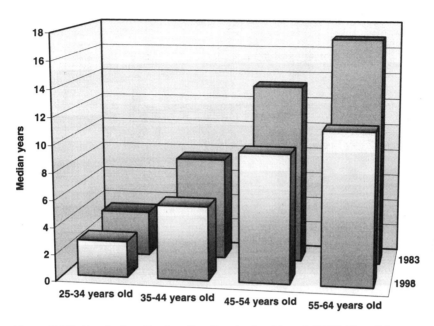

(*Source:* EBRI, *Databook on Employee Benefits,* 4th ed., table 21.8; EBRI, *Notes,* February 1999, chart 1.)

cial insurance around specific employment relations may have made more sense than it does today. Yet the support of "voluntary," employment-based insurance has always failed to cover all workers, particularly those most in need of protection. As figure 2.5 shows, very few workers have spent their entire working lives with only one employer and even fewer will do so in the years ahead.

In today's dynamic capital and labor markets, employer-based social insurance arrangements are increasingly problematic. The profitability of firms often depends on their capacities to trim labor costs through "downsizing" workers or through wage and benefit reductions. These activities may contribute substantially to efficient resource allocation, but they rapidly erode employment-based insurance protections.

### Demographic Shifts

Demography may not be destiny, but it surely sets the agenda from which alternative futures can be chosen. The baby boom, followed by the birth

Fig. 2.6.    U.S. population, by age

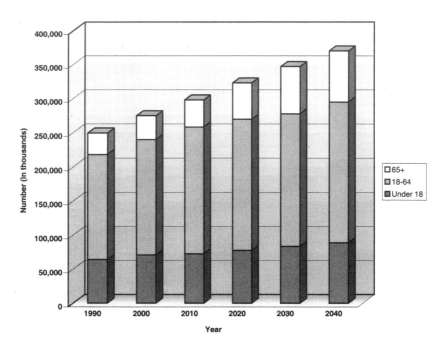

(*Source:* U.S. Census Bureau, *Population Projections of the United States by Age, Sex, Race, and Hispanic Origin: 1995-2050,* February 1996, P25-1130, table F.)

dearth, now influences everyone's thinking about how to cope with an aging population (fig. 2.6). Add increased longevity to these fertility shifts, and the promises made in our current programs of Social Security retirement pensions and Medicare look potentially very difficult to keep. As figure 2.7 shows, the ratio of the population over age sixty-five to the working population will increase dramatically beginning in the year 2010. The question then is whether changes in the transparency, security, and diversity of financial markets provide opportunities to maintain these commitments through alternative financing mechanisms, or, as some have argued, offer reasons to abandon them in whole or in part in favor of radically different approaches. At a minimum, some shift away from pay-as-you-go financing (where retiree benefits are financed by taxes on current workers) toward more "prefunding" (where workers put aside amounts to be invested and fund subsequent benefits) seems attractive.

But whatever the effects of changing demographics and family compo-

Fig. 2.7.    65-plus dependency ratio

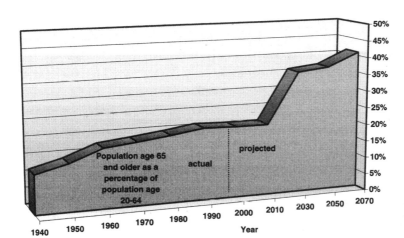

(*Source:* Authors' calculations based on data from *1998 Economic Report of the President,* table B-34, and Congressional Budget Office, *Long-Term Budgetary Pressures and Policy Options,* May 1998, table 1-1.)

sition on social programs, their effects on individual families' capacities to provide intergenerational security have been enormous. True security once resided in having a large and closely linked family that could orchestrate a dense system of intra-family transfers—not only from parents or grand-parents to children when young, but also from children to their parents when old. Those transfers are still crucially important, particularly for children. But existing family structures, themselves a response to changing economic demands and social aspirations, have changed our perceptions of how much reliance can reasonably be placed on family responsibility for its own members.

Family size has plummeted as birth rates have fallen and divorce rates have risen. Urbanization, industrialization, and demands for worker mobility have sharply reduced the percentage of the population living in "extended families"—a percentage that throughout the history of American social insurance was much smaller than popular mythology imagined it to be.[3] But whatever the realities of the past, Mom is now at work, and Grandma is not there to take care of the children. Nor do parents now expect to be supported by their children in old age. And many children must look to the fragile capacities of the law to enforce the support obligations of their absent parents.

### Price Increases for Necessities

The escalation of costs of various necessities also changes the way we should and do think about risks to income security. The aging of the population, for example, will produce only mild financial trouble for the pension system, but because of skyrocketing health care costs, enormous financial problems for Medicare. Those same accelerating health care costs fall on the non-aged as well, a population with rising, but far from skyrocketing, family incomes (fig. 2.8). The result has been increased risks combined with steadily shrinking private insurance coverage. The Committee on Economic Security recognized in 1935 that protection against health care expenses was important, but no action was taken. In 1965 Congress provided universal protections for the aged and the poor, but left most working families with whatever protection was made available by tax-subsidized, employer-based insurance. At century's close, the non-

Fig. 2.8.   Wages and medical care costs

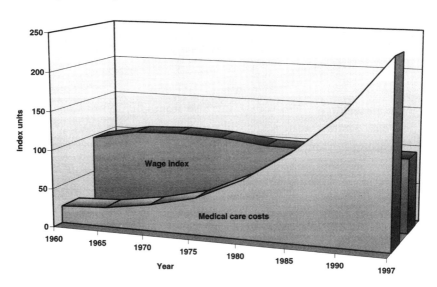

*Note:* Wage index based on average weekly earnings in constant 1982 dollars indexed so 1982–84 = 100. Medical care cost is indexed to 1982–84 consumer price index = 100. (*Source:* Authors' calculations based on data from *1998 Economic Report of the President,* tables B-47 and B-61.)

aged middle class remains the group most in need of relief from potentially devastating health care costs.

Nor is health care the only arena in which family incomes have not kept pace with the rising cost of necessities. As we detail in Chapters 6 and 12, child care, and for some groups, housing, provide other major examples. These are not independent risks that social insurance should recognize. They do, however, highlight a social insurance technique—consumption subsidies to help fund necessary expenditures—that the social insurance vision of 1935 scarcely imagined. Current programs employ this technique for low-income populations in providing food stamps and Medicaid, and for a portion of the population at all income levels in a melange of housing and child care subsidy programs. The time has come to recognize the commonalities implicit in our social supports in these areas and to unify these programs structurally by asking straightforwardly what consumption subsidies are necessary to produce true security for American families.

### Time and the Recognition of Insurable Events

We have been discussing changes that shape our understanding of the risks that social insurance might protect against and the techniques through which protection can be accomplished. But it is also important to recognize that social insurance has certain attributes that distinguish it from common forms of private insurance such as insurance against property or casualty losses. One is that "risk" from a social insurance perspective includes family circumstances that stretch over time and that may not be traceable to some particular "event."

To be sure, some social insurance risks begin with a relatively discrete occurrence—the onset of a disability because of illness or work injury, for example. But old age has no obvious "onset" and its effects on labor income depend importantly on the background environment of workplace demands and social expectations. In addition, as we have remarked, being the child of impoverished parents seems more like a "status" than an occurrence.

The interaction of time and background changes are even more dramatic when one thinks about risks that now are only partially recognized by social insurance arrangements. Persistent low wages is a good example of an "event" that may stretch across time and be the product of complex shifts in such things as family composition, labor market returns to schooling, and changing wage structures. And as we shall see, because of anticipated behavioral effects or "moral hazard," low wages may require amelioration only in part and via techniques that are indirect, partial, and conditional on work effort.

Hence, as we consider what risks to insure to give American families a measure of true security, we must confront the changes since the 1930s in three ways: first, the risks we were concerned with then may be more or less salient, differently or similarly distributed. Second, new risks may have emerged that demand independent attention and novel forms of social insurance intervention. Third, social insurance covers risks that arise from circumstances as well as from discrete events. But this breadth of application carries with it some special concerns about behavioral effects. Not every risk that fits within the general category of a threat to family economic security can be insured directly or fully without unacceptable effects on individual incentives and on individual and family responsibilities for their own well-being.

## WHO SHOULD BE COVERED BY SOCIAL INSURANCE?

Social insurance's aspiration to universalism may be the feature that distinguishes it most from private insurance. Income security is a purpose that applies to the whole of society and across each member's entire life cycle. Indeed, social insurance is a contract across generations. It presumes that its institutions are durable across time and that its coverage will come to include generations as yet unborn.

The aspiration to universalism in social insurance protections also carries with it some important practical advantages. One is the economy that results from avoiding adverse selection, a dynamic we often see at work in private insurance. Individual disability insurance, for example, is very expensive because of the concern of insurers that those who seek to purchase it know something about their own susceptibility to work disability that they are concealing from the insurer. Disability insurance becomes much more affordable if it is group insurance organized by a large employer. While buying the insurance is voluntary on the employer's part, if a group policy is purchased, coverage is usually mandatory for all employees. This guarantees the insurer that it is not getting a group of self-selected, high-risk insureds. Making social insurance mandatory, and therefore universal across the whole society, has a similar and even greater effect in limiting the problem of adverse selection.

Universal participation can also limit moral hazard. For example, for many years Australia had only a means-tested public pension system. The basic idea was that most Australians would provide for their own retirement, but some would be needy in old age and participate in the public program. In order to provide a reasonably dignified standard of living in retirement, however, the benefit payments under the means-tested scheme were set well above the level of bare subsistence. As it turned out, most Australian workers found that the annuities they could buy with their individual retirement savings provided little, if any, income above the means-tested program's benefit levels. The result was a pattern of "spending down" savings near retirement so that the majority of retired Australians became eligible for the means-tested program. In the end, Australia responded to this widespread moral hazard by instituting a mandatory public pension scheme for all.

While we will develop these ideas in much more detail later, the aspiration to universalism in social insurance has significant implications for our critique of existing programs and our proposals for social insurance for the future. Several recurring themes bear mention: first, the American system's current reliance on employer-based, voluntary protections has not produced universal coverage in any domain. And, as our discussion of the changing nature of employment suggests, these arrangements are likely to be less durable and to produce even spottier coverage in the future. Further evidence is offered by the growing number of workers who each year find themselves without health insurance. Our general approach is to rearrange public social insurance expenditures by removing the tax-based subsidies that now support voluntary employer-based income security regimes and devoting those public funds instead to mandatory, universal programs.

This does not mean that all employment-based income security arrangements will disappear. In some cases, they will serve as a way to satisfy individual mandates (for example, health insurance) or will substitute for a public scheme (such as short-term disability insurance). In the retirement context, we leave the tax subsidies for employer-based pensions in place because they serve there not as a first level of social insurance coverage, but rather as a supplement to a mandatory public Social Security pension program (which we would bolster with an additional level of mandatory individual retirement savings). In addition, we favor a tax system friendly to savings.

But as a general matter, we believe Americans have received a bad social insurance bargain from tax-subsidy investments in employer-sponsored insurance protections. To put the matter slightly differently, as subsequent chapters make clear, we view tax-supported employment-based benefits programs not as something separate from American social insurance arrangements, but as a currently defective part of those arrangements. We would modify them to more closely approximate the aspiration to universalism that is a hallmark of social insurance provision.

We find similar problems with programs that leave the financing of social insurance protections to the individual states—often with some federal financial incentive.[4] Given diverse state political cultures, one could imagine different social contracts about social insurance in different state jurisdictions. But this is generally an inefficient and inequitable approach in a national economy. Most of the policy instruments that affect the performance of the economy are within the exclusive control of the federal government. The states cannot regulate interstate or foreign commerce, modify the money supply, or control migration in or out of their jurisdictions. Yet all of these things bear importantly on the level of economic risk experienced by their citizens. And unlike a private insurance company, states that create good social insurance policies cannot protect themselves from ruinous costs by preventing high-risk populations from moving in. While the effect of "welfare magnets" may be oversold in the popular imagination, there clearly are some such effects among neighboring states. Moreover, perceptions may matter more than reality. Fear that the migration effects may be strong can fuel "races to the bottom" in which social insurance protections unravel as a means of improving the states' "business climates."

In short, we believe that devolution of financial responsibility for social insurance programs to the states is generally a bad idea. Our proposals, therefore, systematically nationalize finance and coverage requirements of social insurance, but do not necessarily nationalize administration. In many cases, implementation of national social insurance arrangements can be contracted out to state or private parties. Contracting out permits efficiencies in administration where local knowledge is important and allows the integration of income supports and services in some programs. And when the question is services (such as job training or vocation rehabilitation, for example) rather than income security, states, localities, and private entities are often superior providers.

Finally, universalism for us requires emphasis on the social contract features of social insurance. To be effective for all Americans, promises to provide income security must be both intragenerational and intergenerational. The returns to the productivity of today's workers must be shared between those workers who have not encountered the standard risks to income security and those who have (intragenerational sharing), as well as between those who are in the labor force and those who are either too young or too old to work (intergenerational sharing). Otherwise the risks to adequate labor income that we have identified across the life cycle will continue to undermine Americans' security.

This is hardly a novel idea. But, surprisingly, it is an idea that has never been systematically applied to the income security requirements of children. Americans have tended to think of children's income security needs as being met by some different regime of "welfare" or "social assistance," not by social insurance. We will argue that this is both a conceptual error and a formula for programmatic ineffectiveness.

The conceptual error lies in believing that the recipients of social insurance in retirement have "paid for their own benefits." That is simply not how Social Security pensions in the United States work. To be sure, most of today's retirees paid payroll taxes into the Social Security pension program during the whole of their working lives. But those monies were used to support a prior generation of workers during their retirement. Today's retirees are supported not by "savings" in the Social Security Trust Fund, but by the current payments of America's workers.

To put the matter in different terms, Social Security operates on the belief that it is more effective to make all of today's workers responsible for the retirement security of all of the previous generation's workers than to make each individual family responsible for the support of its own elderly relatives. The dramatic reduction in poverty among the elderly resulting from the full implementation of the Social Security pension system makes clear that this belief was correct. How that effectiveness can be maintained for the future will be addressed later.

Recognizing the needs of children in the social insurance system requires exactly the same move: a shift from believing that the income security of children is solely the responsibility of their parents to the belief that the risk of income inadequacy in childhood can, at least in part, be spread across all families and borne by the whole of the working-age population. Indeed, only by making the social insurance contract intergenerationally complete in this way can we provide true security to America's children.

### HOW MUCH SOCIAL INSURANCE IS ENOUGH?

Having described the risks that social insurance should cover and who should be covered, we now come to perhaps the most controversial question of social insurance design: how much social insurance is enough?

Clearly, this question cannot be answered once for all time. As we have shown, a society's needs for social insurance will change over time as economic and social circumstances change. For example, demographic shifts and changes in work and family circumstances affect people's needs for social insurance protections. Likewise, how much social insurance is affordable will depend on the level of a nation's output and other demands on a society's resources; military needs during the twentieth century provide a prime example of radical changes in demands over time.

Looking to private insurance offers limited insight into this question. In a private insurance contract, the level of insurance provided—the degree to which the full risk of loss is covered—is a function of two things: (1) the purchaser's desire for security—for protection from the risks at issue, and (2) the insurance company's concerns about adverse selection (the migration of bad risks toward insurance) and "moral hazard" (the likelihood that "full compensation" might make the insured indifferent about whether the risk occurs). Private insurance contracts, therefore, rarely provide as much coverage as the insured can afford to buy. Rather, they limit the insurers' potential losses, typically by putting a ceiling on the amount of coverage and also by leaving some of the burden of loss on the insured person through "deductibles" or "copayments." All of these techniques tend to protect the insurer from the prospect that the risk will substantially increase simply because it is insured.

To be sure, some sorts of private insurance coverage are often complete or nearly complete. Homeowners, for example, can usually purchase insurance for the complete value of their homes. So long as the house is not "over-insured" in relation to its market price, insurers can rely on some combination of criminal sanctions against arson and fraud, homeowners' concerns about personal injury, and widespread behavioral norms to protect them against the prospect that insured homeowners will torch their own premises. In other circumstances, private insurance leaves people significantly underinsured or completely uninsured. Individual disability income policies, for example, seldom provide replacement rates for lost income above 50 or 60 percent. Even then, such policies are so expensive that few people can afford them. These affordability and moral hazard constraints result in some rather peculiar looking contracts, such as disability insurance contracts to pay people particular amounts of money for each day that they are receiving treatment in a hospital. Such contracts are a proxy, and a poor one at that, for the disability income insurance that was really desired.

Social insurance, in contrast, is designed explicitly to counteract the "what the market will bear" limitations of private insurance contracts. It provides insurance for people who could not otherwise afford it and in markets where moral hazard and adverse selection make private insurance unavailable or of limited value. Social insurance nevertheless can face the same problems concerning how much is provided that pervade private insurance markets. Some levels of protection may be "unaffordable" collectively as well as individually. And because social insurance is directed specifically to the problem of inadequate labor income, it suffers from a peculiar form of the moral hazard problem: the tendency of social insurance to interfere with work incentives and the accumulation of labor income by saving. Many of the debates swirling around social insurance programs are concerned with the potential loss of productivity from replacing labor income with insurance benefits.

Avoiding moral hazard in social insurance is a question that we address continuously as we analyze existing programs and advance our own proposals for reform. In our view, the moral hazard issue explains much of the heterogeneity of existing programs and the need to pursue social insurance through many different techniques. We will have more to say about that question in Chapter 3, when we address the question of whether income security might be provided by one overarching social insurance policy. But responding to moral hazard raises difficulties about how to realize true security through social insurance, not about the question of what social insurance is or what it should be.

Ultimately, answering the question "how much social insurance is enough?" turns not only on a society's needs and desires for protection against the common risks to labor income, but also on how much as a society we are willing to pay to support social insurance protections. A society's willingness to pay for social insurance depends both on what it can afford and, more fundamentally, on how it draws the line between collective and individual or family responsibility. As we have remarked, before the 1930s this nation regarded the well-being of its elderly as a private family or charitable responsibility. Eventually, however, we came to regard keeping retirees out of the poorhouse as a societal obligation and introduced Social Security pensions. There is no turning back on that commitment. On the other hand, as we have explained, the economic well-being of children continues to be left to their parents, even in circumstances where the resources available to the child are inadequate although her parent or parents are working full-time. We view this situation as producing serious but remediable gaps in our nation's social insurance coverage.

The question "how much social insurance is enough?" is further complicated because, as we have described, social insurance attempts to spread income both over the lifetime of particular individuals and across families. These two aspects of social insurance raise distinct issues. In its effort to smooth income over a person's lifetime (or among different generations of the same family), social insurance must ask how big a shock to current income families can tolerate. Society must trade off the benefits of additional levels of protection against the costs of replacing increasing percentages of lost income.

This question may be answered differently with respect to different risks. For example, risks that result in a temporary loss of wage income might be insured at a lower "replacement rate" (the percentage of lost income replaced by the benefit amount) than risks that have more long-lasting effects. Presumably families can defer larger amounts of current spending over short periods than over longer ones. Thus, for example, we may want to replace higher levels of income for persons who are permanently disabled than for persons who are temporarily unemployed. Similarly, we may want to use a lower replacement rate for retirement than for disability pensions because older workers have more time to amass personal savings that will provide a buffer against being "retired" from the workforce. Indeed, we may want to require individuals to put aside some amount of their current wages in personal savings accounts to serve as an element of income replacement when unemployment strikes or retirement occurs.

When considering social insurance across families and, in particular, how much higher-income workers should subsidize the insurance of lower-income workers, we have to ask a somewhat different question. How much is enough tends to be addressed in terms of some social standard of "adequacy" or "decency." Here, of course, there is widespread dispute about what these terms might or should mean. It should be emphasized, however, that social insurance provision does not generally gauge its success only by its capacity to prevent abject poverty. To be sure, social insurance programs celebrate their anti-poverty effectiveness. But, as we have urged, social insurance should protect the incomes of all members of society, not just insure the poor. In aspiration, social insurance hopes to provide income security for the whole population, not just the bare necessities to help the poor keep body and soul together.

In the end, the overall affordability issue is something of a "how high is up?" question, and we have no special insight into how much in the aggregate Americans are willing to pay for social insurance. In this book, we ultimately sidestep the aggregate "how much is enough?" question by imposing a budget constraint on the total costs of our proposed system that is roughly equal to the total cost of existing social insurance programs. Some people will say we should do more; others may claim we can do with less. What is the "proper" amount is not a question on which we have been able to get much purchase. We are convinced, however, that Americans can enjoy much greater security without incurring much additional cost.

## SUMMARY

In our reasonably straightforward vision, the basic purpose of social insurance is income security. In order to realize that purpose, social insurance must cover common risks to income security across the life cycle of individuals. If it is to fulfill its social purposes effectively, social insurance must be universal in coverage. And to provide an adequate level of protection, social insurance must recognize and facilitate two different forms of redistribution—redistribution of resources across the lifetime of individuals, and redistribution from families that have not incurred the risks insured to those that have.

We have also explored some of the implications of this vision for the construction of successful social insurance regimes. They include mandatory participation, a national risk pool and financing, and the development of an intergenerational social contract. These ideas will provide major organizing themes for our critique of existing practice and our proposals for the future.

We begin that task by addressing two issues that have plagued income security debates for decades. The first has to do with the use of unitary versus heterogeneous methods of providing income security. We have described social insurance as designed to deal with one risk—inadequacy of labor income. Does that mean that a single program can provide social insurance for all Americans? Our answer is no, but the reasons for that response are not so obvious that the question can be dropped without additional discussion.

Second, if we believe that social insurance is to be realized by a set of heterogeneous programs, which programs count as social insurance and which programs do not? Put slightly differently, this issue also breaks into two questions: First, how is social insurance distinguished from the broader realm of domestic social policy? After all, most social policy is designed to make American families better off, and in that sense more economically secure. What is special about social insurance? Second, how do we respond to those who take a more conventional view of social insurance, defining it as limited to a much narrower set of universal, mandatory, contributory programs modeled essentially on the basic characteristics of Social Security pensions? Answering these queries is the work of Chapter 3.

# Chapter 3 Providing Social Insurance

Describing the risks that justify social insurance intervention is straightforward. Families live almost exclusively by labor income; they therefore demand protection against circumstances and events that take them out of the workforce and cut off labor income. The principal risks to economic security in a market economy have been understood for over a century: Age—both youth and advanced age—is almost certain to produce economic dependency. And within the prime working years, both individual incapacity (death or disability) and involuntary unemployment threaten to interrupt labor income either temporarily or permanently.

Although these risks have been stated as if they cut off labor income completely, that is often not the case. Many children have some earnings, and many of the elderly work at least part-time. Disability may be partial, and most systems for paying benefits for total disability ignore some low level of earnings when determining eligibility. Unemployment merges into "underemployment" when workers cannot find jobs suitable to their education and training.

Given these considerations, there is nothing inherent in the logic of social insurance that prevents the risk from being generalized in a more comprehensive fashion as the risk that circumstances or events will make one unsuccessful in a free market for labor. And if that is true, then social insurance logically extends to cover the risk that individuals or families will suffer from low income or low wages. The obvious remedy for those risks is to supplement either income or wages. Moreover, the techniques for addressing these risks could be relatively straightforward. Low income could be addressed by the so-called negative income tax (NIT), under which taxpayers with low income get monetary payments from the Treasury rather than sending the Treasury a check. Low wages could be dealt with by a government supplement to wages earned in the marketplace, either in a way similar to the Earned Income Tax Credit (EITC), which sends families checks based on wage levels and family size, or directly, by passing wage subsidies through paychecks in the form of direct additions to wages or the forgiveness of wage taxes.

## THE NEGATIVE INCOME TAX

That no nation has ever adopted a comprehensive NIT as its principal means of protecting family incomes suggests that there must be some serious problems with this seemingly elegant approach.[1] Indeed, a quick look at those problems and their solutions helps explain why we have the types of social insurance provision that we actually observe.

One basic problem with the NIT is that, when made available at a level sufficient to make sure that no one has inadequate income, it undermines work incentives (why work at low wages rather than take the NIT's guaranteed annual income?) as well as savings incentives (why save for retirement if your nest egg is unlikely to do better than the NIT's guaranteed annual income?). The response to these moral hazards can proceed in a number of directions: (1) limit payments to persons satisfying conditions that put them out of the workforce anyway—involuntary unemployment, disability, old age, or youth, (2) limit payments to persons currently working or to persons with a substantial past attachment to the workforce, (3) limit payments to persons who have contributed (mandatorily or voluntarily) to the fund from which benefits are paid, (4) calibrate payments to past earning or contributions, (5) set payment levels low enough, or make eligibility periods short enough, that cash assistance will not substantially affect work or savings, (6) make identical payments to everyone—or everyone in particular groups (such as the aged, or workers with dependents)—without regard to other income and resources, or (7) all of the above.

The negative income tax has a second drawback; we call it "consumption hazard." While libertarians and welfare economists may value the consumer freedom that cash transfers provide, most of us are not concerned simply that our fellow citizens may have insufficient cash. Instead, as contributors to the well-being of the disadvantaged, taxpayers seem concerned about material deprivation with respect to basic necessities such as food, shelter, child care, and medical care. People often are willing to transfer more of their own wealth to others if they know that these necessities are what is being provided for families with inadequate incomes. The obvious solution is to make transfers in-kind, by vouchers or by tax credits for qualified expenditures.

Individually, or in combination, these responses to moral hazard and consumption hazard explain much of the structure of all countries' social insurance provision. Which responses are chosen determine the peculiar character of a nation's social insurance regime.

The United States has leaned heavily on (1) the use of contributory and/or earnings-related programs (Social Security's Old Age, Survivors', Disability, and Health Insurance ["Medicare"] programs [collectively known as "OASDHI"], unemployment insurance, and workers' compensation); (2) means-tested programs for persons out of the workforce (Supplemental Security Income for the aged, blind, and disabled; public assistance; and, for poor mothers with small children, Aid to Families with Dependent Children [AFDC]—now replaced by Temporary Assistance for Needy Families [TANF]); and (3) tax subsidies tying benefits to work or savings (the Earned Income Tax Credit, dependents' tax credits and exemptions; the non-taxability of employer-based health, illness, and pension contributions or private individual retirement accounts; and the deductibility of certain medical expenses from taxable income). Indeed, the first and third categories account for the vast majority of all American social insurance spending.[2]

As we shall see, the choices among these strategies for providing social insurance have been fateful for the adequacy of protections for various age groups in the population, for the distribution of benefits across income groups, for the costs associated with particular protections, and for the political popularity and stability of funding. For example, the heavy reliance on tax subsidies to voluntary employer-based benefits has never produced adequate coverage and threatens now to create more and more gaps in social insurance coverage. As companies downsize and rely increasingly on part-time or "contingent workers," and as families rely more and more on two incomes, one of which is sometimes not full-year, full-time employment, it becomes more and more chancy to count on tax-subsidized employer-based social insurance coverage for protections. These changes in the labor force also are causing many deserving workers to fail the contributions, earnings, or work-force-attachment tests for public social insurance protections, particularly unemployment insurance. These developments suggest needs for reform, but the NIT is no cure-all. What about wage subsidies?

## WAGE SUBSIDIES

The difficulties with the negative income tax do not necessarily carry over to programs that subsidize low wages. In a wage subsidy scheme, built-in work requirements somewhat limit moral hazard. Wage subsidies, of course, will not protect those completely out of the labor force because of age, disability, or unemployment. But so long as some family members are working some of the time, as is true for most families, would it make sense to make wage supplements the backbone of the income security system?

The arguments for this approach are substantial.[3] Many who have low wages may be at the margins of the categories that would otherwise be supported through disability or unemployment insurance programs. Surely there are many workers who have relatively limited education, poor health status, or modest cognitive abilities that limit their earning potential, although not so severely as to make them completely unemployable. And in a labor market with weak demand, many with the skills to earn more will find themselves in low-paid work. Subsidizing wages would thus recognize that the specific risks to income security now buffered by disability and unemployment insurance program are a matter of degree, not the question of kind that disability or unemployment benefits adjudication suggests.

These are indeed good arguments for programs that support low wages, either through direct wage subsidies or in the form of an annual income subsidy like the current EITC. Nevertheless, we do not support generalized wage subsidy programs beyond the role now played by the current EITC, which is directed at families with children. We have multiple reasons for this position, but they will not persuade everyone. There is nothing in the logic of social insurance that precludes general wage subsidy approaches. Making wage subsidies the cornerstone of social insurance, however, would, in our judgment, undermine individual incentives, create labor market distortions, and contradict deeply held notions of personal responsibility, thereby risking undermining the legitimacy of the social insurance enterprise. In addition, strange as it may seem, current low wages or low income may be a poor proxy in many cases for the sort of material deprivation that social insurance benefits seek to redress.

Let us take the last issue first. We know that most people earn less at the beginning (and end) of their work lives than in the middle. Hence, many low-income or low-wage workers are simply young workers beginning their working lives or older workers phasing out earnings on the way to retirement. The latter group is engaging in what looks like voluntary labor income reductions and may well be doing so because of greater and greater reliance on income from savings. The former group, young workers, may be living at home, doubling up living arrangements with a roommate, and engaging in all the other strategies that young people use to live reasonably well while earning relatively little. Professors commonly say that their ambition is to regain the standard of living that they enjoyed as graduate students. A wage subsidy program, whether organized as a direct subsidy to wages or like the Earned Income Tax Credit, would want to avoid payments to these people for a straightforward reason: there is no good story to tell taxpayers about why they are receiving benefits.

A wage subsidy system need not be powerless in the face of this problem. It could put age brackets around payments so that, for example, only persons between thirty and fifty-five would be eligible. To be sure, these are arbitrary limits, but that is not their only difficulty. Arbitrary age limits still fail to solve the more general problem that a wage subsidy program faces—distinguishing between those who have material deprivation because of involuntary low wages and those who have either voluntary low wages or no material deprivation.

On the material deprivation side, we confront many couples who are likely to qualify for wage subsidies if their wages are evaluated separately, but because they pool income and resources are not suffering material deprivation. We can, of course, deal with this problem in relation to married couples, but only at the cost of creating yet another marriage penalty. Widespread criticism of the Aid to Families with Dependent Children program and of the Internal Revenue Code make clear that marriage penalties can seriously de-legitimate tax and transfer programs. To many, perhaps most, Americans, tax or transfer disincentives to marriage are simply bad social policy.

Support for low wages will also cause some people to accept low wages voluntarily. In many cases this voluntary choice may carry no social stigma, and may even be praiseworthy. Some people may want to devote themselves to voluntaristic causes, spend more time caring for their families, or develop their talents in ways that have no obvious market payoff. There is no social "bad" created by such behavior, but taxpayers as a whole are quite likely to balk at paying increased taxes to allow some of their fellow citizens to make choices that they, too, may find attractive, but unavailable.

Once again, wage subsidy schemes can be designed to ameliorate these problems, but the complications multiply. Attempting to determine whether households are in fact sharing economic resources although they have no formal family relationships is a very difficult business. It either involves highly arbitrary presumptions (such as whether people share the same address) or extremely intrusive investigation. The same is true for determining whether the acceptance of low wages is "voluntary" or "involuntary." We could use some proxies such as education, I.Q., and health status to try to separate the voluntary from the involuntary low-wage worker. But again, these proxies would be only partial indicators of what we really want to know and would also often entail arbitrary measures and subjective and intrusive administrative investigations.

The foregoing reasons are significant objections to wage subsidy programs, but we have not yet even begun to consider problems of work incentives and potential labor-market distortions. Nor have we considered the problem of fraud. Indeed, these three objections are somewhat intertwined.

While many may doubt that wage subsidies will provide strong incentives for most persons to withdraw labor effort, they surely create a substantial incentive to understate returns to labor effort in order to obtain the subsidy. In a program like the Earned Income Tax Credit, the incentive to understate labor income is provided to the "taxpayer." Where subsidies are provided directly through employers, the incentive is for the employer to understate the wage that would be paid in the absence of the existence of subsidies. If this employer incentive, or moral hazard, is significant, it can create serious distortions both in the labor market and in the market for goods and services. Taxpayers will, in effect, be subsidizing the production of certain goods and services, although no explicit rationale has been (or perhaps could be) given for such a subsidy. Moreover, because the subsidy is to labor costs, it distorts the choice between incurring capital and labor costs at the margin, which could again contribute to significant inefficiencies.

The incentives problem for employees, however, is not just the incentive to misrepresent earnings. Employees progress up the pay scale not just by longevity, but also by effort and compliance with expected work norms. Subsidies to low-wage or low-income work reduce the incentive to make those efforts or bear those conformity costs. We have no idea just how significant this problem might be, but in a labor market in which it is recognized that there are substantial returns to "work experience," tampering with the incentives to make experience yield higher productivity is treacherous.

For all of these reasons, we believe that it would be extremely difficult to use wage subsidies as a primary approach to social insurance protections. The problems are sufficiently numerous that we would expect some combination of inadequate subsidy rates, high administrative costs, and political disaffection to plague such programs and perhaps destroy them.

We should be careful, however, to state clearly the lessons that we draw from this analysis of wage subsidy approaches. Our conclusion is that this is not an approach that could provide a generalized core for social insurance protections. On the other hand, we believe that wage subsidies (and consumption subsidies) can be used in certain circumstances where moral hazard is less prominent and material deprivation is clear.

Hence, for example, we believe that the social insurance component of old-age pensions should be considered in substantial part as insurance against having low lifetime earnings that prevent adequate savings for retirement. We are extremely doubtful that workers will engage in voluntary income limitation over the course of a working life in order to get a better deal (in terms of returns on contributions) from the old age pension system. And falsifying a lifetime work history is a much more difficult matter than underreporting annual earnings.

Similarly, we believe that the Earned Income Tax Credit is an appropriate way to supplement the incomes of families with children. We are not here dealing with young adults who are doubling up or living at home, nor with people easing into retirement. We are subsidizing the incomes of parents with children in order to avoid material deprivation of the children—and only to the extent that the parent or parents are working. There is still considerable moral hazard here, to be sure. No income support program is without moral hazard, but some risk is worth taking when the alternatives are either high rates of childhood poverty or even riskier forms of income support. We are sufficiently concerned with moral hazard, however, that rather than increasing the EITC for families with children, we ultimately argue for subsidies for certain necessities.

### MORE COMPLEX CONTEMPORARY SOLUTIONS

Given the problems with unitary approaches to providing social insurance, such as the negative income tax or wage subsidies, it is likely that a society designing social insurance interventions will engage in a host of differing types of efforts. America is certainly not exceptional in its choice of a multifaceted system.

Public provision is clearly one option; the government can run a social insurance program and require participation by all workers. This is the current U.S. approach to risks of old age, death (survivorship), disability, and medical expenses in old age—the familiar OASDHI programs embodied in the Social Security and Medicare acts. But even these familiar social insurance programs employ more heterogeneous mechanisms than are generally acknowledged.

Medicare Part A (hospital care) and Part B (physician services) are important examples. Part A is a mandatory program financed through a wage tax on employers and employees. Part B is a voluntary program financed through relatively small premiums coupled with substantial subsidies from general federal revenues. Both programs were designed to ameliorate the threat to family income security that medical costs pose for the retired population. Normal insurance market segmentation in the private health insurance markets would produce high costs for a group that, on average, combines high risks with low incomes.

When Medicare was enacted, hospital care posed the largest threat to the financial well-being of the elderly. Mandating hospital coverage advanced social insurance purposes while solving significant adverse selection problems. Insurance for physician care, by contrast, was thought important but not crucial for family economic security. Potentially high administrative costs and premiums seemed to justify public administration and a subsidy, but not a mandate.

Over time, the Part B subsidy became more and more generous—growing from 50 percent of premiums to 75 percent—so that today Part B coverage is nearly universal. And shifts in medical treatment modalities over time have made out-of-hospital care both medically more important and financially more burdensome. The current scheme may be outmoded—indeed, we believe it was poorly designed from the beginning—but the point of the example remains. Public provision of insurance coverage need not be of one type, either in its regulatory or in its financial arrangements.

Nor is public provision the only game in town. Carrying insurance can simply be mandated by law. Some current American social insurance programs use mandates, either to require employer-based coverage or to compel individual participation in a state-run scheme. Workers' compensation offers a ready example of the employer-mandate mode. But mandates can be used as well to require individual purchases of private insurance protection. Automobile liability insurance is a standard American example. Automobile liability insurance is not usually considered social insurance, but individual mandates are quite common in the pension and health insurance regimes of other nations. Many now advocate reforming Social Security pensions by including mandatory individual accounts that function somewhat like Individual Retirement Accounts (IRAs).

The IRA suggests yet another common technique for socializing insurance markets: public subsidies. Medicare Part B may be our most conspicuous and successful example of social insurance financed, in substantial part, by subsidies out of general revenues. But direct subsidies are not the only alternative; much social insurance protection is subsidized through targeted tax breaks. For example, active workers in the year 2000 will receive more than $80 billion per year in tax subsidies for their health coverage and another $100 billion or so annually in tax relief for private pensions and IRAs.[4] Meanwhile, about 20 million low-income families get wage subsidies totaling nearly $30 billion each year under the Earned Income Tax Credit.[5] We believe tax subsidies for voluntary employment based regimes tend to work badly, but they are a way for government to "sponsor" social insurance without making "government" appear bigger.

Not all subsidies to social insurance are from general revenues. Cross-subsidies within insurance pools are a common response to unwanted private insurance market segmentation. Higher earners can subsidize lower earners through premium or payment arrangements in virtually any social insurance scheme, just as high earners subsidize low earners in the current Social Security pension system and low-risk elders subsidize those with high risks in the Medicare system. Nor are cross-subsidies limited to public insurance programs. Mandated "community rating," for example, can force cross-subsidies within private insurance pools that would otherwise generate differential premiums.

## SOCIAL INSURANCE, SOCIAL POLICY, AND
## THE "CONVENTIONAL CONCEPTION"

So far so good. Social insurance is a means for providing income security for a set of common risks that shift over the life cycle and that loom larger or smaller depending on the changing backdrop of general social, economic, and demographic developments. Because the core idea is to provide income security, straightforward solutions like negative income taxes and generalized wage subsidies have intuitive appeal. But on reflection, the world turns out to be a complex, indeed messy, place. Meeting our complicated income security goals while avoiding unwanted economic, social, and symbolic side effects tends to drive us toward some heterogeneous package of social insurance interventions that utilize a medley of techniques—direct cash transfers, in-kind transfers, premium subsidies, mandates, regulatory cross-subsidies, and "tax expenditures," to name but some of the more prominent.

Yet we have thus far ignored a host of other ways to ameliorate the income security risks that we have described. Public health activities protect against disease, accidents, and disability. Fiscal and economic policies help to limit unemployment. Education increases earning capacities. Regulation makes possible secure life insurance and annuity policies. Are all of these things social insurance? Surely social insurance does not encompass all (domestic) public action.

In contrast, many would limit social insurance to a small subset of the policies that we have discussed. In this conventional conception of social insurance, the risk insured against is loss of individual or family income or of some fringe benefit that is a standard feature of wage or salary packages.

Participation is mandatory, and coverage is nearly universal. Eligibility, however, is closely connected to work and to the payment of taxes or "contributions" imposed on wages. Amounts received should the risks materialize are related to prior earnings. The insurer is the government (or some specialized governmental entity). And the government's commitment to pay is emphasized by having dedicated taxes or contributions held in a "trust fund." In a sentence, under this view "social insurance" is mandatory, earnings-related, near-universal protection against loss of wage income and fringe benefits, provided to contributing workers and their families through a publicly administered system financed by dedicated taxes.

We view social insurance as much broader than the conventional conception, but considerably narrower than all the public activities that might be said to support American family income. Getting the idea of social insurance fixed in a reasonable way is not just a semantic quibble. If the definition is too broad, "insurance" becomes a useless metaphor—a synonym perhaps for "assistance." Important ideas about good program design—identifiable risks, moral hazard, adverse selection, and so forth—lose their salience. If the criminal justice system qualifies as "social insurance" (protection against loss of income or assets through theft, embezzlement, extortion, and the like), the concept fails to define a distinctive arena of public policy. On the other hand, if the concept is too narrow, we fail to understand both what we have done and what still needs doing to provide adequate security against risks to family income.

### Social Insurance versus Social Provision

If social insurance is not all social provision, what is it? By a social insurance commitment, we mean to encompass only collectively determined and legally binding promises to pay defined amounts to or on behalf of particular beneficiaries given the occurrence or continuation of an event or condition that impairs the adequacy of current family income.

Breaking down this lengthy definition into its components will clarify its meaning. Note, first, that this definition does not encompass all public programs designed to increase family economic well-being. Social insurance entails a legal commitment to pay on the occurrence of a defined event—remembering, of course, our extended understanding of "event" to include a substantial period out of the workforce due to youth or old age. Provision of emergency assistance to flood victims *if and when* the

Congress appropriates specific funds is not a social insurance commitment. It could become social insurance, but only if the promise of relief were made unconditional. Post hoc funding of an entitlement to relief from a disaster works if you have the power to impose taxes.

Second, the event insured against is a current loss of economic well-being due to inadequate labor income. Current access to schooling may be crucially important to future economic well-being, but this is investment in future opportunity. Educational opportunity, even if provided in the form of vouchers or tax breaks for the purchase of education, does not create a social insurance program. Further, while an ounce of prevention may be worth a pound of cure, the latter may be social insurance while the former is not. Workers' compensation is social insurance; occupational safety and health regulation are not. Disability Insurance is social insurance; the nondiscrimination requirements of the Americans with Disabilities Act are not.

To be sure, private insurers sometimes engage in preventive activities and impose contract provisions to avoid future losses. In that sense we have come to think of insurance as having a prophylactic dimension. But there is an important difference between these private regulatory activities and governmental programs of public education, health and safety regulation, and nondiscrimination. The government has other policy reasons for these programs that would justify engaging in them whether or not it were also insuring the populace against the associated risks. These are independent governmental activities, not parts of an insurance contract.

Indeed, we believe that the failure to make clear distinctions between income security purposes and other social goals seriously limits the efficacy of some existing social insurance programs. For example, workers' compensation's goal to create a safer workplace gets in the way of covering a broad range of risks to income from injury or illness that cannot be connected to the operations of any particular employer. Its effort to serve compensatory justice forces workers' compensation programs to adopt an inappropriate and inefficient adversarial process for deciding claims. Similarly, unemployment insurance is burdened by a financing structure that emphasizes regulating employers' managerial practices through differential insurance rates. In our view, that system of firm-specific "experience rating" is a central cause of unemployment insurance's current inadequate coverage of unemployment risks. Finally, the goal of universal medical *in-*

*surance* has usually been conceptualized as the goal of providing universal access to medical *care*—a very different purpose than protecting family economic security in the face of large medical care expenditures. We argue that this conflation of purposes has hampered the achievement of income security for many Americans.

Keeping our eye on the goal of income security also permits us to distinguish between governmental actions that affect the structure of insurance generally and social insurance itself. The government is, of course, involved in virtually all insurance markets. Special legal rules apply to the interpretation of insurance policies and limit enforceability to those having an "insurable interest." State and federal laws regulate the form of insurance contracts, the financial soundness of insurance companies, the structure of insurance pools, the extent of allowable underwriting, and a host of other attributes of insurance coverage. Once one leaves the relatively clear cases of direct government provision of insurance against loss of family economic well-being, distinguishing between "private" and "social" insurance is not easy. Why isn't mandatory automobile liability insurance, which includes payment for lost income of an injured party, social insurance? What about private Medigap insurance, whose terms and availability are closely regulated by federal and state law?

Indeed, when considering even governmentally provided insurance, problem cases come easily to mind. Are crop insurance, flood insurance, and federal deposit insurance social insurance programs? These are, after all, public insurance programs that protect individuals and families against substantial risks to economic status and income continuity.

Unless virtually all insurance is to be considered social insurance, we must give more discriminating substantive content to "social" than just substantial involvement of government in an insurance market that protects individual or family income. No abstract criteria will provide a foolproof guide to concrete categorization, but meaningful distinctions can still be drawn. The critical issue in separating social insurance from other types of insurance evidencing substantial governmental involvement is the *purpose* of collective provision, subsidy, or regulation.

Consider three broad purposes of government intervention in insurance markets. First is the assurance that insurance markets are efficiently and fairly structured. This *consumer protection* goal is the rationale for most special legal rules governing interpretation of insurance contracts and for much state and federal regulation of insurance markets. Assuring that consumers get the "benefit of their bargains" supports private insurance markets, including insurance that compensates for loss of family income. But this sort of intervention does not transform private insurance into social insurance any more than the application of state "lemon laws" to used car sales transforms the family car into public transportation.

A second purpose is the use of insurance or insurance regulation to foster *economic development*. Some of these interventions are easily excluded from the social insurance category. For example, insuring commercial contracts with foreign entities protects firms and their employees, but the principal purposes here are clearly the fostering of foreign trade or some other foreign policy objectives. Other situations are harder to classify. Federal deposit insurance protects individual wealth, but it is also designed to create confidence in banking institutions and maintain sufficient levels of commercial bank liquidity to finance a dynamic private economy. Crop insurance protects farmers' incomes in disastrous years, but it also, like farm price supports, maintains continuity in the resources devoted to farming. Flood insurance protects individuals against the loss of economically valuable resources, but it is also a device for exercising indirect regulatory power over the use of flood plains, where the federal government is legally unable to act, and where states and localities are politically incapable of implementing optimal regulatory regimes.

We are uncertain how to classify deposit, flood, and crop insurance, although because our focus here is on social protections of labor income, not programs to protect capital assets, this uncertainty is of little moment. We are convinced, however, that in principle the answer should turn on whether the basic purpose of the program is to protect individuals or families from common risks to family income adequacy. Moreover, we will argue in several different social insurance domains that the key to providing adequate social insurance coverage lies in separating out other social goals when they impair the achievement of true security.

Our analysis is devoted to a third broad category of governmental interventions in insurance markets: those programs designed to cope with the risks to family income security that we discussed in Chapter 2—the risks attached to youth and old age, illness, injury, disability, death, and involuntary unemployment. Whether a program is currently recognized as social insurance and how well it works depends crucially on whether and how the program pursues this particular income-security goal.

### The Limits of the Conventional Conception

Although we have now cut social insurance down to size, the vision we have offered is still much broader than the "conventional conception" we previously outlined. We have not limited social insurance provision to public entities, insisted on trust fund financing, or demanded that entitlements be premised on (or benefits measured by) prior worker contributions. Nor have we declared that, as a definitional matter, all such programs should be mandatory or universal. These may, indeed, often be desirable design features for social insurance programs. But to limit social insurance provision to these design parameters would be stifling. Indeed, it would exclude from the realm of social insurance many of the programs that we noncontroversially associate with the social insurance idea.

As we have remarked, the conventional conception is tightly connected to the structure of Old Age Survivors', Disability, and Health Insurance (OASDHI), the familiar protections of the U.S. Social Security and Medicare acts. When Americans say "social insurance," they tend to mean Social Security pensions and Medicare. Yet a moment's reflection reveals that the conventional conception only partially describes the American system of social insurance. To take but one feature of this view, many social insurance programs do not premise benefits on prior contributions to an insurance fund or calibrate benefits in relation to prior earnings.

Part A Medicare benefits (hospital coverage), for example, are financed by payroll taxes, but benefits are not earnings related. Everyone has the same health insurance policy, no matter what their level of prior contributions or earnings. Part B of Medicare (physicians' coverage) is a voluntary program subsidized from general federal revenues at such a high level to achieve virtually universal participation by the eligible population. State and federal workers' compensation programs require no taxes or contributions from employees, and benefits usually are paid through private insurers or employers' self-insurance, not out of a public fund. And whatever the ultimate economic burden of the tax, unemployment insurance involves no worker contributions.

Moreover, much social insurance protection for income during retirement and much health coverage during the working years are provided through employer-sponsored pension plans and health insurance, which are subsidized through targeted tax cuts. No one examining retirement income security or health insurance in the United States should fail to take these tax subsidies into account. To be sure, their coverage is far from universal, turning on the worker's connection to a particular employer. Their spotty and inadequate coverage, however, only signals that this kind of social insurance is inadequate; it does not negate such subsidies' social insurance nature.

Finally, means-tested, noncontributory programs for dependent children and the aged were a part of the original Social Security Act. Indeed, old age assistance based on need is Title 1 of the Social Security Act of 1935, and is the part of the act that had the broadest public support when the statute was enacted.[6] Title IV of the 1935 act granted a federal subsidy to state means-tested "mothers' pensions"—programs that were recognized at that time as America's primary innovation in social insurance provision. Means-tested support for the blind as well as the totally and permanently disabled were part of the Social Security Act nearly a decade before contributory, earnings-related disability insurance was added.

As a matter of history, protection against current low income because of defined personal or family circumstances, irrespective of past contributions or past earnings, has long been a cornerstone of American social insurance arrangements. The original Social Security Act was a complex compromise between those who thought social insurance should be structured primarily as a protection against low income and those who saw it primarily as a protection against loss of prior economic status and wanted social insurance closely tied to workforce attachment.[7]

These variations on the social insurance theme are not minor curiosities. Indeed, careful analysis reveals that none of the features of the conventional conception of American social insurance are necessary aspects of a social insurance package. Assuming that they are requires historical amnesia and induces contemporary policy myopia. In fact, when one looks at the full panoply of social insurance transfers and tax expenditures, the narrow or conventional conception—mandatory, contributory, earnings-related universal (or near universal) programs—accounts for only 56 percent of all social insurance transfers and less than half when both transfers and tax expenditures are taken into account (figs. 3.1 and 3.2).

Moreover, treating the conventional conception as the full measure of social insurance induces both analytical and political mistakes. High-wage workers, covered by a generous employer-sponsored pension plan, may believe they are getting a relatively poor deal from federal retirement insurance protections if they look only to Social Security as providing pro-

Fig. 3.1.    Social insurance transfers

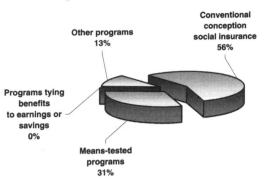

(*Source:* Authors' calculations based on FY 1996 figures contained in budgetary appendix.)

Fig. 3.2.    Social insurance transfers and tax expenditures

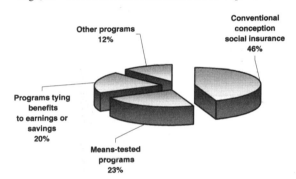

(*Source:* Authors' calculations based on FY 1996 figures contained in budgetary appendix.)

tection. But if they also take into account the government subsidies to their pension plans through the tax system, they would recognize that their deal is substantially better than they thought. Likewise, in an overall assessment of public policy, social insurance protections for retirement income look substantially more progressive if tax-subsidized employer-based pension plans are ignored. But they shouldn't be ignored.

For decades social insurance advocates and administrators have sought to distance "social insurance" from "social assistance" by denying that anything with a "means test" (eligibility based on income, wealth levels, or demonstrated need) could be social insurance. Given the unpopularity of AFDC, which came to be a placeholder for all of "welfare" or "public assistance," this political strategy was understandable. In our view, however, it has been a serious mistake.

This artificial and ahistorical division of the social welfare world between "contributory" and "non-contributory" schemes strands crucial poverty reduction programs in political backwaters. It creates confusion in both public discourse and public perception whenever progressive benefit and contribution formulas for social insurance are proposed or discussed. This political separation poses political dangers for "contributory" schemes as well. It highlights "individual equity" or bank-account considerations in social insurance arrangements—represented recently by the ubiquitous calculations of each individual's "money's worth" from Social Security pensions—while submerging the social adequacy commitment that should be the fundamental norm in the design and defense of social insurance.

Indeed, the flight from all income or means testing as a part of social insurance makes comprehensive protection virtually impossible. Insurance against discrete risks through programs consistent with the conventional conception cannot protect against other less well-defined hazards to family income adequacy: sporadic work histories, persistent low wages, borderline incapacities, the opportunity costs of child rearing, the inadequacies of family and community support structures—to name but a few. A social insurance system without some broad-based means-related programs cannot cope with these hazards. On the other hand, as our specific proposals will make clear, we believe that, for both economic and political reasons, programs should be structured wherever possible to avoid explicit means or income testing. There is much political and economic wisdom in designing social insurance regimes to reduce the economic disincentives and the corrosive we/they politics of explicitly means-tested regimes.

This concession to political and economic reality implies that social insurance cannot cover all risks to family labor income any more than private liability insurance can cover all liability risks. Social insurance will not accept the moral hazard (the incentive to incur the risk once insurance is available) of voluntary unemployment any more than private liability policies will insure against liability for intentional torts. Proposals for social insurance reform, ours or others, must be judged, therefore, by whether they are improvements over the status quo—not by whether they eliminate all gaps and provide adequate incomes for every living American.

## A PATH TO TRUE SECURITY

Social insurance is a distinctive set of programs designed to moderate the risks of current income loss or inadequacy by providing secure cash or near-cash entitlements on the occurrence of defined risks. Although the general risk to be insured is simply the lack of labor income, the ways that risk materializes are diverse and change during the life cycle of individuals and families. Risks also may be different for each individual and family, and may shift over time as social and economic conditions evolve. While this diversity justifies multiple techniques for providing social insurance, it should not become an excuse for abandoning basic principles or for failing to look at social insurance as a whole.

In 1999, for example, President Clinton received bipartisan praise for his proposals to shore up the finances of Social Security pensions and Medicare by devoting more than three-quarters of the next fifteen years' projected budget surpluses to that task. By comparison with truly goofy proposals, such as using the surplus to eliminate all estate and capital gains taxes, this suggestion looks statesmanlike. But as an approach to dealing with the most important issues in American social insurance, the proposal is an outrage.

No sensible analysis of which age groups require greater attention to their social insurance protections could possibly conclude that 77 percent of the excess dollars in the federal treasury should be devoted to programs for the elderly. Indeed, no sensible assessment of the fiscal problems of Medicare and Social Security pensions could conclude that 62 percent of the surplus should go to bolster pension finances and 15 percent to Medicare because Medicare's fiscal problems dwarf those of Social Security.

At our most generous, we can only ascribe the appearance of this proposal in this form to the arbitrary agenda-setting mechanisms embodied in current financing mechanisms. Legally required actuarial projections for the Social Security Retirement Trust Fund project a "crisis" in 2032. Hence a felt need arises in 1999 to act as if projections to 2032—indeed 2074—were reliable. The projections themselves have frightened beneficiaries and emboldened ideological opponents to propose radical dismantling of the Social Security system. Hence, the issue is joined.

Children, who are three times as likely as the elderly to be poor, have no federal entitlements program. They have no trust fund projections to catapult their income security needs onto the national agenda. No one seems even to be entertaining the question of whether massive surpluses should be devoted to the needs of children, the unemployed, the disabled, or those without health insurance.

In short, the existing structures and techniques of provision, particularly the existence of a particular set of financing structures and budget accounting rules, seem to be driving the nation's thinking about what really needs reforming in American social insurance. Means are determining what ends are even considered. This is not as it should be. In assessing American social insurance provision, we must first ask what it is that we are trying to do and evaluate how well we are doing it. Only after examining whether our existing efforts are adequate to our overall purposes do we turn to the specific means by which those purposes might be better served. We begin by looking at current social insurance protections during the working years.

Part Two **Pathologies of American Social Insurance**

## Chapter 4 Insuring a Working Life

The principal source of income for virtually all American families is wage or salary work. Family economic units are remarkably heterogeneous. But in all families, earnings by one or more members of the family group pay for food, clothing, and housing for all. We also know that the reserve financial resources of most American families are exceedingly thin. More than half of American families with incomes below $50,000 per year have less than $12,500 in financial assets; many have much less. Even in the middle of the income distribution, most people have some assets, but as figure 4.1 shows, their financial assets are modest. And most are held in forms that are not easily converted into current income.

When work and earnings stop, income stops. It should be no surprise, then, that families wish to insure against the primary risks to their income streams—involuntary unemployment, illness, accident, and early death. Moreover, the nature of the risks involved virtually assure that effective insurance will be social rather than private.

Fig. 4.1.    Financial assets, by income

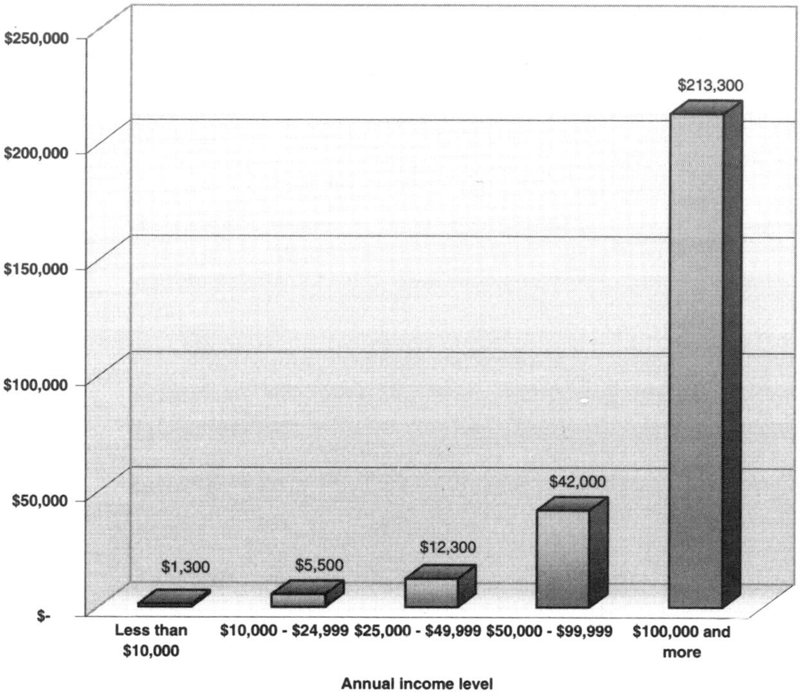

(*Source: 1998 Statistical Abstract,* table 798.)

## THE LIMITED CAPACITIES OF PRIVATE
## INSURANCE MARKETS

Both unemployment and disability insurance suffer from severe adverse selection problems. Insured persons have much better information about their risks than do insurers. A private insurer with its corporate head screwed on straight should be extremely skeptical of anyone showing up at its door to buy an individual unemployment or disability insurance policy. It would have to assume that such a person was looking at a high risk of the occurrence of the insured event and charge an appropriate— that is, a very steep—premium.

Unemployment insurance and some types of disability insurance are also especially prone to moral hazard. People will be far more likely to find reasons to stop working if the cost of doing so is cushioned by replacement of most of their wages. There inevitably is a tension between protecting workers against shocks that leave them without their wage income and encouraging them to keep working and pursuing alternative jobs.

While the moral hazard issue is always important in designing unemployment insurance, disability insurance presents more subtle challenges. People are not going to become seriously disabled simply to collect insurance, but disability is a very heterogeneous condition with varying effects on people's ability to earn a living. Some disabilities prevent people from working only for a short time; some limit the kinds of jobs one can do, or require special help from others to hold a job; others make any work at all impossible. Individualized determinations are an essential feature of disability insurance.

Basic insurance principles—concern with adverse selection and moral hazard—suggest that private, individual insurance against these risks will be unaffordable for most, and indeed, it always has been. Individual unemployment insurance is virtually unknown. And insurers who have attempted to write individual disability policies have often had disastrous experiences.

The most recent cautionary tale involves insuring doctors for total disability. Insurers thought that they had identified a group of professional compulsives who would work through virtually any disabling condition and collect only from their life insurers. Alas, insurers did not count on the growth of "managed care." Bureaucratic hassles recently drove so many middle-aged doctors from the profession that insurers suddenly found their clients virtually unrecognizable. Instead of stoic compulsives, they were faced with bitter early retirees—who also had precisely the right knowledge and connections to get themselves diagnosed and documented as unable to carry on their normal work.

Group disability insurance is more feasible. But, as might be expected, insurers can provide it at reasonable cost only to large groups of workers who are thought to have stable employment in relatively low-risk occupations. Groups at high risk of injury or disease, either through workplace exposures or otherwise, can obtain private disability insurance, but at very high rates. Hence, if disability or unemployment insurance is to be supplied to substantially all of the population of working families, workers must be forced into a common pool by government action. Moreover, if socially adequate replacement rates are to be provided for low-wage workers without having similarly high replacement rates attract too many high-wage workers out of the workforce, there must also be redistribution in the benefits scale between high-wage and low-wage workers. That is the domain of social insurance.

As if this were not enough, unemployment and disability insurance are unattractive to private insurers because of the extremely high covariance of the risks. It is well known that involuntary unemployment follows the business cycle. And if recessions are reasonably long and deep, private insurers might expect to go bankrupt even if they had somehow solved the adverse selection and moral hazard problems endemic to unemployment insurance. (The alternative, of course, would be to charge premiums so high that no one would buy.)

It is less widely known that the major determinant of disability claims is also the business cycle. Disability is not a precisely definable event. Whether individuals having certain conditions can continue to do their current jobs, or any job in the national economy, turns out to be a highly uncertain prediction in individual cases. There are many workers with physical or mental conditions that might qualify them for disability payments. In robust economic times, these workers are sought by employers and at wages that motivate them to overcome their impairments. As demand for workers becomes slack, however, the marginally productive will be let go. Many will rationalize their inability to find other work in terms of their medical condition. And many who do so will be found eligible for disability benefits.

As figure 4.2 reveals, disability claims in the Social Security Disability Insurance (SSDI) system have tended to track the unemployment rate. The major exception is the period of the early 1980s, when stringent administration was combined with deep recession. But this position was not politically sustainable. When the years 1982 and 1983 are removed from the data, the convergence between unemployment rates and disability insurance claims rates is striking.

Once again, this problem might be solved in private markets were business cycles predictable. But as one Nobel laureate economist famously quipped, "The stock market has predicted nine of the last five recessions."[1] If insurance against unemployment and disability is to cover a substantial portion of the workforce, it needs government's taxing and spending power behind it in some fashion. And disability insurance, like unemployment insurance, is wage replacement insurance. Once again, social adequacy will demand a redistribution from higher-wage to lower-

Fig. 4.2.    Disability applications and unemployment rate

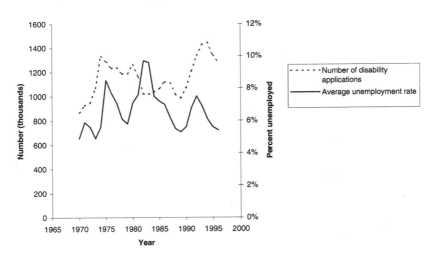

(*Source: 1998 Green Book,* tables 1-27 and F-1.)

wage earners in order to meet the joint purposes of reasonable levels of support and reasonable costs for the program as a whole.

Finally, we should not forget that the provision of unemployment and disability insurance is of interest to governments for reasons beyond the interest in protecting workers against hazards that are difficult to insure in private markets. Many analysts believe that downturns in the business cycle can be ameliorated by government spending, financed if necessary during recessions through government borrowing. Unemployment insurance may be a useful countercyclical macroeconomic tool. And because disability claims and awards also tend to follow the business cycle, these programs are countercyclical as well.

The case for unemployment and disability insurance as social insurance is virtually overwhelming. But as we shall see, the programs that we currently operate are not overwhelmingly successful.

## THE STATE OF UNEMPLOYMENT INSURANCE

American unemployment insurance was one of the centerpieces of the original 1935 Social Security Act.[2] Indeed, perhaps more than any other section of that statute, the unemployment insurance provisions addressed the critical problem of the moment. Within the ensuing decades, unemployment insurance has provided enormously important support for American workers, particularly during downturns in the business cycle. Nevertheless, American unemployment insurance has grave deficiencies. Because it was badly designed at the outset, it has had extreme difficulty responding to the massive transformation in the American labor market over the past sixty-five years.

Economic logic strongly suggests that unemployment insurance should be a national program. In a unified national economy with a single currency, macroeconomic shocks and cycles ripple throughout the nation as a whole. Because one of the functions of unemployment insurance is the maintenance of purchasing power to dampen the effects of recession, unemployment insurance is a part of the overall package of economic steering devices that should be available to the national government. Moreover, because economic cycles have regional variations both in timing and intensity, it makes sense to include the whole nation in the insurance pool. The demands on particular regions will be greatest just at the time that their fiscal capacity is weakest. Regional unemployment figures always diverge, and with some lag, they diverge the most in times of national recession (fig. 4.3).

Fig. 4.3.   U.S. unemployment rate and state variation

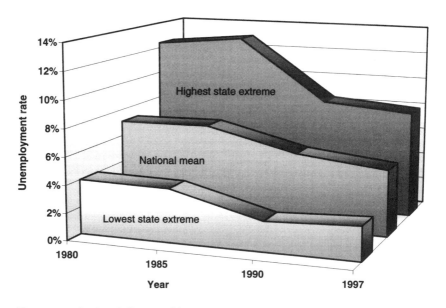

(*Source: 1998 Statistical Abstract,* table 683.)

Yet unemployment insurance, as it was constructed in the 1930s, and as it remains today, is a set of diverse state programs for which the federal government offers a peculiar incentive. For reasons both of politics and constitutional law, the unemployment insurance program was structured as a national tax on employers who fund their employees' unemployment benefits. This tax, however, is waived for any employer whose state imposes a similar unemployment tax and establishes an unemployment insurance benefits program that conforms to the broad contours of the federal statute. Because all states prefer to run their own programs, the federal government's role in unemployment insurance is to assure that states meet the minimum conditions for waiver of the federal tax and to manage a contingency fund from which states can borrow during times their reserves become inadequate.

Franklin Roosevelt understood as well as anyone the difficulties with this design. While governor of New York, he attempted to convince his fellow governors to institute parallel unemployment insurance systems in every state. As he told them then, unless we all act together, none of us can act at all.[3]

Roosevelt's reasoning was unassailable. The inexorable logic of interstate competition for mobile business capital makes it dicey for states to go it alone in a program like unemployment insurance. That is why the federal tax was necessary to goad states into action. Indeed, the federal tax is set sufficiently high that states can virtually always make their employers, or at least some substantial number of them, better off by having a state system of their own. But the same logic also suggests that states will continuously be tempted to improve their "business climate" by reducing the burden of unemployment insurance on existing and prospective employers. This so-called race to the bottom tends to undermine both the economic security and the macroeconomic stabilization purposes of the unemployment insurance program.[4] National averages mask great diversity among the states. The rate of unemployed persons receiving unemployment insurance benefits in 1995 was 17.6 percent in Virginia, but 65 percent in Rhode Island. As these highly divergent numbers suggest, states have remarkably different unemployment insurance systems.

Employers are only the first payers of the unemployment insurance tax. Some or all of these costs may be shifted to labor through reduced wages and to consumers through increased prices. But these reallocations of the burdens of the unemployment insurance tax occur only in the long run.

And in an experience-rated program like unemployment insurance (in which employers pay taxes based on how much unemployment insurance compensation is collected by their employees), they are unlikely to be shifted fully.[5] Every employer remains vulnerable to an idiosyncratic experience that may substantially increase its unemployment insurance costs under market conditions that prevent it from passing those costs back to workers or forward to consumers. Because employers really do pay some of the freight here in the form of increased labor costs, there is reason to believe that interstate competition will erode unemployment insurance protection.

Erosion has surely occurred, but it is an erosion that is invisible from the point of view of legislated coverage. Since 1935 the percentage of the workforce *nominally* covered by unemployment insurance has consistently increased. Well over 90 percent of Americans are now in covered employment. But coverage by statute is only a small part of the story. In every state, in addition to being in covered employment, an employee can collect unemployment insurance during a spell of unemployment only by meeting certain monetary and nonmonetary conditions. The monetary conditions relate to length of attachment to the workforce and average earnings; the nonmonetary conditions relate to reasons for unemployment and current availability for reemployment. The manipulation of these conditions over time has produced results that diverge startlingly from the steady statutory expansion of covered workers.

In 1947, 80 percent of workers in covered employment actually received benefits during a spell of unemployment. By 1995, that proportion had dropped to 38 percent. This amazingly low percentage is actually an improvement over the situation in the 1980s (fig. 4.4). These numbers alone suggest that American unemployment insurance is currently an inadequate set of protections for America's workers.

Moreover the percentage of unemployed workers actually receiving benefits bounces around erratically over time. These variations are the result not only of state policies and the unemployment rate, but also of the degree to which Congress has been willing to fund extended periods of benefits in times of national recession. The clear correlation between the unemployment rate and the number of workers who exhaust their unemployment insurance benefits suggests that effective action to counteract the effects of general recessions has not been the dominant pattern of congressional reaction.

Fig. 4.4.    Unemployment insurance coverage compared to actual receipt of benefits

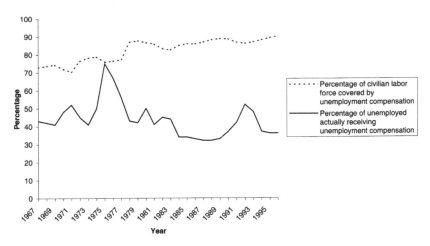

(*Source: 1998 Green Book,* table 4-2; *1998 Economic Report of the President,* tables B-35 and B-45.)

The reasons for the long-term decline in participation rates for unemployment insurance have been difficult to quantify.[6] Explanations include at least the following:

### Demographic Shifts

The workforce has become younger, at least during some of the relevant period. Younger workers tend to have lower wages and less secure employment. They are therefore less likely to meet prior work and earnings requirements during a spell of unemployment. There has also been a general shift of the population to southern and western states, which traditionally have lower participation rates in their unemployment insurance programs.[7]

### Workforce Changes

The increase in secondary workers, primarily women, who often work at lower wages and part-time, is also a part of the explanation. These again are characteristics that are likely to result in disqualification for benefits during a spell of unemployment. Full-time workers in stable employment are, in every state, most likely to receive benefits should they become unemployed. Part-time workers, workers who tend to be in and out of the workforce, and workers in lower-paying positions are least likely to receive benefits. There has also been a substantial decline in the percentage of unionized employees—and union membership has been found to be highly positively correlated with unemployment insurance participation rates.[8]

### Economic Changes

A number of analysts ascribe the decline in participants to a decline in the manufacturing sector and the rise of the services sector.[9] The notion is that the manufacturing sector offers more stable employment and fewer part-time or temporary positions. Downsizing and contracting out have created large numbers of "contingent workers" who once enjoyed relatively stable employment in large firms.[10] Wage stagnation, and in some cases decline, is another economic change that bears on unemployment insurance eligibility because a certain level of earnings during the relevant base period is required for eligibility in all states.

### Policy Changes

There has also been a tendency over time to make state eligibility rules more restrictive concerning the involuntariness of unemployment, the period for which leaving one's job voluntarily disqualifies one for unemployment insurance, and the rules about searching for a job.[11] Even without these rule changes, many observers believe that changes in state administration or practice have had similarly restricting effects. This is part of the "race to the bottom" that interstate competition for employers predictably creates.

Many of these causes for the decline of unemployment insurance participation rates are interconnected. There is continuing dispute in the literature about what is going on and which variables are most important in explaining the long-term decline in coverage. But whatever the true causes and their relative importance, this much is clear—unemployment insurance is becoming less relevant to the current world of work. Those workers who most need unemployment insurance are least likely to be eligible for benefits.

### EXPLAINING FAULTY DESIGN

Faulty initial design has prevented American unemployment insurance from meeting the challenges of the second half of the twentieth century.

That design will do no better in the twenty-first. As with most failures of institutional design, the federal-state nature of the unemployment insurance program was not a simple mistake. The technical committee on unemployment insurance of the Committee on Economic Security recommended a national system. But political logic sometimes leads where economic logic would not. President Roosevelt did not believe that a national unemployment system could pass in the U.S. Congress. Here, as in other aspects of New Deal legislation, Roosevelt was hostage to southern Democrats.[12]

To be sure, the federal government might have imposed additional conditions that would have limited state competition. But down that road lay potential invalidation of the program by the Supreme Court. Indeed, the technique of a federal tax to be waived in the face of state legislation, but with few conditions on state discretion, was suggested by Supreme Court Justice Louis Brandeis. A similar approach had been used to induce the state of Florida to adopt an estate tax to halt Florida's increasingly effective campaign to capture the residency of wealthy individuals by advertising its lack of any death taxes. The Federal Estate Tax Act of 1926 imposed an estate tax, but forgave 80 percent of it if a state enacted a tax of its own. The next year the Supreme Court declared the federal law constitutional.[13] The decision was unanimous at a time when many other aspects of New Deal programs were in deep constitutional trouble.

Both constitutional law and federal policy toward state-based discrimination have changed dramatically since 1935. Nevertheless, the inertial force of its beginnings has kept unemployment insurance primarily a state program. The federal government has made inroads in recent years, particularly through new conditions attached to federal payments for extended benefits in times of prolonged recession, but stopping the long downward spiral of unemployment insurance requires more effective reforms. Such reforms must recognize contemporary changes in the labor market, in the workforce, and in the risks that unemployment insurance should insure against.

For example, because a majority of American women now work, loss of income through pregnancy has become a major family problem. Similarly, shifts away from lifetime employment to employment by multiple employers often in differing locations, combined with geographic transfers by large national employers, cause critical problems for two-earner families. Virtually no state provides pregnancy benefits as a matter of course.

And leaving your job because your spouse has had to move is almost never "good cause" for a resignation under state unemployment insurance rules.[14]

There may, of course, be good reasons not to cover these sorts of risks in schemes structured as unemployment insurance currently is. For if such risks are to be covered, they will substantially change our view of the degree to which taxes for unemployment insurance should be borne entirely by the employer and should be experience-rated. Socializing these risks requires a move away not just from state policymaking and administration, but also from the relatively strong employer-financing and experience-rating principles that have always been part of the unemployment insurance program. The new world of unemployment risks requires substantial rethinking of current arrangements.

## THE MANY WORLDS OF DISABILITY INSURANCE

Work disability is ubiquitous.[15] Virtually everyone misses days of work because of illness or injury. Eighty percent of all workers can expect to lose ninety or more consecutive days of work to illness or injury sometime during their working lives. But work disability is also highly heterogeneous. Bouts of work disability range from a day out with the flu to career-ending and life-threatening conditions. Moreover, disability carries with it not only highly variable threats to the continuation of wage or salary income, but also a wide spectrum of needs and expenses for medical care, rehabilitation, and personal assistance. We should hardly be surprised, therefore, that disability insurance is not provided by a single program.[16]

For convenience, the world of disability cash benefits can be divided into three parts. The first is compensation for injury on the job provided by workers' compensation or veterans' compensation. The second category encompasses other work-based and work-connected cash benefits: sick leave, temporary or short-term disability insurance, Social Security Disability Insurance, private long-term disability insurance, and disability pensions as a part of employer-based defined-benefit retirement plans. Finally, there are means-tested benefits, including Supplemental Security Income and veterans' pensions. Even this listing is far from exhaustive. Many state and local cash-benefit programs have eligibility criteria based in part on disability. And a period of work disability often provides the occasion for receipt of cash benefits from programs such as unemployment insurance or general assistance that have nondisability-based eligibility criteria.

The ubiquity and heterogeneity of disability insurance in some sense matches the risks. And as might be expected, private and social provision for disablement has a long history as well as a wide scope. We have already mentioned that workers' compensation is generally recognized as the earliest modern social insurance program. But provision for disability stretches back to the dawn of human civilization. It has been an arena of public policy virtually from the time that nations came into being.

Given this long history and the existence of multiple interventions, one might easily imagine that risks of work disability are well insured for most American workers. One might also imagine, given this long experience with disability provision, that we would have learned to manage the costs of disability programs in some acceptable fashion. Alas, neither of these happy conclusions is warranted.

It is hardly surprising that coverage should be inadequate through purely private insurance markets. As we mentioned earlier, disability is a difficult event to define in objective terms. Work disability consists of a complex interaction between a worker's impairments, the demands of work, and the broader social and economic environment that either facilitates or inhibits rehabilitation and continued productive activity. As a consequence, only a minority of American workers have short- or long-term disability insurance, other than workers' compensation, as a part of their employee-benefit package. Roughly one-quarter of American workers hold jobs that provide sick leave and short-term disability insurance. And about that same proportion have private (usually group) insurance that covers long-term disability, which amounts essentially to early retirement.

On the other hand, almost all workers, roughly 95 percent, are covered under Social Security Disability Insurance. And more than 90 percent are covered by mandatory workers' compensation. These major social insurance programs thus broaden disability coverage, of some sort, to virtually the whole population. Nevertheless, as we shall see, this breadth of coverage is not matched by depth of insurance provision. Many disability risks remain uninsured, eligibility conditions restrict coverage for those who incur nominally insured risks, and income replacement rates are often meager.

The relative inadequacy of disability insurance coverage is in many ways merely the inevitable outcome of the difficulties of cost containment when insuring income loss due to work disability. Some commentators have theorized that disability insurance simply has an inherent tendency to grow more and more costly over time.[17] It is certainly easy to find examples of growth that have destroyed insurance systems or required their drastic modification. The relatively tight connection between unemployment and disability insurance claims, combined with judicial reluctance to interpret policies to the disadvantage of impecunious insureds, drove virtually all private disability insurers out of business in the United States in the 1930s. More recently, explosive growth in the Dutch disability insurance system has given rise to a term of art in the disability policy community called "The Dutch Disease."[18] Before recent reforms, cost projections for the Dutch disability system looked dramatically worse than our current scary projections for Medicare.

Yet the lack of a precisely defined risk that makes insurance schemes subject to economic shocks and uncontrolled growth is not the whole story of the difficulties of disability insurance. The adequacy-affordability tradeoff is real, but here again we find situations in which insurance is simultaneously inadequate and unaffordable. This sort of pathology has additional causes that we will sketch briefly by describing our two broadest disability insurance programs—workers' compensation and Social Security Disability Insurance.

### Workers' Compensation

Workers' compensation began in 1908 with the passage of the predecessor of the current Federal Employees' Compensation Act. The first state statute was passed in 1911, and by the early 1920s virtually every state had followed suit.[19]

The standard explanation for workers' compensation programs is that they were a necessary response to rapidly increasing industrial accidents and the incapacity of the tort system to provide timely and adequate compensation. More recent research suggests that, as usual, this "tort reform" began to make progress when plaintiffs began to win suits.[20] The increasingly sympathetic hearing that workers received before judges and juries brought employers to the bargaining table and produced workers' compensation's great compromise—limited liability in return for prompt payment without requiring a demonstration of the employer's fault.

In any event, the workers' compensation revolution of the early part of the century was hailed at the time as a triumph for the economic security of workers. A stingy, uncertain, and administratively cumbersome tort system was replaced by a secure entitlement to immediate assistance. Looking back at this victory from the perspective of the century's close, workers might rightly wonder whether Faust was bargaining for their side. Legislated levels of compensation have been slow to change in the face of both inflation and wage growth. The progressive shift in risks from industrial accident to industrial illness have been only haltingly and partially reflected in most state workers' compensation programs. Finally, because workers' compensation is experience rated, employer resistance to awards has produced a form of "adversarial legalism" that mocks the original promise of rapid and secure payment of insurance benefits for many workers.

This story sounds a lot like the story of unemployment insurance, and it is in two crucial respects. Workers' compensation, like unemployment insurance, features state administration and policy development, as well as funding through "experience-rated" premiums or taxes. In our view, these design features are critically implicated in the inadequacy-unaffordability crisis that besets both programs.

Workers' compensation has been described as serving three pivotal social purposes: [21]

1. By promptly providing workers with medical and disability benefits and establishing reasonably certain employer liability, it seeks to cushion the effects of worker-related injury and illness.
2. By requiring employers to pay compensation, it forces them to incorporate the cost of work-related injury and illness in marketing services and products. It thus seeks to create a significant incentive to improve occupational health and safety conditions.
3. By delivering no-fault benefits through an administrative process, workers' compensation is designed to operate as a relatively litigation-free system, providing prompt delivery of benefits at low administrative cost.

Yet in the early 1970s, the National Commission on Workers' Compensation described a system that was failing to meet all of these stated social purposes. And while there was some improvement in state programs in the 1970s, in the late 1990s American workers' compensation systems still provide inadequate coverage at great administrative costs.[22]

To be sure, most workers are now nominally covered by a workers' compensation insurance policy, which generally promises to pay them 67 percent of their prior weekly earnings if they are disabled on the job. But the 67 percent of prior earnings is "capped" by a maximum benefit amount that, in most states, makes actual average replacement rates fall well below 67 percent.

A host of other features of eligibility for workers' compensation restrict real coverage. Temporary total disability benefits are discontinued under workers' compensation policies after a prescribed period unless the worker can demonstrate permanent total disability. Most workers cannot, and are then left with absolutely no income replacement from workers' compensation. Time limits that are perfectly reasonable with relation to the filing of accident claims are also applied to workplace illnesses. The effect is to deny claims where exposures long antedate illness. Attempts to adjudicate particular claims fairly have built up an arcane workers' compensation jurisprudence that has rendered more and more areas of workers' compensation claims controversial and made their payment uncertain.

The combination of these and other factors means, quite simply, that workers' compensation makes a very modest contribution to the replacement of lost earnings due to work disability. All sources of disability income, public and private, replace only about 25 percent of total national income lost to disability.[23] Workers' compensation does not, to say the least, make a huge contribution to this low replacement rate.[24] But the program is far from cheap. Total benefits paid in 1993 were nearly $43 billion, and total costs to employers were nearly $14 billion more. In 1997, workers' compensation cost employers about forty cents per hour per employee, but given the difference between employer costs and workers' benefits, coverage was worth only twenty-seven cents an hour to covered employees.[25]

This disparity between costs and benefits strongly suggests that the original idea of an administratively efficient system run by disinterested specialists to produce prompt payment of claims has turned out to be another program planner's "Rosie Scenario."[26] State industrial accident commissions are not the efficient apolitical machines that danced in the heads of Progressive reformers. In recent years, litigation has reached epidemic proportions.[27] The result has been that over one-quarter of workers' compensation premiums are eaten up in administrative costs.[28]

Finally, requiring employers to pay compensation through the workers' compensation system has uncertain effects on the rate of industrial accidents or illnesses. By the 1950s scholars were questioning whether the workers' compensation program actually affected the rate of workplace injury. These claims have been challenged, but doubts have persisted. There are even claims that, on balance, workers' compensation discourages safety and increases injury levels.[29]

The question, of course, is how such an inadequate system can be so costly. Three answers are routinely given: lawyers, doctors, and legislators.

We have already commented on the increasing litigiousness of the workers' compensation system. Situations vary across states, but clearly some states have seen cost increases because of litigation. In 1988 and 1989, claims litigated were equal to nearly 12 percent of claims filed in California and included a whopping 44 percent of all claims involving any lost work time—that is, the real work disability cases. In Illinois, litigation expenses amounted to the same percentage of recoveries as those in fault-based automobile injury cases. And, in Rhode Island, 80 percent of total claim costs resulted from cases involving attorney representation.[30] This litigiousness could be blamed on attorneys. But it is really the fault of systems that have failed to make attorneys unnecessary.

Doctors were never thought to be unnecessary to the treatment of workers' injuries or to the processing of claims, but they certainly were not anticipated to be so costly. Workers' compensation has suffered from the same cost inflation in medical care that has buffeted all public and private health insurers. Evidence suggests, however, that workers' compensation medical cost increases have been much greater than in health care generally. A recent study finds, for example, that beneficiaries of workers' compensation receive nearly four times the duration of treatment and twice as many medical encounters as others with the same diagnosis. The result is that it costs 1.7 times more to treat a covered workers' compensation injury than that same injury outside the workers' compensation system. These peculiarly high medical costs have yet to be explained.[31] We confess to the suspicion that they are caused in part by the adversarial character of disputes. Many medical services covered by workers' compensation may be as much for evidentiary as for clinical purposes.

Cost increases clearly also resulted in part from liberalizations of benefits that occurred mostly in the mid- to late 1970s. But whatever the reasons for the growth in workers' compensation costs, the perception of runaway expenditures has led to retrenchment. One state legislature after another has been importuned to do something about rising insurance rates. They have responded by a new round of benefit limitations, time limits, maximum earning caps, and administrative reforms. The cost of cutting costs will, of course, be a further reduction in adequacy.

If the cost overruns of the 1980s are traceable in considerable degree to the liberalizing reforms of the 1970s, and the contemporary retrenchment is a response to the spiraling workers' compensation costs of the prior decade, what do these expansions and contractions tell us about the economics or politics of workers' compensation as a social insurance program? Put in historical perspective, the message is relatively clear. Left to their own devices, states are forced into a race—really a slow crawl—to the bottom in terms of the adequacy of workers' compensation coverage and benefits.

In short, where states must respond to the "non-competitiveness" claims of employers facing rising employee benefit costs and of insurers unable to get premium relief from state regulators, they are unlikely to produce or maintain an adequate workers' compensation package. Benefits rose during the 1970s in the face of a credible threat of federal intervention. When that threat faded, retrenchment began, and it has generally continued to the present.[32]

Workers' compensation and unemployment insurance are major examples of two of the reform themes we highlighted in Chapter 2: the problematic role of state finance, and the danger that pursuit of other social goals—regulating employers' employment practices in unemployment insurance and deterring accidents while providing compensatory justice in workers' compensation—will undermine a program's effectiveness as social insurance. The effective ingredients for stable workers' compensation reform, therefore, seem to be the same as those we encountered in our discussion of unemployment insurance: an increase in national presence, and a decrease in the tight connection between employee compensation and employer costs. More generally, it seems increasingly sensible to fold workers' compensation protections into a comprehensive scheme of illness, disability, and health insurance.

We will not develop the contours of these ideas further at this point. It is worth noting, however, that neither of these reform directions is utopian when viewed in cross-national perspective. Only three of the 136 countries with workers' compensation programs have state- or province-run systems—Australia, Canada, and the United States. Nor is the simple fact of constitutional federalism a barrier to a national scheme. Brazil, Argentina, Austria, Switzerland, and other federations all have nationally run workers' compensation programs.

Moreover, while there is usually some greater payment level for work-related injuries, and some contribution by employers to the workers' compensation portion of disability insurance, in most countries workers' compensation is part of a general social insurance system financed primarily through taxes other than employer payments. Indeed, in most countries workers' compensation has been decoupled from its tort reform history and made a part of disability insurance more generally.

### Social Security Disability Insurance

Looking at disability "whole" is clearly a good idea. Eliminating gaps in coverage that result from programmatic fragmentation is only one of the advantages. A holistic approach to disability insurance also permits the pursuit of other important goals. After all, some disability can be avoided, and some can be made temporary rather than permanent. Even if permanent, sometimes consequences of an "impairment" may be avoided so that the "disability" is partial rather than total. With appropriate care and support, some impairments that affect personal capacities may pose no serious limitations on self-support.[33]

There are existing models of the holistic approach to disability policy. Those workers lucky enough to be covered by comprehensive health and disability insurance at their workplace (about 25 percent of all workers) sometimes get the advantages of integrated "case management." Health care is immediately available; rehabilitation services are provided; income support during the period of recovery is a part of the package. Access to a pension for long-term disability is delayed until all of these efforts at rehabilitation and return to work have been exhausted. Integrated supports and services have traditionally characterized the public systems of some European democracies—for example, of Germany and Sweden.[34]

Why is this not the system created by the disability provisions of the Social Security Act? Once again, an ounce of history, particularly political history, is worth a pound of logic.

Disability insurance was recognized as a crucial part of the total social insurance effort in the early 1930s. But the disastrous consequences for private disability insurers during the Depression gave Social Security planners pause. Their caution was strongly reinforced by the medical community's strident political opposition to a federal role in disability insurance. Apoplectic about the possibilities of public health insurance, the American Medical Association viewed a disability program as a first step toward "socialized medicine." In the collective imagination of association members, the use of physicians as sources for treatment and information in a federal disability system would metastasize rapidly into a full-blown national health insurance scheme.

As a consequence, public disability insurance in the United States was long delayed. It crept into our Social Security scheme as a form of early retirement. The disability program began as a waiver of Social Security (FICA) taxes for disabled workers. The idea was to ensure that workers who had a disability that precluded all substantial gainful employment, but who were otherwise qualified, received retirement benefits. The progressive logic of moving toward cash payment was then irresistible, for there was no good answer to the question, "What are these people to live on in the meanwhile?"

As a result, by 1960 we had a disability retirement insurance scheme with coverage as broad as the pension scheme. But because of its origins and focus, it dealt only with a complete disability that was expected to keep a worker permanently out of the workforce. The federal scheme contained no temporary or partial disability payments, nor were medical benefits available. Rather than featuring early intervention, there was a waiting period of five months before a person was eligible to apply. All of these features have been retained. Although medical insurance is now available through Medicare, coverage is delayed until two years after a determination of eligibility for receipt of cash benefits. No one can mistake this for an integrated or coordinated scheme.

The only integrating element worth noting is the requirement that disability beneficiaries be referred to state vocational rehabilitation agencies. But these agencies generally find that they can do nothing to assist recipients to return to work. In fact, the test for work disablement under the Social Security disability statute is so stringent that a large number of applicants who have been denied Social Security disability cash income are rejected by vocational rehabilitation services as too disabled to benefit from any such retraining. And there is no national insurance program for those disabled either temporarily (for less than twelve months) or partially.

The position of applicants denied disability cash benefits is particularly dire. Every study of the future work history of denied applicants finds that fewer than half of the surviving denied applicants are working. Those who are working are not doing particularly well. And those without work are living primarily off the income of other family members or some form of state general assistance.

The economic position of those who receive cash benefits is better, but replacement rates are quite low in relation to prior income. For example, only workers having annual earnings of less than $20,000 (in 1995 dollars) are eligible to receive benefits equal to 50 percent or more of their prior earnings. These replacement rates drop sharply as one goes up the income scale. Social Security disability cash benefits are thus inadequate to keep many families out of poverty, much less to maintain something close to their prior standard of living. Nearly 20 percent of disability insurance recipients also receive means-tested Supplemental Security Income (SSI) payments.[35]

Notwithstanding serious inadequacies in disability insurance coverage and the level of disability benefits, contemporary concerns with the disability insurance program have focused almost exclusively on combating increasing costs. Fewer than 4 million Americans received disability insurance payments in 1984, but that number had risen to over 6 million in 1996. Indeed, 8.5 million Americans now receive benefits under the disability insurance, SSI, or dependents' benefits provisions of the Social Security Act. Expenditures for disability cash payments and medical care for disabled beneficiaries is now over $100 billion per year and projected to grow rapidly as the baby boomers age.

The causes of growth in these programs are difficult to isolate. Clearly the aging of the population is part of the explanation. Work disability is highly associated with advancing age. There is also a rising incidence of disability among younger workers affected by various mental or nervous disorders. Mental disorders represented 11 percent of disability insurance awards in 1982, but 22 percent in 1996 (down from 26 percent in 1993). In the SSI program, mental illness (29.9 percent) and mental retardation (27.8 percent) accounted for a whopping 57.7 percent of those receiving SSI payments in 1996. Not only is mental illness now treated in "deinstitutionalized" settings, thus making those with mental disabilities eligible for cash payments, but the movement to an information and service economy also may make working with a mental illness more difficult than it was in the past.

There have also been significant cutbacks in other areas of social support—cutbacks that put pressure on impaired persons to apply for disability benefits. And private disability insurers all reduce their disability pension payments by amounts received from public programs and require that their clients apply for public disability cash payments.

As if perceptions of unaffordability combined with problems of inadequacy were not enough, many advocates are increasingly impatient with the structure and focus of disability insurance. The new politics of disability features "inclusion" and services, and steers away from labeling people as "disabled" and presuming that they will be "dependent." Hence while disability cash benefits are a crucial protection for millions of Americans, a vocal constituency to support these programs is hard to find.

The "insider" politics of disability benefits could prove to be a major liability. While disability policy has been crowded off the congressional agenda by crises in Medicare and a projected crisis in the pension program, disability's day in the congressional limelight will surely come. Congress is already showing considerable interest in reform proposals designed to move more disability beneficiaries off the disability rolls and into the workplace. But it remains to be seen whether these reforms will "balance security with opportunity," as the title of a recent National Academy of Social Insurance report suggests, or stress the enthusiasms for beneficiary terminations that have characterized recent rounds of welfare reform.[36]

### SUMMARY

Insuring a working life—roughly the years between twenty and sixty-five—requires insuring risks related mostly to discrete events in workers' lives, not to their long-term experience or slowly emerging trends in the economy. Private market failure is pronounced for these events, and private voluntary insurance plays a very small role. Recognizing the high moral hazard that is present, programs protecting against income loss during the working years have historically and conceptually been tightly linked with ameliorative efforts to improve functioning or job prospects and to promote return to the labor force.

Unemployment insurance and workers' compensation benefits are funded by state taxes or mandates combined with experience-rating—modes of finance that create severe political impediments to adequate funding. Even though these programs are not experiencing the kind of fiscal strain that we shall see in connection with social insurance for the retirement years, there are serious gaps in coverage. American social insurance programs have failed to maintain insurance that responds to today's real risks. Our worries here should probably be more about spending too little than spending too much.

The crucial issues for unemployment insurance, workers' compensation, and disability insurance vary, but in all of them the problems are structural, not fiscal. Destructive interstate competition, excessive levels of adversarial behavior, high administrative (including medical and legal) costs, and lack of coverage integration are all implicated in the inadequate protections now afforded American workers against the risks of unemployment, illness, and disability. In this arena there is every prospect for providing better social insurance with little increase in insurance costs.

## Chapter 5 Insuring
the Post-Work Years

As the twentieth century comes to a close, Congress has em-
barked on a major effort to reform the nation's least troubled and
most successful social insurance program, Social Security. Today,
95 percent of all U.S. workers are covered by the retirement, disability, and survivors' benefits of Social Security (OASDI) and
when retired due to age or disability will enjoy health coverage
through Medicare. Close to 50 million Americans—one of every
six—receive a monthly benefit check (or direct bank deposit)
from the Social Security Administration.

Unlike unemployment and disability insurance, insuring retirement income is plagued by neither adverse selection nor
moral hazard. Insurers need not fear that people will age faster to
collect their retirement checks, and, although determining a
person's age was once challenging, now doing so is easy. To be
sure, many workers retire sooner than they would without retirement income insurance, and some save less for retirement than

they otherwise might. But insuring income during retirement is straight-forward compared to insuring unemployment or disability. Here the problems principally lie in deciding what retirement protections we want and how to finance them.[1]

The Social Security and Medicare programs for retirees are immensely popular, but they are also budgetary behemoths. Health and retirement benefits together account for more than half of the total annual outlays of the federal government. These costs have grown rapidly over the last six decades (fig. 5.1), and the aging and increased longevity of the population guarantees even greater growth in the years ahead (fig. 5.2).

Indeed, the imbalance between projected benefit costs and dedicated OASDHI taxes propelled both the creation of a bipartisan Medicare commission that reported in 1999 as well as a spate of presidential and con-

Fig. 5.1.    Federal expenditures

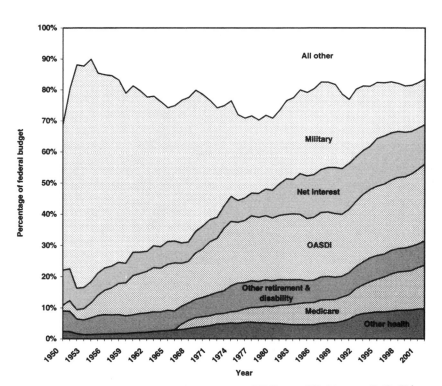

(*Source:* C. Eugene Steuerle et al., *The Government We Deserve*, Washington, D.C., Urban Institute Press, 1998, fig. 4.6.)

Fig. 5.2.    Projections of federal expenditures on Social Security, Medicare, and Medicaid

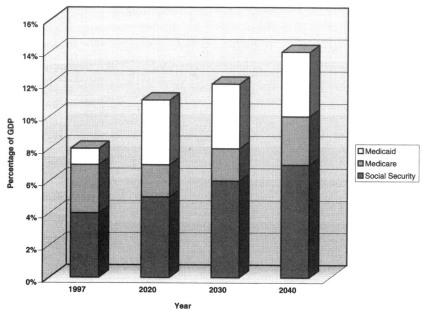

(*Source:* Congressional Budget Office, *Long-Term Budgetary Pressure and Policy Options,* May 1998, table 2-1.)

gressional proposals to make Social Security more financially secure over the long term. But, as we noted earlier, such financial concerns tend to motivate relatively superficial consideration of programs alleged to be in "crisis." In thinking about social insurance as a whole, we need to ask more fundamental questions about the appropriate role of collective and individual responsibility for retirement security in old age. Is all the governmental attention to the end of the life cycle justified? If so, are our current approaches doing a good job? At acceptable costs?

## WHY IS RETIREMENT AN INSURABLE EVENT?

Although we now take the existence of Social Security for granted, it is somewhat surprising that Social Security has become the nation's largest social insurance program.[2] Living to enjoy one's retirement may seem an odd thing to insure. Unlike premature death, disability, injury, illness, or unemployment during one's working years—events that tend to strike

Fig. 5.3.    Earnings over the life cycle

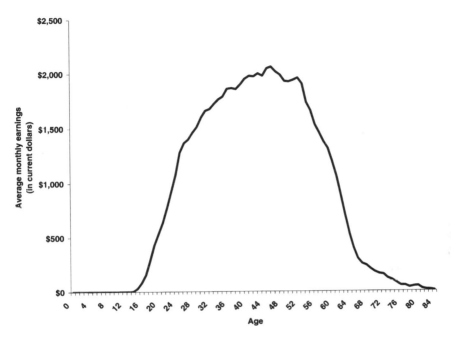

(*Source:* Authors' calculations based on U.S. Census Bureau, *1993 Survey of Income and Program Participation.*)

suddenly—the loss of earnings due to retirement is routine and, on average, predictable. As figure 5.3 illustrates, people tend to have little or no earned income both at the beginning and end of life.

In a nation that venerates self-reliance, why isn't retirement a proper occasion for self-protection through thrift, an event we should each plan and save for? There is no crisp, simple answer to this question. But a host of considerations have led every developed nation, and many underdeveloped ones, to take collective governmental action to promote retirement security.

First, planning for an adequate income during retirement is not as straightforward as it might seem. What length of retirement, for example, should one expect? Unlike the risk of premature death, which life insurance protects, the risk to income security in retirement is living too long. Each worker is uncertain, perhaps happily so, about the time of his or her own death. People are not all "average," and outliving the average may mean outliving one's savings.

People face considerable uncertainty not only about their own life expectancy, but also about the average life expectancy of their age cohort. For every worker entering the labor force, assessing that expectation involves projecting mortality rates half a century later. If mortality unexpectedly improves—because of medical advances, for example—even far-sighted and thrifty workers will not have sufficient savings when they reach retirement age. In 1950, for example, workers could hardly have anticipated that people over age eighty-five would today be the fastest growing segment of the population.

Second, there is great uncertainty about both future economic conditions and one's place within the national economy. Greater economic progress will improve living standards, but at the same time require additional resources to maintain preretirement standards of living. No individual can be certain where her own earnings pattern will fit within the overall economy. This is obvious at the beginning of a working life. But as many "downsized" middle- and upper-income employees have learned to their great dismay, even during the middle years it may be a bad bet to rely on one's employer for consistently increasing incomes and a generous retirement package.

Predictions of investment returns are also uncertain. Although long-term trends can be discerned, markets from time to time make large "corrections." For a retiree, the timing of such corrections may be critical. For example, we might pity those who retired in November 1987, just after the stock market had made a mid-course "adjustment" that cost it one-third of its value. The market romp of the nineties was of no avail for many of these people. The simple point is that market returns will vary for different age cohorts.[3]

Inflation also presents a planning problem. Slightly higher than expected inflation rates can have a big effect on fixed incomes. If inflation averages 7 percent a year, the purchasing power of a monthly retirement check will be reduced by half in a decade, and by three-quarters in two decades. It is impossible for people ten or twenty years into their retirement to recoup by saving more or working harder. Nor, as figure 5.4 shows, is inflation stable or predictable.

Moreover, despite the natural expectation of retirement, some people are simply unable to save adequate resources to protect themselves against a major decline in their standard of living—or even from poverty—after they can no longer earn a living from employment. Most of us seem inca-

Fig. 5.4.    Inflation

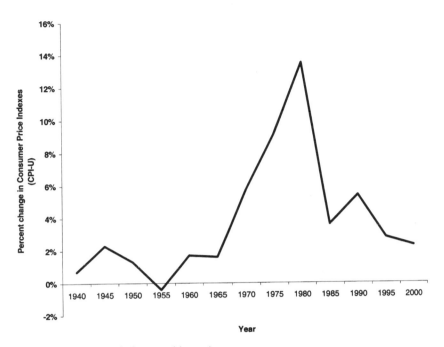

(*Source: 1998 Statistical Abstract*, table 772.)

pable of imagining ourselves retired until retirement is so close that saving enough to maintain our lifestyle is virtually impossible.

Myopia is not the only reason for deferring retirement savings until relatively late in life. Given the low incomes of most younger workers, it is difficult, perhaps selfish, to deprive children of current resources so that the parents can save for their own retirement years. In thinking about ensuring an adequate standard of retirement living, we cannot ignore the economic reality of our nation's workers. The vast majority struggle daily to make enough income to meet their current needs.

Finally, the predictable loss of salary income during retirement is so large that people commonly underestimate the resources a reasonably comfortable retirement will demand. For example, if a married couple with earnings of $60,000 a year wants to maintain an income of two-thirds that amount, $40,000, they will need $500,000 in assets at age sixty-five to finance that level fully from private savings. This is the amount that an insurance company required in 1995 to fund a $40,000

Fig. 5.5.   Median net wealth of householders age 65 and older, by income

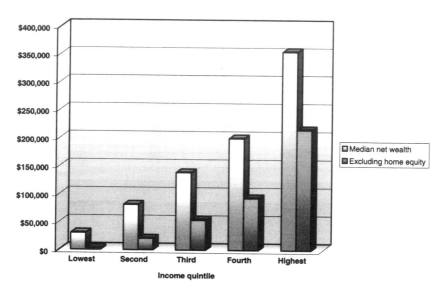

(*Source: U.S. Census Bureau, Current Population Reports, Asset Ownership of Households, 1993,* Washington D.C., 1995, 70-47, table D.)

single-premium two-life annuity. *Fewer than 3 percent of the population have assets this large.* (Figure 5.5 provides additional information about the size of people's assets by income quintile.) In almost comical economist-speak, a recent article in the prestigious *American Economic Review* attributes systematic shortfalls in resources for retirement to "information shock"—in plain English, the sudden discovery that you don't have enough money to live on during retirement.[4]

These difficulties with individual provision for retirement security do not, however, tell us that the United States must maintain the form of social insurance for retirement security that it has. For example, mandatory private retirement accounts, with subsidies for low-income workers' accounts and required conversion on retirement into government-insured, inflation-protected annuities, could theoretically meet the income security goals that underlie our current Social Security pension scheme. We will have much to say later concerning the mix of techniques that we believe to be most desirable when providing retirement security. The crucial point, nevertheless, remains: individuals' uncertainty, myopia, and differential capacities to save make a substantial public role in retirement security inescapable.

## THE ROLE OF PRIVATE PENSIONS

The inability of private savings and insurance to do the whole job of ensuring retirement security does not mean that government must do the entire job instead. Indeed the architects of Social Security pensions presumed that employer-based pensions and private savings would complete the "three-legged stool" of retirement security policy. But these sources of retirement income, particularly employer-based pensions, have had a troubled history. Their partial coverage and limited relevance to many low- and middle-income workers make them an inadequate line of defense against insufficient income in old age.

### The Troubled Past

Beginning in the 1870s, railroads and certain other large American businesses created private pensions as a way to retain experienced workers in their forties and fifties and to encourage retirement of older workers.[5] In 1921, when about three hundred employer pension plans had been established, covering 15 percent of the nation's wage earners, Congress provided a major tax boost to private pensions. Employers were allowed to deduct current contributions to a pension plan, pension trusts were made exempt from any income tax on their investment income, and employees were permitted to defer all taxes until they received pension payments. This income tax treatment made pension promises more valuable than cash compensation, not only because pension funds accumulate earnings tax-free in contrast to the normal current income taxation of investment income, but also because the deferral of taxation of compensation until retirement may produce taxation at lower rates.

By 1932, however, a total of only 300,000 to 400,000 people were receiving employer-based pensions, with less than half of those from private for-profit companies.[6] The employer pension movement was limited to government employers and large firms. During the 1920s, four firms—AT&T, U.S. Steel, and the Pennsylvania and New York Central railroads—employed one-third of all pension-plan participants.[7] Even in these companies, only those workers who stayed until retirement received a pension. The companies provided no guarantee that pensioners' benefits would not be reduced or eliminated, and protection against postretirement inflation was unheard of. Employees of small and medium-sized businesses had no pensions to look forward to.

Moreover, workers bore the risks of their employer's insolvency, a risk made all too real by notorious collapses—such as when the Morris Packing Company ceased operations in 1923 and terminated its pension plan, ultimately leaving workers unable to recoup even their own contributions to the plan.[8] Public suspicion about the value of employers' pension promises was raised again four decades later by the collapse of the Studebaker auto company.[9] Jimmy Hoffa's raids on the assets of the Teamsters Union's multiemployer pension plans in the 1950s and 1960s offered further proof that an unregulated private pension system could not be counted on to protect retirees' income.

The failures of the private pension system pushed public policy in two directions: Social Security was enacted in 1935 to provide a public system for ensuring a baseline measure of retirement income security, and in 1974 extensive federal regulation of private employer pensions was added to protect legitimate employee expectations. To qualify for favorable tax treatment today, defined benefit pension plans must have a broad participation base among employees, meet specified minimum levels of funding, and provide for vesting of benefits after a prescribed period of employment. These employer plans now must also purchase solvency insurance from the federal Pension Benefit Guarantee Corporation.

### The (Non)-Coverage of Lower-Income Workers

Private pensions had always favored highly-paid employees, but when Social Security pensions were added to the mix, employers "integrated" their pension plans by reducing employer-provided benefits by some proportion of Social Security benefits. Because Social Security pension calculations favor low-wage workers, the advent of Social Security pensions had the ironic effect of making integrated employer plans favor the higher-paid even more.

But the lower a family's income, the greater proportion it must save to avoid poverty during retirement. And low-income families find it difficult to save anything. Without a mechanism to guarantee at least some minimum level of retirement income, many elderly Americans would find themselves in poverty. To provide true security in old-age retirement, insurance protection must insure against the effects of low lifetime wages. This requires that social insurance benefits upon retirement for low-wage workers constitute a higher percentage of their preretirement salary than those of high-wage workers. Private insurance and private savings alone are inadequate to this essential redistributive task.

Nor is a system that provides greater replacement rates for lower-income workers necessarily a bad deal for higher-paid workers. Their realistic choice is to subsidize the retirement income of low-wage contributors to the retirement system, or pay the full costs of subsistence pensions for people who make no provision for their own retirement security. Given the limited coverage and checkered history of employment-based pensions, higher-paid workers can hardly rely on the employers of low- and middle-income workers to provide them with an adequate retirement package.

### Public Pensions and Poverty Rates

While accurate statistics are elusive, in 1930 before Social Security was enacted, at least 40 percent of the elderly population had less than $1,000 in assets and $300 in income and therefore were dependent on family, friends, or charity to live.[10] Public almshouses and limited cash relief from the states as well as private charitable homes for the aged were commonplace. Social Security completely changed this landscape, but transformation did not come overnight. In 1960, twenty-five years after the enactment of Social Security, the poverty rate among the elderly (over 30 percent) was still about twice as high as that for the rest of the population.

By 1992, in contrast, only 13 percent of the elderly were in poverty, about the same proportion as for other adults. Looking at levels of consumption, rather than income, the elderly now apparently have the lowest poverty rate of any demographic group.[11] The effects of Social Security in shaping this result are dramatic. More than half of the elderly—56 percent in 1994—would have incomes below the poverty level without their Social Security benefits. Fifty-nine percent of Social Security recipients obtain more than half their income from Social Security and, as figure 5.6 shows, the importance of Social Security to family budgets is inversely correlated with income throughout the income distribution.

The central role of Social Security in ensuring a decent standard of living in retirement is now obvious. But although Social Security is our most important mechanism for funding retirement income, it provides, on av-

Fig. 5.6.   Income sources for individuals age 65 and older

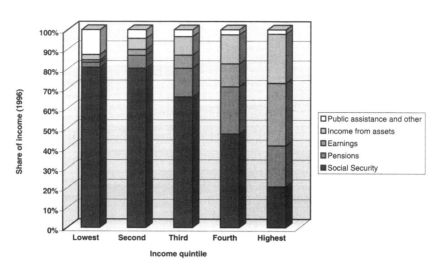

(*Source:* Social Security Administration, *Income of the Population 55 or Older,* April 1998, table VII.)

erage, less than one-half of the income needed to fund an average worker's preretirement standard of living (fig. 5.7). The other half must come mostly from earnings, personal savings, and/or employer-sponsored pensions. While virtually all elderly persons now receive Social Security income, however, fewer than 40 percent receive any other pension income and fewer than 20 percent have any earnings. Nearly 70 percent of the elderly have some income from personal savings, but for most of these their annual investment income is quite low.[12]

While savings and pensions are both generally regarded as "private" and "voluntary" and, as a result, typically are omitted from discussion of social insurance, government plays such a large and critical role in regulating and providing tax incentives for these forms of retirement savings that any discussion of social insurance for retirees is radically incomplete if it omits them. Most larger employers view the provision of tax-favored pensions as a necessary part of their compensation packages, and their employees have no option but to take some of their compensation in the form of pension benefits. The huge public subsidy and significant regulation of employer-provided pensions make the common label "private pensions" misleading. These are not arrangements freely chosen by individuals in a competitive

Fig. 5.7.   Income sources for total population age 65 and older

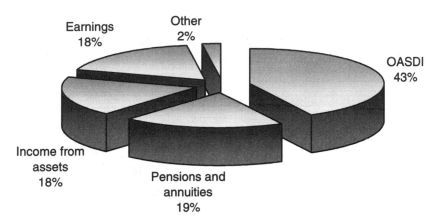

(*Source:* EBRI, *Databook on Employee Benefits*, 4th ed., table 7.4, 1995 data.)

market for pensions. Public policy has made employer-based pensions a virtual necessity for employers who have a substantial workforce. And the choice of how and how much to save is largely determined by employers, not employees.

Retirement security policy thus raises two types of questions for social insurance reformers: (1) How should we structure the mandatory scheme for assuring basic adequacy? and (2) How and to what extent should we subsidize and regulate "voluntary" savings for retirement to assist families in maintaining preretirement standards of living?

## THE CHALLENGE FOR MANDATORY PENSIONS

The 1935 Social Security Act provided monthly retirement income at age sixty-five, scheduled to begin in 1942, and a lump-sum death benefit to the estates of these workers. Amendments in 1939 extended benefits to retired workers' spouses and dependent children, added survivors' insurance, and moved the payment of benefits forward to 1940. The first four decades of Social Security were years of growth: eligibility was expanded in the 1930s and 1950s; insurance for disabled workers, disabled children, and dependents of disabled workers was added in the 1950s; benefits were increased in the 1950s and 1970s, and automatic cost-of-living increases were introduced in 1972. Social Security coverage has expanded from 60 percent of the workforce in 1935 to about 95 percent today. But the past two decades have produced some retrenchment: in 1977 benefits were scaled back, in 1983 the normal retirement age was scheduled to gradually increase from sixty-five to sixty-seven (beginning in 2002), and in the 1990s the benefits of many Social Security beneficiaries were subjected to income taxation. Payroll taxes to finance Social Security have increased from their 1937 level of 2 percent on the first $3,000 of wages to 12.4 percent on the first $72,600 in 1999.

Until now, Social Security has enjoyed a rather benign demography, with the proportion of the population over age sixty-five increasing relatively slowly. The ratio of Social Security–covered workers to beneficiaries fell from 16.5 to one in 1950 to 3.8 to one in 1970, largely through expansions of Social Security eligibility.[13] Now America's population is aging: first, the large baby-boom generation—people born between 1946 and 1964—will begin to retire early in the twenty-first century, just as the smaller baby-bust generation that follows reaches its peak earning capacity. By 2050 about 35 percent of the population is projected to be fifty-five or older, compared to less than 15 percent in 1970 (fig. 5.8).

Moreover, retirees' life expectancies after age sixty-five are increasing

Fig. 5.8.    Changing size of population age 55 and older

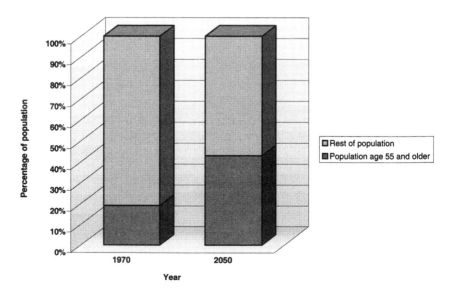

(*Source:* Authors' calculations based on EBRI, *Databook on Employee Benefits,* 4th ed., table A-1; *1997 Statistical Abstract,* table 17, middle series.)

dramatically. The fastest growing age group in America is persons eighty-five or older. While the specifics of all such predictions should be taken with a pound—not grain—of salt, the population over age sixty-five is expected to increase by 23 percent during the period 1993–2010. But those over age eighty-five are expected to increase by about 80 percent. The number of people age eighty-five and over is expected to grow by over 400 percent, from less than 4 million to nearly 19 million people by the year 2050, and will be a greater share of the population (fig. 5.9).

The Social Security Administration (SSA) projects that the ratio of payroll tax contributors to recipients of benefits will decline from the current level of 3.3 workers per recipient to 2.0 by the year 2030. If current benefits were financed entirely from current taxes, this demographic shift would imply that if three workers today are required to pay thirty-three cents each for every dollar of benefits, fifty cents each will be required from two workers to fund a dollar of benefits in 2030. Alternatively, if payroll taxes are not increased, benefits would have to be cut by one-third.

Fig. 5.9.    Percentage of population age 85 and older

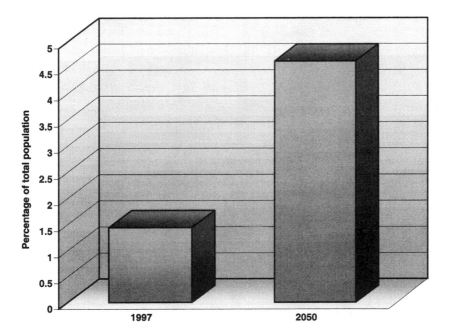

(*Source:* Authors' calculations based on *1997 Statistical Abstract*, table 17, middle series.)

Because the Social Security Trust Funds have been accumulating surplus funds for a number of years and because this demographic shift will occur gradually over time, SSA has estimated that, without changing Social Security financing, after about 2030 current tax revenues will pay for about 76 percent of benefits now promised to OASDI beneficiaries.[14] Likewise, these demographic forces imply an average annual deficit equal to 2.17 percent of covered wages over the next seventy-five-year period—the lifetime perspective over which Social Security finances have typically been viewed. That number increases annually as current years of surplus are replaced by future years of deficits. If no changes are made, Social Security benefits in 2070 are projected to exceed taxes by about 5.5 percent of taxable wages.

Traditionally, when faced with such adverse financial projections, Congress has responded with a combination of payroll tax increases and benefit cuts. In 1983, for example, benefits were reduced, in part by gradually raising the "normal" retirement age from sixty-five to sixty-seven (beginning in 2002) and by accelerating planned tax increases. But, unlike 1983, today's debate involves no short-term financial crisis for the Social Security Trust Funds. In fact actuaries in 1998 estimated that, at current tax levels, the Social Security Trust Funds can finance all benefits promised until the year 2032 and about three-quarters of such benefits thereafter.

Paradoxically, changing circumstances have broadened the agenda of potential responses to Social Security's long-term demographic and financial challenges. Until now, all Social Security retirement beneficiaries, regardless of their wage level, have received large benefits relative to the payroll taxes they paid. Workers who retired at age sixty-five in 1995, for example, turned twenty in 1950 when the payroll tax rate totaled only 3 percent, applicable to a maximum of $3,000 of earnings.[15] They can expect, on average, to receive nearly 120 percent of what they would have gotten had they invested both their employers' and their own share of their Social Security taxes in long-term government bonds. Today's workers, particularly high-wage workers, cannot expect nearly as great a return on their payroll tax contributions. On average, workers born in the 1950s are projected to receive only about 75 percent of the rate of return they could have received from long-term government bonds. As a result, workers may resist payroll tax increases—despite opinion polls purporting to show their willingness to pay more—and Congress is skeptical of increasing any taxes of any sort. On the other hand, the elderly are expected to fight any retirement benefit reductions, and they are a potent political force.

The search, therefore, has been for proposals that avoid or minimize both benefit reductions and tax increases. It is no easy trick to guarantee average- and high-wage workers a greater return of benefits relative to taxes without impairing retirement security for lower-wage workers. One idea is to try to increase the "rate of return" on Social Security Trust Funds, which are now invested in Treasury debt instruments, by shifting some portion of these funds into investments in corporate equity.

In addition to proposals linking the financial future of Social Security to the performance of the private equity market, debate about the future of Social Security has also inspired a number of serious proposals to "privatize" some part of the program. The basic idea is to shift away from the current system of taxes and benefits toward mandated individual retirement savings accounts, where funds would be invested based on workers' choices, and retirement benefits in turn would depend on investment returns. We evaluate these alternatives in Chapter 13.

The larger lesson of projected fiscal difficulties is, nevertheless, clear. There is a danger in tying the financial health of retirement security financing solely to the size of the wage base. Either demographic shifts or shifts in the relative returns to wages and capital can jeopardize the soundness of the system. Put in more prosaic terms, we have insured retirees' economic well-being by giving them a claim on one factor of production, labor income. Because of demographic shifts and other (somewhat mysterious) economic developments, wages have not grown fast enough to fund projected liabilities at current tax rates. It appears that we would have been better served had we devised a retirement scheme that gave workers a diversified portfolio of claims against both labor and capital. Our history thus lends plausibility to current enthusiasms for mandated equity investments—in the form of individual retirement accounts or by investing Social Security Trust Fund assets in corporate stocks.

## THE CHALLENGE FOR PRIVATE PENSIONS

As figures 5.6 and 5.7 have shown, private pensions and individual savings contribute substantially to retirement income, although low-wage workers have enjoyed relatively little of either. Employer-based pensions (and annuities) and personal savings each account for nearly one-fifth of the elderly's income.[16]

Employer-based retirement plans cover about 40 percent of all retirees and today reflect a mix of defined-benefit plans (where the employer promises a specific retirement benefit based on the retiree's wage level) and defined-contribution plans (where the employer provides an opportunity for the employee to save and invest in a tax-favored manner and sometimes also contributes to the employees' accounts). In recent years, participation in defined-contribution plans has been growing faster than participation in defined-benefit plans, but the latter still account for the greater share of employment-based retirement assets.[17] While employees bear investment risks in defined-contribution plans, which are borne by employers in defined-benefit plans, defined-contribution plans better serve a mobile workforce. Moreover, larger employers, who have been the principal sponsors of defined-benefit plans, are accounting for a dwindling portion of the workforce. Workers not covered by employer-sponsored plans are permitted to establish their own tax-favored individual retirement accounts (IRAs), but these have been utilized primarily by higher-paid workers.

According to estimates of tax expenditures (that is, the revenue losses attributable to federal income tax provisions), the exclusion for employer-sponsored pension contributions and earnings will be the largest tax expenditure for individuals during the years 1999–2003, costing nearly $400 billion in lost revenues during that period.[18] Tax incentives to employer-provided pensions have inspired both employers and workers to substitute retirement income payments for current compensation and have produced a substantial shift away from other savings toward pensions. Private employee pension assets total about $3 trillion, and public employee pension plans now hold more than an additional $1 trillion of U.S. investment capital.

As figure 5.10 shows, the distribution of government-provided benefits for employer-provided pensions contrasts significantly with the targeting of Social Security benefits to low- and moderate-income workers. The tax savings attributable to private pensions disproportionately benefit higher-income workers, and the distribution of benefits from private pension plans is skewed in the same direction. One study shows, for example, that the 5 percent of households with incomes above $100,000 received 24 percent of the pension tax savings, and the 25 percent of households with incomes between $50,000 and $100,000 received an additional 43 percent.[19]

Fig. 5.10.    Participation in employer-based retirement plans

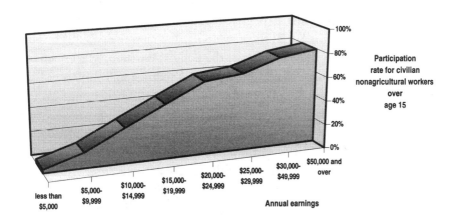

(*Source:* EBRI, *Databook on Employee Benefits,* 4th ed., table 10.5, 1993 data.)

In short, two-thirds of the public subsidy for employer-sponsored pensions is paid to the top one-third of wage earners.

In principle, the combination of defined-benefit and defined-contribution pension plans, along with IRAs, should give most workers a tax-preferred vehicle for financing their retirement. Because the system is voluntary, however, many employers have no plan, and many employees are not covered. Lack of coverage is concentrated in smaller firms, where high per-employee administrative costs and a more mobile workforce may make pension-plan sponsorship much less attractive to employers. Participation in employment-based retirement and savings plans has declined in recent years, and fewer than one-half of all civilian workers participate in any plan. In addition, many workers raid their retirement funds rather than using them to provide annual income during retirement. In 1990, for example, $108 billion was paid from retirement accounts as lump-sum distributions when workers changed jobs or retired, compared to about $127 billion in annuity payments to retirees from such plans.[20] Preretirement withdrawals from IRAs have also increased.

Moreover, even those who have enough disposable income to save and an employer retirement plan in which to invest fail to anticipate the amount required to fund a long retirement. This leaves far too many workers with inadequate assets to prevent a substantial decline in their standards of living during retirement.[21]

Because private pension and individual retirement savings are funded by a combination of employer and employee contributions, rather than out of the earnings of the next generation of workers, the demographic challenges confronting Social Security do not threaten the private pension system in the same way. The aging of the population, along with steep inflation of medical costs, has, however, caused many employers to restrict or retract promises of health benefits for retirees to finance medical expenses not covered by Medicare. Some analysts have also expressed concerns about the economic consequences of the major liquidation of pension assets needed to fund the forthcoming retirement of the baby-boom generation. In prosaic terms, if the supply of assets sought to be liquidated by retired boomers exceeds the demand for those assets by baby-bust generation workers, asset prices will fall. The value that the boomers thought they had in their private accounts will simply not be there when they need it.

The highly skewed distribution of retirement assets is part of a broader picture of wealth holding in the United States. Six percent of earners account for 70 percent of the net worth of all families, and families with incomes of $50,000 or more account for 87 percent of all wealth holdings. Tax subsidies and regulatory protections for employer-based pensions and individual retirement saving are obviously not doing an adequate job of topping off Social Security benefits for most American families. Social Security in addition to personal meager retirement assets are keeping many out of poverty, but millions still hover near the poverty line.

**SUMMARY**

Despite its great accomplishments, the three-legged stool for retirement income security seems a bit wobbly. The historically strongest and only universal leg, Social Security, faces long-term financial difficulties and questions about its continuing political support, particularly from young and high-income workers. The voluntary employer-based pension system has apparently reached a ceiling in its participation rate at about one-half the working population. It remains vulnerable to disruptions from independent changes in tax policy, and it is shifting more responsibility and financial risks (and rewards) to individual workers. Private savings has always served as a retirement income resource, but principally for the well-to-do. Without some major economic and/or political change to increase both the national savings rate and the dispersion of income from capital, private savings seems unlikely to provide retirement security for a much broader population.

There is good news for retirees as well. Those with assets now find that the individual annuity market is becoming wider and more competitive. And the Treasury Department has recently started issuing inflation-protected bonds, thereby making it easier to purchase individual insurance against the risk of outliving one's assets and to guard against inflation during retirement. In addition, longer life spans and increased years of relatively good health suggest that continued earnings at reduced rates can provide an increasing share of "retiree" income. The three-legged stool actually has four legs, and one of them has become somewhat stronger on its own.

# Chapter 6 Social Insurance
## Prior to Work

The poverty statistics tell a simple truth about the risk of economic need in the American economy. Young children have a startlingly higher risk of living in poverty than any other age cohort of the population.[1] In 1995 one of every five children under age eighteen in the United States lived in poverty, and one of every four children under age six. The poverty rate was over 59 percent for children under age six living in families headed by a single female.[2] Politicians, social scientists, and the media remind us regularly that children hold the key to the nation's future economic well-being. The extraordinarily high levels of childhood poverty we now tolerate threaten their chances of leading successful and productive lives.

Changes in the labor force and in family structures and responsibilities make social insurance protections for children in low-income households imperative. The "Ozzie and Harriet" economy, in which Ozzie's "family wage" provided a comfortable standard of living for the family while Harriet devoted herself to household work, no longer exists. As figure 6.1 shows, a sharp in-

Fig. 6.1.    Labor force participation rates of mothers

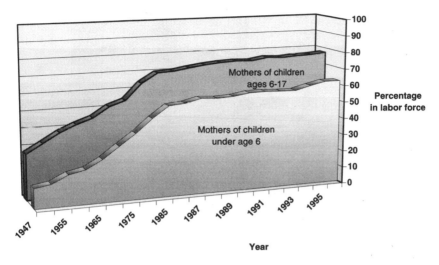

(*Source: 1998 Green Book,* table 9-1.)

crease in the proportion of women with children who are working has occurred since World War II.

Changes in family structure, particularly the increase in the number of
children living with only one parent, have also been dramatic. Nearly one-
third of live births in the United States are now to single women, and in
some minority groups the proportion is roughly one-half. When this
trend is combined with high divorce rates, the result is predictable—a
major increase in single-parent families, most of them headed by women.
In 1996, there were about 11.7 million single-parent families with children
under age eighteen, 84 percent maintained by the mother. One-parent
families accounted for nearly one-third of all families in 1996, a much
greater share than in 1970, when that number was 13 percent.[3] Figure 6.2
depicts how the composition of American families has changed since 1950.

At least half of all children born in the United States in the late 1970s or
early 1980s will live with a single parent before becoming adults.[4] Providing adequate income to support and raise children has become difficult
for most American families even when mothers hold full-time jobs. For
unmarried mothers, the difficulties are staggering.

By comparison with married couples, as figure 6.3 shows, the incidence
of poverty among single-parent families headed by women is extremely

Fig. 6.2.    Changing family composition

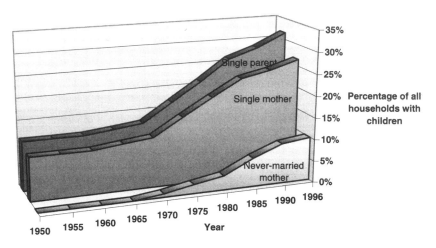

(*Source:* U.S. Census Bureau, *Historical Statistics of the United States,* series G148-53; *1996 Green Book,* table G-4; *1998 Green Book,* table G-4.)

high. Most have incomes below the median for all families, and very few are to be counted among the prosperous. Indeed the disparity in the incomes of two-parent and female-head families has widened substantially since 1970.

Being born into a family with parents who are unable to provide a decent standard of living is a complex risk. In some cases, inadequate income results from the occurrence of an event for which the parents already have social insurance protections—such as disability, temporary unemployment, or the death of a family breadwinner. Here the need is for some means for "topping off" family income should those benefits prove inadequate. In other cases, the parental breadwinner or breadwinners may be out of the labor market or suffer from persistent low wages because of low skill levels or chronic, but not disabling, health problems. The persistent low-wage problem may be exacerbated by the increased costs of basic necessities, such as housing, medical care, and the child care necessary to permit parents to work.

The core difficulty in delivering adequate social insurance protection to children is that the virtually universal desire to help these children is accompanied by suspicion of, and sometimes even antipathy toward, their parents. A public policy grounded in the view that parents are indifferent

Fig. 6.3.    Distribution of families, by income

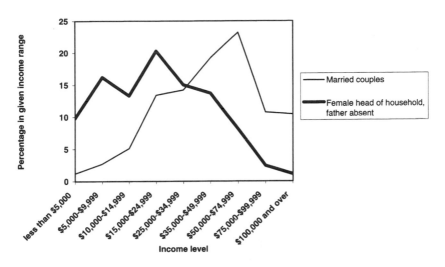

(*Source:* EBRI, *Databook on Employee Benefits,* table B-5, 1994 data.)

toward their children's well-being is a prescription for disaster. This carica-
ture is not simply demeaning and erroneous. Successful policies cannot be
developed in a political climate that offers greater rewards for characterizing
parents as "welfare queens" than for taking into account the real conditions
in which they live. Even Newt Gingrich abandoned his 1994 suggestion for
resurrecting orphanages as the primary way to care for poor children.

## THE ROLE OF SOCIAL INSURANCE IN
## COMBATING POVERTY

Data on the effects of social insurance payments suggest a straightforward
conclusion: social insurance provision dramatically reduces the incidence
of poverty. In 1959, when only a bare majority of adults over the age of
sixty-five received Social Security pensions and Medicare had not yet been
enacted, the poverty rate for adults sixty-five years and over was above 35
percent. By 1996, when our pension and medical care systems for the elderly had reached maturity (and coverage was nearly universal), only 10
percent of those between ages sixty-five and seventy-four lived in poverty
(fig. 6.4). The 14 percent poverty rate for those older than seventy-five remained high, but it was about half of that for those younger than six. By

Fig. 6.4. Poverty rate and retiree benefits of people over age 65

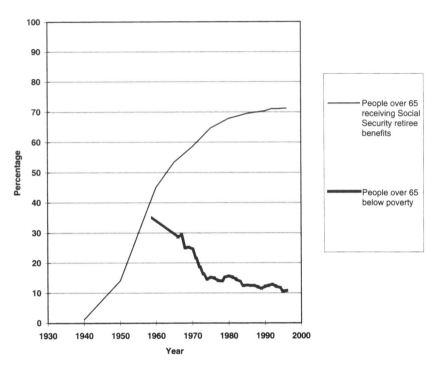

*Note:* Spouses of retired workers receive Social Security benefits, but are not included in these calculations due to data limitations. Including recipients of spousal benefits would further highlight the correlation between the expansion of Social Security receipts and the reduction in poverty. (*Source:* Authors' calculations based on U.S. Census Bureau, *Current Population Reports,* P 60-198, table C-2; *1997 Annual Social Security Statistical Supplement,* table 5, B5; and Social Security Area Population Projections, *1997 Actuarial Study,* no. 112, table 23.)

contrast, in the thirty-seven years under discussion, poverty for those under age eighteen was reduced by only about six percentage points (fig. 6.5).

While many factors affect the incidence of childhood poverty, income support affects the poverty of families with young children just as it does the poverty of the aged. Figure 6.6 tracks the year-by-year incidence of childhood poverty and the real value of payments to families with dependent children under Title 4 of the Social Security Act. These curves turn out to be virtually mirror images of each other. As the real value of AFDC payments went up from 1960 through 1970, childhood poverty dropped dramatically. A roughly 30 percent increase in AFDC payments during this

Fig. 6.5.    Poverty among children and the elderly

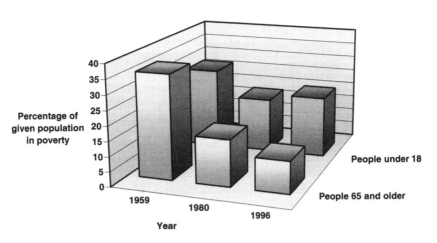

(*Source: 1998 Green Book,* table H-4.)

period is associated with a nearly 60 percent decrease in the incidence of childhood poverty. From 1973 to 1995 the real value of AFDC payments declined by about 40 percent, and during those same years poverty for children under age six climbed back almost to 1960 levels.

These skeletal data on poverty and social insurance payments tell an important story: while families face a multitude of risks to economic well-being during their prime working years, the largest risks to family income occur when breadwinners are either too old or too young to earn a living. American social insurance policy has dramatically dampened the risk of neediness in the postwork years, but has done much less well with respect to children.

Once again, assignment of primary responsibility to the states is a big part of this story. Federal, state, and local government expenditures for each elderly person are more than double those per child. In 1995, these expenditures amounted to nearly $15,000 per elderly person, but only $6,000 per child.[5] For the elderly, $14,000 of this amount comes from the federal government, principally through Social Security and Medicare. In contrast, two-thirds of government spending on children is by state and local governments, mostly for elementary and secondary education.

This situation is not some "natural" aspect of the life cycle in capitalist democracies. The incidence of childhood poverty in the United States is

Fig. 6.6.    Average monthly AFDC benefits and child poverty

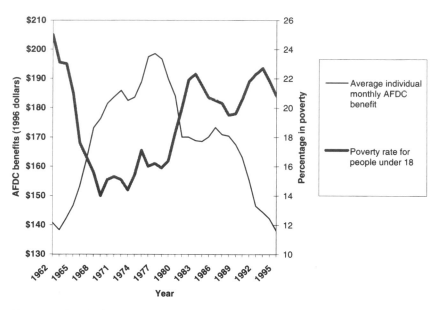

(*Source:* Authors' calculations based on *1997 Annual Social Security Statistical Supplement,* table 9. G1; U.S. Census Bureau, *Current Population Reports,* P60-198, table C-2; *1997 Statistical Abstract,* table 752; and U.S. Bureau of Labor Statistics.)

more than twice as great as the next closest OECD nation, Canada. It is nearly three times as great as the incidence of childhood poverty in the United Kingdom and roughly eight times as great as the figure for Germany.[6]

The moral hazard problems of insuring children are severe. Children, after all, are in no position to have "contributed" to their social insurance coverage. Nor can we deliver income to children directly; it must go through their parents. Indeed, even though children, like retirees, are predictably out of the workforce for fifteen to twenty years, many deny that protecting them against inadequate income is an appropriate task for social insurance. We cannot here canvass the many reasons for this reluctance, nor will we describe the history of the multitude of social welfare interventions currently directed at poor children or poor families with children. Our interest, instead, is in how social insurance will have to be reshaped in order to make headway against America's largest poverty problem.

For now, we need merely note that designing social insurance protections for children confronts virtually all of the structural problems we have seen in earlier contexts. Moral hazard is high, even for perfectly behaved children, because funds must be funneled through their parents. And some of the natural and most effective means of combating moral hazard in other contexts—such as requiring large copayments or contributions—are not available. Nor is there a discrete event—such as being laid off from a job—triggering the insurance payments. Rather it is a status we are insuring. We believe that these problems can be overcome. But, as our proposals in Chapter 12 will reveal, only at the cost of considerable complexity.

## THE CONCEPTUAL PROBLEM: WHO IS TO BE
## INSURED AGAINST WHAT?

Income security for children is routinely framed as a problem of childhood poverty. From that perspective, the insured population is the population of children—say those between birth and eighteen years of age. The risk to be insured against is the risk of being born into and raised in a poor household. Income supplements payable to a poor family with children, sufficient to eliminate or ameliorate the risk of poverty, would presumably constitute the appropriate social insurance program.

There are, however, serious difficulties with this idea. Because the family is an economic unit, society cannot lift the poor child from poverty without making the family non-poor. The insured population could then as easily be characterized as the population of poor families with children, as the population of children with poor families. If that is true, the risk insured against may seem to be more like "having children to raise while poor." And, because having children and raising them is viewed as voluntary, insuring against that "risk" seems a strange form of "insurance." This is insurance fraught with moral hazard, not to mention moral judgments about whether people too poor to raise children should be having them.

Moreover, the risk of being poor is a generalized risk stretching across the whole life cycle. From this perspective should we not wish to insure against poverty whenever that risk might materialize in our lives?

The answer to that question could be "yes," but, as we have discussed previously, our concern to maintain personal responsibility for economic outcomes counsels against treating poverty alone as an "insurable event."

Poverty status in general is too dependent on personal incentives and actions to be a good candidate for aggressive social insurance interventions. But from this perspective childhood poverty is different. Children's actions are not implicated in their poverty. For those not expected to be in the labor market—the young, the old, and the disabled—the question of how to provide insurance protections without undermining present or future market effort does not completely disappear. But it is far less critical than the problem of work disincentives when providing income support to able-bodied people of working age.

In addition, society has a special stake in preventing childhood poverty. A nation wants its children to become productive adults—people who are self-supporting and who contribute to the general welfare. We know all too well the association of childhood poverty with low levels of educational attainment and a substantially increased likelihood of low productivity as an adult. Poor children are twice as likely as non-poor children to repeat a grade in school, to be suspended, or to drop out of high school.[7] From this perspective, the insured is not just the poor child or the poor family with children, but also the society as a whole. The risk to be insured against is the prospect that "future workers" will not turn out to be productive workers. Income support might be given to the child, or the poor family with children, as a means for protecting the interests of the society in general.

Finally, the "risk" that children pose to family income has changed dramatically over the years. In an agrarian economy, children could be a source of income within a few years after their birth. Industrialization, along with child labor restrictions and compulsory schooling requirements, radically altered the understanding of a child's place in the economy of the household. Children shifted from earners to dependents. More recently the disappearance of the "family wage" and the widespread necessity for two-earner households have increased the opportunity costs of childbearing. For many young families today—particularly single parents—the availability of free or subsidized child care is the difference between maintaining an adequate income and not having "ends meet."

Each of these visions of social insurance for families with children says something important about why we are inclined to think about "childhood poverty" as a risk that should be insured, and why it is so difficult to insure. These conflicting views about who is insured, for what, and why, complicate the understanding of the goals of social insurance in this context and create ambivalence about the instruments that should be employed in developing an acceptable social insurance policy.

If the child is the insured, how do we provide assistance without producing unwanted disincentives for parental responsibility? If the family is the insured, hasn't it "voluntarily" assumed the opportunity costs of child rearing? If the society is the insured, wouldn't aggressive service provision be better than cash assistance in producing self-reliant adults?

### PROGRAMS SUPPORTING CHILDREN

The policies that Americans have chosen to deal most directly with "childhood poverty" reflect our multiple, complex, and contested historical purposes. Programs to protect society by developing the potential of future workers have fared reasonably well in budgetary wars over scarce public funds. While we often complain about its effectiveness, expenditures for public education are massive, and public schools are universally available.

We have also been quite willing to insure workers against loss of income sufficient to support their families because of disability or death. Our largely noncontroversial programs of disability and survivors' insurance pay modest, but decent, benefits and carry little social stigma (although many people with disabilities find the "disabled" label abhorrent).

As originally conceived, the survivors' insurance program was designed to protect the spouses and children of male wage earners in a labor market characterized by pervasive discrimination against women. It also supported the social objective of having children grow up in the care of a full-time homemaker. Indeed, it was the Social Security planners' dream that disability and survivors' insurance would ultimately render the Aid to Dependent Children program virtually irrelevant. But time and change have not been kind to these original aspirations. To be sure, disability and survivors' insurance now provide important support for a substantial number of American families, but disability and survivors' insurance have little relevance to the population most at risk of family and childhood poverty—divorced and never-married women and their children. Because these women and children have no legal relationship to a deceased or disabled injured worker, they have no entitlement to disability or survivors' benefits. Alternative forms of support are essential if their children are to be lifted out of poverty.

American income security policy has sought to deal more generally with the problem of low wages for workers with dependents through the Earned Income Tax Credit. Where the insured is a worker, and the risk is lack of capacity for family support because of low income from work, we have been relatively willing to provide these cash income supplements. But where the goal is protecting children from poverty whatever its cause, and encouraging their development, we have been reluctant to provide substantial cash payments and have turned instead to in-kind provision of food, housing, medical care, and schooling. Along with assistance to families for the costs of child rearing, such as through child care subsidies or family leave programs, these efforts remain partial and fragmented. Moreover, all of these transfers are deeply controversial and are far from universal.

Indeed, simply being a child in poverty or being a family in poverty with children has always been an underinsured event. The Aid to Dependent Children, or Aid to Families with Dependent Children, program was never happily or heavily funded; it has always been less than one-half of one percent of GDP (fig. 6.7).

It has now been replaced by the program of Temporary Assistance to Needy Families (TANF), which strictly limits the years of assistance that any family can receive. Prior emphasis on supporting dependent children and caretaker adults has shifted to providing temporary assistance for

Fig. 6.7.    AFDC as a share of GDP

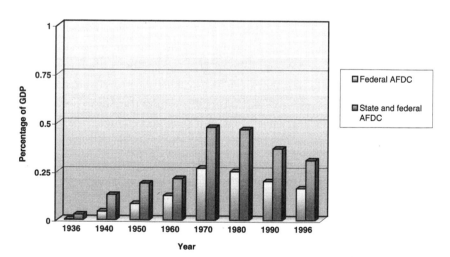

(*Source: 1998 Green Book*, table 7-2; *Survey of Current Business*, August 1997; table 1, gross domestic product.)

nonworking adults with children. Programmatic focus has shifted from income support for children to moving parents into the workforce as rapidly as possible. "Success" now seems to be measured by how fast the "welfare" rolls decline, not by the adequacy of family incomes.[8]

While many view recent welfare "reforms" as simple abandonment of the poor, the evolution of AFDC into TANF is not a radical departure from traditional goals. The AFDC program was originally understood in investment terms. The Committee on Economic Security was not engaging in polite circumlocution when in the 1930s it described the purpose of AFDC as primarily to free mothers from "the wage earning role" so that they could keep their children from "falling into social misfortune" and "more affirmatively to rear them into citizens capable of contributing to society."[9] The "mothers' pension" laws that AFDC replaced were described by Abraham Epstein in his magisterial treatise on social insurance as premised on the simple idea that "the government should aim to preserve family life by paying the mother for the services rendered in rearing future citizens."[10] Such a system was both more effective and cheaper than institutional care.

But so viewed, the state's payment was limited to "worthy" mothers, largely widows. As the Massachusetts Commission on the Support of Dependent Minor Children of Widowed Mothers put it in 1913, the state should adopt: "The principle of payment by way of subsidy for the rearing of children. . . . The term 'subsidy' implies that a condition exists which, aided, will result in positive good for the state. Subsidy makes it feasible that children should stay with their worthy mothers in the most normal relation still possible when the father has been removed by death. It is intended not primarily for those with least adequate incomes under the present system of aid but for the fit and worthy poor." At the time of the adoption of Title 4 of the Social Security Act, only four states provided mothers' pensions to "unworthy" (that is, never-married) mothers, although many covered divorced or abandoned women.

By the mid-1990s, the widowed mother as a recipient of AFDC had all but disappeared. Of the 30 percent of children being raised by a single parent, those being reared by widows and widowers accounted for 1 percent. The remainder were in the homes of never married (58 percent) or divorced or separated (42 percent) mothers and fathers. The "worthy poor" covered by the early state mothers' pensions and AFDC had vanished. In 1996, its clientele gone, the program vanished too.

The fundamental presumptions underpinning the program of Temporary Assistance to Needy Families that replaced AFDC are that every parent can become a worker and every worker can earn an adequate income. Both presumptions are heroic. Recent attempts to determine how post-welfare recipients will fare suggest that they can get by on the wage rates that most will command only if they have access to both subsidized housing and subsidized child care. But only a relatively small percentage of families who meet the income guidelines are currently served by programs providing housing or child care. For people leaving welfare, if these benefits are provided at all, they usually terminate after a relatively short period of work. Others struggling to leave poverty or to maintain a middle-class life often receive nothing.

Congress has recently extended health care benefits to poor and near-poor children under Medicaid, but although some states have responded aggressively and creatively, health care coverage for the children of low- and moderate-income workers remains spotty. The reason for the reluctance of legislatures to expand these programs is not difficult to fathom: many families with children feel they need help with these major expenses and they are reluctant to fund provision of these large benefits for persons only marginally worse off than they are.

### SUMMARY

Protection against the risk of poverty in early childhood, and especially the poverty of children of one-parent families, requires a reconceptualization of traditional American approaches to social insurance. The relentless concentration in our social insurance programs on workers who have strong attachment to the labor market, and their families and dependents, leaves out a group that now seems most in need of assistance. Hence Senator Patrick Moynihan's call for reconceptualizing the risk insured as the risk of being born into the wrong family. We agree with that basic characterization.

But while conceptually coherent, we also recognize that this rethinking of the insured event is deeply controversial. Many have moral objections to the family composition that puts so many children at risk of childhood poverty. Others are concerned about the work disincentives that would be provided to single mothers by securing an adequate entitlement to social insurance provision. The working poor, and even the working middle class, have understandable objections to paying higher social insurance premiums to support the nonworking poor.

American political preferences focus more on preventative or punitive measures for this population than on the palliative of income support. Many believe that education, training, and other intensive social services are the answer—not cash benefits. Insuring the preworking life—insuring children—asks more poignantly than other domains of social insurance not what is or can be insured, but what we as a society want to insure.

The ineffectiveness of American social supports for children revealed by our staggering levels of childhood poverty are, of course, not all attributable to a tendency to conceptualize the insurable event as the occurrence of parental irresponsibility. Structural issues also loom large. As with unemployment insurance and workers' compensation, much of the social responsibility for children has been left with states and localities. This is understandable, perhaps even wise, if the goal of programs is understood as behavior modification rather than income support. But on the understanding of social insurance that we are urging here, it is the latter purpose that is most critical. State-by-state income support encounters, once again, a well-documented race-to-the-bottom problem as well as a simple fiscal reality—poor states will have less capacity to assist their poor people. States fear becoming "welfare magnets," however weak academic studies suggest that the magnetic field might be. Combating childhood poverty requires significant redistribution from haves to have-nots within the insurance pool. And, for that purpose, state insurance pools are the wrong pools.

Equally critically we believe that the confusion over the goals of assistance to poor families with children has been a confusion of ends and means. The goal of social insurance should be to insure children against living in a family with inadequate income during a period when they are expected—indeed legally required—to be out of the workforce. The challenge is to provide assistance in a form that does not unduly impair parental responsibility for self-support and that gives assurance that the most important material deprivations for which "inadequate income" is a proxy are avoided. Those questions go to the appropriate means for providing social insurance, not to the questions of who is the insured and what is the risk.

To put the matter starkly, we believe that from a social insurance perspective children should not be viewed as "future workers" in whom we are investing so that they can be productive adults. Children are leading current lives, not just preparing for some future one. To be sure, we want them to prepare for a productive work life, and our economy demands that they engage in a lot of preparation in order to be successful. But that is a reason for recognizing youth as a risk factor in a modern capitalist economy, not for treating necessary insurance protections only as investment expenditures.

# Chapter 7 The Special Case of Medical Insurance

No domain of American social insurance rivals the incompetence of American health insurance. While spending nearly twice the average for OECD member nations (14 percent versus 7.5 percent of GDP), we manage to leave 43 million Americans without insurance. Yet no other developed nation lacks universal (or near universal) coverage. As figure 7.1 demonstrates, this spending disparity is not some artifact of America's GDP growth.

Nor are we necessarily leaving out only hard-to-insure populations. Most of the uninsured are both working age and working at least part-time or part-year (fig. 7.2). But Americans' chances of being uninsured are much higher if their incomes are average or low (fig. 7.3). Nowhere in America's social insurance world does the combination of unaffordability and inadequacy loom larger than in health insurance.

Fig. 7.1.    Per capita health expenditures

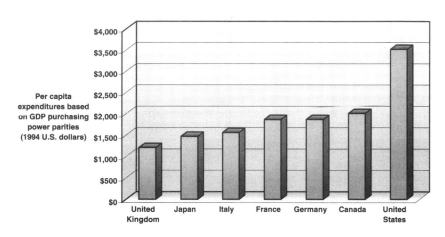

(*Source:* EBRI, *Databook on Employee Benefits,* 4th ed., table C-10.)

## SOME HISTORY

This poor record has hardly gone unnoticed by reformers who have peppered the populace, state legislators, and the Congress with proposals. How this sorry state of affairs developed has been the focus of numerous excellent studies.[1] We need here recount the story only in broad strokes.

During World War I, a group called the American Association for Labor Legislation tried to persuade a number of state legislatures to adopt health insurance, but to no avail. The effort was doomed by an odd and powerful political coalition. The American Medical Association opposed

Fig. 7.2.    Employment status of nonelderly uninsured population

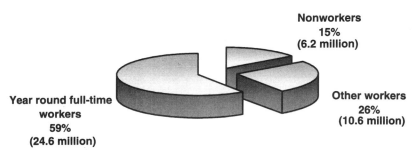

(*Source:* EBRI Issue Brief 192, December 1997, chart 2, based on *Current Population Survey,* March 1997.)

Fig. 7.3. Uninsured portion of nonelderly population, by income

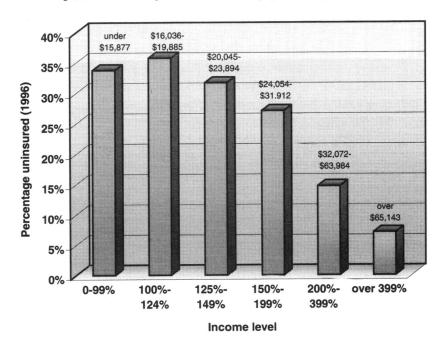

*Note:* Income-level distribution is based on income as a percentage of the 1996 federal poverty threshold, which varies by family size. Income equivalents for a family of four are provided as a guideline. (*Source:* EBRI Issue Brief 192, December 1997, chart 6, based on *Current Population Survey,* March 1997.)

any compulsory insurance against illness provided, controlled, or regulated by any state or federal government. Meanwhile Samuel Gompers, the president of the American Federation of Labor, regarded any form of compulsory insurance, health care or otherwise, as government controlling labor. Every subsequent attempt to enact universal health care insurance has been eerily reminiscent of this first clash between health insurance reformers and politically potent interest groups.

The AMA's opposition to a single, seemingly innocuous, sentence in an early version of the Social Security Act, which stated that the Social Security Board should *study* the problem of inadequate health insurance coverage and report to the Congress, threatened passage of the Social Security Act. The offending sentence had to be deleted.[2] Franklin Roosevelt's 1944 call for an "economic bill of rights" including a right to adequate medical care got nowhere.

FDR's successor, Harry Truman, consistently supported national health insurance. He proposed action in 1945; made health insurance the center-piece of his legislative program in 1949; and repeated the effort annually until 1953. Truman was never able even to muster a vote on the floor of the House or Senate. Determined and strident AMA opposition, marching under the then disingenuous banner of protecting patients' freedom to choose their doctors, combined with Republican and southern Democratic resistance to all expansion of federal government programs for individuals, nullified Truman's efforts.

To make this repetitive story short, presidents Nixon, Carter, and Clinton all advanced plans for universal health insurance. None fared any better than Truman or Roosevelt, although their plans and their political opponents were different. The one constant was the AMA. Although by the 1990s its power had waned, its role as defender of American patients' freedom to become impoverished by medical costs was ably filled by the private health insurance industry.

Because any effort to remake the American health insurance system potentially affects the overlapping and often antagonistic interests of doctors; hospitals; medical equipment manufacturers; pharmaceutical manufacturers and distributors; other health services providers; private insurers; organized labor; employers, large and small; and their employees, the difficulty of change should not be underestimated. Commenting on the Clinton plan, Charles Schultze, former president Carter's chairman of the Council of Economic Advisors, remarked that President Clinton was attempting to remake an economic entity as large as the economy of France in one legislative stroke. Moreover, while fears of losing or being denied health insurance coverage have been widespread in the United States, virtually all Americans over age sixty-five enjoy health insurance coverage under Medicare, and nearly 85 percent of other Americans have some coverage, mostly through employer-sponsored health insurance plans and Medicaid. A political system crafted by the founders to resist large-scale reforms, coupled with public and politicians' fears of a "government takeover" of health care, has entrenched our health insurance patchwork in the face of obvious inequities and absurd levels of expenditure.

Following the defeat of President Clinton's health insurance proposals and the Republican takeover of Congress in 1994, which it may have precipitated, no national politician has had any interest in even talking about comprehensive restructuring of the nation's health insurance system.[3] Instead, the political process has returned to its traditional path of incremental change. In 1996 Congress passed federal legislation both adding regulatory protections so that people don't necessarily lose their health insurance when they change jobs or because they have preexisting medical conditions and addressing some of the short-term financial problems of Medicare. In 1997 Congress provided new federal funding to reduce the number of uninsured children from 10 million to 5 million over the next several years through state-based health insurance programs. And in 1999 both Democrats and Republicans supported a "patients' bill of rights" to protect the American public from the alleged depredations of the "managed care" revolution—developments in the private insurance market that regulate doctors' and patients' freedom in ways potentially more draconian than any national health insurance plan ever proposed.

## MEDICARE: THE TRIUMPH OF FAILURE

Health insurance for the elderly was proposed as a response to President Truman's failed efforts to obtain universal health insurance coverage. Shortly after that defeat, the first modest Medicare bill was advanced to provide sixty days of hospitalization coverage for Social Security beneficiaries over age sixty-five.[4] But given the politics of public health insurance in this country, another decade of struggle was required to bring any plan to fruition. Here, as elsewhere in the health insurance world, the United States was unique. No other industrialized country initiated government health insurance coverage by covering the aged.

Given the longstanding American emphasis on self-reliance and individual responsibility, the elderly are appealing beneficiaries in our political process. They cannot be expected to return to the labor market to take better care of themselves. They also face a particularly difficult problem in acquiring private health insurance because, on average, per capita health costs of the elderly are greater than those of other segments of the population. Large uninsured medical expenses threaten the retirement security that Social Security pensions were designed to protect. Moreover, Medicare was crafted originally to avoid any interference with doctor-patient relationships. The program simply promised to pay the customary charges for most medical procedures. And with much of its day-to-day administration contracted out to private insurance carriers, Medicare threatened no new large federal bureaucracy.

Part of the moral hazard problem of health insurance was also solved by insuring the elderly. People cannot age faster just to become eligible for coverage. But Medicare's capacity to expand the costs of medical care by increasing both patients' desire for medical services and providers' willingness to provide them was enormous, as future events would reveal.

Given ten years of hard work by supporters and the Democrats' landslide victory in the 1964 elections, Medicare was signed into law in 1965. Its proponents believed that Medicare was but the beginning of a scheme that would eventually cover the whole population. In this ambition, as we have seen, they were to be disappointed.

Medicare coverage initially was—and remains today—divided into parts A and B. Part A provides hospital insurance, financed by a payroll tax on employers and workers—a tax that is transferred into a government trust fund from which Medicare hospital costs are paid. Currently, the payroll tax rate is 2.9 percent (1.45 percent each for employers and employees) on all wages and salaries without any limitation. Part A provides insurance coverage for inpatient hospital services, short-term nursing home care, certain home health services, and hospice care. Virtually everyone over age sixty-five is automatically entitled to Medicare Part A, and people under age sixty-five who receive Social Security disability payments for at least two years are also covered under Part A. Patients are required to pay a sizable deductible out-of-pocket for hospital admissions more than sixty days apart, as well as a large daily charge for posthospital skilled nursing facility care after the first twenty days (the initial period is fully covered by Medicare).

Medicare Part B—so-called supplementary medical insurance (SMI)—is a voluntary program available to all persons over age sixty-five and covers physicians' services along with certain other nonhospital-based care. A monthly premium now equal to approximately 25 percent of the insurance costs is paid by beneficiaries ($45.50 in 1999). The remaining 75 percent of Part B costs are paid out of general federal tax revenues. Virtually everyone who is enrolled in Part A is also enrolled in Part B.

The bifurcation of Medicare into two parts reflected the mid-1960s pattern of private health insurance. At the time Medicare was enacted, hospital insurance and physicians' coverage were treated separately under Blue Cross and Blue Shield. And because most expensive medical care was done in hospitals, coverage of physicians' charges under Part B was something of a legislative afterthought, added toward the end of the legislative process. Hospital and physicians' insurance has long since been merged under Blue Cross and other private health insurance arrangements, and the division of Medicare coverage into two parts no longer makes sense, if it ever did. The principal effect of the bifurcation of Medicare is budgetary. Part A is financed from the Medicare Trust Fund, which periodically is described as facing insolvency, thereby creating occasions for revisions in the Medicare program and inspiring political arguments about the appropriate boundaries of Part A and Part B. In 1997, for example, one way chosen to strengthen the financial solvency of the Medicare Trust Fund was simply to transfer some home health care coverage from Part A to Part B. Part B seemingly faces no binding budgetary constraint.

The aging of America is causing even greater financial stress for Medicare than for Social Security. When it was first enacted, Medicare covered fewer than one in ten Americans; today it covers one of every eight, a proportion that will continue to grow as the nation's population ages. The Congressional Budget Office estimates that Medicare will cover one of every four Americans in the year 2070.[5] More importantly, health care costs have been growing much faster than either prices generally or wages. When originally enacted, Medicare's principal focus was on broadening health insurance coverage. Its potential costs were given modest attention. The past two decades' continuous concern with costs hardly reflects anything of Medicare's origins, when the political fixation was on convincing retirees and providers to participate.

Together, Medicare parts A and B now amount to about 2.6 percent of GDP. Depending on what one assumes about the future pattern of health care cost increases, Medicare will grow to somewhere between 6 and 7.5 percent of GDP by the year 2030, and to nearly 8 percent by 2070.[6] Although predicting changes in the nation's health care costs over the long term requires even more heroic suspensions of disbelief than does predicting demographic shifts, hospital insurance under Medicare Part A is now estimated to face an average annual deficit of about 3.5 percent of payroll over the next seventy-five years. The projected long-term financial difficulties Medicare faces are clearly much greater than those confronting Social Security pensions.

Surprisingly, despite its high costs, Medicare health insurance coverage has many important gaps. Prescription drugs are not covered (except during hospitalization), for example, and there is no ceiling on catastrophic medical expenses. In total, Medicare pays only about 55 percent of the total health care costs of the elderly. Like retirement income, health insurance for the elderly is financed through a multiple-legged apparatus, although calling it a stool would make the methods currently used to finance the health expenses of the aged seem better structured than they really are. The remaining 45 percent of these costs are paid through Medicaid coverage, employer-sponsored retiree health programs, individually purchased "Medigap" insurance, and out-of-pocket payments by patients.

Out-of-pocket costs and premiums for all persons over age sixty-five were estimated to average $2,605 in 1996. The 10 percent of beneficiaries who had the highest out-of-pocket costs spent an average of about $8,800.[7] On average, noninstitutionalized elderly Medicare beneficiaries spend about 21 percent of their income on health care. For that substantial group just above the poverty line, with incomes below 125 percent of the federal poverty level but without Medicaid, health care and insurance expenditures exceed 30 percent of income. The amount of out-of-pocket costs paid by beneficiaries tends to increase with age, even though this is when income is usually falling. In short, Medicare is a very costly program that still leaves its beneficiaries at risk of becoming impoverished by large medical expenses.

### MEDICAID

The Medicaid program provides access to medical care for poor persons who are aged, blind, disabled, or members of families with dependent children, or are pregnant women or children who meet certain specified eligibility requirements. In 1996 Medicaid covered 12 percent of the U.S. population, including nearly 45 percent of those with incomes below the official federal poverty level. Some Medicaid recipients have double coverage, often through Medicare.

Medicaid is a joint federal-state program. The federal government provides both substantial financing and some coverage requirements and guidelines, but each state designs and administers its own Medicaid program. This structure has produced great variation among states in both the scope of health insurance coverage offered and the benefits provided. Because the inclusion of poor elderly patients under Medicaid often turns on income and asset tests at the state level, there is considerable variation in coverage across the nation. Why Social Security pensioners left without sufficient health care assistance by Medicare should be the responsibility of states is hardly obvious.

Six million Medicare beneficiaries are eligible for both Medicare and Medicaid insurance because they are poor and also either elderly or disabled. These so-called dual eligibles make up 16 percent of the Medicare population and 17 percent of the Medicaid population, but the $50 billion spent on them annually represents 30 percent of total Medicare expenditures and 35 percent of total Medicaid spending.[8] Medicaid and Medicare together also finance more than half of all spending on long-term care of the elderly. Given this pattern, Medicaid also faces serious financial stress from an aging population. Because of the widely varying age distributions of state populations, and significant differences in state fiscal capacities, the financial pain of increasing Medicaid costs will be haphazardly distributed across the country.

For example, Medicaid accounted for more than one-third of the total state expenditures of New Hampshire in some recent years, and about one-quarter of the total state expenditures of several other states. But Medicaid has not caused fiscal problems everywhere; it has amounted to only about 5 percent of the total expenditures of the state of Alaska, and less than 10 percent in certain other states, such as Delaware and Wyoming. The federal share of Medicaid expenditures also varies across the states, ranging from 50 percent to 80 percent, with an average of about 60 percent of total Medicaid expenditures. In an effort to gain financial control over federal Medicaid expenditures, legislation enacted in 1996 capped the federal payments to states and in exchange expanded state flexibility in determining eligibility, coverage, and other aspects of the program. This expanded autonomy for the states is certain to produce additional geographic variation in coverage and benefits.

## LONG-TERM CARE

As the number of "old elderly"—those over age eighty or eighty-five—increases, expenditures for long-term care will pose a serious financial threat both to their families and to the budgets of federal, state, and local governments. Nearly one-fifth of people over age eighty-five live in nursing homes.[9] The number of people over age sixty-five who will need nursing home care is projected to grow from its current level of less than 3 million to just under 5.5 million by the year 2030.[10] Millions more will require medical and personal help in their homes or an adult daycare facility (fig. 7.4).

Currently, long-term care is financed through a combination of Medic-

Fig. 7.4.    Projected total nursing home expenditures

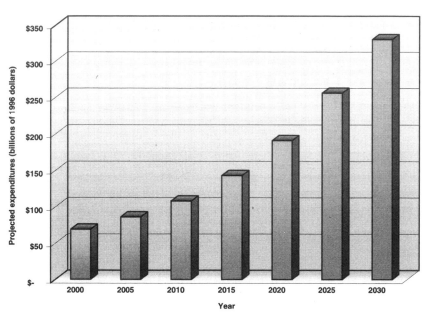

(*Source:* American Council on Life Insurance, *Who Will Pay for the Baby Boomers' Long-Term Care Needs?* Washington D.C., ACLI, March 1998, fig. 3.)

aid, Medicare, and out-of-pocket expenditures. Medicaid is the principal source of insurance for nursing home care (fig. 7.5); Medicare is the primary payer of home health expenditures of the elderly (fig. 7.6). Private insurance currently covers only 1 percent of these expenditures.

Neither Medicare nor Medicaid has been structured or financed to cover the future explosion of long-term care costs. Medicare faces huge financial pressures even for the inadequate insurance protection it now offers. Medicaid does not become available until one becomes impoverished, and it faces serious financial stress as well. Significant future increases in the demand for long-term care are inevitable. Substantially improving social insurance protections for these costs is essential.

Improvement here may well involve "de-medicalizing" the long-term care risk. Social insurance now provides protection largely through medical care budgets. But the needs of the long-term care population include accessible shelter, assistance with personal hygiene, prepared meals, and a host of other aids, not just medical care. For those who need long-term

Fig. 7.5.    Sources of elderly nursing home expenditures

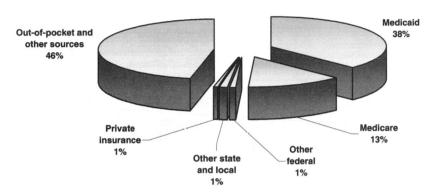

(*Source:* Congressional Budget Office, *Long-Term Budgetary Pressures and Policy Options,* May 1998, box 4-1, 1995 data.)

care, it is as if, in old age, virtually all of the risks that social insurance is designed to cover, and then some, have occurred simultaneously. Handling this coalescence of risks as a medical problem misdirects our attention from both real needs and adequate remedies.

## EMPLOYER-SPONSORED HEALTH INSURANCE

### Retired Workers

Approximately one-third of Medicare beneficiaries enjoy some additional health insurance coverage through employer-provided retiree health insurance policies. As with pension income, retirees who worked in higher-paying jobs and for unionized and larger firms are more likely to be covered through retiree health insurance. About 45 percent of full-time workers in medium and large private firms are offered retiree health insurance. That figure drops to about 18 percent for workers with small firms.[11] Yet employer-sponsored retiree health insurance is the principal source of insurance coverage for retirees younger than age sixty-five.

Retirees have fared worse than workers, but not much worse, in the recent decline of employer-sponsored health insurance coverage. But overall, because of Medicare, retirees' health insurance protections are more secure than those for the remainder of the population. Eighteen percent of the nonelderly population had no health insurance in 1996, compared

Fig. 7.6.    Sources of expenditures for elderly home health care

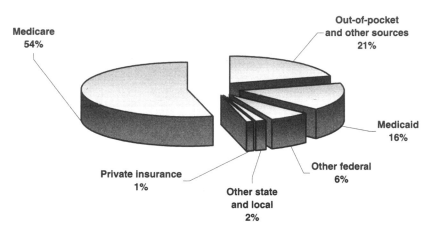

(*Source:* Congressional Budget Office, *Long-Term Budgetary Pressures and Policy Options,* May 1998, box 4-1, 1995 data.)

to only 1 percent of those over age sixty-five. Between 1987 and 1993, the percentage of nonelderly people without health insurance increased from just under 15 percent of the population to just over 17 percent, an increase of 7.5 million uninsured persons.

### Current Workers and Their Families

For the nonelderly population, the source of health insurance coverage varies significantly by the individual's level of income.[12] For example, in 1993, 70 percent of individuals whose family income was below the poverty level were covered by health insurance, and three-quarters of those who were covered were insured through a public plan. Employer-sponsored health insurance coverage rises steadily with income. Fewer than 11 percent of poor families are covered compared to more than 80 percent of the overall non-elderly population having incomes above $50,000 (fig. 7.7). Voluntary tax-subsidized group insurance is not a good vehicle for increasing the economic security of lower-income families.

Like Medicaid, employer-sponsored health insurance also shows considerable regional variation, principally because coverage is concentrated among larger employers. More than 70 percent of Connecticut, Wisconsin, and Utah residents, for example, had employer-sponsored health insurance coverage in 1993, while fewer than half of Louisiana residents had

Fig. 7.7.    Nonelderly population with employer-based health insurance, by income

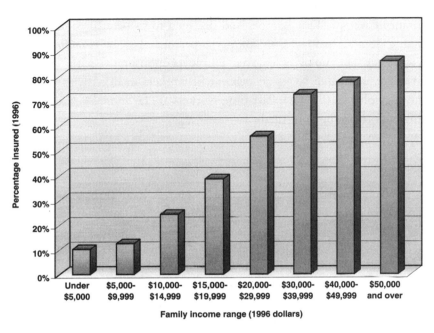

*(Source:* EBRI Issue Brief 192, December 1997, table 6, based on *Current Population Survey,* March 1997.)

coverage. Although the states have regulated health insurance plans—for example, by mandating community rating and specific benefits that must be included in health insurance policies issued in the state—these regulations do not apply to most health insurance provided by employers. Because of an important policy mistake—enacted without debate but never corrected—virtually all firms with one hundred workers or more self-insure and are exempted from state regulation by the Employee Retirement Income Security Act of 1974 (ERISA).

Prior to World War II, there was remarkably little private health insurance coverage in America; only 9 percent of the population enjoyed such coverage in 1940. By 1950, half of the U.S. population was covered by private health insurance, largely because employment-based health insurance had become a desirable form of paying wages—it was exempt from wartime wage control limitations. Federal income and payroll tax exemptions further stimulated employment-based health insurance coverage as a way of compensating workers. Employer-based coverage, however, has experienced a steady decline beginning in the 1980s. In 1979, for example, 82 percent of full-time civilian employees had employer-sponsored health insurance coverage. That number had declined to 73 percent in little more than a decade. In 1997, only about 30 percent of workers in firms with fewer than 25 employees enjoyed employer-sponsored health insurance coverage, compared to 65–70 percent of workers in firms with 1,000 or more employees (fig. 7.8). Part-time workers are far more likely than full-time workers to be uninsured.

### SUMMARY

A smaller proportion of employees and retirees have employer-provided health insurance today than even a decade ago. Such plans seem likely to become a less and less important component of retirement income security. Further, as Medicare and Medicaid's fiscal challenges grow, public

Fig. 7.8.   Nonelderly population with employer-based health insurance, by firm size

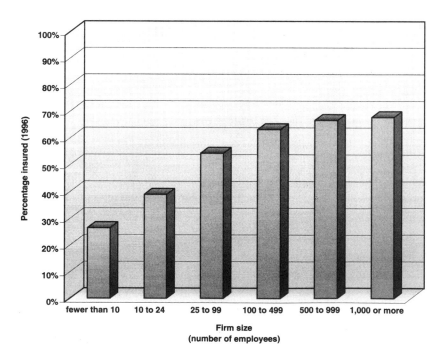

(*Source:* EBRI Issue Brief 192, December 1997, table 5, based on *Current Population Survey,* March 1997.)

programs are having increasing difficulty taking up the slack. Declining retiree health coverage by employer-provided plans has combined with the peculiarities of Medicare insurance to produce an apparent anomaly—retirees now pay a slightly larger proportion of health care costs out-of-pocket than they did before Medicare was enacted in 1965. Even for the elderly—the segment of our population that enjoys the most universal health insurance coverage—the twin curse of unaffordability and inadequacy looms large. For the non-elderly and non-poor, the situation is worse.

The contemporary pattern of American health insurance reveals once again the limits of voluntariness, federal tax subsidies, state financing, and employer-based insurance when seeking to fulfill conventional social insurance goals of universality and progressivity. To be sure, when the subsidy is big enough and is financed by a progressive tax, near universality with some progressivity can be achieved. That is the story of Medicare Part B. But elsewhere in the American health insurance world, we find the gaps and regressivity that we have come to expect of systems that rely on private markets supported by tax-expenditure subsidies and by state willingness or ability to fund redistributive programs. On the distributional side the oddity here—replicated to some degree in the cases of unemployment and disability insurance—is that the worst-off group consists of those families struggling to join or remain in the middle class, not those below the poverty line.

The special pathology of American health insurance arrangements is, of course, their tendency to fuel inflation in medical care costs without increasing insurance coverage. Other developed nations have combined universal coverage with cost control by structuring or regulating a universal system to effectively monopolize the financing and purchase of medical care services. By exercising governmental power in this strong form over the medical care sector, these countries have avoided the costly and inadequate health insurance system that has been our fate, at least until now.

But pointing to successes elsewhere will not change either our political history or the real institutional impediments to creating a universal medical care program for American families. As Chapter 9 details, we believe that reform requires a different way of thinking about the purposes of medical care insurance within the overall system of social insurance protection. Health insurance reform should focus on income security, not on ensuring equal access to medical care. If it were to be so focused, we believe that universal coverage could be provided within the constraints of current total expenditures. A reconceptualization of the function of medical social insurance as we urge may or may not produce substantial progress toward adequate, affordable, and universal health insurance protections. But as a political strategy, that approach can hardly do worse than recent reform efforts.

Part Three  **From Problems to Proposals**

# Chapter 8 The New Social Insurance Contract

Our current social insurance arrangements are a cause for celebration as well as concern. But Americans are impatient people. Pausing briefly to acknowledge success, we move on. We hunger for progress, for individual and social improvement. Like the self-help books that cluster at the top of the best-seller lists, this book too has a reformative impulse. Writing a social rather than a self-help essay, we have emphasized current social insurance problems more than successes. We turn now to proposed remedies.

Prior chapters articulate our beliefs about the reach and rationale for social insurance arrangements as well as the successes and failures of current programs. A framework for rethinking the social insurance contract is implicit in those discussions. The work of this chapter is to make more explicit our beliefs about the role of social insurance and the shape of the world that it is likely to inhabit. Having articulated the domain and context of what we are calling the "new social insurance contract," and the risks against which it should provide assistance, we turn in later chapters to the particulars of the insurance policies that we believe should be available at the various stages of each American's life.

## THE DOMAIN OF SOCIAL INSURANCE

We addressed the domain of social insurance in Chapter 2. We offer here only a reminder that social insurance, for us, neither encompasses the whole of social provision, nor is confined to existing programmatic expressions of social insurance principles.

The conventional idea of social insurance is a collectively organized scheme that promises to pay money (or "near money," such as tax credits or vouchers) either to or on behalf of a family economic unit when some specified risk to labor income occurs. The programmatic implementation of this conventional understanding often involves a government-administered program supported by mandatory "contributions" that provide income-related benefits to a very broad, near-universal, population.

Remember, however, that this conception neither exhausts the idea of social insurance nor accurately describes the heterogeneous programs that we currently operate. In fact, as we demonstrated in Chapter 3, it accounts for only about half of U.S. social insurance. We understand social insurance to include programs that are not only income-related, but also income-tested. We include programs funded out of general revenues as well as those financed by participant contributions. And we include within the instruments available to social insurance the creation of mandates or tax subsidies that either support family income directly or facilitate the provision of private insurance.

To put the point more purposefully, it is the job of social insurance to protect family income streams against absolute inadequacy and ameliorate the drastic decline in living standards that may attend the realization of some risk to labor income. But we hasten to add that even though the cause of the loss or inadequacy of family economic well-being is in principle irrelevant to the broad purposes of social insurance, this does not mean that all such risks will turn out to be insurable in a prudent social insurance system.

Nor is it the business of social insurance to ensure economic growth, assure every child a useful education, or decrease the incidence of infectious disease. All of these things may bear on family economic security, however, and the design of social insurance regimes should not impede achievement of these purposes. Social insurance arrangements play a large role in protecting family economic security, but they are only a part of the overall social contract. Social insurance can undermine true security by attempting to do too much as well as by doing too little.

No discussion of social insurance (or anything else) is free of underlying assumptions about the shape of the world or from commitments to normative propositions. Nor is it always easy to disentangle factual presuppositions from moral or political values. As we have attempted to unravel and reconstruct the complex system of income supports that compose American social insurance policy, we have been guided, sometimes only implicitly, by a host of underlying assumptions and commitments. We can hardly identify or discuss all of them here, but it is time to make some of the more important ones explicit. We begin with our own normative beliefs and then proceed to describe our assumptions about the more general normative and factual environment that provides the backdrop for our proposals.

## COMMITMENTS

### Limited Altruism

We share the conventional American belief in the primacy of personal and family responsibility for individual well-being. We, like most Americans, recognize our membership in groups broader than the self or the family, but we believe that allegiances outside the family are more attenuated than those within it. We all recognize responsibilities to our fellow citizens (or perhaps to all people), to other living things, and to "the environment." But when push comes to shove, these are responsibilities to be satisfied only after we satisfy our responsibilities to ourselves and our closest kin.

At the level of economic organization, this understanding of mutual support obligations translates, we believe, into a simple further understanding: Everyone (at least each healthy adult) is responsible for his or her own economic well-being and, to a somewhat lesser degree, for that of family dependents. Families are expected to be "self-supporting," and most of us are most of the time.

### Shared Luck

The idea that we are responsible for our own economic circumstances, however, can be extended only so far. We all operate within an economic system that binds us together by its particular rules for promoting economic cooperation and settling conflicts over access to resources. No matter how wedded we are to Horatio Alger stories of personal triumph, our success in the economy is also a function of the success of the economy—of the economic, legal, and social system as a whole. Our capacity to support ourselves depends crucially on others' willingness to participate with us in productive activity by sharing responsibilities and opportunities, successes and failures.

In any system of market capitalism, such as those in place in western democracies, there is typically considerable dispersion in individual returns to economic participation. These returns depend on the public's demand for the product or service being supplied. People who work or risk their capital in endeavors where demand proves strong will do well; people in enterprises where demand proves weak will do poorly. Luck also plays a role: being born into a family of wealth or education rather than a family of poverty or ignorance often produces lifelong advantages. And market returns depend critically on well-functioning government institutions, police, civil and criminal courts, and laws against fraud and deception, to name a few. Surely, some substantial share of the nation's output—of income from both labor and capital—is a societal rather than an individual creation. But those returns will end up in some individuals' pockets and not in others. In order for this dispersion of economic rewards to be acceptable to all—that is, for the system to maintain its legitimacy—variations in outcomes must seem to be "fair."

We believe that fairness requires attention to at least four aspects of the system. First, the rules of the game should support *equal opportunity* for all participants. Second, the principle of *just desserts* should be respected: effort and risk-bearing—the engines of economic growth—should be rewarded; force, fraud, neglect, and the depletion of common resources should be deterred and punished. Third, substantial risks to economic well-being that are not individually controllable should be buffered by collective *social insurance,* arrangements that reduce these economic risks to a tolerable level. Those risks include systemwide events or changes (for example, recession, inflation, or technological change), common features of human nature (such as tendencies to overdiscount the future and to undervalue small risks), and personal shocks that are difficult to insure against individually (for example, disability, unemployment, or being born into a poor family). Fourth, financing collective arrangements to ensure equal opportunity, enforce the system of just desserts, and provide social insurance should be *progressive*. Those who benefit most from participation in the economic system should bear greater responsibilities for its maintenance.

The ways in which "fairness" is assured in any social and economic system are complex and diverse, as are the interpretations and priorities assigned to the various domains of fairness. We cannot here argue for the soundness or comprehensiveness of our understanding of fairness, but it is important to see something of the "big picture" in order to understand the domain of our discussion. This book considers primarily the third arena of fairness, the system of social insurance—a system for increasing security by sharing "luck" both within economic units (within families) across time and across families at any particular time.

Moreover, it is crucial to understand that, in our view, social insurance is a device for buffering risks to individual or family income streams in a market economy, not for transforming that economy by pursuing egalitarian aims or for "decommodifying" labor income by uncoupling economic rewards from economic productivity. To be sure, insuring against some risks to family income—for example, the risk of low lifetime wages—clearly requires transfers from the more to the less affluent. But much of the work of social insurance involves the smoothing of family income over the life cycle in the face of risks such as unemployment, illness, or death of a breadwinner—events that can produce dramatic losses in living standards. Because these losses may often also entail a family's falling below basic standards of income adequacy, it is impossible to specify just what proportions of social insurance provision are directed toward income-smoothing, on the one hand, and redistribution to avoid poverty, on the other. The income adequacy and income stability goals of social insurance are inextricably intertwined. While many have argued that this gives social insurance a set of confused purposes that render its goals incoherent, we do not share that view. Individuals and societies have multiple, not unitary, goals. The demand that programs have only one purpose is a demand for both the impossible and the undesirable, not a demand for coherence.

### Flexible Intervention

Given the inevitable tradeoffs at the margin between arrangements that promote opportunity and those that promote security, the design of social insurance regimes is critical to the true economic security of the populace.

And providing security from economic misfortune—while simultaneously maintaining an appropriate sense of personal responsibility and avoiding excessive constraints on free market activity—is no mean trick. The proposals in this book favor security arrangements organized as cash income replacements or supplements, mandated individual savings, and certain forms of stop-loss insurance to assure access to particular necessities.

These types of interventions obviously have incentive effects, and we will be attentive to those issues. They are substitutes, however, for much more interventionist policies that tend either to rigidify factor markets (such as by high minimum wages, job guarantees, price supports for declining industries, and trade restrictions to protect domestic jobs) or to preclude the emergence or evolution of private markets (for example, by public provision of health care or child care, or the creation of substantial numbers of public-sector jobs). We believe that policies based on transfers rather than structural intervention are markedly superior in terms of their impact on the economy as a whole. Security does not lie in destroying the adaptive capacities of the private economy.

The line between opportunity-enhancing programs that increase economic productivity and social insurance that guards against the risks of economic distress is hardly a bright one. Potential negative effects on personal effort and family responsibility create important constraints on the design and financing of social insurance arrangements. And societies engage in many efforts to prepare people for work and to assure that they have opportunities to employ their talents. Obviously, the better connected people are to the workforce and the more human and material capital they acquire, the better off they will likely be in a market economy. In this sense they are "more secure" because they have more economic power.

Our concern in this book, however, is with protections that take hold when labor markets fail to produce adequate income for particular families or when families experience specific threats of sharp declines in their standard of living. Such protections are crucial to a society's ability to structure economic risks in ways that are energizing rather than demoralizing. They also maintain the society's sense of identity and solidarity in the face of individualized or more widespread economic misfortunes.

We believe that this is a discrete policy domain worthy of separate and sustained attention notwithstanding its imbeddedness in a much broader system of economic relations. For if it is well constructed, social insurance will sustain and bolster a market economy.

### Program Effectiveness

Given our belief that true security resides in an appropriate balance between personal and collective responsibilities, our programmatic commitments are eclectic. The reader of these pages will find advocacy of a host of techniques (cash benefits, vouchers, mandates and subsidies, to name a few), activity at multiple governmental levels, and approaches that are sometimes "public," sometimes "private," and sometimes in combined forms. No single technique or institutional arrangement is likely to be the best solution for each instance of economic insecurity generated by a divergent set of economic risks. Our goal is to promote true security, not to satisfy some simple ideological formula about appropriate forms of government interventions.

Nevertheless, the history of America leads us to certain presuppositions concerning program efficacy: we are convinced that private markets are terrific means for wealth creation, but we are doubtful that private institutions are very good vehicles for the effectuation of redistributive policies. We are, therefore, skeptical that tax subsidies for voluntary private "employee welfare" activities can provide effective income security for most American families, unless they are a part of a broader scheme of public provision or mandates that universalize protections. On the other hand, "privatized" arrangements may often permit flexibility and choice, experimentation and competition that enhance individual security. They should be retained so long as core income security goals are not compromised.

Similarly, we believe that societywide income security schemes are likely to be more effectively financed through national than through state or local efforts. But we believe that the scale of national programs limits the degree to which national officials can engage in highly individualized discretion and decisionmaking. This is to our mind a strength in providing cash income replacements or supplements, but a weakness with respect to the provision of individualized ameliorative services that demand discretionary judgment. The latter should generally be left to, or contracted out to, states, localities, and private entities.

Finally, while we concede that most policies serve multiple purposes, we believe that core income security goals must be kept in the forefront when designing social insurance programs. Where subsidiary purposes seriously impair the capacity of programs to provide true income security, they should be separated from social insurance and pursued through independent means. As our prior and subsequent discussions of workers' compensation, unemployment insurance, and health insurance reveal, pursuing multiple goals through a social insurance program is sometimes an important reason for the failures of existing arrangements.

### Budgetary Realism

Like many who are concerned to strengthen the economic security of American families, we often believe that too little is being spent to accomplish particular purposes. But we are not at all persuaded that too little is being spent in the aggregate to finance a well-functioning social insurance system. To switch fairy tales, the idea is not to spend more or spend less but to spend in ways that are "just right."

We, therefore, propose to be realistic about budgetary matters in two ways. First, we seek to avoid interminable squabbles about "how high is up?" by making proposals that can generally be accomplished within the boundaries of current overall expenditures for existing income security programs. In that sense our proposals should in aggregate seem financially "realistic" to all except those few who believe that current expenditures for these purposes are unsustainable. (Given the strength of the American economy, this is not a very plausible position, but some hold it nevertheless.)

Second, for us a current dollar spent to support family income against the risks that we propose to cover is just that—a dollar spent. For purposes of determining current aggregate outlays we do not care whether that dollar is in a trust fund or is part of general revenues, is in an "entitlement" or a "discretionary" program; is in the form of a direct outlay, tax expenditure, or unfunded mandate; or is located in a federal, state, local, or even nongovernmental budget. We are concerned with public economics and public finance, not public accounting. We are thus talking about what is "really" spent in the aggregate as the result of governmental policies directed at income security.

We are, of course, not so naive as to believe that how much is spent is independent of how the expenditure is labeled or whose budget (if anyone's) reflects the expenditure. But that is a point about politics or political economy that our principle of budgetary realism ignores. Our primary interest is in analyzing what should and can be done given current resource commitments, not in the budgetary accounting rules and strategies that have shaped current arrangements. We will return in Chapter 15 to the question of how these structural arrangements affect the politics of reform.

### Achieving True Security

Ignoring politics is dangerous but conventional for many economically oriented policy analysts and some other students of public policy. By contrast, the programmatic ambitions of others in the policy community often seem to be driven almost entirely by an appreciation of what is immediately politically possible. Both positions have their merits, but they run very different risks. The first risks irrelevance, either because it ignores stable political commitments or, alternatively, treats existing but malleable political preferences as fixed. The second courts incoherence and inefficacy as it seeks to satisfy momentary coalitions of interests through complex compromises that imperil the achievement of any sensible set of policy goals.

The proposals in this book attempt to occupy an uneasy middle ground between these camps. On the one hand, we are mindful of certain structural aspects of the American political system. We try to avoid proposals, for example, that are likely to unravel because of interstate competition or to be nonstarters because they involve massive transfers of novel authority to public-sector officials.

Yet much of our criticism of existing programs may be described as criticism of once-necessary political compromises, and many of our new proposals have an uncertain political viability. We are not attempting to design a scheme that might pass in the next Congress. Our goal instead is to fashion a coherent and attractive vision of social insurance and to illustrate how that vision might be implemented.

Our ambition is an integrated understanding of the ends and the means of a social insurance regime that would provide true security for America's families. This leads us to offer a comprehensive and tightly integrated set of reform proposals. Some of our discrete suggestions demand the acceptance of others, although the scheme is not designed as an all or nothing proposition. The whole package should appeal to many Americans. Its fundamental purpose, however, is to inform reform efforts that in a democracy must, almost of necessity, be partial and incremental.

We want to convince you that our overall scheme makes sense in terms of the economic security needs of American families, that it is consistent with widely held social values, and that it is workable within the sort of economic and governmental system that we have. If all of that is true, we will have presented a coherent set of aspirations for a social insurance regime, and we will have demonstrated that true security is more than a fuzzy ideal.

## ASSUMPTIONS

Beyond the authors' personal commitments, any elaboration of a general approach to social insurance must also make a large number of assumptions about existing and future states of the world. Indeed, any such attempt indulges in so many assumptions that not all of them can cogently be made explicit. We sketch here only some of our more important assumptions, those that bear directly both on the needs that should be met by a new social insurance regime and the approaches that we deem feasible for structuring the new social insurance contract. All of these political, moral, social, and economic "facts" are contestable to some degree, but extended discussion of their philosophical and social presuppositions is not warranted here. This is a book about reform within the context of an existing but malleable regime, not a book about regime change or social, economic, or political revolution.

### Political and Moral Commitments

We assume first that Americans will remain committed to representative democracy and to a form of government that entails pragmatic accommodation of the trade-off between accountability and competence. While rigid ideological positions are often the stuff of constitutional debate, the path of American constitutional practice has been quite different. We have a commitment to limited, local, and accountable government *combined* with a commitment to activist and ambitious central initiatives when the need arises. Our constitutional structure has not always yielded instantly to the felt necessities of the time—it could hardly do so and remain a constitutional regime. But our stable constitutional system has remained so by engaging in substantial, occasionally radical, change. There are legal constraints on the shape of social insurance arrangements, but given time and ingenuity, we believe that virtually all of what Americans democratically decide that they want can be designed to be consistent with our basic constitutional commitments.

We believe, second, that whatever the constitutional necessity, Americans will continue in their historic preference for a limited national bureaucratic presence—a preference that is seldom frustrated outside of Washington, D.C., and the environs of military bases and federal public lands. Federal civilian employment as a percentage of the population has never been large and has been decreasing steadily since the end of the Korean conflict. State and local public employment has more than doubled in the same period (fig. 8.1). Hence, while decentralization is one of the pathologies of our current social insurance arrangements, we do not imagine that new arrangements that feature highly centralized implementation—beyond record keeping and check writing—are likely to be attractive. We will propose new central government initiatives, but they are designed to limit the presence of central government administration.

Third, we believe that Americans will remain committed to a market economy with free movement of the factors of production. Indeed, it is this commitment that makes an effective social insurance system so important. Economic security can be guaranteed, at least in the short run, by rigid controls on factor mobility, centralized planning, a massive public sector with substantial featherbedding, extensive regulation of labor contracts, and so on. This is not the economy we have chosen, for good rea-

Fig. 8.1.    Civilian government employment

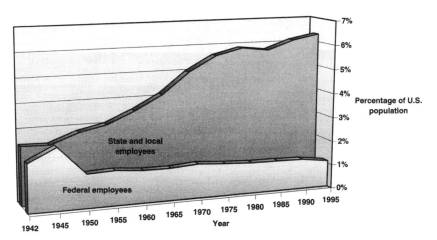

(*Source:* Scott Moody, ed., *Facts and Figures on Government Finance,* 32d ed., Washington D.C., The Tax Foundation, 1998, 27; *Statistical Abstract,* 1997, 1981, table 506; and 1956, table 482.)

son. But having not chosen it, we expose ourselves to a number of risks that generate the need for social insurance protections. Indeed, while historical comparisons are always treacherous, the dynamics of current economic arrangements, in particular movement from a manufacturing to a services economy, seem to create risks and insecurities that are at least as important as those that arose in the great age of industrialization that spawned the first round of social insurance provision.

Fourth, we believe that Americans will retain their expectation that a family's receipt of income will result primarily from present work by family members or returns to the investments of past savings. Families will always remain principally responsible for their own well-being. The key role of social insurance is both to support work and to ameliorate the risks inherent in a free market for labor.

Finally, we assume that Americans will maintain a social commitment both to protecting basic income adequacy and to helping maintain prior living standards where insurance against loss of income is funded directly or indirectly by personal contributions. As we have said, we do not believe that the "adequacy" and "equity" values that were much discussed by the designers of America's current social insurance arrangements are obsolescent ideals. They must both be part of an acceptable and enduring system of social insurance for the future.

### Contextual Continuity

Supreme Court Justice Oliver Wendell Holmes famously remarked, "Continuity with the past is not a duty, only a necessity." In accordance with this wisdom, the new social insurance contract that we envision imagines that historic trends in demographics, economic performance, labor market participation, and family income patterns will persist.

On the demographic side, we assume that America's population will remain relatively stable in overall number, but that it will gradually be weighted more heavily toward the elderly. There is much dispute about whether the increases in life spans that we have witnessed over the past four or five decades will continue. It seems hard to imagine them continuing at the same rate. But it would have been difficult in 1940 to imagine the average life span that has been achieved by the end of the twentieth century. In any event, absent some drastic shift in our ecological fortunes, over the next four or five decades America is destined to have an older and older population (fig. 8.2).

Fig. 8.2.    Life expectancy at age 65

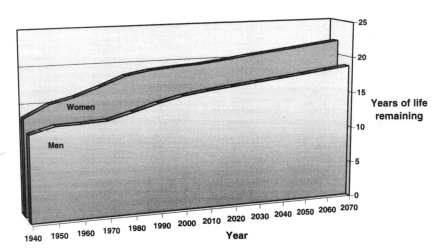

(*Source:* Social Security Administration, *1998 OASDI Trustees Report,* table II.D2.)

Second, we see no reason to anticipate a reversal of the rate of family formation that has occurred over the last several decades or a radical decline in the rate of family dissolution. Whatever we may wish, we expect a continued high incidence of divorce and single-parent families, a status highly correlated with families' economic distress.

Third, we assume that the business cycle still cycles, and we suppose that we will be about as bad at predicting the timing and extent of downturns and upturns as we have been in the past. Involuntary unemployment is not over, and planning for it within the family will remain difficult, if not impossible.

We also detect no necessary relationship among the growth rates of inflation, wages, or returns to capital. Economic security cannot be assured, therefore, by pegging social insurance benefits or funding to any one of these sources or indices. Nor is it prudent to predict that wages or family income will keep pace with the costs of all basic necessities. Prices and wages can move in opposite directions and generate needs for specific consumption subsidies in addition to more generalized wage or income subsidies.

Fourth, with respect to labor markets, a number of factors seem particularly salient in thinking about the appropriate scope of an adequate social insurance regime. We see no reason, for example, to foresee a norm of lifetime employment by the same employer. The radical destabilization of work may have been oversold by both academic and political commentators. Nevertheless, we no longer inhabit a world in which workers spend thirty-five years with the same employer and retire with a gold watch and a defined-benefit pension.

In addition, there is no reason to believe that competitive pressures on wages will abate. The struggle to keep wage costs down will affect wage rates, fringe benefits, and the size of the workforce employed by particular companies. These trends will render employer-based social insurance increasingly problematic.

We also expect that pressures on wages, along with the entry of married women into the workforce, will mean that the two-earner family is the dominant family economic unit. Whether that structure of labor force participation will become nearly universal remains to be seen. After all, many families have only one earner to earn. Planning for a two-earner norm is important. Planning exclusively for that norm will further marginalize the economic position of the one-parent household.

Fifth, with respect to income distribution we expect a number of historic trends and stabilities to continue. We assume, for example, that there will continue to be high returns to education measured by years of schooling. As figure 8.3 shows, in recent years these returns have increased substantially. If "information workers" become even more prominent, and job mobility requires frequent adaptation, the returns to generalized education may climb even higher.

We also assume that accumulations of wealth resulting from voluntary market activity and family transfers will remain highly concentrated. We should not be misled by the reports that more and more middle-aged Americans are salting away ever more in treasury bonds and mutual funds. An increase in average family financial holdings does not mean that we have become a nation of wealthy capitalists. Although the concentration of wealth in contemporary America is so great that the numbers are somewhat difficult to believe, our assumption is that no radical redistribution of that wealth is on the horizon (fig. 8.4). In the future, the top 1 percent of wealth holders still will not need social insurance, but the rest of the population still will.

On the other hand, we believe that broadening the base of worker-capitalists can have important effects on the success of social insurance arrangements. We propose, therefore, to require each worker to con-

Fig. 8.3.   Returns to education

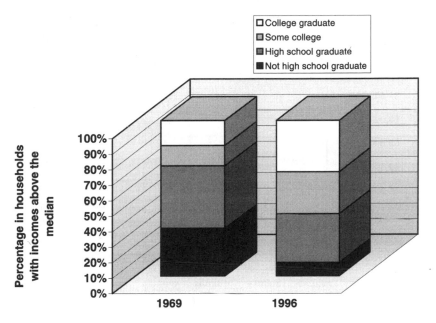

(*Source:* Authors' calculations based on data from U.S. Census Bureau, *Current Population Reports, Changes in Median Household Income: 1969–1996,* July 1998, P23-196, table 2.)

tribute 3 percent of wages into a Universal Security Account. As we explain later, that account will increase retirement security by giving workers a more diversified portfolio of pensions linked to the capital market and labor market. It is also designed to be used during spells of unemployment as a form of copayment for unemployment benefits. When functioning in that way, these accounts will reduce moral hazard in the unemployment insurance system and permit more liberal eligibility rules than might otherwise seem prudent.

Finally, with respect to family income, we assume that a general life-cycle pattern of income and savings will remain broadly descriptive of family histories. Younger workers, particularly younger workers with children, will have relatively low per capita incomes by comparison with workers in their prime earning years. And as workers reduce their work effort and move into retirement, their incomes will decrease.

We hasten to add that none of these background assumptions are foolproof predictions. But the social contract implicit in a social insurance

Fig. 8.4.    Wealth distribution

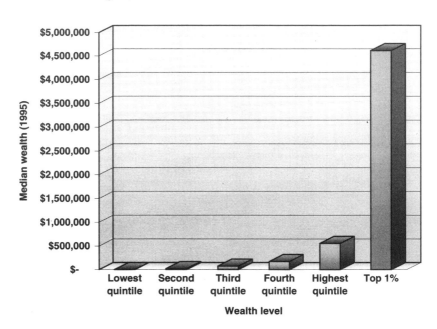

(*Source:* Bruce Ackerman and Anne Alstott, *The Stakeholder Society,* New Haven and London, Yale University Press, 1999, table 3, 225.)

regime stretches over long time periods. This makes it necessary to make some assumptions about what the underlying characteristics of the economy and society will be. We should expect that these predictions will prove wrong in some particulars in the short term and in most particulars in the long run. Social insurance provision must be capable of adjusting to confront new or emerging realities. Stable commitments demand the ability to change programmatic arrangements.

### SUMMARY

Our vision of the new social insurance contract is in some ways quite simple. Americans should expect to live by work and to consume from what they have earned or saved. But Americans should also expect that a society that provides opportunity will recognize that opportunity entails risk. Not all will succeed, and few will succeed all of the time. For market risks to provide incentives rather than occasions for demoralization, they must be made tolerable. The income stream of the family economic unit should depend on the market, but not solely on the market. It is the straightforward role of social insurance to cushion risks in ways that maintain decent and/or customary living standards when statistically, but not individually, predictable risks undermine family economic security.

The generality of this vision has significant virtues. It is not wedded to particular methods of implementation as the defining attributes of social insurance provision. It is open to the discovery of new risks and to changing approaches for protection against old ones. It focuses on a straightforward objective—protecting family income in the face of a lack of adequate labor income.

Unhappily, a simple vision of purpose does not lead to simple programs. Differing risks demand differing interventions. Moral hazard, for example, is a serious problem in insuring workers and children; it is far less important in insuring retirees. Resources are not inexhaustible. Restructuring programs to face the financial challenge of providing security to an aging population without depriving workers and children is a daunting task. Other social purposes compete with social insurance for our collective attention. Administrative and political difficulties abound. And the balance among personal responsibility, economic opportunity, and social insurance is inevitably precarious and contestable.

Were this not the case, we would, like others before us, offer up a simple solution—a negative income tax. As we wrote in Chapter 3, the NIT is elegant in its simplicity and breathtaking in its simplemindedness. For it assumes that we believe that all risks should be insured in the same way and in the same amount and that income adequacy is the only purpose of social insurance (or, at the very least, that maintaining living standards is relatively unimportant). It imagines that truly adequate income support can be provided without substantial work disincentives.

This is not the world that we inhabit or one that is likely ever to be available to us. As a consequence, we must approach a simple task through complex means. In the following chapters, therefore, we sketch the elements of insurance against particular risks that together might constitute the new social insurance contract.

Lest we be misunderstood, we should emphasize that the programs that we propose in the next four chapters are only possible ways to fulfill the true security goals that animate social insurance provision. We cannot develop them here in the fiscal and administrative detail that would provide an adequate template for specific legislation. We offer them to demonstrate more concretely that progress is possible and to show how the design of social insurance regimes is crucial to achieving overall social insurance goals. We hope to persuade you that an American society motivated to achieve true security in its social insurance arrangements can do much better than we are now doing.

# Chapter 9 Social Insurance and Health Care

As we recounted in Chapter 7, American health insurance policy is a mess. The aggregate costs of our health care insurance system are the highest in the world, the payment of those costs responds to no one's definition of fairness, and a large number of Americans lack secure health insurance coverage. While our politicians often claim that Americans have the "best health care in the world," it is hard to know what that statement means. Not only do many Americans lack access to the high-cost technological marvels that the statement seems to embrace, but even larger numbers lack access to the type of care that they need—such as mental health care, prescription drugs, and home care. Or to put the matter more precisely, their insurance policies do not cover needed care. Further, more than 43 million Americans lack health insurance. The families we have called the "struggling middle class," particularly families that earn between a poverty-level income and 200 percent of the poverty-level income, are those most likely to lack health insurance.[1]

Americans' complaints about their health care system are not exhausted by concerns relating to access, quality, and cost. While most Americans value choice (most of the time), as insurance purchasers and patients they are increasingly limited in their selection of affordable plans and physicians. And while Americans bow to no one in their hatred of bureaucratic wrangles, the difficulties of managing medical insurance claims are probably greater in the United States than elsewhere in the developed world.

Even at the most basic level of social insurance protection—the ability of a social insurance system to protect against inadequate income or dramatic losses in standards of living—the American medical insurance system fails to provide security. Many private insurance policies have annual and lifetime maxima that fall below the costs of major bouts of illness. Medicare coverage is riddled with payment limitations, many of which are routinely exhausted by its beneficiaries. So-called Medigap policies respond to an enormous demand for insurance covering the copayments and deductibles for Medicare patients, but nevertheless fail to fill important gaps in Medicare coverage that continue to be paid out-of-pocket. Medicaid has no cap for covered services, but you must become impoverished in order to be eligible. A substantial number of the elderly and disabled find themselves in just that position because of limitations on Medicare coverage. For the uninsured, financial disaster is but one hospital visit, or expensive out-patient procedure, away.

**IF IT'S SO BROKEN, WHY DON'T WE FIX IT?**

When encountering a policy calamity like the American health care system, one's first instinct might be to search for some incompatibility among the goals of universality, quality, choice, administrative simplicity, and reasonable cost. To be sure, tradeoffs are to be found among these goals. At some point, coverage and quality must be traded off against cost. Maximizing choice may well be both costly and inconsistent with administrative simplicity. Yet these crucial tradeoffs do not stand in the way of major improvements in the American health insurance system. From our current starting point, every dimension of the health care system can be improved simultaneously. We confront serious design flaws, not inevitable policy dilemmas.

To see that this is true, we need but notice some very general facts about the medical insurance systems of other OECD countries. All of these systems provide (near) universal access at aggregate costs—both per capita and as a percentage of GDP—below American expenditures. In some cases our costs are greater by as much as 5 percent of gross domestic product. To be sure, certain high-tech wonders are available to some Americans that are not available elsewhere. But quality measured in more meaningful terms—real resources (physician and hospital time) devoted to patient care, breadth of covered services, continuity of care, and gross indicators of health (like infant morality and longevity)—points in the direction of at least equal, and sometimes higher, quality care abroad. Basic health indicators like life expectancy at birth and the percentage of babies with low birth weights bear virtually no relationship to a country's health care expenditure level (fig. 9.1). This suggests that the United States is not getting a significant health quality bang for its huge health care bucks.

Nor are patients better off in other ways. Administrative difficulties for

Fig. 9.1.   Comparative health expenditures and health indicators

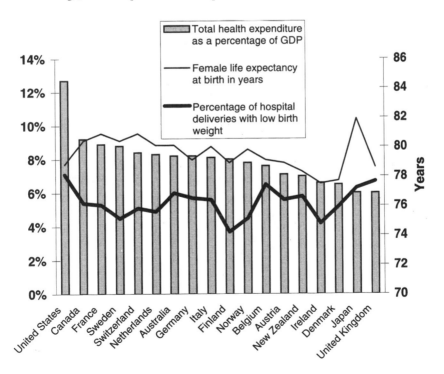

(*Source:* Authors' calculations based on 1990 OECD data. Combined male and female life expectancies are not available, so only female life expectancies are depicted.)

patients and medical providers tend to be more limited in other OECD countries than in the United States. And in most countries, patients' choice of providers is effectively broader than that available to virtually all Americans outside of the Medicare system.

In a candid assessment, the American system may rank ahead of others only on the proximity of high-tech medical equipment and the ability of consumers to choose their insurance carrier. For those who require high-tech procedures, proximity is surely an advantage. But the putative benefits of being able to select an insurer are often purely theoretical and, where real, relatively trivial. Medicare and Medicaid beneficiaries have no plan choice (although Medicare is now experimenting with the substitution of plan choice for provider choice). Most working Americans who get their insurance through their employer are offered a single plan, or a menu in which cost differentials make only one or two plans a realistic option. Even where there is a realistic choice of plan, it is hard to know how to value the availability of these options. Most people have great difficulty predicting what they will need and, therefore, which plan to choose—even if they can understand the differences among them. Moreover, alternative systems, such as those available in many OECD countries, where virtually any needed service is covered at a price that all families can afford, make one wonder how important it is to be able to choose one's insurance carrier.

The programmatic features that produce these results abroad are relatively straightforward, although the variations on these themes from country to country are substantial. A short list of features seems to make up the common core of institutional designs: mandatory coverage of the whole population; tight regulation of insurance contracts to insure breadth of coverage and the unavailability of competition by risk selection; the utilization of substantial (or in some cases sole) buying power and/or per-patient, rather than per-medical-service, payment; and financing mechanisms that generate redistribution from high- to low-income families and from low- to high-risk beneficiaries.

The failures of American health insurance policy are thus not explained by the technical incapacity of any system to meet our countervailing goals. The story here is a story of political failure—and it is frequently told elsewhere and in great detail. Each analyst, to be sure, offers up a different villain—entrenched interests, reckless politicians, institutional inertia, misleading misinformation campaigns, ideological firewalls, or simple incompetence, to name a few favorites. But our purpose here is not to sort out why health insurance reform has failed to produce universal coverage at a reasonable cost for American families. We want instead to redefine the problem. It may be possible to get different answers, and better results, by asking a different question.

## TWO VIEWS OF HEALTH INSURANCE AS
## SOCIAL INSURANCE

Most previous discussion of American health insurance policy has explicitly or implicitly agreed that health care provision is a vital aspect of social insurance policymaking. According to the dominant view, the state should make sure that everyone has access to comprehensive health care at a reasonable cost. This vision of the appropriate role of health insurance tends both to multiply state responsibilities and to build them into the social insurance scheme itself. There are some good reasons for this dominant vision, but it is not the only one available to us. The functions that now compose our image of a national health care system are multiple and, at least in principle, separable.

Imagine for simplicity that there are three basic functions involved in the orchestration of a national health care system: The most direct activity is providing health care itself. This function is carried out by a host of professionals, subprofessionals, and commercial public and nonprofit institutions—doctors, nurses, lab technicians, hospitals, clinics, pharmaceutical companies, university-based medical schools, public health organizations, and so on.

The second function involves the creation of some system for purchasing medical goods and services. These activities, once again, take a variety of forms: patient, third-party-insurance, employer, single-payer (as, for example, in Canada), and combinations of these purchasing approaches. Moreover, the methodology of purchase may range from fee-for-service payments by individual buyers or insurers, to systems based on per-patient payments for individual patients or groups, to global budget specifications for all or particular segments of health care provision. The possible combinations of purchasing institutions and purchasing methods create a rich array of possible arrangements.

Finally, all of this purchasing and providing must be financed. Financing can be accomplished by household out-of-pocket expenditure, private individual insurance, private group insurance, and public budgets. The public budgets themselves, may, of course, be made up of differing sorts of revenue streams, ranging from earmarked "contributions"—usually in the form of wage taxes—to general revenues. The levels of contribution to the overall financing scheme by particular households or entities and the degree to which those contributions are "voluntary" or "mandatory" can vary both across and within financing systems.

In short, a health care system is an arrangement for financing, purchasing, and providing health care goods and services. The choices that are made concerning the organization of these three functions and their relation to each other define a nation's approach to assuring its population's access to health care. More importantly for our purposes, the dominant vision of health insurance as the provision of universal access to comprehensive health care implies that social insurance protection against health risks requires the orchestration of all three health care functions—finance, purchase, and provision—within the social insurance system itself.

This combination of functions is perhaps most obvious in systems like the British National Health Service or our system of Veterans Administration hospitals. If the government is in the business of providing health care, it is necessarily in the business of purchasing the goods and services necessary for that task and raising the money to finance those purchases. One can imagine a system of public provision with private purchase and finance, but one never observes such systems in the developed world.

Where government is not the provider of medical goods and services, disaggregation of the financing, purchasing, and providing functions is commonplace. Yet pressures to combine these functions are quite strong even where the initial policy impulse (public or private) is merely to assist in the organization of the financing of needed medical care.

Private employers, unions, and other associations often provide or purchase group health insurance as a means for reducing members' costs. Group insurance is an obvious antidote for some of the adverse selection and risk segmentation of private individual health insurance. But once into the financing role, it is hard for group sponsors not to take on responsibilities for purchasing decisions and even the organization and the provision of care.[2] Much of contemporary "reform" in the American health care system, whether in public programs like Medicare and Medicaid or in private group-sponsored insurance, has been in combining financing with purchasing responsibilities. Financing inevitably leads to a concern with costs, and costs must be controlled either through modifications in coverage or through reductions in prices and/or the rates at which patients utilize medical services. If coverage is to be maintained, the use of purchasing power to negotiate or impose lower prices and/or reduced utilization becomes the dominant strategy. Finally, even if these issues have not emerged before, the effort to control costs through collective purchase leads inexorably to concerns about the maintenance of quality. The result is a relentless merging of purchasing functions with the provision of care.

An employer-sponsored health maintenance organization (HMO) is perhaps the extreme form of this private merger of functions. Just as the Veterans Administration might be conceptualized as running a large HMO for veterans, many universities, and some other large employers, sponsor HMOs that put the employer in the position of financing, purchasing, and providing health insurance and care in an integrated fashion. This was industrialist Henry J. Kaiser's great innovation, a system that still covers millions of Californians.

Even where complete integration does not occur, there are strong tendencies to take on responsibilities for the quality of health care provision through the details of purchase arrangements, or, when the purchaser is a public entity, by regulation. Medicare reimbursement policies, for example, are designed not merely to limit moral hazard in the use of health care resources, but also to promote a series of additional policies: medical education, cost sharing across low- and high-cost jurisdictions, the subsidization of hospitals providing significant charity care, and the steering of medical professionals into general or specialty practices, to name a few. In addition, reimbursement policies seek to pursue various public health goals by allocating resources to preventative versus curative interventions and the like.

We have little doubt that there is a role for the state in pursuing all these sorts of policies. We question, however, whether the best way to pursue these policies is through regulations, subsidies, and cross-subsidies *within* the social insurance system. And we suspect that the overload of goals and functions built into current social insurance arrangements impedes reform.

Under the current system, every attempt at change influences not just beneficiary access and cost, but also a whole range of other policies that have their own constituencies and issue-specific concerns. It is not too surprising, therefore, that prior failed attempts at universalizing health insurance in the United States have been viewed not only as substituting governmental control for market choice, but also as interfering with medical practice, undermining medical education, reducing support for charity care, interfering with state and local prerogatives and responsibilities in both the provision and regulation of medical care, and threatening the continuation of tax-preferred employee medical benefits. When all of these potential objectors are rolled together with the medical insurance industry—for whom the stakes are highest—the political impediments to comprehensive reforms seem almost insurmountable.

There are a number of explanations for this vision of government's responsibilities. For many, health care is a "merit good" that demands strong governmental intervention to assure access in accordance with need, rather than on the basis of social class, ability to pay, job, residential location, or any other "arbitrary" factor. For others, it is a matter of equal citizenship in which governmental responsibilities to all citizens should mimic the special responsibilities that have been undertaken for governmental employees and, in particular, for military personnel and veterans. On either of these views, the state has at least three types of responsibilities: to protect against the economic costs of health care; to manage the health care market in the interests of quality, overall cost, and equitable access; and to promote public health by steering health care expenditures toward more beneficial interventions. Given that view, it is difficult to disentangle the provision of social insurance from a guarantee of adequate and relatively equal health care for all.

We want, nevertheless, to urge a different view of the role of health insurance in an overall social insurance scheme. Our basic position is that social insurance should be designed to protect income adequacy and to support income stability in the face of large and unpredictable medical expenses, as well as to guard against loss of income due to illness (among other contingencies). This income security goal is both narrower than the notion of securing access to health care and broader than the mere provision of health insurance. From this point of view, illness or injury carries with it two major threats to income security: the potentially high cost of medical treatment, and a possible loss of wages during recovery and rehabilitation. The question is whether an attempt to provide Americans with security concerning the economic costs of illness or injury has a better chance of fulfilling the basic purposes of social insurance—protecting all American families against the standard risks to family income—than does an attempt to make universal access to health care a part of a comprehensive social insurance package.

Putting the question this way, of course, loads the dice in favor of our preferred vision of health insurance and social insurance. A program targeted on income security in the face of illness or injury has a better chance of serving that goal than does a multifaceted health care policy that seeks to promote that goal along with many others. Hence we treat it as a constraint on the attractiveness of our proposal that it not produce substantial negative effects on such other health care goals as broadening access, insuring quality, promoting the public health, and contributing to a fair allocation of health care costs. To add fiscal realism, we will also impose an additional constraint: such a plan should not increase the aggregate costs now devoted to health care provision. In 1996, personal health care expenses in the United States totaled more than $900 billion, about 90 percent of the nation's total health expenditures of almost $1.035 trillion, or 13.6 percent of GDP (including, in addition to personal health care expenditures, such outlays as medical and development expenditures and subsidies to medical education). For the moment we will put aside what is often called "sickness" insurance—the provision of substitute income when illness or injury prevents work—and concentrate on a scheme to pursue the straightforward goal of preventing medical expenses from impairing income adequacy or from causing dramatic declines in standards of living. (Sickness insurance is taken up in Chapter 11 in connection with disability and workers' compensation arrangements.)

## AN INCOME-SECURITY HEALTH INSURANCE POLICY

### The Demands of Social Insurance

Given our understanding of the general purposes of social insurance, the role of health insurance should be to protect families against two types of risks to income: (1) the risk of income falling below some social requirement of decency at any point in the life cycle, and (2) the risk of encountering an unacceptably steep decline in living standards because of large medical expenses. With respect to adequacy, health risks are similar to risks resulting from unemployment or incapacity due to old age. The only difference is that a health insurance policy would be required to top off income measured not just by some fraction of income loss, but also by the amount of large medical expenditures. Similarly, protection against steep declines in standards of living would require the establishment of some "maintenance rate" that would be the analogue of the "replacement rate" in systems such as unemployment or disability insurance and old age pensions.

Social insurance in relation to health risks also implies that financing and benefits taken together should be progressive (that is, insurance coverage should not be limited by ability to pay), and that insurance pools should cover persons having heterogeneous rather than homogeneous risks. The basic idea is a society-wide pool in which the risks covered are those to which everyone is susceptible, although not necessarily to the same degree. Unlike casualty insurance, where we may wish to allocate insurance costs in accordance with levels of chosen risk, we will view health status here as stochastically distributed. To be sure, there are behavioral aspects to health risks, but as a normative matter we prefer to deal with those issues through education, regulation, taxation, and social norms. Sanctioning lifestyle choices by withholding health care or insurance coverage is an available policy choice, but not a desirable one. We would heavily tax cigarettes, alcohol, guns and bullets, or motorcycles, for example, rather than denying care to people with lung cancer or heart disease or to victims of violence or accident. Finally, any social insurance scheme must take account of fiscal and administrative realities. It must be run at a "reasonable" fiscal and administrative cost.

### A Tax Credit Strategy for Economic Security

If the straightforward social purpose is to protect against inadequate income or steep declines in standards of living due to health care costs, a refundable or transferable tax credit for "excess" medical expenses has much to recommend it. By filing the requisite tax forms, anyone having an income below the established level of adequacy could receive a tax cut or refund to cover medical expenses incurred during the year or could transfer the tax reduction to an insurer or health care provider in exchange for health care coverage or services. For those above the defined income-adequacy level, the amount of medical expenses exceeding some specified percentage of income would be credited against taxes owed and refunded to the extent that the credit exceeded tax obligations. This system would build on and extend the existing provisions for the deductibility of medical expenses exceeding 7.5 percent of income. A credit, however, eliminates the more favorable treatment of higher-bracket taxpayers inherent in a deduction, and refundability or transferability extends the benefits to people who owe no income taxes.

Building incrementally on current tax code provisions, nevertheless, raises some relatively serious problems. One is the definitional breadth of "medical expense" for tax purposes. At least as currently drafted, the Internal Revenue Code coverage goes well beyond any public or private medical insurance scheme. To some degree adopting this expansive definition of coverage would make sense given the purposes that we have specified for health insurance as a part of social insurance. When maintaining income, a medical expense is a medical expense, whether it is for open-heart surgery or for aspirin, eyeglasses, fertility treatments, or psychotherapy. It seems likely that for social insurance purposes we would want to draw the line short of the current expansive tax code approach. The German medical system may cover trips to the spa, but Americans are likely to raise their eyebrows at paying for such things as prescribed spa vacations or physician-directed lap pools. Nor should insurance pay for small routine expenses, such as purchases of over-the-counter drugs.

The tax credit approach also tends toward a year-end settling up process. This can be a major problem for those with inadequate or barely adequate incomes. It might be difficult to finance heavy medical expenditures solely on the promise that reimbursement from the IRS will become available some months hence. Experience with efforts to provide advance funding through employers of their workers' Earned Income Tax Credits is not encouraging. Making tax benefits transferable to health insurers or health care providers offers a potential solution but is an untried experiment.

It may be feasible to solve problems of definitional breadth and year-end accounting within the context of the tax system. A simple tax credit approach, however, tends to lead to a relatively open-ended commitment to pay for care of whatever type and whatever extent patients and their physicians choose. Moreover, at least as currently understood, tax credits would be available for any expenditures for medical insurance. Given recent experience with fee-for-service medicine under both Medicare and private group plans, such a commitment seems rash.

There are, of course, ways to deal with these issues by regulatory policies within the tax code. But we have by now encountered a sufficient number of problems that are specific to health insurance to make the wisdom of pursuing all of these matters through the Internal Revenue Code questionable even though financing income-based health insurance premiums through tax credits does have the advantage of using income data supplied routinely on tax returns rather than setting up separate and administratively objectionable means tests. There are often ways of dealing with things through the tax code that should not be chosen, both because of the increased burden of complexity that is introduced into tax compliance and because of the shift of policy enforcement from political actors—who specialize in and are knowledgeable in these matters—to the IRS, which does not and is not. As the simple tax credit strategy has become more complex, the reasons mount for setting up health insurance as a separate institutional domain and limiting any role of the tax code to a financing mechanism.

### THE BASE LINE OR "CATASTROPHIC" POLICY

The health insurance that we have in mind is a policy that insures incomes. The social insurance guarantee would be that no family would in any year be required to expend resources for medical care that (1) brought its annual income below a predetermined level of decency (say 100 to 125 percent of the poverty line) or (2) produced dramatic losses in standards of living. This latter standard would in fact be a sliding scale of percentages of income. From this perspective, a 15 to 20 percent allocation of income to medical care might be bearable for higher-income individuals, whereas a 5 percent expenditure could be unduly burdensome for a family living at the margin of decency.

Because this system guarantees against larger than bearable individual or family medical expenditures, the primary funding source—the first payer—for medical care will be individuals. This is not as strange as it may sound. As we described in Chapter 7, the most densely covered group of beneficiaries in the United States—Medicare beneficiaries—now pays a large share of medical costs out of pocket. And Medicare-covered workers and their employers contribute nearly 3 percent of wages to the system as Medicare "premiums." Moreover, if one believes, as most economists do, that the current costs of employment-based group health insurance should be allocated approximately two-thirds to employees and one-third to the government (because of tax subsidies), then approximately 60 percent of total medical expenses in the United States are currently "individ-

Fig. 9.2.    Health care financing sources

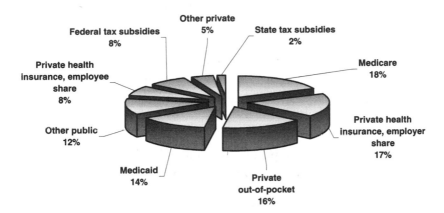

(*Source:* C. Eugene Steuerle and Gordon B. T. Mermin, "A Better Subsidy for Health
Insurance?" in Galen Institute, *A Fresh Approach to Health Reform,* Washington, D.C.,
1997, FY 1996 data.)

ually funded." These payments are made as copayments or deductibles,
funded by (often implicit) private insurance premiums, or are paid
through mandated public insurance premiums. Figure 9.2 breaks down
current financing arrangements by source.

We favor providing social insurance protection against excessive health
care expenditures by requiring all individuals and families to purchase a
"catastrophic" (high deductible) health insurance policy. A variety of such
policies would satisfy our income protection goals, but we will illustrate
our plan with a specific policy for which the American Academy of Actuaries has estimated the premium costs.[3] This policy has the following
characteristics: covered medical services are broad (as under the Federal
Employee Health Benefits Program [FEHBP] or Medicaid), but not all-
inclusive. Individuals would be responsible for the first $1,500 of health
expenses and for copayments of 20 percent for expenses above that deductible amount to an annual maximum of $2,500. For family policies,
total expenses would have to exceed $3,000 before the policy would begin
to pay benefits, and the family would be responsible for 20 percent copayments up to a maximum of $4,000 in total out-of-pocket costs. The
Academy of Actuaries estimates that such policies would cost individuals
approximately $2,000 annually and families about $4,850.

For those people whose policy costs would threaten their income adequacy, the government must provide a subsidy to help defray premiums. In addition, to meet our social insurance income-protection goal, neither premium amounts nor out-of-pocket health expenditures can, separately or in combination, cause too great a shock to family income. Thus, for some families both premiums and out-of-pocket expenditures must be subsidized. Although some level of contribution might be required from everyone, for the purpose of illustrating our scheme, we have chosen the following income security policy goals: (1) Families and individuals with income below 100 percent of the poverty line will have their health insurance premiums and out-of-pocket costs fully subsidized, and (2) No family, however high its income, will be required to spend more than 15 percent of its income on health care in any one year. This means that subsidies will phase out gradually between the poverty level and about $60,000 of family income.[4]

With these protections, workers earning the minimum wage would have their families' entire premium and any out-of-pocket expenses fully paid for through government subsidies. If workers' wages increased from the current minimum wage of $5.15 an hour to $7.50 an hour, they would be required to contribute about $20 a month toward their health coverage. At $10.00 an hour, workers would pay $50 a month for their families' health insurance coverage.

This basic outline leaves open at least the following questions: Who exactly is covered? For what? Financed through what mechanisms? Enforced and administered by whom?

### Who

Coverage would be mandatory for all citizens and all aliens legally resident in the United States. We will not engage in any extended justification of this choice. Succinctly put, we see no reason to exclude from coverage any citizen or legal resident. In our view, it is virtually axiomatic in a social insurance scheme that benefits and burdens should be as widely distributed as possible.

### What

As a first approximation, we anticipate that coverage will be for all physician, outpatient, and hospital expenses, and for prescription drugs. The scope of required coverage must be defined broadly enough to be sure that income security goals are met. Those who desire more details should look to the kinds of health care coverage now provided by employers to their employees—the Federal Employees Health Benefits Program offers a good example of a variety of options—or even to the coverage currently offered by the Medicaid program (putting aside, for now, Medicaid's nursing home coverage). Medicaid offers a relatively broad coverage package, broader than Medicare and many private insurance policies. Moreover, while it does not go as far as the current tax code definition of medical expense, a Medicaid-based package of coverage would include most of the health care expenses that are threats to family income adequacy or stability. (By the Medicaid package, we mean any package permissible for states to adopt under the federal matching formula for the Medicaid program, not what any particular state has adopted.) We would exclude items not typically covered by health insurance, such as over-the-counter drugs, eyeglasses, fertility treatments, and elective cosmetic surgery.

### How

The system we propose would impose no greater aggregate individual responsibility for funding such direct private health care expenditures than do current arrangements. The remainder would come from general revenues—very likely some combination of payroll or income taxes and special excise taxes (for example, on products that generate high health risks such as guns, motor vehicles, cigarettes, and alcohol). In accordance with the budgetary practice of Medicare hospital insurance and Social Security pensions, these revenues should probably be allocated to a "trust fund." There is little economic meaning in this accounting move, but there seems to be political magic associated with it, at least in the United States.[5] In its most complete version, these general revenue funds would substitute for all "non–public health" direct and tax expenditures now devoted to the provision of health insurance or medical care. In short, a comprehensive plan would substitute for Medicare, Medicaid, workers' compensation medical payments, tax subsidies for employer-sponsored group health insurance, and a host of smaller government programs and for private individual insurance and private out-of-pocket payments. (We ignore here the system of veterans' and seamen's hospitals.)

It is far easier to imagine universal purchases of health insurance than to actually enforce a requirement that all individuals and families purchase a catastrophic health insurance policy. The states' experience with mandatory auto insurance policies, enforced through denying drivers licenses or automobile registrations, demonstrates the difficulties of designing an effective enforcement system. Of course, in this case, since all or a substantial portion of the costs of policies for many families will be subsidized, insurance companies and health care providers should prove to be quite effective at enrolling people, either directly or through their employers. In addition, we propose delivering subsidies through the tax system in the form of tax credits transferable to insurers or health care providers and requiring individuals and families to demonstrate that they have obtained the required coverage when they file their tax returns. Tax refunds would be denied to the uninsured, and enrollment could be accomplished for subsequent years by requiring increased withholding. To the extent that people nevertheless remain uncovered, health care providers would be required to enroll them in insurance programs whenever they show up to obtain health care.

Make no mistake: an individual mandate, whether to obtain automobile liability insurance, vaccinate your children before sending them to school, or pay your income taxes both encounters evasion and sometimes entails intrusive enforcement. This is a public "bad" that must be weighed against the public "goods" of universal health insurance protection and a fair distribution of the costs of coverage. A humane nation does not allow its residents to become impoverished by medical expenses. A prudent one cannot allow them to evade paying their share of the costs of their medical care.

The organization of administrative responsibilities of such a program will, of course, depend upon the level of detail that Congress enacts and the financing mechanisms chosen. For example, some entity rather like the Health Care Financing Administration (HCFA) might have the responsibility to fill in the details of the insurance contract left open by statute and to organize the disbursement of funds. Most of this latter function could be carried out through private intermediaries as is currently the case in the Medicare program. Because revenues come from general taxes, this HCFA-like agency would have no responsibility for fund collection, but might take on other health-related responsibilities outside the social insurance sphere, such as providing subsidies to medical education, funding specialized clinics used for public health purposes, and the like. Disbursement of funds to providers would occur through private intermediaries, including employers and private insurance companies. We recommend that the income-related subsidies might be provided to individuals and families through refundable or transferable tax credits, but alternatively, subsidies could be transferred in voucher form by this HCFA-type agency or another social insurance agency.

In any event, under the scheme as we envision it, the new HCFA would have no responsibility for specifying the forms of medical provider organizations or regulating the quality of medical care. Moreover, while the pertinent statutes and regulations would specify the required contents of the mandated "catastrophic" health insurance policy, that mandated policy might be purchased from a wide array of private providers. Those providers could compete for clientele both on the basis of price and on the basis of additions to the goods and services covered under the catastrophic scheme. But they would not be allowed to compete by segmenting health risks. Insurers would be required to "community rate" their policies, to take all comers at the same price.[6]

Purchasing arrangements or attempts to regulate the quality of and access to medical care are not trivial matters. We do not, however, believe that they need be a part of a social insurance scheme. Attempts to achieve economies through various purchasing arrangements can, in our view, be left to market competition in the provision of "catastrophic" or "catastrophic-plus" insurance packages. And in this regard, employment-based or other group-based purchasing or insurance schemes should have continuing advantages.

The government's promise to pay costs above the catastrophic ceiling could not, of course, be left open-ended in a scheme that permits fee-for-service contracting. Either bidding for acceptable contracts, as under the Federal Employees' Health Benefit Plan, would need to occur, or something like the existing price-cap mechanisms for hospital and physician services under Medicare would have to be in place. While we are attempting to simplify the administrative role of the government in insuring against private catastrophic health care costs, our scheme may have to remain saddled with a substantial regulatory apparatus to guard against public fiscal catastrophe.

Quality control regulation has historically been left to the states, which have been subject in recent decades to the extraordinarily broad preemption of state authority for employer-based self-insured plans by the Employment Retirement Income Security Act (ERISA). Our proposal makes no explicit change in this provision, although we view this preemption as having had adverse consequences that were not foreseen when it was enacted. We are very skeptical of a federal statute that preempts state authority and then fails to exercise national authority. To be sure, there are dangers in both state and federal regulation, but the ongoing federal "hands off" policy seems less a considered judgment than a concession to powerful economic interests.

Described in this very sketchy way, the program we envision has certain obvious advantages. Protections are universal, coverage is comprehensive, and the distribution of costs cannot help but be more progressive than under current arrangements. Figure 9.3 illustrates the extraordinarily perverse distribution of the current benefits of federal tax subsidies for employer-provided health insurance.

As we have described the system, the overall sharing of expenditures between government guarantees and private payments and premiums remains essentially as it is today. The difference lies in the broader distribution of benefits and the more progressive allocation of costs. There is nothing in the scheme that necessarily affects the organization of medical care, the availability of private medical insurance, or aggregate expen-

Fig. 9.3.    Per capita value of federal subsidies for employer-based health insurance

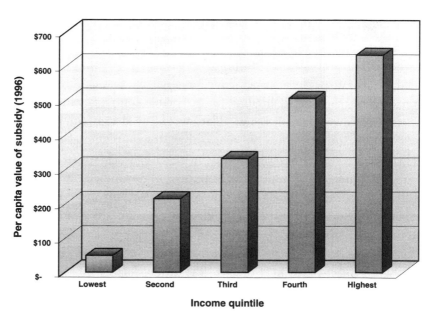

*Income quintile*

(*Source:* C. Eugene Steuerle and Gordon B. T. Mermin, "A Better Subsidy for Health Insurance?" in Galen Institute, *A Fresh Approach to Health Care Reform,* Washington, D.C., 1997.)

ditures for health care. Yet serious repercussions may ensue for all these dimensions of current arrangements. To see what happens requires a somewhat more detailed analysis. We turn first to the issue of overall expenditures for health care.

## WHAT WOULD INCOME-SECURITY HEALTH COVERAGE COST?

Before looking closely at the general system that we propose, we should at least notice that there are ways to creep up on this plan without instituting it for the whole population at once. One possibility would be to make the system applicable on a mandatory basis only to individuals not currently covered by Medicare. Financing would be provided by a combination of the existing funds from Medicaid and the recapture of federal tax subsidies for health insurance and medical expenses. As we have explained, this kind of income-security health insurance plan requires funding both "catastrophic" (high-deductible) health insurance and out-of-pocket expenditures on an income-related basis. No reliable comprehensive estimates exist for the aggregate costs of such a departure from current practices or for the distribution of these costs. Back-of-the-envelope estimates suggest, however, that a version of our catastrophic coverage program could be instituted for a total cost that would not exceed current expenditures.

In some sense, demonstrating this proposition is straightforward. All analysts of "high-deductible" or "catastrophic" insurance policies estimate either no change in aggregate expenditures or savings ranging from the modest (4–6 percent) to the implausible (50 percent).[7] And as we discuss later, we see no reason to predict significant increases or decreases in medical care utilization consequent upon our proposed shift in the financing mechanism. The major changes have to do with how costs are allocated. Yet lest the coverage of 43 million additional Americans at zero cost seem like an exercise in pure "smoke and mirrors," we should walk through the basic calculations.

The American Academy of Actuaries has estimated the premium costs of a variety of high-deductible health insurance policies, including the one we recommend here.[8] The Actuaries do not assume any substantial savings in aggregate costs from such a restructuring of insurance coverage. Because the only reliable estimates for high-deductible policies exclude the over-sixty-five population, we will, for the moment, assume that

Medicare remains unchanged. Based on the Actuaries' per-policy cost estimates, we assume that the aggregate cost of such policies for the approximately 230 million Americans under age sixty-five would total about $385
billion (at 1995 levels).[9]

Assuming no change in overall medical expenditures, this would mean
that approximately $200 billion would be spent out-of-pocket. (About
$600 billion total expenditures for the under-sixty-five population, less
$385 billion in insurance payments.) Under our proposal part of these pre-
miums and out-of-pocket costs would be paid from public funds. How
much is needed?[10]

Because of data limitations, we have estimated these costs in a rough-
and-ready way by looking at the costs for the Medicaid population under
age sixty-five and then by using income categories based on multiples of
the poverty line. In summary the situation is this: insuring the Medicaid
population and fully subsidizing its out-of-pocket costs require about $75
billion to $80 billion of public funds. Subsidizing medical expenditures
by non-Medicaid families to protect against expenses exceeding 15 percent
of income requires some subsidy for individuals and families up to about
400 percent of the poverty level (nearly $60,000 of family income), cost-
ing an additional $75 billion to $100 billion.[11] Total subsidy costs are thus
in the range of $150 billion to $180 billion.[12]

Where does this money come from? Medicaid expenses for people
under age sixty-five are approximately $100 billion. Income tax expendi-
tures for employer-provided group insurance, insurance for the self-
employed, and medical expense deductions total about $60 billion, and
payroll taxes are reduced about $20 billion. Hence, our required public
revenues are in the same ballpark as current public expenditures. Further
refinement may demonstrate that the balance is better or worse, but for
present purposes we are reasonably confident that our proposal would not
"break the bank." (If we counted the 4–6 percent savings projected by the
Urban Institute, for example, we would have another $24 billion to $36
billion.)

We have not, of course, shown that shifting to our income-security
health insurance plan would be politically feasible. Achieving a great
enough increase in the number of winners versus losers in such a shift
might well require additional sources of revenues. Other alternatives designed to garner public support for this kind of a shift in health insurance
arrangements, such as mandating that employers maintain their current

levels of contributions to employee health insurance (about $265 billion currently) through a pay-or-play type requirement, have proved to carry serious political and economic liabilities in previous efforts to restructure national health insurance policy, although the relevance of such precedents in the context of our overall proposals is not clear. We also might consider imposing a "maintenance of effort" requirement on employers to ensure that they do not drop existing coverage. Perhaps moving in the direction we urge could begin by replacing Medicaid and extending income-security health insurance to the currently uninsured, a step that also is financially feasible.[13] We have undertaken here only to show that income-security health insurance based on social insurance principles could achieve universal coverage and a more progressive distribution of costs and benefits within current fiscal restraints.

Finally, while we have no current ability to offer detailed financial estimates for the population age sixty-five and over, there is no principled reason to exclude retirees from our proposal. Under current arrangements, the elderly generally have only Medicaid to protect them against catastrophic medical expenses. While double eligibility for Medicaid and Medicare may offer the elderly ultimate protection against falling below minimum level of adequacy, it does not kick in until an individual or family becomes impoverished. Except for those elderly who are able to obtain private catastrophic coverage, therefore, current arrangements fail to ensure that health expenditures will not cause a precipitate decline in people's current standard of living.

Nor are current Medicare financing arrangements progressive. Hospital insurance is financed by a flat-rate payroll tax on all wages and self-employment income at a total current rate of almost 3 percent. The federal government subsidizes approximately 75 percent of premiums for Medicare's physicians' services (Part B) regardless of the beneficiaries' level of income or wealth. In addition, Medicare has major gaps in coverage not only for overall levels of expenditures, but also for important health expenditures that are covered under most private policies and Medicaid.

### EFFECTS ON RISK SEGMENTATION
### AND COMPREHENSIVE INSURANCE

Proposals for catastrophic insurance coverage are hardly new, and most voluntary programs have been criticized for their predictable effects—

massive increases in risk segmentation in health insurance markets and in the costs of comprehensive health insurance coverage. We agree that simply providing the option to choose catastrophic coverage, combined with a tax-preferred "medical savings account" (MSA), would have the predicted consequences. The young and healthy are more likely to choose catastrophic coverage with an MSA; the old and sick would prefer comprehensive coverage, but will find the premiums for that coverage rising. Indeed, relatively small shifts toward catastrophic coverage have been estimated to produce substantial effects on comprehensive insurance costs. The American Academy of Actuaries has estimated, for example, that introducing a high-deductible plan of the sort we have described here on a voluntary basis, along with tax-preferred MSAs, would boost the cost of a low ($200) deductible plan by more than 150 percent (from $2,699 to $4,343 for an individual plan).[14]

A system that segments risks, shifts high costs to the sick, and favors those with high income (through a tax-preference for MSAs) is hardly a strong candidate for a desirable social insurance scheme. But these are not the features of our proposal. We envision a universal mandate with income protection for the costs of a broad set of medical interventions. Once deductibles and copayments are exhausted, coverage is the same as a good, first-dollar comprehensive insurance plan. The potential unavailability of first-dollar or other forms of comprehensive coverage should not be a concern so long as the premiums, deductibles, and copayments for our mandated catastrophic plan are affordable for all.

Moreover, because our approach subsidizes these costs based on family income differentials, the system is not skewed in favor of the wealthy. To be sure, the mandated coverage will be cheaper for the young and healthy. But this should not be objectionable. A health insurance "price break" for younger families puts more money in the pockets of those who, in general, have lower incomes and asset holdings. And, no one, young, middle-aged, or old, will be required to pay medical costs that render their family's resources inadequate or that severely depress their living standards.

Some may find it objectionable that younger or healthier workers may be able to purchase comprehensive coverage for the price that older workers would have to pay for the mandated catastrophic plan. Hence, not everyone will necessarily have the same health care coverage. We understand this concern, but we do not view it as decisive. It merely illustrates the different normative commitments of an equality-based or merit-goods-based approach to health insurance and our vision of the role of social insurance as directed primarily at income security.

## EFFECTS ON HEALTH CARE DELIVERY
## AND UTILIZATION

Some might characterize catastrophic insurance plans as combining two bad insurance policies into one truly horrible one: Within the deductible range, the patient is uninsured; then, when the policy kicks in, the patient is covered for everything. (This is not quite our proposed policy, which requires copayments, but for present purposes we will address this worst case scenario.) Lack of insurance, critics charge, will discourage utilization of effective, low-cost preventative care; full insurance will encourage profligate use of high-cost interventions. This is a plan, in short, that may impair the public health while simultaneously fueling medical inflation. Who could be for such a dopey scheme?

"Dopes" is the obvious, but we believe wrong, answer. We already have medical inflation in a medical insurance world in which one can find only few pure "catastrophic" policies. The open-ended "catastrophic" feature of our proposal adds only marginally to overutilization risks. Most insured patients will have expenditures well within policy limits. Concern and conflict about existing health insurance contracts is mostly about what is covered, not how much.

Moreover, insurance companies issuing "catastrophic coverage" will be able, probably impelled by cost control concerns, to use the same sorts of managed care approaches to controlling costs as they now use for "comprehensive" policies. In addition, we anticipate that many insurers will offer comprehensive coverage for a price that is less than the total of the catastrophic premium plus the full amount of deductibles and copayments. To the extent that preventive care, including regular checkups, is actually cost effective, there will be large financial incentives for making sure that such care is utilized. The more comprehensive policies may take many forms, including per-patient priced HMO plans and other arrangements that promise not only to contain costs but also to maintain health through effective preventative measures. Our best guess is that "managed care" would be as likely to continue its central role in the delivery of American health care given a financing shift of the sort we propose as under current financing arrangements. Managed care and related techniques may or may not work over the long run to keep costs under control, but they should be no more or less successful under our proposal than they are today.

Underutilization risks should be less with our scheme than they are under current arrangements. Out-of-pocket costs for the poor will be fully subsidized with public funds, as will any substantial out-of-pocket costs for the struggling middle class. These are the groups most likely now to lack any insurance and hence most likely to be deterred from routine examinations and other preventative care.

"Covered" middle income workers and Medicare beneficiaries already face substantial deductibles and copayments. Moreover, to the extent that workers want to keep their comprehensive group insurance without a tax subsidy, they remain free to do so under any policy that also provides at least the coverage envisaged by the mandated catastrophic plan. This is not an empty opportunity. The availability of a tax subsidy explains only a portion of the extent of employer-sponsored plans. Most such plans would continue because they provide other important advantages.[15]

We also anticipate that cost-effective preventative measures will be encouraged by the pricing of policies included in provider contracts negotiated by managed-care catastrophic insurers. And, to the extent that true public health threats are involved—as with communicable diseases—other governmental interventions (such as information and vaccination campaigns, mandates, and subsidies) will remain as likely as they are today.

We recognize, of course, that there are alternative approaches to comprehensive health care provision, including some presently in place in other industrialized countries, that might do as good a job, or perhaps even a better job, of ensuring the availability of all needed care at reasonable costs. But the failed struggle to move in those directions is an integral part of the sorry history of American policy toward health insurance. Recasting the issue as social insurance protection against income loss due to health expense may offer an opportunity to extend health insurance coverage to the currently uninsured while improving income security.

But we do not offer our plan because of political expediency. We believe it represents a coherent approach to social insurance provision understood as the protection of income security, not as the assurance of the availability of particular goods or services. Here, as in our later discussions of long-term care, shelter, and child care, we employ insurance or consumption subsidies targeted on access to specific goods or services. But we do so not because of their attributes as "merit goods," but because of the way these expenses affect family income.

## Chapter 10 Unemployment Insurance

In the early 1930s the Upjohn Pharmaceutical Company, like most employers, could no longer employ its full workforce. Distressed by the plight of the workers he had to lay off, W. E. Upjohn, Jr., donated a substantial tract of land near the company's offices to be dedicated to household food production by his displaced workers. Recognizing the industrial economy's failure to maintain full employment, Upjohn attempted to recreate a microcosm of a more stable preindustrial past for the benefit of his former employees.[1] Four hundred fifty years earlier, Henry VII had attempted to deal with English unemployment in much the same way. He responded to the plight of farmers displaced by sheep herding by making it illegal to convert tilled land to pasturage.

Both Upjohn and King Henry failed to turn back the tides of technological and economic change and the involuntary unemployment that such changes always bring. Nor, in the centuries that separated their actions, had unemployment been solved by any other strategy. Yet the idea that we can determine the causes of unemployment—and stop it—dies hard. From the 1349 Statute of La-borers, through the late nineteenth century, English legislation alternated between intervening in the market to create work (often through public workhouses) and punishing the unemployed (with penalties that from time to time included enslavement, transportation, and death). The two techniques were often combined: failure to get a job or go to the work-house was the occasion for punitive action.

Unemployment has also been attacked through physical violence and virtually every variety of aspirational legislation.[2] The Luddites famously confronted the industrial revolution by smashing the machinery that would displace them. And a majority of French voters in the late 1990s still seem to believe that unemployment can be solved by legislating re-ductions in the work week unmatched by reductions in wages.[3]

The notion that employers can be forced to maintain employment lev-els by visiting the full costs of maintaining unemployed workers on the offending firms provides the distinctive American contribution to the his-tory of failed attempts to abolish unemployment. The United States has also embraced child labor laws, regulation of the hours of work, statutory and contractual featherbedding, macroeconomic steering of the economy, a largely hortatory "Full Employment Act," public works, public employ-ment, and more or less aggressive employment and training services.

Some of these efforts may actually do more good than harm. Yet unem-ployment persists, and its persistence makes the need for unemployment insurance clear. Despite all of our efforts, useful or silly, many workers will still suffer a spell or more of unemployment during their working lives. And despite all our exhortations to workers that they should save against the proverbial "rainy day," many, if not most, families will continue to have inadequate reserves to tide them over during periods of involuntary unemployment.

In 1993, for example, only 71.1 percent of American households had any savings in interest-bearing accounts at financial institutions, and the me-dian value of any such assets was slightly less than $3,000. In addition, surprising as it may seem, less than one-half of households had checking accounts, the median value of which was less than $500. When income stops, most families have very little ready cash. Moreover, the distress of these families is not just an individual matter. Maintaining purchasing power during cyclical downturns in the economy may be important for prompt economic recovery. It has been estimated, for example, that in the deep recession of 1992 the current inadequate unemployment insurance system prevented a loss of an additional 4.1 percent of real GDP and 14 percent of personal income.[4]

These straightforward wage-replacement and countercyclical macro-economic objectives do not tell the whole story of the goals of American unemployment insurance. In the United States, unemployment insurance has also been used to stabilize employment and encourage the search for a new job through a series of subsidiary policies: the experience rating of unemployment insurance taxes, stringent conditions to assure the "involuntariness" of unemployment, and close ties between the provision of unemployment insurance benefits and job search services. The structure of unemployment benefits has also sought to assure that job seeking and reemployment are preferable to continued receipt of unemployment compensation by limiting both the replacement rate of wages and the duration of benefits. Contemporary unemployment insurance policy is thus a balance between preserving workers' incomes in the face of economic hazard and reducing the overall costs of the unemployment insurance program by attempting to prevent unemployment in the first place and to limit its duration. Where the risk insured against is unemployment, the social purposes of income adequacy and consumption smoothing necessarily come into sharp conflict with the goals of encouraging employers to stabilize employment and employees to maintain their level of work effort.

The tradeoffs in unemployment insurance policymaking between promoting work and providing income security are real; they are not just legacies of our nation's peculiar political history. But such tradeoffs can be managed in better or worse ways. In our view, the current unemployment insurance system is not managing the inevitable tensions of the system effectively. We agree with the underlying approach to risk definition embodied in the current unemployment insurance regime. Unemployment insurance should be designed as wage replacement for those who are *in* the workforce and who suffer a spell of temporary, involuntary unemployment. But current eligibility requirements, payment levels, financing structures—and indeed, the overall allocation of state and federal responsibility—are producing a program that violates other fundamental principles of good social insurance. The protections of unemployment insurance are now far from universal. The financing structure is regressive. And those with the greatest risks of inadequate incomes tend to receive less rather than more protection. These failings call for very substantial changes, or—to put the matter more optimistically—offer the opportunity for very substantial improvements in our unemployment insurance policies.

## THE LIMITS OF CURRENT POLICIES

### Wage Replacement Adequacy

The question of whether unemployment insurance does an adequate job of wage replacement is really two quite distinct questions: First, are the benefits paid to eligible workers during a spell of unemployment adequate to support their families and facilitate their search for a new job? Second, does the system replace wage income for most workers who become unemployed? The current system does a reasonable job, on average, with respect to the first dimension, but is quite poor in relation to the second. Average payment levels—approximately 50 percent of gross wages up to about $200 per week—are satisfactory, but coverage is both limited and declining. Moreover, averages, as usual, can be deceiving. As figure 10.1 shows, states vary significantly in the "generosity" of their unemployment insurance benefits. A more unified, national schedule of payments is necessary to provide adequate payment levels for workers irrespective of their place of residence.

### Payment Amounts

What percentage of wages should be replaced by unemployment insurance? The current conventional wisdom, which we adopt for lack of a superior alternative, goes something like this. Most spells of unemployment are expected to be of reasonably short duration. Hence the standard limitation of payments, both in the U.S. system and abroad, is to periods ranging from six months to a year. During such periods, it is assumed that families will be able to defer certain expenditures, but not others. In developed countries, unemployment insurance benefits replace from as little as 40 percent to as much as 70 percent of average wages (fig. 10.2).[5] But how much of a family's expenditures are recurrent and nondeferrable, and how much can be put off to the time when wage income has been restored?

Surprisingly few studies have attempted to determine empirically the answer to this question. In its 1995 report, the Advisory Council on Un-

Fig. 10.1.    Variation in state unemployment insurance wage-replacement rates

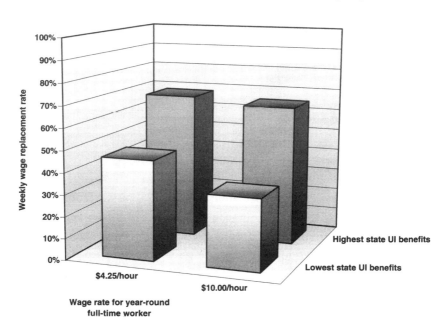

(*Source:* Advisory Council on Unemployment Compensation, *Unemployment Insurance in the United States: Benefits, Financing, Coverage,* February 1995, tables 10-1 and 10-2. The numbers shown are duration-adjusted.)

employment Compensation estimated that average households spend between 33 percent and 49 percent of their income on "necessary" items.[6] The estimates vary depending on the definition of "necessary." They also vary widely by income category. Lower-income families spend the bulk of their income on necessities, while those at the high end of wage and salary receipts allocate most of their income to "discretionary" spending. In the middle range, $20,000 to $40,000 per year, estimates of necessary expenses range from 31 to 62 percent of income. If that range brackets the "average" family, then, on average, something like 50 percent of wages must be replaced to provide an adequate wage replacement. This rule of thumb has often been cited as the political aspiration of the unemployment insurance system. But recognizing that upper-income wage earners do not really need a 50 percent replacement rate, the goal has been expressed as replacing 50 percent of wages for 50 to 75 percent of covered workers.

Current state payment levels come close to realizing this conventional goal. As of 1994, a majority of states provided 40 to 60 percent replace-

Fig. 10.2.    International UI replacement rates for manufacturing wages

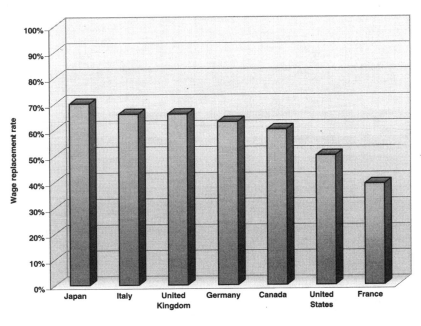

(*Source:* Authors' calculations based on data from Advisory Council on Unemployment Compensation, *Unemployment Insurance in the United States: Benefits, Financing, Coverage,* February 1995, table 3-1; and *United Nations Statistical Yearbook,* 42d issue, 1998, tables 33 and 84.)

ment rates for workers with wages up to $15.00 per hour—that is, workers having gross incomes around $30,000 per year. Moreover, replacement rates as a percentage of past wages are considerably better for low- and middle-income workers than for higher-income workers. This results from the common benefit structure in most states, which pays a flat percentage of past weekly wages with a cap or maximum benefit amount indexed to a given percentage of state average wages.

But making the benefit structure progressive above the cap does not produce adequate replacement rates for lower-income workers, whether these rates are measured by poverty guidelines or by estimates of necessary expenses. The Congressional Budget Office estimates that while unemployment insurance benefits prevent 25 percent of unemployed families from falling below the poverty line, almost 20 percent of long-term recipients of unemployment insurance are living in poverty.[7] And, as a comparison of state benefits with necessary expenditures for families in

Fig. 10.3.    UI coverage of necessary expenditures

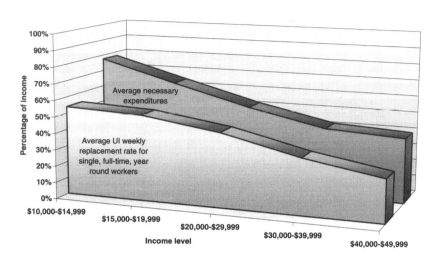

(*Source:* Authors' calculations based on Advisory Council on Unemployment Compensation, *Unemployment Insurance in the United States: Benefits, Financing, Coverage,* February 1995, table 9-2 and fig. 9-2, 1992 and 1994 data.)

differing income categories makes clear, low-income workers must find additional support from other programs in order to meet necessary expenses (fig. 10.3).[8]

These data suggest some straightforward adjustments to insure greater adequacy of unemployment insurance payments for workers who qualify for compensation. One is the unification of payment levels across the United States. That more than half the states have, on average, adequate payments levels means that slightly less than half do not. In 1994, a full-year, full-time worker in Oregon earning $10.00/hour would have received unemployment insurance benefits replacing 65 percent of lost wages, but the same worker in Nebraska would have been given only 39 percent.[9] While this heterogeneity is not itself a cause for alarm, downward pressures on state policies suggest that continued interstate competition is unlikely to produce an upward move toward adequacy. At the very least, federal minimum-payment standards seem necessary to insure wage replacement adequacy.

Second, the concept of "prior wages" needs to be altered to recognize wage subsidies that support the incomes of lower-paid workers. While we do not advocate replacing lower-wage workers' wages at higher percentages than other workers receive through the unemployment insurance system, we do believe that the system should recognize the true wage base for lower-income workers. Hence prior wages should include any wage subsidy that would have been received through the Earned Income Tax Credit. (This could conceivably be accomplished by adjustments to the EITC itself, but changing the wage base for unemployment insurance seems a simpler approach.) Policies designed to "make work pay" should not require low-income workers to accept greater proportional reductions in their standards of living than higher-wage colleagues when they become unemployed. Our proposed reform will not make unemployment insurance an adequate income support system for workers who are marginally attached to the workforce, but it will help bolster adequacy for low-income workers.

**Coverage**

Insuring adequate wage replacement rates by increasing the effective coverage of the system requires more dramatic reforms. The current system pays benefits to only about 38 percent of workers who suffer a spell of unemployment—down from nearly 80 percent fifty years ago. In short, there has been a steady erosion of the promise of income security that was embodied in the original design of the unemployment insurance program. This decline in coverage has been the result of a decline in the percentage of the unemployed who are eligible for benefits, rather than of reductions in either replacement rates or the duration of potential coverage.

For some workers other programs could provide assistance during periods of unemployment including the program of Temporary Assistance to Needy Families (described in Chapter 12) and the protections we propose for health care, child care, and housing in Chapters 9 and 12. Unattached individuals and couples without children are ineligible for TANF. Provided that these persons are "in the workforce," as evidenced by prior labor force participation at levels insufficient to qualify for unemployment insurance, and that they register for job search assistance (and job training, if needed) with the relevant employment service, we propose to make them eligible for a new unemployment assistance benefit. We will describe that program in more detail at the end of this chapter when we turn to the characteristics of our revised unemployment insurance program.

## EXPLAINING THE DECLINE OF
## UNEMPLOYMENT INSURANCE COVERAGE

### A Changed Reality

Declining eligibility results from the interaction of a series of factors: demographic shifts, changes in the general economy, changes in workforce composition, and modifications in eligibility rules or administrative practice. Indeed, demographic, economic, and workforce changes could produce a decline in participation rates even if unemployment insurance rules and practices stayed the same. Hence, at one level, the explanation lies in the interaction of state monetary and nonmonetary eligibility criteria with shifting work structures and changes in the nature of the workforce. Monetary requirements—such as the requirement that a claimant have a certain level of earnings within the relevant base period (usually the first four of the last five quarters)—tend to disfavor those with low wages and those with mostly recent earnings. In an economy that has been experiencing stagnant wage rates and increases in temporary and part-time work, these two features of monetary requirements should be expected to exclude increasing numbers of workers from receipt of unemployment insurance benefits.

Consider, for example, workers Joe and Moe. Joe works at the minimum wage; Moe makes $10.00 an hour. In order to qualify for minimum unemployment benefits, Moe need only work fifteen hours per week, fifty-two weeks per year, in order to qualify in all fifty-two U.S. jurisdictions (the fifty states, the District of Columbia, and Puerto Rico). Joe, on the other hand, would qualify in only thirty-five jurisdictions working those same hours. To qualify in every jurisdiction, he would have to work more than twenty-five hours per week in each of the fifty-two weeks of the year. Obviously, in some jurisdictions Moe would be eligible for benefits when Joe is not, even though Joe may have worked twice as many hours per week over the course of the preceding year. Surely it is bizarre to suggest that a Joe working twice as many hours as a Moe has less attachment to the workforce and therefore is properly excluded from unemployment insurance coverage.

Additional exclusionary effects result from workforce changes and the so-called nonmonetary requirements—criteria that seek to insure that unemployment is involuntary and that recipients are available for and seeking employment. Under the rules in virtually all states, it is not "good cause" to quit a job because the employer has changed one's hours of work. Nor is it acceptable to refuse job offers of otherwise "suitable" work because the hours of work interfere with family responsibilities. Hence, when Jane has to quit her job at the convenience store because she has no child care for shifts outside the usual 8:00 A.M. to 6:00 P.M. workday, she will be ineligible for unemployment benefits in most states. In the legal vernacular, she is not "able and available for work." Were she seeking part-time work for the same reason, she would be ineligible in virtually all states.[10] When these rules are combined with the treatment of pregnancy as a medical condition making one unavailable for work, the pattern of disqualification is clear. Women with child-rearing responsibilities, whether single parents or in a dual-earner household, are quite likely to run afoul of one of these nonmonetary eligibility requirements. Predictably, as more and more women have entered the workforce, the percentage of workers who are eligible for unemployment benefits when unemployed has declined.

Most states also exclude other "personal" reasons for leaving a job from the "good cause" category, such as quitting to remain with a spouse whose job has been relocated.[11] The effects of these exclusions on "second" workers, again usually women, are dramatic. As the dual-earner family has become the norm, with the wages of the second earner becoming more and more important to family income adequacy, unemployment insurance coverage has been moving in precisely the opposite direction.

These same rules have similar—perhaps even greater—effects on single-parent households. And while a few states have taken a more liberal attitude toward pregnancy, refusal of "shift work," and the recognition of other family imperatives that make unemployment "involuntary," most states have not. The tendency, indeed, has been toward strengthening these disqualifications and making them last for the duration of a spell of unemployment rather than for some shorter period.

### The Political Economy of Eligibility Rules

That the current rules do not comfortably fit the current workforce and the changing structure of the economy tells us why the population of unemployed people who actually receive unemployment benefits is declining, but it does not tell us why those rules remain in force. Long-time structural characteristics of unemployment insurance in the United

States—its financing mechanism and the allocation of primary policy responsibility to state governments—provide much of the answer.

Unemployment insurance benefits are financed by a tax on employers. But unlike flat-rate wage taxes, which generally are thought to be passed on to employees, the unemployment insurance tax is experience-rated. Employers who make more charges on the system pay higher taxes, and there is evidence that both labor and product markets are sufficiently competitive to prevent a significant portion of these experience-rated taxes from being passed on to either workers or consumers.[12]

Experience-rated, employer financing thus creates a strong business constituency for restraint in unemployment insurance benefits. State legislatures attentive to the "business climate" of their states must be responsive to that constituency. Moreover, to the extent that the nonmonetary eligibility rules that limit recipiency seem to relate to conditions outside of employers' control, relaxing those requirements in an experience-rated system seems unfair.

Employers have also pressured state legislatures to extend the periods of disqualification that result when a worker is either fired "for cause" or quits without "good cause." Although at one time workers were permitted to purge themselves of these disqualifications by registering for and seeking work for some meaningful period, virtually all states today treat voluntary quits or justified firings as disqualifying workers for compensation for the duration of that spell of unemployment. While these rules seem harsh from the worker's perspective, employers understandably object to paying additional taxes to finance benefits for workers whose unemployment they clearly did not "cause."

The "race to the bottom" that is fueled by employer demands for tax relief is reinforced by other political incentives for state legislators. One is the states' capacity to shift unemployment benefit costs to the federal government by reducing the eligibility of low-wage workers who might then qualify for food stamps and other programs that have federal matching funds or 100 percent federal funding. The 1994–96 Advisory Council on Unemployment Insurance found strong evidence both of the existence of the race to the bottom in unemployment insurance benefits and of the effects of cost-shifting motivations in state legislatures.

There is yet another quirk to the Federal Unemployment Tax Act (FUTA) that keeps the program "underfunded." When originally enacted, FUTA taxed all wages up to $3,000 per year, at that time 92 percent of the wage base. Current federal law sets the minimum cap for state systems at $7,000, a figure that captures only about a third of total wages—a sharp contrast with the Social Security wage base, which also started at $3,000 in 1937 but had risen to $72,600 by 1999. The low FUTA tax base not only reflects a declining effort to fund an adequate unemployment insurance system, but also imposes the greatest burden for support of the system on employers with predominantly low-wage employees.[13]

## THE PATH TO REFORM

From the perspective of program design, reform of unemployment insurance seems straightforward. First, the national interest in adequate wage replacement and countercyclical efficacy must be reasserted by updating eligibility requirements, unifying payment levels, and assuring advance funding at an adequate reserve level. These objectives could be accomplished either by "federalizing" the system while contracting out administration (as is currently done in the disability insurance program), or by a much tighter set of federal conditions under the Federal Unemployment Tax Act. As we discuss in Chapter 15, budgetary accounting conventions might well make the latter course the prudent one.

Second, experience-rating of employers should be abandoned, tax rates should be lowered, and 100 percent of the wage base, as with Medicare financing, should be taxed or general revenue financing secured. Finally, eligibility rules, both monetary and nonmonetary, should be revised to assure better coverage of low-wage, part-time, and contingent workers and to recognize family imperatives, such as child care responsibilities, as good cause for leaving or declining a job. Pregnancy should be recognized as a temporary medical disability. Under the system of temporary disability insurance that we propose in Chapter 11, this would excuse a failure to be immediately available for work because of childbearing. (Under current federal law any firing because of the taking of maternity leave should already make such unemployment "involuntary.") Let us consider these reforms in turn.

### Federalizing Finance

There is little or nothing to be said for state financing of unemployment insurance. Because unemployment experience in different regions of the country varies, an effective insurance pool is a national insurance pool.

State-level financing is the insurance equivalent of requiring that insurers insure covarying risks. And states have little capacity to take action that furthers national macroeconomic goals.

Nor is it obvious why states, employers, or employees should resist increased federalization of unemployment insurance. The current structure is a historical accident, born of archaic constitutional necessity, irreconcilable differences concerning the goals of an unemployment compensation regime, and the insistence of 1930s southern Democrats on state control over benefit levels. All of those original precipitating factors have either vanished or substantially abated. More important, it is difficult to see who would be big losers in a system that was federalized and therefore uniform, that avoided experience-rating of employers, and that decreased or eliminated federal incentives to "steal" funds for administration of the system.

While federal eligibility rules are unlikely to be as generous as those currently in force in jurisdictions with high recipiency and high replacement rates, most workers would get better unemployment insurance coverage in a unified system. Employees of state unemployment insurance agencies would lose if the federal government took over administration, but there is little reason to make that move. To the extent that help with finding new work remains an important function, local knowledge is superior. And although disability insurance administration through contracting out to the states is not without its difficulties, it is workable and lowers administrative costs.

A shift to a flat-rate tax, without employer-by-employer experience rating, would give all employers in the same industry a "level playing field." As is the usual case with flat-rate taxes, these levies should be expected to be passed on to employees. Indeed, we believe that these taxes should have the usual 50/50 structure of other payroll taxes. The question then would be whether the incidence of the unemployment insurance tax was fair to workers.

In the national system that we propose, workers with lower lifetime risks of unemployment would pay more to support a system that better insured workers with higher risks. But the overall increase in wage taxes, or decline in wage rates (or, alternatively, contribution from general revenues), to finance this charge would be very modest. Moreover, this form of progressivity is common in social insurance.

On the other hand, it would be perverse if the workers whose unemployment insurance benefits were being subsidized had higher incomes than those with a low risk of unemployment. Unfortunately, this is a plausible effect of a completely flat-rate scheme. Certain traditionally high-wage sectors, such as manufacturing and construction, also have higher than average risks of unemployment. But so do sectors that are characterized by relatively low wages, such as retail sales. We recommend, therefore, a financing scheme that "experience rates" industries both by the average rate of unemployment in the industry and the average incomes of that industry's workers. This will maintain income progressivity in the tax scheme, avoid cross-subsidies from low-risk to high-risk industries, and still provide subsidies to groups that have both high risks of unemployment and relatively low incomes.

### Abolishing Firm-Specific Experience Rating

There is little doubt that experience rating, perfectly applied, would have some impact on unemployment levels. Estimates vary, but it is plausible to believe that perfect experience rating would reduce overall unemployment rates by as much as 1 percent.[14] The catch, of course, lies in the use of the adjective "perfect." Current experience rating is far from perfect. It therefore probably has some effect on employment stability, but those effects are difficult to quantify.

Why not then go to "perfect" experience rating? The answer is simple: we cannot believe that such a system is a realistic prospect. Our disbelief proceeds from several grounds. First, much unemployment is outside employers' control. The unpredictability of the business cycle and the vagaries of market competition make the stabilization of employment through "scientific management" a hopeless aspiration, and demanding impossible behavior has no moral or political appeal. Second, getting blood from turnips is a lost cause. Employers who fail, and many do, will create unemployed workers. But because in this case there is no employer left to experience rate, perfect experience rating is clearly not feasible. Finally, because all unemployment is to some degree "voluntary"—there is probably some job out there for every able-bodied worker however unsuitable and unremunerative—perfect experience rating would visit "unfair" costs on employers. "Perfect" experience rating requires that employers bear the unemployment compensation costs not just of impersonal market or technological forces, but also of personal choices by employees that the unemployment insurance system rightly encourages them to make. In short, "perfect" experience rating can be neither effective nor fair.

Given these considerations, it is hardly surprising that state legislatures have balked at making contemporary experience rating "perfect." We do not believe that the real world of imperfect experience rating's uncertain, but probably positive, effects on employment stability justify its apparent costs in inadequate coverage and imprudent financing.

Experience rating cannot be judged, however, on its employment stabilization potential alone. Current experience-rating approaches may also reduce moral hazard by increasing employer monitoring of employees' unemployment claims. But whether employer monitoring leads to greater accuracy or merely to greater adversariness remains a mystery. While there is no systematic evidence that employers abuse the appeals system to keep down payments, employers gain the same advantage from erroneous denials of claims as from accurate ones.

The somewhat speculative employment-stabilization and employee-monitoring gains from experience rating must also be balanced against its probable costs. Employer economic incentives, resulting from experience rating, clearly feed back into state coverage policies. Experience rating is therefore implicated in both the current low levels of effective coverage and resistance to relaxing eligibility criteria to qualify workers whose unemployment is not within the employer's control. Experience rating, and the relatively high taxes that it imposes on certain employers, also contribute to resistance to adequate forward funding of the unemployment insurance system.

For all of these reasons, we believe that firm-specific experience rating should be abandoned. It has problematic effects on both employment stability and "fairness," and seems heavily implicated in the decline in effective unemployment insurance coverage that the United States has experienced over the last five decades. While some may be unpersuaded that experience rating is undesirable in unemployment insurance financing, it surely is not necessary. Of the G-7 nations, only the United States uses employer-specific experience rating as a part of its mechanisms to finance unemployment insurance.[15]

### Expanding Coverage

A system that covers 38 percent of unemployed workers does not provide adequate protection against the risk of involuntary unemployment. Yet many may worry that relaxing rules in ways that will insure more low-wage workers—including part-time, contingent, and secondary workers—will substantially increase the moral hazard inherent in the system. If so, that will ultimately affect the costs both of financing unemployment insurance and of lost productivity due to increased unemployment. Moreover, the elimination of experience rating could exacerbate these problems by eliminating employer incentives to monitor employee claims. How do we confront these difficulties?

First, we must be clear at the outset that a system of adequate coverage is likely to be more expensive than a system of inadequate coverage. While the current unemployment insurance system in the United States is increasingly ineffective, it does not appear to contain large inefficiencies. Some money can be saved by eliminating the administrative expense, including some appeals, necessary to implement experience rating. Reducing duplication of effort among state unemployment agencies and lowering benefits for some workers in high-paying states will also produce savings. But all together, these economies will not cover the increased costs of more universal protections against the risk of unemployment. Total tax collections must go up in order to finance the system we contemplate, although with a broadened tax base and the elimination of experience rating, the tax *rate* faced by virtually all employers will go down. We have been unable to estimate the increased funding requirements for our unemployment insurance proposals, but we are convinced that the increased costs will be relatively modest.

One reason for this confidence is that our proposals will decrease moral hazard. First, we propose to combine expanded unemployment insurance coverage with a system of individual accounts—a "universal security account" (USA) for each worker. Each employee will contribute 3 percent of wages to this account while working in order to help fund both periods of unemployment and retirement. (These accounts are discussed in more detail in Chapters 13 and 14.) If the worker experiences a period of compensated unemployment, his or her account will be debited with 20 percent of the costs of the compensation paid. Workers whose accounts are insufficient to fund the required copayment will face a surcharge on their wages when reemployed, which will be paid until such time as the individual's account has an adequate balance. Upon retirement or death, amounts left in the worker's account will be paid in retirement benefits, or as a death benefit to the worker's heirs.

Second, as is explained in more detail later in this chapter, we propose to reduce wage replacement rates as the period of unemployment increases. The straightforward implication of this change is that it gives workers a greater stake in maintaining employment and in reducing the duration of periods of unemployment. Because much unemployment is in some sense "voluntary," either in terms of its incidence or duration, we would anticipate that this form of worker experience rating will reduce unemployment claims and payments amounts. The exact magnitude of this reduction is obviously speculative.

In addition to these savings, there will be decreases in unemployment benefit costs that now show up in the disability insurance and SSI programs, food stamps, TANF, and general assistance programs that assist unemployed workers currently ineligible for unemployment insurance. Again no one knows what these costs are, but many observers believe that they are substantial. Hence, when potential savings are taken into account, we do not believe that the broader, more progressive, and more prudently funded system of unemployment insurance we propose here will impose significant net aggregate costs, either on our social insurance system or on the economy as a whole.

## OUR REVISED SYSTEM IN OUTLINE

While we cannot here address every detail of unemployment insurance reform, the revised unemployment insurance system that we contemplate has many of the features of the existing one. Most centrally, it insures workers against involuntary unemployment. It therefore assumes that workers are in the workforce, that they will return to it, and that their temporary unemployment is involuntary. Hence, like the current system, our revised system must have rules concerning workforce attachment— the current "monetary" eligibility criteria—and rules concerning reasons for separation from past employment and availability for and willingness to resume work—the "nonmonetary" eligibility criteria.

### Workforce Attachment Requirements

As many have pointed out, the current monetary requirements for unemployment insurance have two significant defects. First, because they look only at earnings amounts, they measure attachment to the workforce as much by wage level as by work effort.[16] As we have pointed out, a low-wage worker who worked more hours in the relevant qualification period than a higher-wage worker can find himself or herself without coverage while the higher-wage worker receives benefits. In addition, current rules tend to ignore the worker's most recent work experience. States that take account of the most recent three months' work have monetary qualification rates nearly 10 percent higher than states that do not.[17]

Responding to these concerns, we contemplate workforce attachment requirements having the following characteristics: In order to qualify for benefits, workers would be required to have some earnings in two of the last four quarters or to have earnings in all three months of the most recent quarter prior to the application for benefits. In addition, workers would have to demonstrate that they have earnings equivalent to the definition of substantial gainful activity in the disability system (currently $500 per month) in each month of at least one of the last four quarters, *or* that they have at least twelve weeks of work within the last four quarters that was full-time (thirty-five hours per week). Those twelve weeks of full-time work need not be consecutive.

While no set of workforce attachment requirements can establish foolproof criteria for determining whether a worker is truly "in the workforce," these standards have certain advantages over current rules. They count recent work, and they permit workers with quite different work histories (but arguably equivalent workforce attachments) to qualify for unemployment insurance benefits.

### Separation and Continuation Requirements

As with the current scheme, we would disqualify workers who voluntarily quit their jobs. This would include being fired for misconduct related to the workplace, staying away from work due to a strike or job action, making a fraudulent claim for benefits, or quitting without "good cause."

"Good cause" will forever remain a contested concept. Three issues, however, seem to dominate current controversies about good cause resignation: pregnancy and childbirth, quitting to follow a spouse who has relocated, and caretaking responsibilities either for a child or for an ill or aged relative.

As is detailed in the next chapter, if the worker is incapable of continuing in her customary occupation, our approach to pregnancy and childbirth is to treat this as a temporary disability. Hence it would be good cause to quit and to remain unavailable for work for a period certified by a physician to be necessary to complete a successful pregnancy and recover from the effects of childbirth.[18] We also believe that caretaking responsibilities, including the necessity of caring for an infant, should be good cause for quitting a particular job or rejecting jobs whose time demands are inconsistent with those responsibilities.

We do not believe, however, that family caretaking responsibilities should excuse general requirements of being available for work, engaging in a job search, or accepting "suitable employment." Hence, caretaking responsibilities would disqualify workers from the receipt of unemployment insurance benefits, if the caretaking responsibilities made them unavailable for work generally. Such workers must then be assumed to be out of the labor market and ineligible for unemployment insurance benefits so long as they maintain that status.

Finally, while the prospect of temporary unemployment because of the necessity of following a relocating spouse creates poignant choices for two-earner families, we believe that these should be considered family choices about what maximizes family welfare, not a risk of involuntary unemployment. Families should not accept transfers, or new jobs requiring relocation, unless they anticipate that they will be better off in the long run by making that decision. We see no reason why the cost of temporary unemployment, gauged against the prospects for spousal reemployment in the new location, should not be a part of that calculation. To put the matter slightly differently, while the "following" worker's separation from employment is in some sense involuntary, it is a voluntary choice of the marital economic unit. And from that perspective, the provision of unemployment insurance for persons who quit their jobs to follow a relocating spouse looks more like a subsidy for the pursuit of greater family economic opportunity than insurance against the risk of involuntary unemployment.

By contrast, we do not believe that resignation from a job because of an employer's demand for relocation should be treated as a voluntary quit. The worker's job has disappeared over the horizon for reasons beyond his or her control. And while the economy may be global, most people are intensely local. The demand that workers uproot their lives or become unemployed is precisely the sort of risk that should be insured in a modern market economy.[19]

**Duration of Benefits**

The duration of coverage should be limited to twenty-six weeks, absent a general unemployment rate of 7.5 percent or so, which would automatically trigger an extension of benefits for up to fifty-two weeks. We believe, however, that other restrictions should be put on both the duration and the amount of benefits. Although workers would be eligible for twenty-six (or occasionally fifty-two) weeks of benefits, no worker should be eligible for more weeks of unemployment insurance benefits than one-half of the weeks worked during the fifty-two-week period prior to the application for benefits. Moreover, we believe that workers should be given greater incentives to resume employment quickly, along with greater replacement rates in the earlier weeks of unemployment. Hence we would propose to pay 60 percent of past ("high quarter") wages for the first ten weeks of unemployment; 50 percent of past wages for the second ten weeks of benefits eligibility; and 40 percent of past wages during the last six weeks of payments. If receipt of benefits occurs during a period when extended benefits are available, replacement rates would not drop below 50 percent after twenty weeks, but would remain at that level throughout the covered period. As with current practice, we would cap benefits to any worker at 50 percent of the median wage for workers in that worker's state (or locality, if wages are substantially higher there).

### Unemployment Assistance

We also propose to create a new program of unemployment assistance for workers who have exhausted their unemployment insurance benefits or who have a prior workforce attachment that does not satisfy the requirements of earnings, duration, or recency that would qualify them for unemployment insurance compensation.

As with unemployment insurance, unemployment assistance would be limited to a maximum period of one year. Workers would have to be registered with the employment agency and actively seeking work, or certified as excused from that requirement by their participation in an acceptable job-training program. Because many of these workers could not be expected to have substantial prior work histories, their benefits would have to be calibrated in terms of some other standard. We would propose to set the benefits at either 40 percent of past wages in the highest-earning quarter of the last four quarters (a rule applicable primarily to workers who had exhausted their unemployment insurance compensation) or 75 percent of the current minimum wage, whichever is greater.[20]

### Financing

We would finance the unemployment insurance system by a wage tax that is "experience rated" by industry. The tax would be on the whole of the wage base and, like the FICA tax, divided equally between employers and employees.[21] In addition, a mandatory savings account equal to 3 percent of employees' wages would fund worker's individual accounts, which would be debited to pay a part of that worker's unemployment insurance benefits and used to fund additional retirement and death benefits. We would place unemployment tax receipts, like those from FICA, into a special trust fund. The unemployment assistance program would be financed from general revenues.

### Promoting Reemployment

In its 1995 report, the Advisory Council on Unemployment Compensation exhaustively reviewed the literature on demand-side and supply-side incentives for reemployment of unemployed workers and the effects of various forms of services on workers' successful return to work. The council's conclusions are easily summarized: A tight labor market has very substantial positive effects on re-employment. All other techniques, ranging from wage subsidies to reemployment bonuses, job sharing, job search services, and job training, have very modest effects and seldom produce demonstrable and substantial savings to the unemployment insurance system.

Given this record, we are not motivated to attempt to develop bold new reemployment policies. We are aware that some other countries, notably Sweden and to a lesser extent Germany, have been quite successful in using a combination of intensive social services and public job creation to limit unemployment. But we are far from confident that these techniques can be transplanted to the United States. In any event, recent German unemployment experience also suggests that these efforts may be swamped by other macroeconomic factors.

We are not, of course, advocating that the federal and state governments give up on experiments with various techniques for increasing reemployment of displaced workers—or for preventing displacement. These efforts clearly should continue, particularly if they are done in a way that allows careful evaluation of their efficacy. Our point is merely that the history of reemployment initiatives in the United States provides little support for the notion that employment stabilization and reemployment of displaced workers should be the principal goal of the unemployment insurance system.

Existing analyses of reemployment efforts reinforce our belief that the unemployment insurance (and unemployment assistance) system—like other social insurance protections—should be concerned primarily with the protection of workers' incomes against the risk of involuntary unemployment. Both the current unemployment insurance system and the revised one that we propose are constrained in their generosity by the need to avoid serious disincentives to continuing in or returning to employment. But constraints on the way in which the risk of unemployment can be prudently insured should not undermine the primary goals of the unemployment insurance system.

## SUMMARY

The workplace and the workforce have changed remarkably since 1935. Unemployment insurance arrangements have changed only modestly and generally in directions that have reduced coverage and shrunk the taxable wage base. The wage-replacement objectives of the 1935 vision of unemployment insurance were sound. But the institutional choices made during the New Deal—and constrained by the constitutional, political, and economic understandings of that era—have proved to be dysfunctional.

We have provided here a sketch of a revised unemployment insurance system, although we are under no illusion that we have solved, indeed even mentioned, all of the problems of constructing and running a system of income replacement for the unemployed. Our goal is more modest—to point the way toward a new approach that is consistent with our understanding of the basic functions of social insurance.

From this perspective, we believe that our general approach is appealing. A national system with broader coverage and a uniform benefits formula has a much better chance of meeting the twin goals of adequate wage replacement and countercyclical macroeconomic effects than does the current state-based arrangement. Broadening coverage to include more of those most at risk for unemployment, and eliminating employer experience rating while broadening the tax base to make financing more secure, are both improvements in our nation's social insurance scheme. By combining these changes with a new system of individual accounts and a benefits formula that provides increased incentives for workers to remain at work or to find new employment promptly, we believe that we can provide better protection for America's workers without substantially increasing costs or abandoning other goals, such as stabilizing employment and facilitating the search for new work.

# Chapter 11 The Risk of

# Work Disability

Public policies in aid of the ill or disabled have a very long history. "Invalids" were among those exempted from criminal prosecution for begging by the earliest Elizabethan Poor Laws. And the modern era of social insurance is often said to begin with worker protections against medical expenses and income loss from industrial accidents. Disability and sickness insurance was originally organized by guilds, but that source of relief disappeared as these associations were swept away by the industrial revolution. Some employers tried to fill the gap left by the disappearance of the guilds. And illegal trade unions began to reassert their influence by hiding behind relief funds that were established largely to pay workers' sickness and death benefits.

In the end, however, private efforts during the nineteenth century were insufficient to deal with the problem of loss of wage income due to injury and illness. Germany made sickness insurance compulsory for industrial workers in 1883 and by 1885 had also covered commercial and agricultural workers. Sickness insurance laws spread rapidly throughout Europe, and by the early 1920s were in place not only there but also in Japan and Chile.[1]

Notwithstanding the vast historical and transnational experience with disability programs, the maintenance of income security for persons temporarily or permanently out of the workforce due to illness or injury has been one of the most troubled programs of modern states.[2] A brief look at the issues that complicate the design of disability policies sets the stage for our proposals and simultaneously reveals why heroic efforts may yet leave both policy planners and affected populations dissatisfied with the outcomes of disability programs.[3]

Disability policy designers must ask and answer at least the following questions: What level of medical impairment (injury, illness, or congenital impairment) should qualify someone for assistance? To what extent should factors other than medical impairment—age, education, work experience, the nature of work environments, and so on—be considered in determining eligibility for benefits? What is the appropriate "replacement rate" for income lost due to disability? What part of the opportunity costs or lost income due to work disability should be met through personal or family effort, including private insurance? To what extent should the problem of inadequate income due to disability be relieved by programs that do not rely on disability status as an eligibility criterion? What role should "compensatory justice" play in disability income support where impairments can be traced to the conduct or activities of others? To what degree should policies that provide income security be integrated with services and support (such as medical care, rehabilitation, vocational education, retraining and placement efforts) that seek to provide opportunity for continuation of work or reentry into the workforce? What balance should be struck between these opportunity aspects of programs in aid of the disabled and our basic income security goals?

None of these questions is easy; indeed, all are controversial. Moreover, many suggest aspirations that are at cross-purposes with each other. An emphasis on security may not only downplay opportunity; it may also inhibit reintegration of persons with disabilities into both economic and social life. Relying on personal and family responsibility will leave many without support, but broad and generous coverage of disablement has a tendency to produce runaway costs and withdrawal of individual work effort. Making those who cause injury or their insurers pay through compensation arrangements supports compensatory or corrective justice, but it also leaves major gaps in protections against the risk of loss of income through injury or illness.

## SHOULD SOCIAL INSURANCE
## COVER DISABILITY?

Given these difficulties, many question the wisdom of a social insurance scheme to protect against risks of work disability. Disability insurance skeptics, however, have various perspectives on the issue. Some wonder why risks of work disability cannot be handled by private insurance markets. Others question whether the inability to work because of a medically determinable impairment is a sufficiently discrete event to be carved out for special treatment in a social insurance scheme. Yet others doubt the utility of the concept of "disability" and favor schemes that would compensate for "impairments" without attempting to pursue the more complex question of how impairments affect capacity to work.

### The Possibility of Private Coverage

The argument for leaving disability insurance to private markets is weak. Coverage by private carriers is certain to be restricted, because disability insurance confronts all the major impediments to widespread, affordable, and actuarially sound private insurance provision: adverse selection, moral hazard, and covariance of risks. Indeed, adverse selection is so prominent that there is virtually no market for individual disability insurance policies. Many insurers write group policies, but they differentiate strongly between groups with high and low risks. Some groups are treated as essentially uninsurable. Where risks are high, prices are high as well. The result is that private disability insurance tends to be available only to those groups who need it least; others are priced out of the market.

Figure 11.1 plots the striking differences in the coverage of distinct occupational groups and the clear segmentation of coverage by firm size. According to Department of Labor statistics, nearly 80 percent of managerial employees are covered by sick-leave benefits and more than that have short-term disability insurance through their employers.[4] Long-term disability benefits, however, even for managerial employees, cover less than half of the managerial workforce. Clerical, sales, and blue-collar workers do much less well—fewer than 20 percent have any coverage—although these workers are better covered for sick leave and short-term disability

Fig. 11.1.    Employees with private long-term disability insurance

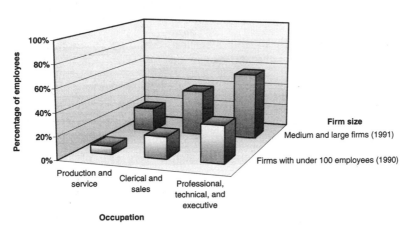

(*Source:* National Academy of Social Insurance, 1996 Disability Policy Panel Interim Report, *The Environment of Disability Income Policy: Programs, People, History and Context,* table 2-4.)

than for long-term disabilities.[5] These data strongly suggest that a broad market for disability insurance can be constructed only by mandatory pooling of low- and high-risk populations—the traditional role of social insurance.

Hence, while all countries have difficulty managing public disability schemes, the need for protection and the shortcomings of private insurance markets have led all industrialized nations to provide social insurance against loss of income due to work disability.[6]

### Work Disability as an Insurable Event

Disability insurance skeptics have also wondered whether disability, or, more accurately, work disability, should be viewed as a separable category for purposes of income replacement or income maintenance programs. People have medical impairments, but whether those impairments result in work disabilities depends upon other characteristics of the person (for example, education, work experience, and motivation), the particular structure of labor markets, the demands of particular jobs, and the degree to which individuals' general social environment provides them with supports that will help to compensate for their medical impairments. Because many of the "environmental" factors and nonmedical personal attributes that influence the existence of work disability are equally relevant to the job success of persons without medical problems, these critics argue that there is a certain arbitrariness to the identification of "disability" as a separate, insurable event.[7]

There is much truth to this assertion. Although research into the causes of changes in the incidence of long-term disability claims and awards in the United States is scientifically challenging and its results controversial, most investigators agree on a series of propositions: First, changes in disability benefits claims and awards are not the result of significant changes in the overall health of the population. Second, the incidence of work disability is strongly influenced by a series of "nonmedical" factors: the unemployment rate, structural changes in the economy, changes in the physical and cognitive demands of jobs, the availability of alternative sources of income support for those who are unemployed or out of the job market, and changes in disability benefits policies and administration.

Some of these causes relate fairly directly to matters that should be an aspect of work disability benefits policy. For example, a reduction in the physical demands of jobs, combined with increases in cognitive demands and requirements for cooperation with coworkers or contacts with the public, will affect the sorts of impairments that produce work disability. In this context, policymakers should expect a reduction in the incidence of work disability based on physical factors and an increase in the number of persons with mental disorders or low cognitive capacities. On the other hand, the downsizing of firms, changes in the general unemployment rate, and changes in the availability of alternative nonmarket sources of income should not, in principle, affect the prevalence or nature of work disability. That these things do seem to have powerful effects suggests that the boundaries between disability insurance, unemployment insurance, retirement insurance, and general income maintenance programs are quite permeable. Moreover, where, as in the United States, the percentage of the labor force that is unemployed can change quite rapidly, and unemployment insurance and public assistance supports are relatively weak, major pressures are put on disability insurance that, strictly speaking, it should not have to bear.

One response to these realities would be to abandon disability insurance entirely in favor of some more general income support program. For reasons detailed in Chapter 3, we do not believe that a one-size-fits-all social insurance regime (the negative income tax or general wage subsidies) is a workable approach. Nevertheless, we do believe that it is important to strengthen other programs, such as unemployment insurance and income support for families with children. Otherwise disability benefits programs inevitably become residual income-maintenance programs for those with nowhere else to turn. Our proposals, therefore, strengthen those income supports and provide a more comprehensive unemployment insurance system. Under those conditions, we believe that disablement is sufficiently distinguishable from unemployment—and from more generalized bases for lack of labor market success—that it can and should be treated as a separately insured risk.

This is not to say that disability administration will ever be able to distinguish perfectly between persons who are not in the workforce because of a serious medical impairment and those who simply have a serious medical impairment and are also not in the workforce. Adjudicating disability claims is the most difficult and contestable aspect of American social insurance provision.[8] But the fact that these judgments cannot be made with perfect confidence does not mean that they cannot be made at an acceptable level of reliability.

The technical capacity to distinguish disability from other risks to market income is not a sufficient ground for recognizing disability as a separate insurable event. But over a century of social provision in all developed (and many undeveloped) societies attests to the desire of families to be insured against a breadwinner's involuntary total exit from work, whether due to death, old age, or disability. Moreover, because disability is a socially legitimate ground for exiting the workforce, and can be financed in substantial part through contributory taxes, virtually all societies are prepared to provide more adequate replacement rates for income lost due to disability than in more universal, and usually means-tested, income support programs.

### Substituting Impairment Compensation

Finally, concerns about the trade-off between disability payments and work effort (which are particularly troublesome in the means-tested disability programs), combined with concerns about the "labeling effects" of disability benefits, lead some analysts to favor an impairment compensation system that focuses exclusively on medical conditions or anatomical losses with no attempt to determine whether those conditions affect individuals' capacities for gainful employment. There is surely something to be said for such a scheme, but we do not consider it a feasible substitute for disability insurance.

If income security is the goal of disability "compensation," then determining which impairments are compensable is as difficult as determining who is "disabled." Indeed, it's hard to imagine making a decision about the compensability of an impairment (outside of a corrective justice context) without considering its effects on work capacity and earnings. The level of compensation for impairment must necessarily bear some relation to the anticipated economic loss—medical expenses and lost earnings. Indeed, a social insurance system designed to protect people's incomes against absolute inadequacy or sharp decline should compensate impairments *only* to the extent that they give rise to those economic risks. Hence it is hard to see how an impairment-based system that pursues social insurance goals could avoid making the same sorts of determinations that a disability insurance scheme must make.

To the extent that the disability insurance skeptics' concern with "labeling" is a concern with the effect of a finding of disability on subsequent work effort, the proposal outlined later is substantially superior to the current system. Because we compensate shorter-term disabilities through the unemployment insurance scheme, persons involuntarily unemployed for health reasons will not be forced to apply for long-term disability payments because of ineligibility for unemployment insurance payments. This should limit the number of persons for whom recovery and return to work are possible, but who nevertheless accept the "disabled role" and become early retirees. To the extent that the concern with labeling is one about general stigma, we frankly are skeptical that benefits determinations contribute substantially to that problem or that being designated "impaired" is a significantly smaller assault on personal dignity or social standing than being determined eligible for "disability" benefits.

Thus there are, indeed, good reasons for including disability among the risks covered by social insurance provision. But as the preceding general discussion makes clear, disability policymaking requires hard choices. We are under no illusion that the choices that we have made will persuade everyone that we have somehow discovered the optimal disability insurance scheme. When in doubt, our choices have been driven principally by our overall conception of the role of social insurance. We believe that the proposals that follow provide a coherent approach to protections against the risk of disablement within the context of that overall vision.

We first sketch our basic approach to insuring income streams against the risk of work disability due to physical or mental impairments. In the course of that description, we touch briefly on the reasons for the choices that we have made and on the relationship between social insurance for disability risks and other aspects of the overall social insurance system that we propose. Once the basic outline is in place, we will turn to a discussion of some of the details of our disability insurance scheme, anticipating some of the objections that might be leveled at our approach.

## DEFINING WORK DISABILITY

Physical and mental impairments are of many types, and they interact with the demands of work and the general social environment to produce work disabilities that vary enormously both in character and severity. For purposes of income security policy, we must work with a few broad categories.

### Partial Disablement

Divide the world first into partial and total disability. The former, partial disability, is not a risk that we will cover as a part of our disability income security policy. There are multiple reasons for this exclusion.

Partial disability is exceedingly difficult to adjudicate. This is the most contentious arena of workers' compensation benefits' determination and the one generating the highest administrative costs.[9] To be sure, administration might be divorced from American-style adversarial proceedings. But down that road lie other dangers. The inclusion of benefits for partial disabilities in nonadversarial adjudicatory settings elsewhere has tended to produce explosive growth in benefit rolls. Much of what has come to be called the "Dutch Disease"—exponential growth in the costs of disability benefits—can be attributed to the way that the Dutch system once treated partial disability.

The Dutch disability benefits scheme recognized seven different levels of disability, including six partial disability categories. This broadening of the availability of disability benefits, combined with relatively high replacement rates, produced staggering increases in the incidence of disability in the Netherlands. Immediately prior to reforms instituted in 1994, one in every ten Dutch citizens of working age was receiving some disability benefits, and nearly 40 percent of Dutch workers between fifty-five and sixty-four were out of the labor force and receiving disability pensions. The average age of Dutch disability beneficiaries was quite young—forty-three—and most were expected to remain on the rolls until they died or automatically shifted to the retirement program at age sixty-five. Labor force participation rates in the Netherlands dropped to twenty percentage points below that of most industrialized countries, and the number of disability benefits recipients per one thousand active labor force participants was nearly three times the level in countries like Germany or the United States.[10]

Systems that maintain fiscal balance while providing partial disability benefits, such as the veterans' benefits program in the United States, do so largely because they have a constrained universe of beneficiaries. It is possible to run a disability system with partial disability benefits, as some European nations have demonstrated, but it is a challenging task that generally requires very aggressive social service and job creation efforts, the setting of very low levels of support, or both.

Our principal reason for leaving partial disability out of the disability insurance portion of our social insurance scheme, however, is derived less from fears of administrative or fiscal crisis than from a conviction that partial disability is not conceptually distinguishable from a host of other factors that may make a person more or less successful in labor markets. Low educational attainment, poor cognitive skills, low motivation, demoralization due to personal losses, changes in the work environment, declining energy levels—all may contribute to low wages, a decline in wage levels, or repeated bouts of unemployment. An attempt to separate out the existence and role of partial disability in contributing to these occurrences and to compensate them in a partial disability scheme seems to us an unnecessary, if not a hopeless, task.

Persons with partial disabilities should not, of course, be left without support if their impairments limit their earning capacity or their job security in ways that produce inadequate incomes or temporary but sharp drops in income streams. But those concerns should be dealt with through other income security interventions: wage subsidies for low-income workers with children, the unemployment insurance scheme, and residual means-tested public assistance programs. (We are assuming that the tort and other compensation systems will provide compensation where other private or public parties have direct responsibility for the injury or illness that produces a partial disability.) These interventions will not provide assistance for every worker with an impairment and low wages, but as we argued earlier, social insurance has its limits.

### "Total" Disability

That a scheme focuses on total work disability, either temporary or permanent, does not tell us which disabilities will qualify for social insurance payments or how those payments are to be structured. Our approach to these questions is relatively conventional. Total disability, defined either as inability to do one's customary work (temporary disability), or as inability to engage in substantial gainful activity in the economy as a whole (permanent disability), can be segmented by duration. We are all prone to routine or short-term illnesses that keep us away from our jobs for brief periods. These short periods of "sickness," lasting two weeks or less, make up the vast majority of time lost from work. Most of us will also experience longer bouts of illness or injury from which we will recover almost totally and return to our prior jobs, or work of the same general sort. These are instances of temporary total disability. Finally, a relatively small subset of persons will experience a "permanent" disability that takes them out of the workforce as a whole and that lasts until death or until they reach the age of normal retirement. We believe that a social insurance system should approach these varying forms of total disability in differing ways.

We do not see any compelling need to attempt to compensate sickness through a public social insurance scheme. The administrative costs of adjudicating claims related to brief illness, not to mention the moral hazard inherent in such claims, make the construction of such a system imprudent. Many employers will, of course, continue sick leave policies that cover the salaried portion of the population. Hourly wage workers will experience income losses that may be compensated by union sickness funds, and in some cases by employer sickness funds, but often will go uncompensated. If these bouts of sickness are sufficient to produce annual incomes that are low enough to qualify for a wage subsidy or for other means-tested benefits, then income adequacy will be supported in that way. Private savings should also play a central role in smoothing out income loss due to brief spells of sickness.

By contrast, temporary total disability—an incapacity to do one's customary job or occupation that lasts a year or less—is very similar to temporary unemployment. Unemployment insurance, however, is not payable to the temporarily disabled because the claimant is not "available for work." Our approach to temporary total disability is, therefore, quite simple: Where unemployed workers would be compensated but for their unavailability for work due to illness or injury, they will be entitled to temporary total disability payments at the same rate as for unemployment insurance.

As with unemployment insurance, monitoring of the situation will be required. But rather than registering for job search assistance and demonstrating efforts to obtain employment, temporarily disabled persons will be required to provide periodic medical recertification that their situation continues to prevent their return to work and to participate in appropriate rehabilitation programs. As with unemployment insurance, there will be a time limit of twenty-six weeks on benefits from short-term disability insurance (STDI). Indeed, these payments might simply be denominated unemployment insurance benefits, but made payable under rules that are altered in the ways just suggested. Benefits could be extended up to a total of fifty-two weeks for persons expected to return to work after a further period of recovery and rehabilitation.

The California scheme of state disability insurance provides a general model for the sort of system that we contemplate. That system is state-mandated and funded through employee payroll deductions. It is administered by the unemployment insurance agency and has requirements for prior workforce attachment that are similar to the unemployment insurance scheme. Benefits are payable if claimants are unable to perform their regular work and lose wages because of disability. The disability must last at least eight days, and the claimant must be under the care and treatment of a doctor who certifies that he or she is unable to perform his or her regular work. The replacement rate is 55 percent of prior earnings during the relevant base period, with a cap (in 1997) of $336 per week.

Other state schemes for short-term disability insurance in Hawaii, New Jersey, New York, Rhode Island, and Puerto Rico vary in their details and methods of administration. These schemes, however, have been in operation for over forty years in some cases, and they cover nearly 25 percent of the American workforce. Hence there is every reason to have confidence that such a scheme can be run effectively and prudently.

A system like California's can be run at quite modest expense. Although California has a quite expansive definition of temporary disability, which includes leaving work because of pregnancy and childbirth, the system is financed by a 0.5 percent payroll tax on wages up to $31,767 per year. Put another way, the maximum yearly premium in 1998 was $158.83, that is, slightly more than $13 per month for workers making at or above the taxable wage limit. Given that a twenty-year-old worker has an 80 percent chance of having at least one disability lasting ninety days or longer before reaching the age of sixty-five, this looks like a real insurance bargain.[11]

As the twenty-six- and fifty-two-week limits on temporary total disability insurance suggest, we accept the conventional notion that disabilities lasting longer than one year should be considered permanent, although some recipients will recover and return to work. Recipients of STDI may also apply for long-term disability benefits and if determined to be eligible will be shifted to that program after STDI benefits are exhausted. No long-term disability "back benefits" will be payable for any period in which STDI payments were received.

We believe the current Social Security Disability Insurance (SSDI) definition is an adequate one for purposes of assessing permanent or long-term disability. It requires that disabilities last for at least one year (or be expected to result in death) and that a medically determinable impairment makes it impossible for claimants to work at any job in the national economy that would produce a substantial income (currently defined as $500 per month). Here the criterion for disability benefits shifts from inability to do one's customary job—the STDI requirements—to inability to do any job that provides substantial income. Few people who meet this stringent definition ever return to work. The system of long-term disability benefits is therefore both historically and functionally a system of early retirement, and benefit levels are basically the same as for Social Security pensions.

We would also maintain the current system of Supplemental Security Income (SSI) payments for persons with total and permanent disability who have no significant prior attachment to the workforce. This program is means tested and pays a relatively low level of benefits by comparison with Social Security disability insurance. It is also a politically and administratively more problematic program than SSDI. In SSDI, the claimant's prior attachment to the workforce gives a circumstantial guarantee that the medical impairment is the cause of withdrawal from the workforce. That guarantee is not available in the SSI program, and leads to greater concerns about the legitimacy of some claims.

These concerns notwithstanding, we see no good substitute for the SSI program in insuring against the possibility that a person will be unable to develop substantial attachment to the workforce because of medical impairments. This risk is insured to some degree by a special provision in the SSDI program for "disabled adult children," that is, persons who become disabled during childhood and who are then permitted to collect SSDI benefits upon achieving majority, provided their parents have SSDI coverage. But whatever the merits of that scheme, it does not cover the substantial number of persons who encounter serious injury or illness early in their postadolescent years, before achieving eligibility for SSDI, or who have always been marginal workers, never amassing sufficient quarters of qualifying work to be eligible for SSDI benefits.

We are aware that there has recently been substantial growth in the SSI disability program (from about 1.5 million recipients in 1974 to more than 5 million in 1996). The rate of growth has been particularly high in the 1990s, and there has been substantial anxiety about the increase in mental illness claims.[12] Moreover, because serious mental illness is often a disease of the relatively young (or relatively old), SSI benefits are paid to those who are viewed as relatively less deserving than those receiving SSDI benefits, and these people are likely to be on the benefit roles for much longer.[13]

Thus SSI promises to remain a politically embattled program. But these difficulties do not convince us that there is not a real and important risk here that requires social insurance provision. Moreover, we believe that the "moral hazard" involved in SSI disability benefits must be compared with the alternatives that a humane society might choose. The major alternative to means-tested disability payments would be universal, means-tested income payments for persons having income and assets below a certain level. But here the moral hazard problems are even greater, and we have for that reason rejected the notion that a negative income tax (or some similar program) should be substituted for most of our discreet programs of social insurance.

Moreover, a good bit of the moral hazard implicit in the current SSI program may result from its coupling with a nonuniversal system of health insurance. Impaired younger workers, particularly those with mental illness, have very high medical expenses and are likely to be uninsurable in private markets. They are also unattractive to employers who supply employer-sponsored health care benefits. It is widely believed, therefore, that a (perhaps substantial) number of SSI beneficiaries resist leaving the SSI rolls for available work not because they would lose their cash benefits, but because they would lose their Medicaid benefits. If universal medical insurance were available, however, as we propose in Chapter 9, these incentives to acquire or remain on SSI benefits would be removed.

## INTEGRATING DISABILITY BENEFITS WITH
## SERVICES AND PRIVATE INSURANCE

We have until now ignored medical care, rehabilitation, and other services that are designed to ameliorate impairments and promote return to work. Remember, however, that under our general scheme everyone in the population would have medical insurance coverage, including coverage for rehabilitation medicine. Efforts at vocational rehabilitation and assistance with returning to work are also important to persons with disabilities, as are policies against discrimination against the physically or mentally impaired. Strictly speaking, these arenas of public action lie outside the domain of social insurance income supports. Nor do we think that they are so integrally connected to income support payments that it is necessary to construct income supports and social services as a single, comprehensive set of interventions.

Nevertheless there are admirable systems of integrated medical care, rehabilitation, vocational counseling, job placement, and income supports in the private sector in the United States and in certain public disability systems abroad. Moreover, there is much to be said for an "integrated case management" approach as a way of attempting to avoid long-term disabilities as well as of guaranteeing that when long-term disability payments are made, they are being made to the "truly disabled."

Although the ideal system of seamless, integrated supports and services will never be constructed, we believe that the reforms we propose move in the right direction. More universal coverage of unemployment insurance and the addition of temporary disability insurance, combined with the retention of state administration by contract in a uniform national system of unemployment and disability coverage, provides opportunities for increased integration of medical and vocational services with income supports. Hence referral to appropriate state or private service providers could be a part of the administrative requirements for determining state eligibility. Integration of services with supports could also be a part of federal criteria and reward schemes in its grants programs to support state service programs.

There may also be concern about whether our proposals will displace current income supports both at the state and local levels as well as benefits offered through "employee welfare" packages attached to private employment. What will happen to employer-provided sick leave, short-term disability, and long-term disability benefits? What about the mandatory short-term disability insurance schemes in five states and Puerto Rico? What about state vocational rehabilitation and other return to work efforts? What about workers' compensation?

### Radical Reduction of the Scope of Workers' Compensation

To take last matters first, we contemplate the substitution of temporary or permanent disability insurance for most workers' compensation payments. Workers' compensation schemes need not necessarily be abolished, but persons receiving STDI or long-term disability benefits would not be eligible to receive workers' compensation benefits for lost income as well. Moreover, health care benefits would now fall within the universal scheme described in Chapter 9, although workers' compensation might cover the copayments otherwise required under that scheme. Workers' compensation would thus be left with the residual function of compensating for anatomical or functional losses that reduce earning capacity but do not prevent gainful employment.

For reasons detailed in Chapter 5, we believe that this is a very good trade for American workers. The workers' compensation system in the United States has many failings. Its coverage is spotty, its administrative costs are spectacular, and its income replacement effects are very modest. In our view, we can take a substantial step forward by redirecting resources currently used for workers' compensation into the proposed short-term and long-term disability systems, and if necessary, into our program of universal income-security coverage for medical risks. In this way, all workers will be covered for major income loss due to injury or illness, whether or not that injury or illness can be traced to some job.

### Financing Short-Term Disability Programs

Like unemployment insurance, STDI would be financed through a tax on the total wage base. Industry experience rating could be employed, but any "fairness-in-finance" gains here are probably not worth the administrative burdens. SSDI would continue to be financed by FICA payroll taxes.

We imagine that current short-term disability systems run by the states will be folded into the new nationwide scheme. The national system could be organized either in a "pay or play" fashion, as in states like New Jersey, New York, and California, or it could be a tax-and-transfer scheme administered publicly, as in Rhode Island. The tax-and-transfer approach is generally simpler to administer. By allowing qualified employment-based schemes to substitute for the publicly administered system, however, the potential benefits of integrated case management of disability cases might be realized for some workers.[14]

We would, therefore, exempt employers who sponsor short-term disability plans from the STDI tax so long as benefits under their plans are at least as generous as the ones under the public scheme. As under existing state pay-or-play programs, employers covering particularly low-risk groups of employees should be required to make supplementary payments to help finance the higher-risk public pool. Employer-sponsored long-term disability benefits would presumably remain integrated with public, social insurance benefits as they are today—that is, all employers require that long-term disability beneficiaries apply for Social Security benefits. Employer-based benefits are then reduced to the degree that public social insurance payments are forthcoming. As with medical insurance benefits, these arrangements will permit some employees to have fatter packages of disability benefits than others. This may be an inequality, but it is one that need not worry us so long as coverage for the mandatory public scheme is universal and adequate.

The net costs of the new STDI system would be very modest—perhaps even negative. As we have explained, the California program is currently financed by a tax of 0.5 percent of payroll with a wage ceiling that is less than half of the current Social Security (FICA) maximum. Estimates for a proposal similar to ours but with higher average replacement rates (67 percent), made during the Nixon and Ford administrations, suggested somewhat higher total costs of .86 percent of taxable payroll (meaning FICA taxable at that time) or about .72 percent of total payroll. But those estimates did not deduct any costs not currently in the federal budget, such as the reduced workers' compensation costs and the savings from elimination of state-supported STDI (which is currently in place in some large states like California, New Jersey, and New York). And although the risk pools for private insurance companies may not be representative of the total population, MetLife and others report current STDI premiums of roughly $180 per employee per year.

**SUMMARY**

Disability as a social insurance risk should be defined as the interruption of wage income due either to the short-term inability to continue in one's current occupation or the long-term inability to work at any substantial gainful employment. From this perspective, short-term disability insurance becomes an analogue of the unemployment scheme with comparable duration and benefits. Long-term disability, by contrast, is either a form of early retirement, compensated in accordance with the retirement pension schedule, or a legitimate reason for being out of the workforce that therefore makes the worker eligible for subsistence supports. The medical costs of disability will be dealt with through the universal, income-tested, catastrophic insurance plan that we described in Chapter 9.

# Chapter 12 Families with Children

As we detailed in Chapter 6, children are the most economically insecure segment of American society. To provide true security for children, social insurance interventions must do at least four things. First, basic income security must be a right. Security is not to be founded on a legislature's promise that "We will help you until we find something else to spend the money on," or "You are entitled if you live in the right place and got in line early enough." A private insurance contract written in those terms would be a joke. Unredeemable public promises are no better.

Second, social insurance must recognize that children's economic well-being is at risk both because of the temporary or permanent low income of the children's caretakers and because some families must spend a large portion of their income for certain basic necessities such as medical care, child care, or housing. Public policy must use different techniques in order to address these differing circumstances successfully and at acceptable cost.

Third, social insurance provision must be reliably and efficiently administered. This is a major challenge given the heterogeneous situations of the target clientele and the necessity to make entitlements secure. Indeed, it is often thought that a social welfare system must choose between two radically different modes of assistance: either reliable and well-defined entitlements for broad categories of recipients, or discretionary, variable, and legally insecure interventions to meet individualized needs.

Fourth, children's economic security must be assured while respecting both the integrity of family units and the core responsibility of parents to provide for their own offspring. While some children will necessarily be cared for in orphanages or by foster parents who are paid for their efforts, the American public will not, and should not, support a system that breaks up families because they are poor. Nor do we any longer believe, as we did in the 1930s, in paying mothers to stay at home to care for their children. When the majority of families need two earners to make ends meet, policies that promote parental absence from the labor market have limited appeal.

## TECHNIQUES FOR ACHIEVING THESE GOALS

Satisfying the entitlements goal is technically simple. Much administration may take place at the state or local level, but financing and eligibility criteria must be national. This is true for most of American social insurance expenditures, but, as we detailed in Chapter 6, that is dramatically not now the case for many programs of particular relevance to children's economic security.

Heterogeneity of circumstances demands multiple forms of support. The low income of parents can be subsidized by wage supports like the Earned Income Tax Credit (EITC). And parents without jobs for reasons other than death, disability, or involuntary unemployment can be given time-limited economic supports while they prepare to enter or reenter the labor force.

As we shall see, however, generalized income supports will not deal with the problems that confront many families with children—the high costs to some families of basic necessities such as shelter, children's medical care, and child care. These items vary dramatically in their importance to a family's budget depending on the family's composition, the age of children, the place of residence, the place and time of employment, and whether the children are frequently or seriously ill. Here more specific interventions are needed to subsidize consumption of *certain* goods and services for *certain* families with children.

But by such particularized support we do not mean to suggest a system of individualized caseworker assessments and special grants, such as those that historically characterized state Aid to Families with Dependent Children (AFDC) programs and that persist in many discretionary social services programs. We propose instead a series of "catastrophic expenditure" protections, patterned in part after our health insurance proposal, but with a different structure for subsidies and support levels. Although these devices are far from perfect, they combine universal entitlement with sensitivity to differential family circumstances and reasonable ease of administration.

Finally, our proposals seek to reinforce family responsibility by rewarding work effort and avoiding the perverse incentives that have plagued prior means-tested programs and have frustrated both beneficiaries and taxpayers. We also urge increased efforts to assure that absent as well as caretaker parents do their fair share in supporting their children.

The remaining work of this chapter is to put some flesh on this skeletal description of our proposals to provide economic security for families with children—and to persuade you that this approach is both desirable and prudent. Make no mistake; our scheme is no panacea. But it is a vast improvement over current arrangements—arrangements that might with only slight hyperbole be described as writing America's children out of the nation's social insurance contract.


## THE SHORTCOMINGS OF CURRENT POLICY

Two techniques have emerged to mediate between our apparent desire to support needy and deserving children and our reluctance to reward indolent or inattentive parents. The first strategy is to try to limit cash payments to a "deserving group" of parents. As we recounted in Chapter 6, administrators of widows' pensions took this approach beginning in 1911. By 1919, thirty-nine states had adopted legislation to provide widows enough money to keep their children at home rather than sending them to orphanages. Limiting benefits solely to widows and their children, however, proved inadequate as divorce and illegitimacy increased. The AFDC provisions of the Social Security Act of 1935 extended aid to divorced and deserted mothers and their "dependent" children, and also rescued some state efforts from insolvency.

Over time, AFDC lost its political support as it became widely believed to contribute to a cycle of dependency. Moreover, as working mothers became the norm for all families, paying certain mothers to remain out of the labor force looked less and less sensible to the workers who were paying the bills. In 1996 Congress replaced AFDC with Temporary Assistance to Needy Families (TANF) in legislation whose title reflects the continued emphasis on deservingness: "The Personal Responsibility and Work Opportunity Reconciliation Act of 1996" (PRA). In the PRA vision, custodial parents moving toward full-time work represent the deserving poor. PRA also embraced the goal of reducing out-of-wedlock births.

Although no one claims that full-time mothering is idleness, insisting that parents of needy children work has become the mechanism for protecting the public fisc against transfers of cash to "nondeserving" parents. The practical downside of this strategy is that the economy simply does not offer sufficient job opportunities to these parents at a wage level adequate to finance decent living standards for their children.

This gap imposes new demands on social insurance. The fundamental task is to make sure that children whose parents have limited earning capacities will nevertheless have a decent standard of living while their parent or parents are working. Among current policy responses, the Earned Income Tax Credit comes closest to realizing this goal. It too targets the deserving poor—those who work—and provides wage subsidies primarily to families with children. But, as we shall see, the EITC (or more generally wage subsidies) cannot do the whole job.

The second technique for assuring that public support actually benefits children and is not easily diverted by parents to other purposes is to provide benefits to families in-kind, rather than in cash. This is a central reason why in-kind transfers to poor families enjoy far more political popularity than cash benefits. In addition to food stamps (and other food programs) and health insurance (provided to needy children principally through Medicaid), government now provides *some* low-income families with subsidies for home heating, child care, and housing expenses. But these are classic "we-will-help-you-if-you-are-lucky" programs. A very modest proportion of "eligible" families actually receives benefits.

Existing policies and programs address the multiple risks that produce childhood poverty. Yet poverty's persistence demonstrates the inadequacy of current arrangements. The task is to knit together a revised set of approaches that will have the desired effects without displacing the primary responsibility that parents bear for their children's economic well-being.

Although we are currently failing, we can succeed. We already have means-tested supports for poor families whose breadwinner (or breadwinners) is currently out of the workforce but who is expected to obtain a job (TANF). We have wage subsidies for poor workers with children (EITC). We have a host of medical care, housing, and child care supports, as well as a means-tested and work-demanding Food Stamp Program. This collection of remedies for low wages, inadequate labor force participation, and the high cost of certain necessities could constitute an effective, multipronged approach to childhood poverty. We do not need to do anything really "new" to make significant progress. But we do need to make significant changes in the programs that we have. Partial and fragmented efforts must be extended and unified. Both program financing and family entitlement must be made secure. Supports for the affluent must be redirected, at least in part, to the needy. We will look first at reforms in income or wage-support programs and then at the issue of consumption subsidies for necessary expenditures.

## BUDGET PRESSURES ON LOW-WAGE FAMILIES
## WITH CHILDREN

Many analysts have examined budgets for low-income families with children, and we will not repeat those exercises here.[1] Instead, we will fashion a package of social insurance protections based on the lessons they have taught.

Whether low-income families with children can "make ends meet" depends on numerous variables, but five seem the most important:

(1) the number of wage earners in the household,
(2) the number and ages of the children,
(3) the level of housing costs,
(4) the necessity for medical care expenditures, and
(5) the need for child care to permit the parent or parents to work.

Regional variations are most important with regard to the costs of housing, but they also affect the costs of child care. Family structure not only determines the level of family income—most important, whether there are two wage earners or just one—but also shapes the family's need to pay child care expenses in order to enable the parent or parents to work.

Although the quality of public education in many localities is deplorable, public schooling beginning with kindergarten at age five or six does provide child care coverage for a substantial part of the normal working day. Thus the number and age of children, particularly children below age six, critically shape a family's need to pay for child care and often determine whether a parent will find it beneficial to be in the labor market.

Whether the child is living with one or two parents is the single most important variable in the childhood poverty equation. In the 1990s children living with single women have been five times more likely to be poor than children living with two parents. While more than two-thirds of all children currently reside in two-parent families, poor children are more evenly divided between one-parent and two-parent families.

The single-parent family faces two principal disadvantages in comparison to a dual-parent family: First, a dual-parent family, even where both parents work at the minimum wage, can produce twice the level of earned income as a single-parent family. Second, a two-parent family has greater flexibility in dividing child care responsibilities and, as a result, greater choice about what level of child care expenditures to incur.

These distinctions are blurred in poverty-level statistics and in many analyses of families living in poverty. Official poverty levels distinguish among families based on size, but ignore family characteristics. This means that, for example, the poverty level in 1997 for a family of three was stated as $13,330, without consideration of whether the family was composed of two parents with one child, or one parent with two children.[2]

The economic difficulties and insecurities of children living in single-parent families have serious long-term consequences. These children tend to obtain less education, earn less, and are more likely to depend on government income support.[3] In 1995, a total of about 29 million people lived in families headed by unmarried mothers, and the poverty rate for this nearly 10 million families was a staggering 44.5 percent.[4]

The key role of family composition in contributing to children's economic well-being creates a dilemma for public policy. Clearly social insurance should endeavor to eliminate poverty and reduce economic insecurity in single-parent families. Otherwise, we tolerate unnecessary current material deprivation, and we face the prospect of wasting these children's future as well as diminishing our own. On the other hand, an income transfer policy should not make single-parent families unduly attractive, and perhaps more prevalent. This means that any program of social insurance for low-wage families must attempt to minimize economic disincentives for marriage while lowering economic insecurities. Thus, for example, to the extent that allowances for children are provided, they should be based on the number of children, not on the family's composition, and child care subsidies should be made available for two-parent as well as single-parent households. Moreover, because levels of income are higher in dual-parent households, income targeting must be sensitive to these pressures on family composition.

The number of children within a family obviously affects each child's economic well-being. Data concerning average family size can be misleading. More than one-half of single-parent and dual-parent families have only one or two children. But more than one-fourth of low-wage families have three children or more.

Age is also important. At age six, children begin school, and by the time they are thirteen or so, they can stay at home without any adult present. Thus, given current public education policies in the United States, children under age six require child care during the entire workday, while children between ages six and twelve generally require child care only during after-school hours, school holidays or closures, and periods of illness. Generally after a child reaches age twelve or thirteen, child care ceases to be a necessity for a parent to work.

The third major variable affecting the economic well-being of children of low-wage workers is the cost of housing. Housing is typically the largest expense for families at all levels of income. Although nearly 3 million low-income families currently receive some housing subsidy, in 1995 only about one-third of AFDC recipients nationwide lived in a public housing development or received a housing certificate or voucher.[5] Federal housing assistance in either form usually protects recipients against having to spend more than 30 percent of their income for shelter.

The final key variable for family economic security is whether large and unexpected health expenses are covered by insurance. As we noted earlier, Medicaid coverage for children living in low-income families has increased in recent years, but there continue to be important gaps in health insurance coverage, particularly among low- and moderate-income workers. Our program for health insurance coverage would ensure that all families, including all low-wage families, are protected against major financial shocks due to unexpected health expenditures.

We believe that social insurance should generally provide cash rather than in-kind benefits. But there are exceptions. Many families have serious difficulties paying for certain necessities, including health care, child care, and housing. In addition, these expenditures vary dramatically depending on location, family composition, and health circumstances. In order to guarantee families an adequate standard of living, social insurance provisions must address the problems of inadequate income resulting from these particular categories of outlays.

Other major components of the costs of living for low-wage families tend to be reasonably constant across family circumstances. Food costs hover around $100 per person per month, as do family expenditures on utilities and clothing and personal care expenditures, although expenses obviously vary with family size and increase when people have jobs. Transportation costs vary, depending on whether the family lives in a city, suburb, or rural area, but they seem to range from roughly $75 to $100 per month, with those who need to commute to work by automobile paying somewhat more.

Essential expenditures, not including health insurance, housing, or child care payments, total approximately $600 per month for a family of three and $500 for a single parent with one child. At the current minimum wage of $5.15 per hour, the monthly before-tax income for a full-time (forty-hour-a-week) worker is less than $900 a month. That leaves a scant $300 to $400 per month for full-time workers to pay for housing, child care, medical expenses, taxes of all sorts, and all other expenses. This is the "mission impossible" that confronts millions of Americans every day. Moreover, increasing wage rates for these families will not, by itself, yield reasonable income security. Each additional $1.00 an hour of wages will increase monthly income by $150 to $175—a help, to be sure, but often still not enough to afford decent housing and child care. And for most low-income workers, marginal wage increases are the rule—catapulting into high-wage work is exceptional.

SUBSIDIZING INCOMES AND WAGES

### The TANF Approach to Income Support

Previous chapters have described programs for insuring persons who become temporarily or permanently disabled or who suffer relatively brief periods of unemployment. Within a comprehensive program of social insurance, Temporary Assistance for Needy Families (TANF) plays an important role in assisting persons who face long-term unemployment and do not have sufficient income or wealth to support their families at a decent standard of living. TANF also is structured to encourage states to provide income and services to enable poor parents who have no current or recent attachment to the workforce to finance their transition to employment.[6] Given our vision of the proper role and scope of social insurance and of personal responsibility, we regard both the general requirement that able-bodied adults work in order to receive benefits and time limitations for support as appropriate conditions for receiving this category of social insurance benefits.

We do not, however, endorse other aspects of the TANF legislation. While we believe that administration of TANF, particularly its efforts to educate and train workers and to find or provide jobs, must take place at the state and local level, and have no objection to TANF's provisions allowing these services to be contracted out to private firms, federal funding should ensure that there will be no "race to the bottom" in fixing income support levels. In 1998, state TANF benefit levels ranged from $120 to more than $600 a month, leaving many families below a level of even barely adequate income. Moreover, a social insurance benefit should mean that any persons who meet specified eligibility conditions are entitled to the insurance benefits provided. We therefore endorse a time-limited entitlement to benefits for families who qualify. If state statutes setting forth eligibility for the receipt of TANF fail to create a legal entitlement to these benefits for all persons who meet the statutory conditions, reinstatement of a federal entitlement will be necessary.

The emphasis of TANF on entry into the labor market by able-bodied parents does place substantial burdens on states (with federal support) to find or provide job opportunities. While TANF currently emphasizes placing people in jobs as quickly as possible, states should provide education and job training for those individuals who are required to enter the labor force. We assume here that job opportunities will be available for "TANF graduates" through public or private employment—an essential condition for this social insurance protection to succeed. But we recognize both the critical nature and difficulty of creating ample job opportunities.

Such efforts will never be fully successful, but TANF has "loopholes" that allow assistance to continue for some families, and others will be eligible for the unemployment assistance program outlined in Chapter 10. In the end some needy families will be required to rely on state or local general assistance and charity. The sensible goal is to keep these cases to a minimum, not to imagine that they will be eliminated entirely.

Moreover, even if states were successful in creating employment for all TANF recipients, these jobs must necessarily fit within the confines of existing wage structures. The challenge for social insurance then is to make sure that parents who are in the workforce can provide an adequate standard of living for their children. Assuming that sufficient jobs will be available is heroic enough; pretending that parents with inadequate educations and low skills will obtain jobs that pay enough to support their families without further protection would be irresponsibly Pollyannaish.

### The Earned Income Tax Credit

Most low-income working families with children are eligible for the earned-income tax credit, which eliminates their income and payroll taxes and, in some cases, provides a wage supplement.[7] In 1997 the EITC provided a maximum wage supplement of $143 a month for a one-child family, and $246 for a family with more than one child. Rarely, however, does the EITC serve to finance monthly expenditures for these families because the vast majority of eligible workers receive their EITC in the form of a lump-sum refund when they file their annual tax returns. Although an advance-payment system, which entitles workers to receive the EITC in their paychecks, has been part of the law since 1979, only a tiny percentage of eligible workers has taken advantage of this alternative.

### Food Stamps

Even counting the EITC, however, children living with a single parent earning low wages clearly need a further social insurance supplement in order to achieve an adequate standard of living. Current law protects these families against having to spend more than 20–25 percent of their income to provide themselves and their children with adequate nutrition.[8] Low-income households with incomes at or near the poverty level may qualify for food stamps, a special supplemental food program for women, infants, and children (WIC), free school breakfasts, and reduced-cost school lunches. The federal expenditures on these programs in 1996 totaled about $35 billion, of which more than $25 billion was in food stamps.[9]

Politics aside, we are skeptical whether there is any advantage in providing food stamps rather than a wage supplement in cash to low-wage workers. Both empirical data about family expenditures and the maximum benefit levels under the Food Stamp Program demonstrate that the level of food expenditures is relatively constant across households of similar size. In addition, a well-known "gray" market for food stamps has developed allowing recipients to exchange food stamps for cash at about fifty to seventy-five cents on the dollar. This has resulted in increased efforts to uncover fraud, and demonstration projects in a number of states allow the substitution of cash for food stamps. In addition, many states have replaced food stamp coupons with ATM-type electronic cards, a trend that is sure to continue. On balance, we favor transforming food stamps into cash for all who are currently eligible.[10] This could be accomplished principally through increasing amounts of the EITC, TANF, and SSI payments. We recognize, however, that continuing the Food Stamp Program in its current form has considerable support, and we regard converting food stamps to cash assistance as a relatively minor matter.

In any event, the Food Stamp Program's design is consistent with our social insurance goals, and it provides something of a model for our health care, child care, and housing proposals. Food stamps are financed federally except where states want to provide additional benefits, but the states are responsible for the program's day-to-day administration. The Food Stamp Program is designed to protect against disproportionately large expenditures for an essential item and by doing so serves to protect families against food prices rising much faster than wages. Thus a low-wage family can be confident that it will not be required to spend more than 20–25 percent of its income on food.

If the Food Stamp Program were retained, it would require one important reform. Like the current Medicaid program, when a household's assets exceed specified ceilings, they simply lose food stamp eligibility. This creates disincentives for both saving and work, not to mention inequities among families in relatively similar circumstances. While these problems are not nearly so serious as under the current Medicaid program, they could be eased by eliminating the asset test.

## THE LIMITATIONS OF WAGE SUBSIDIES

While we generally prefer that social insurance be provided in the form of cash, we are convinced that insuring a decent standard of living for low-wage families with children cannot be accomplished effectively through wage subsidies or other cash transfers alone. First, as the foregoing analysis demonstrates, there are a number of variables that would have to be taken into account in order to target funds to those families who most need protection. Housing expenses, for example, vary significantly not only across regions but, in some cases, even neighborhood by neighborhood within a single city.

Likewise, child care expenditures can vary dramatically, and various subsidy programs estimate them in very different ways. One study, for example, examined a sample of low-income mothers who on average paid only $63 per month for child care. But the market rate in the locality studied was $331 a month.[11] In calculating net income, the Food Stamp Program allows a deduction for out-of-pocket child care expenses of up to $175 a month per child, $200 for children under age two. Yet the average costs of center-based child care nationally are estimated at about $300 to $400 a month. In 1997, New York State reimbursed child care expenses for families qualifying for subsidies under child care block grants at the rate of $30 a day, or $600 a month ($43 per day, or nearly $900 a month for children under age three).[12] Obviously, a family's child care expenditures can vary greatly, depending on where they live, whether they have friends or relatives available to take care of their children, and, if not, whether they send their children to licensed child care centers or to stay with unlicensed neighbors.

Moreover, as we have shown, any supplement to the income of a low-wage family intended to provide a decent standard of living for children should vary depending upon the numbers of both children and adults in the household. As the refundable Earned Income Tax Credit of current law shows, this can be done in providing cash income supplements, but not without considerable complexity.

Finally, while we do not believe that public policy should be fashioned on the assumption that any class of parents will ignore the best interests of their children, it would be politically naive not to recognize that misuse of cash subsidies by a handful of low-income parents threatens the political sustainability of subsidies for the entire population. Each time Congress is told of a drug-addicted or alcoholic parent who misappropriates funds intended for their children's support—or even of a parent who throws a lavish party to celebrate a child's birthday—huge political and economic costs are imposed on all low-wage families. Even occasional expenditures on alcohol or cigarettes by subsidized low-income people raise hackles in the nation's legislatures.

For these reasons we have concluded that a politically stable and well-targeted social insurance program to protect the living conditions of children, particularly children whose parents earn low wages, should, in addition to income and wage subsidies, take the form of protecting these families against large out-of-pocket expenditures for health care, child care, and housing. While we recognize that child care and housing costs are not as unpredictable as large health care costs and may, in some sense, be more voluntary, we nevertheless believe that providing graduated subsidies for these costs is an important aspect of providing true security for American families. These costs vary dramatically with location and family composition—factors that are only partially susceptible to individual control. But because of the flexibility that many families enjoy with regard to both child care and housing costs, a prudent social insurance scheme for these costs must require substantial copayments from the families themselves.

## SUBSIDIZING CONSUMPTION OF NECESSITIES

### Insurance against Disproportionate Child Care Costs

As both married and single women have entered the labor force, the demand for child care services has increased dramatically. In 1997 the mothers of more than half of the nearly 20 million children under age five in America worked, and nearly 20 million more children between ages five and thirteen had working mothers.[13] Increasingly, child care is provided outside the home, and families' monthly child care costs have risen in real terms by more than 20 percent since 1986.[14]

Even though child care expenditures per child rise with income, low-income families spend a larger percentage of their income on child care than higher income families. The percentage of income spent on child care for preschool aged children declines from about 25 percent of family income for those earning less than $1,200 per month, to about 6 percent of family income for those earning over $4,500 per month.[15]

Both federal and state subsidies for child care vary widely in amount and availability. Thirty-eight of the states that subsidize child care report long waiting lists, and many have given up even keeping such lists.[16] The General Accounting Office reports that more than half of all working families who meet the income requirements for child care subsidies do not receive any subsidy.[17] To get a child care subsidy today requires substantial good luck.

It is difficult to get total estimates on child care expenditures in the United States, but the total amount spent on child care for children under age six may total as much as $40 billion.[18] Somewhere between 70 and 75 percent of that amount is spent directly by families.[19] Government expenditures in the form of tax allowances and direct subsidies constitute about 25 to 30 percent of all child care expenditures. The federal government provides the vast majority of this amount. In 1997 the federal government's contribution to child care expenditures, including both tax allowances and direct outlays, totaled nearly $14 billion.[20] That amount is expected to grow to $17 billion by 2003, without any changes in federal law. This money is estimated to support child care for over 5 million children, half of whom are under age five. A tiny fraction, probably less than 1 percent, is contributed by employers, charities, and religious organizations.

In 1996 there were twenty-two separate federal programs (including tax allowances) supporting child care expenditures (down from ninety such programs identified in 1994).[21] A significant share of this federal funding takes the form of a block grant to states. Under this program the states now enjoy considerable flexibility, but the federal government does require that only families with incomes below 85 percent of state median incomes are eligible for these funds. At least 70 percent of the money must be spent for current or former TANF recipients or for families at risk of becoming eligible for TANF.[22] By contrast, the child care income tax credit and exclusion provide their greatest support to middle- and upper-income families (fig. 12.1).

Current U.S. child care subsidies represent a true hodgepodge of programs. The discretionary nature of much of this spending creates many in-

Fig. 12.1.   Tax reduction from the Child Care Tax Credit, by income

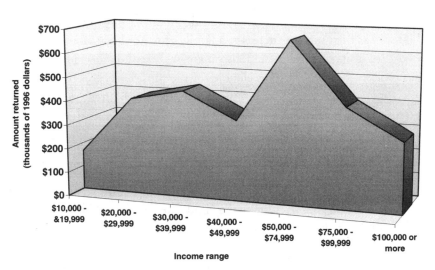

(*Source:* Joint Committee on Taxation, *Estimates of Federal Tax Expenditures for Fiscal Years 1996–2000,* JCS-21-95, table 2.)

equities. Some families obtain substantial subsidies, while others in similar circumstances obtain little or none. And although some programs are progressive, others provide their greatest benefits to the relatively well-to-do.

We propose to rationalize subsidies for child care expenditures in a manner similar to the way that Part B of Medicare finances physicians' services for the elderly, but at a lower level of subsidy. At the current level of expenditures, the federal government could pay 30 percent of each family's child care costs. (Although we would support a subsidy of 50 percent of the cost of adequate child care, to keep within current budget constraints we would begin with a less generous subsidy.) So that public subsidies will not vary depending on the type of care chosen, child care expenditures eligible for the subsidies will be limited to 30 percent of the estimated average costs for child care centers in the area where the worker lives. These data are already available; the Department of Health and Human Services currently determines what level of child care costs would cover 75 percent of the children being served in a locality. The department's data suggest that an average cost in the neighborhood of $400 to $500 a month per child under age six seems reasonable, although the actual level of eligible costs will vary with the age of the child and the type and location of the child care.[23] For children between ages six and thirteen who are in school, the amount eligible for the subsidy would be one-fourth of the base amount. Since families tend to buy more expensive child care as their income increases, a family's financial contribution to the child care of its children would also increase as its income increases, because the level of expenditures eligible for the subsidy is capped.

In Omaha, Nebraska, for example, child care for children under age six is estimated to cost about $417 a month. If a family spends that amount, $125 of the cost (30 percent) would be subsidized for each child. Families that spend less would receive a subsidy for 30 percent of the lesser amount. Families that spend more would still only receive the $125 monthly per child subsidy. Living in New York, of course, is more expensive; for someone who lives there, the child care cost would be about $625, and the subsidy would be $188 (for all parents who spend the average amount or more).[24]

Because the government now finances about 30 percent of total child care costs, this proposal will be no more costly than existing arrangements. It also would be quite easy to administer. Proof of expenditures would entitle the parent to the subsidy, and either vouchers or refundable tax credits could be used to deliver the subsidies. Tax credits seem to have greater political appeal. Compared to current arrangements, this scheme would provide far greater equity among families as well as a more progressive distribution of benefits. The large copayment by families would encourage them to seek good but economical care.

We considered, but ultimately rejected, an alternative form of subsidy for child care expenditures patterned after our proposal for health expenditures. With no greater aggregate public support than is now provided, we could ensure that on average families need not pay more than 25 percent of their income for child care expenditures for any children age five or younger and for after-school care for children ages six to thirteen. A maximum sliding scale limiting out-of-pocket expenditures on child care—along the lines of that described in our health proposal—could be provided, ranging in this case from 15–20 percent of income for low-income workers to a maximum of 30 percent for higher-wage workers. Alternatively, the program could employ a flat ceiling providing that child care expenses not exceed 25 percent of income.

Subsidies at these levels would require families themselves to contribute a greater proportion of child care costs than we proposed for health care, but families' control over child care expenditures often is greater than with health outlays. And like our flat percentage-of-costs proposal, the reasonably large copayment by families would make them cost conscious about child care expenditures, keeping a financial incentive to use grandparents, friends, or other relatives when they are available. Once the ceiling on the percentage-of-income expenditures were reached, however, parents would have no further incentive to be cost conscious.

This income-based sliding-scale scheme fits better with our basic principles of protecting families against large shocks to their income than does our proposal to subsidize a percentage of costs. It also would be more progressive than the constant percentage-of-outlays proposal we advanced. For example, family outlays for child care expenses of a single-parent family earning about the minimum wage would not exceed about $150 per month, no matter where they live.

Notwithstanding these advantages, we favor the constant 30 percent-of-costs subsidy, principally because of the substantial work disincentives that the income-based subsidy entails when combined with other income-based subsidies. This issue is taken up in detail in Chapter 14. For now, suffice it to say that we regard it as essential that social insurance programs be structured so that work pays—so that a family is made better off as its wages increase or when parents work more hours. In combination, income-based subsidies for child care and health (and perhaps housing) would fail that essential test. Because all of these subsidies would be withdrawn simultaneously as income increases, a family could actually be worse off earning $20,000 per year than earning $10,000 annually.

In addition, a subsidy for a flat percentage of child care expenses up to a ceiling is far easier to administer than income-based subsidies and also allows great flexibility in the mechanisms chosen to deliver the subsidy. Income-based subsidies are considerably more complex due to the difficulties in determining and verifying income. They may also carry a stigma that can be avoided by a more universal approach.

By helping to fund an essential and large expenditure for working families with children, child care subsidies are automatically targeted to children whose families need such care and are spending substantial sums obtaining it. In addition, there is evidence that subsidizing child care expenditures allows parents to earn more income. A study of low-income families in Dade County, Florida, where the typical family was composed of an unmarried single mother, age thirty-two, with two children, con-

cluded that an additional $40 of child care subsidy resulted in $60 to
$100 of additional wages.[25] The potential effect of child care subsidies in
stimulating additional earnings offers a further reason to prefer this
method of aiding low- and moderate-income families over wage subsidies.

### Funding the Opportunity Costs of Parental Child Care

By recognizing the need to provide some protection against excessive child
care costs, we do not mean to take a position that either denies the valid-
ity of decisions to exit the workforce (wholly or partially) in order to provide parental child care or underappreciates the economic costs of such
decisions (fig. 12.2). On the other hand, there is clearly some personal
value to raising one's own children. Thus, it hardly makes sense to pay
parents to raise their children as if they were just another commercial
child care provider.

Given these considerations, we propose to convert the current income
tax credits and personal exemptions for children into a refundable tax
credit for children that will provide $1,500 per year, per child to each fam-
ily with a child (or children) below the age of six. Between six and thirteen, the amount will be $750.[26] No credit would be provided for children
older than thirteen. Like unemployment insurance and Social Security

Fig. 12.2.    Women's wages over the life cycle with varying numbers of children

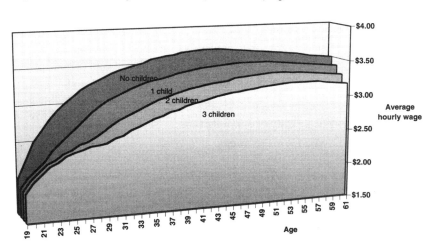

(*Source:* James P. Smith, "Women, Mothers, and Work," in Martha N. Ozawa, ed.,
*Women's Life Cycle and Economic Insecurity,* New York, Praeger, 1989, fig. 3.6.)

benefits under current law, these tax credits will be treated as taxable income to each family and some portion, therefore, will be taxed back—up to 40 percent at the highest income level. In addition, families that do use child care, and that are eligible for the child care subsidy, will have the value of their child care subsidies subtracted from the refundable tax credit. As the previous examples suggest, this means that families using full-time child care will not obtain any additional tax credit for children. We do not propose to permit double-dipping by providing benefits to families for the opportunity costs of parental care while simultaneously subsidizing those families for out-of-pocket costs of nonparental child care. Parents who use less than full-time child care or who are able to have their children cared for by a friend or relative will likely enjoy some benefit from the tax credit. The refundable credit will create benefits for stay-at-home parents roughly comparable to those who use child care, thereby ensuring that all families participate in a program aimed principally at a growing problem—the need for child care by employed parents and the sometimes crushing expenses that care entails.

It would be possible to expand on the refundable tax credit by doubling the amount if a child is disabled, thus substituting a more universal program for the current Supplemental Security Income program for disabled children. The arbitrariness of the tax credit amount, however, and the almost equal arbitrariness of multiplying it by any particular factor to take account of the increased out-of-pocket and opportunity costs of caring for a disabled child, argue against this course. While there is surely also considerable arbitrariness in the amount set for SSI disabled children's payments, by combining family economic status with the requirement to care for a disabled child, SSI for children is at least targeted to the families that are arguably in greatest distress. It also avoids an intrusive (and probably fruitless) search for the facts of just exactly how much each disabled child is costing his or her family in lost income and out-of-pocket expenses.

### Insuring against Large Housing Costs

To repeat what by now is a familiar refrain, the involvement of the federal, state, and local governments in the nation's housing policy is remarkably fragmented and complex. Yet the pattern of interventions is familiar. Direct expenditures have been targeted to certain lower-income families; tax expenditures have benefited primarily the more affluent. Both create substantial gaps in coverage. Less than one-third of low-income families actually receive direct housing subsidies; tax subsidies for housing do not help renters at all and for homeowners increase both as income increases and as their amount of borrowing grows. History, once again, offers the best explanation of how we arrived at the current situation.[27]

Today, there are nearly 1.5 million public housing units, most of which were built between 1950 and 1975. Given its age, much of this housing stock is in poor condition and will require substantial ongoing public funding if it is to be modernized or even maintained.[28] The annual cost of operating and modernizing public housing may have been as much as $5,100 a unit in 1997.[29]

There are also about 1.7 million units of privately owned, publicly subsidized housing. The owners of this property received subsidies for construction and in many cases continue to receive subsidies for operations and renovations. In addition, the income tax contains special benefits for the construction of housing for low-income residents.[30]

Beginning in 1974, federal housing policy shifted from building low-income housing units toward subsidizing housing expenditures of low- and moderate-income families. The 1974 Housing and Community Development Act provided that the federal government would give certain low- and moderate-income families vouchers and certificates, which pay the difference between market rents and 30 percent of the eligible families' income. The federal government establishes the maximum rent it will subsidize based on the costs of modest but decent housing in the relevant locality. The tenants choose the housing, and when the local housing authority approves the lease, the federal share of rents is paid directly to the owner. This program—"Section 8"—currently subsidizes housing expenditures of 1.5 million low-income families.[31]

In 1981, Congress limited eligibility for Section 8 subsidies to families earning 80 percent or less of an area's median income and provided further targeting of such subsidies to households classified as "very low income" (earning 50 percent or less of area median income). The Department of Housing and Urban Development (HUD) laid out $36 billion for housing assistance in 1997, an average of nearly $5,500 per housing unit.[32] The greater cost-effectiveness of vouchers is made clear by the fact that the $625 a month to finance the debt on a $100,000 unit exceeds the rent on a typical newly constructed unsubsidized apartment, ignoring any payment on principal.[33] In 1997, a total of 5.1 million households received some rental subsidy. (This compares to about 10 million households receiving food stamps and about 9 million family house-holds with annual incomes of $15,000 or less.)[34] But despite the existence of these subsidies, in 1995 more than 10 million households spent more than half their income on housing.[35]

HUD periodically reports to Congress regarding the number of house-holds who have no rent subsidy, even though they have incomes less than 50 percent of the area median income and pay at least half of that income for housing. Between 1974 and 1995, the number of households facing such serious housing burdens increased by two-thirds to 6 million house-holds. Of the 5.2 million households with incomes of less than 30 percent of the area median, 3.6 million, or nearly 70 percent, live in housing re-garded by HUD as structurally inadequate, yet pay more than half of their incomes in rent.[38]

For middle-income families, buying a home has become increasingly difficult. In constant (1996) dollars, the cost of a median-priced new home has gone from about $77,000 to nearly $136,000.[36] In 1976, almost half of all families had enough income to buy a median-priced home; in 1996, despite dramatically lower interest rates, only about one-third of families earned enough income to purchase such a home.[37]

On the tax expenditure side, the income tax has long contained subsi-dies to home ownership, principally in the form of itemized deductions for home mortgage interest payments and property taxes. Nearly 75 per-cent of the nearly $50 billion of taxes saved annually through the deduc-tions for home mortgage interest goes to families with $75,000 or more of annual income.[39] This is the nation's largest housing subsidy (fig. 12.3).

The relative success of the Section 8 voucher and certificate program for those families who are able to obtain such vouchers and certificates provides something of a model for insuring families against having hous-ing expenditures take too great a share of their incomes. But today only a small number of families who are eligible are lucky enough to obtain such vouchers. The Section 8 voucher and certificate program in 1996 served only about 1.5 million households, of which nearly 1 million were families with children. The median income of these households was about $7,000.

We propose making housing vouchers (or transferable tax credits) gen-erally available. As with child care, we propose a housing subsidy that would pay for 30 percent of each family's housing expenses, based upon the fair market rents for the median rental unit of the appropriate size in the area in which they reside. Once again the data are already collected by

Fig. 12.3.   Tax reduction from the home mortgage interest tax deduction, by income

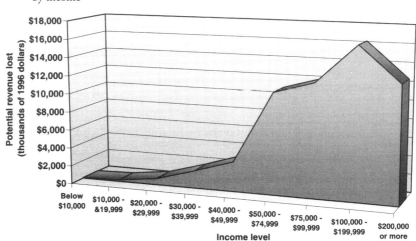

(*Source:* Joint Committee on Taxation, *Estimates of Federal Tax Expenditures for Fiscal Years 1996–2000,* JCS-21-95, table 2.)

HUD. In Omaha, where the fair market rent for a two-bedroom apartment is $503 a month, a family would receive a subsidy of $151. In New York, where the same kind of apartment rents for $862 a month, the subsidy would be $259. Since each family must pay 70 percent of its own housing costs, it will have a substantial incentive to economize, either by finding less expensive housing or moving to a less expensive location.

As with child care, we also considered structuring a housing subsidy based on income to protect families against large housing costs that cause income to be inadequate. The current Section 8 program provides a blueprint for such a program: housing subsidies could ensure that no family with children need spend more than 30 percent of its income on rent, based upon fair market rents.[40] But we regard the amount of housing costs as subject to greater family control than are health expenditures, and as with our child care subsidy, we are concerned about the incentives and administrative difficulties an income-based subsidy entails. These considerations provide four clear reasons to favor an expense-based rather than an income-based subsidy.

First, a subsidy based on the cost of housing provides families a reason to economize on housing expenditures in a way that a subsidy based on income does not. Once a family finds housing that will cost 30 percent or more of its income, it becomes completely indifferent to the amount of rent above that level. Every additional dollar will be paid by the government. Second, an income-based subsidy creates disincentives to earning additional income that a cost-based subsidy does not. With an income-based subsidy, thirty cents of every additional dollar of earnings will go to reduce the amount of housing subsidy. Economists typically regard this kind of subsidy reduction as equivalent to an additional 30 percent tax on earnings. As income-based subsidies accumulate, these disincentive effects compound and can become very serious indeed. Thus, we have limited income-based subsidies to the area where we regard them as most essential, to protect against large shocks to income due to poor health. Third, as we remarked earlier, cost-based subsidies are considerably easier to administer than income-based subsidies: the former require only proof of housing expenditures; the latter also demand determining and verifying income. Finally, cost-based subsidies have an additional advantage: unlike income-based subsidies, there are no marriage penalties.

As with payments to child care or health care providers, to obtain housing, prospective tenants must have the ability to guarantee rental payments to their prospective landlords. Such a guarantee cannot readily be accomplished through tax allowances directed to tenants, but instead requires either tax credits that are transferable to landlords or an expanded use of housing vouchers. As with Section 8, prospective tenants could obtain vouchers and transfer them directly to landlords, who would receive funds from the federal government. Alternatively, transferable tax credits might be used. Housing subsidies for homeowners could continue to be provided through tax offsets. We discuss further the administrative options for these programs in Chapter 14.

We believe that subsidies should be made equally available for renting and home ownership. We would provide subsidies in the same amounts for homeowners as for renters, that is, based on a percentage of fair market rents for the area in question. Monthly housing costs are often higher for owners, reflecting a combination of rental value and investment values. We believe that a social insurance scheme should be indifferent between owning versus renting but should subsidize shelter, not investment in housing.

Implementing our housing subsidy proposals requires (to say the least) substantial and controversial changes in U.S. housing policy. One approach would be to combine all housing programs into a universal housing insurance program. We estimate that subsidizing 30 percent of every child's housing costs would require an average of $2,000 to $2,400 a year for the 35 million U.S. households with children, or about $70 billion to $85 billion a year. In addition to redirecting direct government expenditures on housing to this program, funding a program this size, even just for families with children, would require restructuring a substantial part of the home mortgage interest and property tax deductions. These deductions, which benefit mostly upper-income families, must be converted into tax credits (or vouchers) that would be transferable to a lending institution. Tax credits (or vouchers) would be available for transfer either to landlords or lenders to fund 30 percent of each family's out-of-pocket expenditures on housing, up to a specified maximum outlay. While such a major reorientation of tax incentives for housing would clearly face serious political obstacles, redirection of these tax expenditure deductions is in the spirit of recent legislation that has capped deductions and targeted benefits more toward the middle class.

### REGULATORY CONSIDERATIONS

As we discussed in Chapter 9, subsidizing health insurance demands a considerable regulatory apparatus in order to keep costs under control. Utilization decisions are made as much (or more) by providers as by patients. And competition among providers has limited effects on prices. This is not true for either child care or housing. The markets for both are competitive, and utilization decisions are made by consumers. In this context, the public fisc can be protected effectively by a combination of co-payments and price caps based on existing market prices.

There is the temptation, of course, to engage in much further regulation to protect consumers against inadequate quality. Moreover, existing housing and child care subsidies, like existing public medical insurance provision, often combine quality regulation with social insurance protection. Subsidies are not available unless housing complies with local housing codes, and child care subsidies often require specified levels of "quality."

We do not view this combination of quality regulation with income supports as either necessary or desirable. Hence, as with our health insurance proposals, we would leave housing and child care quality regulation to the states and separate it from social insurance protections. These quality assurance policies are not directly relevant to social insurance purposes. And while the topic is too complex to permit treatment here, we believe that combining support with quality regulation has an expansive logic that leads to quality "floors" that are very close to market ceilings. The result is to require that subsidized parties consume "more" (in the sense of higher quality) of a particular good or service than they may desire. Surely that goes far beyond the goals that we have set for income support through social insurance.

## INSURING AGAINST PREMATURE DEATH OF A PARENT

In Chapters 10 and 11, we described a package of social insurance protections that provide protection against the loss of a parent's earnings due to unemployment and temporary as well as permanent disability. In this chapter, we have described wage subsidies provided via the EITC and the Food Stamp Program (or its cashed-out equivalent) and a redesigned TANF program to buffer long-term unemployment for parents. We have also constructed social insurance protections intended to ensure that children of a working parent or parents will not become deprived of a decent standard of living because health care, child care, or housing costs become unaffordable for their family.

This leaves, however, one significant gap in social insurance protections for young children: insurance against the premature death of a parent. For many children, the Social Security Act fills that gap. Children under age eighteen and students up to age nineteen are entitled to survivors' insurance benefits when one or both of their parents die prematurely. For workers who have paid Social Security taxes during any six quarters of the thirteen quarters prior to the worker's death, Social Security's survivors' insurance provides a monthly benefit equal to 75 percent of the monthly retirement benefit that would have been paid had the deceased parent worked at his or her current wage until retirement. Widows and widowers of deceased workers are also entitled to 75 percent of such a benefit. There is a maximum family survivors' benefit, limited to a total of 150 to 188 percent of the deceased worker's monthly retirement benefit.[41]

Social Security's life insurance protection, however, is often inadequate when a child under age eighteen experiences the death of his or her single parent. Here, the average monthly benefit of less than $500 per child per month simply will not enable the child to maintain a decent standard of living. While in some cases relatives may help support the child or the child may subsequently be adopted, it nevertheless seems appropriate for social insurance to offer greater protection against the premature death of a working parent when that parent's earnings are the sole source of family income.

We therefore propose to increase the monthly benefit in such circumstances to an amount equal to the amount that would be paid by Social Security's survivors' insurance if the deceased spouse had been survived by a widow or widower in addition to the child or children under age nineteen. We would implement this proposal simply by paying the widow or widower's benefit to the child's guardian, whether that caretaker is a relative of the child or an adoptive parent. When such children are in the custody of a state, which will often place them in a foster home, the state pays a fixed fee for their care to the foster parents. In these circumstances, we would pay the widow or widower's benefit to the guardian after offsetting the amount that the state pays to foster parents of children not eligible for survivors' insurance. This additional life insurance protection for orphans should cost very little.

### MAINTAINING PERSONAL RESPONSIBILITY: REQUIRING CHILD SUPPORT

We have proposed to restructure and expand the social insurance contract for families with young children because we believe that changes in family structure and labor markets demand that social insurance be strengthened for these families. Earning an adequate family income, even when one holds a full-time job, is particularly difficult for single-parent families. The growth in divorce rates and single parenthood have clearly reduced financial support from the nonresident parent. Married fathers contribute an average of 20–25 percent of their income to support their children, while nonresident fathers on average (including nonpayers) contribute less than 10 percent of their income.[42] Since 1975, Congress and the states have enacted a number of measures in an effort to identify fathers of unwed mothers and collect child support payments from absent fathers. Although many people were skeptical that these programs could be successful, child support collections have grown steadily since 1978 when

Fig. 12.4.   Child support collections

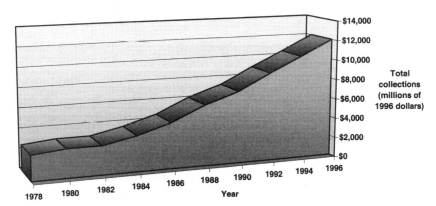

(*Source: 1998 Green Book,* table 8-1.)

these programs first became effective, principally because the IRS has been given the power to withhold child support payments (fig. 12.4).

A society that is prepared to require single mothers to work outside the home should also insist on the economic responsibility of nonresident fathers. Nevertheless, despite federal efforts, there remains great interstate variation in state requirements for child support, particularly at lower income levels.[43] A number of mechanisms for establishing and enforcing more uniform national child support requirements have been adopted, including establishment of a federal parent locator service, and others have been proposed. We need not rehearse these alternatives here. Our central point is a simple one: Enhancing the social insurance contract as we have proposed must be accompanied by additional efforts to improve the levels of personal responsibility of absent parents.

#### SUMMARY

When one looks at the circumstances of American families, particularly of its children, the gaps in current social insurance protection become apparent. Even when their parent or parents are working full-time, far too many children do not have a decent standard of living. We have proposed a social insurance program that has the potential to lift these children out of poverty and to protect virtually all families with children against the risk to their living standards due to disability, unemployment, premature death of a parent, or excessive levels of expenditures for health care, child care, or housing.

These protections are possible without increasing overall government subsidies, but they are not possible without revising priorities and reallocating expenditures. We are not sanguine that mustering a political majority for the kinds of policy shifts we advocate here will be easy, or even possible in the short run. Yet failing to address these problems threatens our nation's future.

Our proposals have important advantages by comparison with alternative strategies. We reward efforts at self-support without imagining that wage levels, even with wage subsidies, will be sufficient to provide adequate incomes for all families with children. We provide universal coverage but redirect existing subsidies for housing and child care to lower- and middle-income families. We do not create "cliffs," which halt social insurance support entirely at some specified level of income or assets, and thus penalize work by operating as if there is a magic difference between being one dollar below or one dollar above some predetermined level of adequate income. And we respect the desire of the more fortunate to assure that less fortunate families not only make ends meet, but do so while meeting their children's basic needs for shelter, medical care, and custodial care.

# Chapter 13 Retirement Security

That people are living longer and doing so in better health is an unambiguously positive development. But an increasing elderly population demands a substantial restructuring of the social insurance protections now available to retirees. Whatever increases in life expectancy occur, retirees must have enough income to live on, income unthreatened by the prospect of catastrophically expensive health care costs or unaffordable expenditures for long-term care. The challenge is to provide this retirement security without imposing a payroll tax burden on working people that they cannot afford or shifting needed resources away from workers or children.

Contemporary hand-wringing to the contrary, this challenge can be met if we are willing to take a realistic view of when retirement protections should begin, how inflation protections are calculated, and what the social insurance role properly entails with respect to medical care costs. We need neither abandon the elderly, beggar the future, nor drastically increase wage taxes to maintain our successful record of social insurance protections for retirees.

## SECURING RETIREMENT INCOME

For retirement income, there are two fundamental issues. First, what level of adequacy—what replacement of preretirement wages—should be guaranteed by Social Security (or an analogous government program)? Second, what role should the government play in mandating, subsidizing, and regulating retirement protections above the guarantee? These basic inquiries necessarily imply a third question: to what extent should we finance retirement income from payroll taxes on current workers (pay-as-you-go financing), and to what extent should the income of future retirees be prefunded either through surpluses in the Social Security Trust Fund or by individual or employer-based pension and retirement savings accounts?

Our answers are straightforward: first, no program of retiree income security worthy of the name can allow income protections to drop below current levels. That level of adequacy must be secured by governmental action that protects workers from both generalized inflation risks and the individualized risks inherent in both labor-market and capital-market returns. Second, because the current guarantee is far from munificent, government should have a larger role in mandating individual retirement savings and insuring broad participation in capital markets. Third, prefunding is not a silver bullet, but a mandated savings program that entails some prefunding can reduce the need for future tax increases or government borrowing. Prefunding may (or may not) increase the national savings rate, which may (or may not) in turn increase economic growth. If savings and growth increase, the pay-as-you-go parts of the program will turn out to be less burdensome on young and future workers.

## ASSURING ADEQUACY IN THE BASIC
## PENSION PROGRAM

### Maintaining a Secure First Tier

Retirement income, as we have explained, is currently provided through a combination of Social Security benefits, employer-based private pensions, and private savings, which together account for about 80 percent of all retirement income. The remainder comes from earnings of the elderly and public assistance programs of state and federal governments. Of the latter, Supplemental Security Income (SSI) is the most important, providing monthly income for 6.5 million needy elderly, blind, and disabled persons.[1]

Even though nearly all retirees today regard Social Security, along with Medicare, as providing a secure baseline of protection that will keep them out of the poorhouse, average Social Security benefits alone supply a far from luxurious lifestyle. Very few elderly are rich. In 1996 three-quarters of all Social Security recipients had total incomes—including their Social Security stipend—of less than $40,000 a year; more than half had incomes below $21,000 a year. Fewer than 12 percent of Social Security beneficiaries had annual family incomes of $60,000 or more (fig. 13.1).[2]

In the 1940s Congress allowed Social Security benefits to fall to levels that undermined its initial promise to ensure a basic guaranteed income for retirees. By the 1950s, it had restored Social Security to its central place as the foundation for an adequate retirement income. Since then, no

Fig. 13.1.    Income levels of Social Security beneficiaries

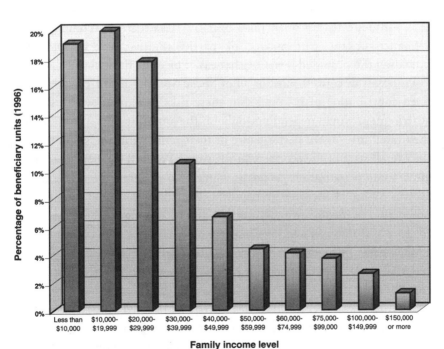

(*Source:* Social Security Administration, Office of Research, Evaluation, and Statistics, *Income of the Population 55 or Older, 1996,* Baltimore, Md., U.S. Social Security Administration, 1997, table II.2.)

Congress has seriously considered legislation to undermine the basic protections afforded by Social Security. Today, Social Security replaces 40 percent of wages on average, but retirement benefits are a higher percentage than that for low-wage earners and a lower percentage for higher-paid workers. We see no reason that the aging of America's population should become an occasion for undermining this fundamental protection.

The first priority in reconsidering social insurance for retirees should be to maintain the fundamental guarantee of Social Security. And because an essential element of this task is to replace a higher percentage of wages for retirees who had low lifetime wages and to insure that rises in prices do not erode income adequacy, a government program is inevitable.[3] A defined-benefit pension that is both mandatory and universal, and that is adjusted upward to reflect increases in prices, protects retirees against outliving their assets, whether due to their own myopia or inadequate wage income during their working lives, and against adverse postretirement changes in economic conditions. It thus provides baseline protection against the fundamental risks of retirement income inadequacy. All citizens—through federal financing—bear the risks that the economy's performance or the performance of particular investments will make providing the promised benefit either easier or more difficult.

Proposals to convert most or all of Social Security into a privatized defined-contribution plan would shift these risks to retirees, whose income at retirement would depend not only on the amounts they had saved and the overall investment performance of their retirement funds, but also on the overall state of the economy at the time of their retirement and thereafter. Some privatization proposals would also threaten the redistributive aspects of Social Security by requiring contributions equal to the same proportion of income from all workers and by linking retirement benefits solely to the amounts and investment performance of such contributions. Among other grounds, these proposals are supported because they will assure that each individual gets his or her "money's worth" from mandated contributions.

Because Social Security provides benefits equal to a greater proportion of lower-wage-earners' preretirement earnings than of higher-wage-earners' preretirement earnings, it is child's play to demonstrate that the retirement returns—or, to use today's fashionable phrase, the "money's worth"—of Social Security tax payments will be greater for low-wage than for high-wage workers. But measuring the equity of Social Security benefits solely in terms of individuals' returns on their taxes ("contributions")—what we earlier termed the "bank account" view of Social Security—mistakes Social Security's function. Social Security pensions not only mandate savings; they also insure against low lifetime earnings. Social Security should continue to provide basic income adequacy for low-income workers, contribute substantially toward insuring an adequate retirement income for moderate-income workers, and offer some assistance in maintaining the preretirement lifestyle of all workers. Proposals for structural changes in Social Security should be measured by how well they fulfill those tasks.

### Dealing with Fiscal Concerns

In sum, Social Security retirement benefits approximating current replacement rates must be preserved for future retirees. But adjustments should be made to put the Social Security Trust Fund on a sounder financial footing. As we discussed in Chapter 5, if nothing is done, seventy-five years from now the gap between promised benefits and taxes is projected to be about 6 percent of payroll. But relatively small changes now could protect the financial well-being of Social Security into the indefinite future.

The 1994–96 Advisory Council on Social Security made a number of consensus recommendations that we support. There is widespread agreement, for example, that the consumer price index overstates inflation, and that a more accurate measure would further improve the financial outlook for Social Security. One congressionally appointed commission, for example, claimed that the consumer price index overstated inflation by 1.1 percentage points a year, which if true would eliminate two-thirds of the actuarial deficit in Social Security.[4] Even if the index only overstates inflation by half that much, a correction of that magnitude would solve one-third of the projected long-term problem.

In addition, eliminating the current exemption of certain state and local employees is a sound idea, but one that Congress so far has refused to enact. Increasing the period of work for which benefits are calculated from the current thirty-five years to thirty-eight or forty years would be consistent with the expected length of working lives. There is some question, however, whether that move would save much money. Any increase in the number of years used to determine benefits would disadvantage women who leave the labor force to have and raise children. Upward adjustments in benefit levels to counteract these effects might eat up most of the projected savings.

Changing the investment mix of Social Security Trust Funds may also offer some potential financial advantages. Even if corporate equity investments were avoided, investing in commercial paper of financially secure corporations may offer some opportunity to increase returns while sticking to investments in debt instruments rather than equities.

We also favor going beyond Congress's 1983 action, which prospectively increased the Social Security retirement age from sixty-five to sixty-seven. This increase will be phased in beginning in 2002 and will not be completed until 2027.[5] Changes in life expectancies since 1965 have dramatically increased the proportion of life likely to be spent in retirement, if retirement begins at sixty-five. Hence, if Congress got the ratio of working to retirement years right in 1935, then it is appropriate to both accelerate the retirement age increases already enacted and extend the normal retirement age to at least age seventy.[6]

Many people may insist that such an adjustment is a "cut in benefits." We disagree with that characterization because we view the social insurance contract across generations as a commitment to provide appropriately for loss of labor income due to retirement, not a commitment to begin benefits at age sixty-five regardless of long-term changes in life expectancies and the health status of the elderly. In any event, a variety of proposals to increase the standard retirement age have been advanced, usually motivated by the desire to enhance the financial solvency of Social Security pensions (and sometimes Medicare). The Congressional Budget Office (CBO) has estimated that one such proposal—which would make the normal retirement age seventy for people born in 1967—would reduce annual Social Security outlays by about 8 percent in 2030, 18 percent by 2070.[7]

While increasing the normal age for eligibility for retirement benefits is an appropriate, if unpopular, policy change in light of changed circumstances since 1935, and one we endorse, we are skeptical that the financial savings will be as large as projected. To be sure, evidence from around the world makes clear that the age of eligibility for retirement income benefits has a major impact on when people leave the workforce.[8] The United States is no exception. And as figure 13.2 shows, the trend toward earlier retirement in the United States tracks the increased availability of Social Security pensions. But as the baby boomers age, we will likely face a labor shortage unless more workers delay retirement beyond today's norms. Higher wages are thus likely to keep more older workers in the workforce.

Fig. 13.2.   Labor force participation rate of men ages 55 to 64

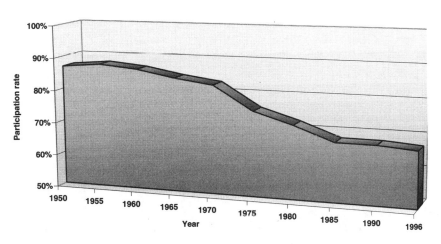

(*Source: 1998 Green Book,* table A-3.)

And, given increasing longevity and increasing years of good health, there is no good social reason for promoting workforce exit by older workers.

Social Security pension policy has recognized these trends by steadily decreasing the Social Security "penalties" on earnings after age sixty-five. We are rapidly moving toward, if we have not already achieved, actuarial fairness in the pension benefits awarded to workers retiring at different ages. It is now much easier for workers to delay retirement or to "partially retire" without giving up the economic gains from continuing work. Moving the "normal retirement age" back to age seventy merely accepts the reasonableness of expecting earnings to play a larger role as the fourth leg of the retirement security stool in a population that is both older and healthier than in the past.

Raising the Social Security retirement age will no doubt increase the contribution of earnings to the income of the elderly. But it will also put pressure on other social insurance programs—disability insurance in particular. Typically, when a government agency, such as CBO, estimates the savings from increasing the retirement age, it focuses on the financial balances of the Social Security Old Age and Survivors' Insurance Trust Funds. Raising the eligibility age for Social Security retirement benefits will improve the solvency of that fund, but will increase the costs of both unemployment and disability insurance. European nations have found that once people pass age sixty, disability benefits often substitute for pen-

Fig. 13.3. Beneficiaries receiving OASDI disability payments, by age

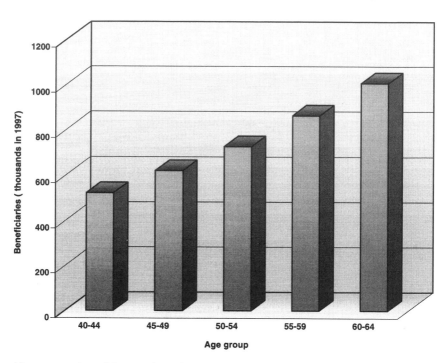

(*Source: 1998 Annual Statistical Supplement,* table 5.D4.)

sions. Our own experience also demonstrates that the proportion of the population claiming disability benefits increases steadily with age until retirement pensions become available (fig. 13.3).[9] Indeed, Social Security disability benefits were originally viewed as early retirement benefits and limited to persons over age fifty.

Our point is simply this: the lines between retirement, unemployment, and disability are necessarily blurry. Some of the savings from increasing the retirement age for Social Security pensions will show up as additional expenditures in the disability insurance and unemployment insurance programs.

All of these changes together may or may not fill the projected gaps in Social Security financing from now until 2075 and put the system on a totally secure footing thereafter. They will surely come close, as measured by conventional techniques of projection and the computations of the 1994–96 Advisory Council's and the 1998 Social Security Actuary's reports. But we think it would be foolish to believe that this contract across generations can, or even should, be fixed now for all time. The Social Security system itself has been in operation for less than seventy-five years. To believe that projections in 1925 would have captured the realities of the year 2000 is absurd. Changes should be made now that improve the fiscal soundness of the program and for which there are sensible, independent reasons of fairness and economy. Further changes will doubtless also be needed in the years ahead as experience proves more or less favorable than we now anticipate.

## MANDATING INCREASED RETIREMENT SAVINGS

Proposals to establish additional, mandatory personal investment accounts, which would accumulate assets throughout a person's working years, offer an opportunity to provide increased prefunding of retirement income protections and a mechanism for increasing personal responsibility for retirement.[10] Such accounts can also be used to reduce the moral hazard attached to other social insurance protections, such as unemployment insurance. We endorse the creation of mandatory individual accounts as a second tier of retirement security protection.

Mandatory personal investment accounts would have the important advantage of allowing individuals who would otherwise have little or no financial holdings to participate in the generally higher long-term returns of investments in corporate securities. This economic benefit could also be achieved if the Social Security retirement trust fund itself made investments in private instruments. Assuming that the same total amount were invested in the same manner, the aggregate, gross returns should be identical regardless of whether individual accounts or trust fund investment is chosen. Indeed, net returns would favor trust fund investment because the administrative costs of individual accounts are certain to be greater.

The politics of these alternatives, however, are quite different. Large direct government investments in corporate equities will tempt Congress to use these assets to further political goals.[11] Alan Greenspan, chairman of the Federal Reserve, regards proposals to insulate these assets from the political process as "not credible and not possible" and regards investment of Social Security Trust Funds in corporate equities as posing "very far-reaching potential dangers for a free American economy and a free American society."[12] Others disagree, but whatever one thinks of the substance of Greenspan's comments, they surely will affect the politics of investing Social Security funds in corporate equities.

Federal budgetary practice also suggests that Congress will find it difficult politically to apply large budget surpluses toward prefunding the Social Security Trust Funds without also using the accumulated funds to increase government spending or reduce income or estate taxes. There are various proposals to "wall off" Social Security from the rest of the budget, but they involve accounting systems that have been changed before and likely will be changed again.

Personal accounts involve a different political risk; experience with individual retirement accounts (IRAs) suggests that Congress will have difficulty limiting individuals' access to these funds prior to their retirement. So long as the basic defined benefit system remains in place, however, this risk does not threaten to make retirees worse off than they are today. Hence we believe that the most prudent course is to put in place supplementary, mandatory, personal investment accounts that will help fund both retirement and periods of unemployment.

While some proponents of individual accounts urge voluntary rather than mandatory accounts, experience with IRAs demonstrates that universality can be accomplished only by mandating that each individual have an account. Low-wage workers, however, will have difficulty funding such accounts if payroll deductions in addition to current Social Security and Medicare taxes are required. Thus some contribution from general revenues seems necessary. We are fortunate that the decade ahead is expected to produce federal budget surpluses (estimated by CBO in January 1999 to exceed $2.7 trillion in the following ten years) that might be used to provide that funding without requiring any tax increases.[13]

Mandatory personal accounts would provide for all workers a second tier of retirement savings that can fill gaps in current employer-based pension coverage—coverage that now strongly favors higher-paid, better-educated and older workers as well as workers employed by large firms (fig. 13.4).[14] Only those whose earnings place them in the top quintile of the income distribution curve currently receive as much private pension income as Social Security benefits, and participation by employees in employer-sponsored pension plans is declining.[15] Employer-sponsored plans thus seem to promise even less security for future retirees than for those now retired.

Indeed, providing true retirement income security for American work-

Fig. 13.4.    Participation in employer-based retirement plans, by firm size

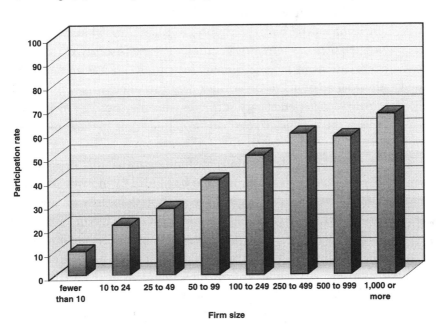

(*Source:* EBRI, *Databook on Employee Benefits,* 4th ed., table 10.5.)

ers through voluntary tax-subsidized and government-regulated voluntary employer-sponsored pensions is virtually impossible. These arrangements are vulnerable not only to shifts in employers' and workers' attitudes about deferred compensation and federal pension policies, but also to other forms of policy shock, particularly to changes in the tax laws. For example, the reduction in the top marginal tax rate in the 1980s from 70 to 28 percent decreased substantially the incentive for high-income employees to bargain for compensation in the form of pensions.[16]

The effectiveness of incentives for employer-sponsored pensions also depends significantly on the presence or absence of other tax-preferred alternatives. For example, if Congress were to replace the income tax with a flat tax, as such prominent advocates as Steve Forbes and Dick Armey have recommended, retirement income savings would enjoy no tax advantage over any other form of savings. This vulnerability to unrelated tax policy shifts is one of the reasons that some analysts have called for mandating employer and employee pension plans or contributions to individual retirement accounts.

Putting in place a mandated second tier of personal accounts is a challenging task. For example, unless funds are shifted from general revenues, such as by using federal budget surpluses to finance individual accounts, prefunding requires the current generation of workers to pay twice—first to maintain retirement income benefits for current retirees and again to fund individual accounts to cover their own future benefits.[17] But given the anticipated federal budgetary surpluses, this may not be a major obstacle. Indeed, the surplus makes this a propitious time to move to such a program.

There are many possible variations for funding mandatory personal accounts. For example, such accounts could be funded by individual contributions equal to 3 percent of wages up to the Social Security ceiling with individuals receiving either refundable income tax credits or credits for payroll taxes (either for the total or a per capita amount) made from each year's budget surpluses. This strategy would require total funding of about $115 billion a year, an amount equal to less than half of the total budget surplus projected by CBO in January 1999 for the next decade. Using more of the projected surplus might permit funding of accounts at 4 or 5 percent of payroll. Such an approach would put in place a permanent system for funding such accounts and create substantial pressures on Congress to maintain budget surpluses as offsets to these accounts rather than diverting such funds to other forms of government spending or to temporary tax cuts. As we described in Chapter 10, we would also use these accounts to fund copayments for our enhanced unemployment insurance protections.

Individual accounts raise a host of further implementation issues, which we discuss briefly in Chapter 14. One aspect of these arrangements, however, requires some comment here. It is critical both to minimize total administrative costs and to distribute costs in a manner that does not unduly burden small accounts. This requires limiting investment options in small accounts and restricting frequent investment changes, and argues strongly for government collection of the mandated deposits. Using the current system for depositing and reconciling payroll and income taxes would make it possible to withhold contributions to such accounts from wages without increasing paperwork burdens on employers.[18] Even with such accounts, employer-based pensions will remain an important source of retirement income, and private savings will continue to play a role in supplying additional retirement income, particularly for higher income retirees.

## REGULATING AND SUBSIDIZING RETIREMENT
## PENSIONS AND SAVINGS

Given our general skepticism about providing social insurance by subsidizing voluntary, employment-based fringe benefits and individual savings via tax deductions, we should take a dim view of employer-based pensions and IRAs. And were we starting the world anew, we would prefer to capture these tax expenditures in a more universal and progressive retirement scheme. But for several reasons we believe that the current approach needs only reform, not abolition.

For openers, employee pensions and IRAs together make a very substantial contribution to retiree income. The tax subsidy is substantial, but the contribution of the increased retirement savings to economic growth may be substantial too. Such growth itself produces additional tax revenue, and if it occurs, the actual net revenue cost of these tax incentives may be relatively small.

More fundamentally, many tax policy specialists believe that savings should not be taxed. From this perspective, the tax-favored status of employee pensions and IRAs moves our income tax in the right direction— toward a consumption tax. Income tax subsidies for retirement savings thus may be good tax policy.

Nor are we much bothered, as many analysts have been, by the steady move away from defined-benefit to defined-contribution plans in the nation's employee pension programs, a trend illustrated in figure 13.5. Workers face different risks in these two types of plans, but we are hard-pressed to determine which risks are preferable.[19] Hence regulatory interventions to require the choice of one type of plan seem to us unwarranted.

We would, however, make one important regulatory change: employees with defined-contribution plans (and less frequently with vested interests in defined-benefit plans) often take their accumulations in a lump sum when exiting employment with a particular employer. This cash can be spent on current consumption rather than being rolled over into another retirement account or annuitized. In fact, only about 40 percent of recipients of lump-sum payments from defined contribution plans roll over any

Fig. 13.5.    Distribution of total private pension assets

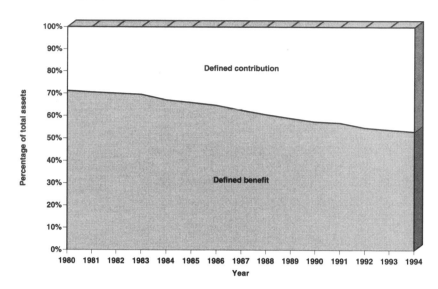

(*Source:* EBRI, *Databook on Employee Benefits,* 4th ed., table 11.1.)

portion into IRAs or another tax-favored retirement savings plan.[20] Both employers and employees like the option to consume previously tax-subsidized retirement accounts, but it is poor retirement policy. Tax-favored status for private retirement saving should require that funds actually remain available to provide retirement income—a mandatory rollover requirement. Such funds should not be allowed to be spent on vacations or a new car, or, in our view, even more "worthy" expenditures like education.

## HEALTH INSURANCE FOR RETIREES

While the aging of America's population creates serious, but solvable, financial difficulties for Social Security, its impact on Medicare spending is potentially disastrous. Medicare must contend not only with more beneficiaries who will draw benefits for longer periods, but also with rapidly rising costs per beneficiary. Even optimistic expectations about the health of the elderly and a slowing of health care inflation do not counteract the projection of extremely large growth in medical care costs for the population over age sixty-five.

For example, both the Medicare Board of Trustees and the Congressional Budget Office assume that the growth in Medicare and Medicaid spending per beneficiary will begin falling in 2008 and by 2020 will begin to mimic the growth in average wages.[21] In effect, this assumption makes all estimates of post-2020 growth in Medicare and Medicaid spending attributable purely to demographic pressures. This projected leveling and decline in the rate of health care spending, however, is anticipated to occur without specifying any policy changes that would produce these results. And, even through these rose-colored lenses, CBO projects that federal spending for Medicare and Medicaid will increase from 4 percent of GDP in 1998 to 10 percent by 2050.

Assessing the future growth of health insurance costs is further complicated by the artifacts of federal budget accounting for Part A (hospital insurance) and Part B (physicians' insurance) of Medicare. As we have explained, Medicare's Part A is funded from a payroll tax, now 2.9 percent of total wages, dedicated to a special trust fund; Part B of Medicare is funded from general revenues. The potential for budgetary smoke and mirrors in such a bifurcated accounting system is virtually unlimited. The 1997 Budget Act, for example, extended the solvency of the Medicare Part A Trust Fund by seven years principally by shifting the costs of many home health services from Part A to Part B of Medicare. This budgetary shift enabled the Medicare Board of Trustees to cut its estimate of the long-range actuarial deficit of the Part A Medicare Trust Fund by half (from 4.32 percent of payroll in its 1997 report to 2.10 percent in its 1998 report). More Medicare funding from general revenues may be a policy improvement, but we should not allow this kind of accounting to conceal the forthcoming financial pressures.

Funding is only one of the problems of our current programs of health insurance for retirees. As we have described in Chapters 7 and 9, Medicare provides limited health insurance, covering neither prescription drugs nor catastrophic health expenditures. Even with Medicare, the elderly pay substantial health care costs out-of-pocket. To qualify for Medicaid's broader health insurance protections, a retiree must become impoverished. In addition, the age-based requirement for eligibility for Medicare coverage creates a sharp split in U.S. health insurance coverage, explicable only by our nation's own peculiar political history. No other industrialized nation makes eligibility for health insurance protection turn on reaching a particular birthday.

We view the key function of health insurance within an overall scheme of social insurance protections as protecting income adequacy and supporting income stability in the face of large and unpredictable medical expenses. We believe that the proper role of health insurance protection is to protect Americans—retired or not—against potentially high costs of medical treatment that can cause a devastating decline in their standard of living. We would therefore restructure Medicare and Medicaid health insurance coverage for the population over age sixty-five in a manner similar to that proposed in Chapter 9 for the population under age sixty-five.[22] In that chapter, we described the details of income-based health insurance protection against catastrophic medical expenses. A similar program can protect those over age sixty-five without increasing either current or anticipated health care spending for this population, as long as other coverage is provided for long-term care to the elderly population.[23]

Although we believe that a shift of the sort we are urging here has great advantages, we have no delusions about the political difficulties of getting there. The path of American social insurance policy is littered with failed proposals for health insurance reform, and substantially revising Medicare will be a daunting political task. In 1988 and 1989, Congress had the gut-wrenching experience of enacting and then repealing a catastrophic health insurance supplement for Medicare beneficiaries.[24] Since 1989, whenever Congress has considered increasing payments required of Medicare beneficiaries or cutting their benefits, someone has shouted "Remember Catastrophic!" Any proposal is then promptly shelved. The failure of "Catastrophic" is a political lesson learned too well.

But despite the political obstacles, the course we are recommending here offers a genuine opportunity to improve health insurance coverage and its financing. The kinds of small adjustments that can solve Social Security's long-term financing gap are simply unavailable for retiree health insurance. Nor do we have any confidence in the recent congressional practice of looking to private health insurance trends as a blueprint for Medicare policy changes.[25] For example, substituting a private health insurance voucher for current Medicare arrangements, as some have suggested, will address the financial problems Medicare faces only to the extent that the eligible private health plans manage to limit rises in health care costs. We are far more confident that such a shift would improve current budgetary estimates than that it will succeed in solving the coming financial crunch.

Despite the large political difficulties, a major restructuring of retiree health insurance seems inevitable. Otherwise, substantial increases in direct cost sharing of medical expenses by the elderly population—expenses that are already large—will have to be coupled with major new inflows of financial resources from both payroll taxes and general revenues. These kinds of changes will undermine even the limited insurance protections that Medicare now offers and also threaten a political revolt by workers, who will be forced to pay extraordinary amounts to fund retirees' health insurance. Our health insurance plan, particularly as applied to retirees, may seem radical today; in the not-too-distant future, it could seem inevitable.

## LONG-TERM CARE

In combination, the general aging of the population and longer life expectancies—particularly the great growth in the population over age eighty—are increasing the need and expenditures for long-term care of the elderly. Long-term care encompasses a wide variety of circumstances, including long-term residence in a skilled nursing facility, community-based adult daycare, and both medical and personal assistance provided to the elderly in their homes, including help with such everyday activities as bathing, cooking, and shopping.

The elderly today obtain long-term care from their families and friends, community-based organizations, and skilled nursing facilities. This care is financed through their own resources, private long-term care insurance, Medicare, and most importantly, Medicaid. An extended period of long-term care, particularly when skilled nursing or other medical help is required, can be very costly, and many elderly confront the question of how to pay for it. In 1995 a year in a nursing home cost an average of $46,000.[26] Some elderly need only to pay for additional services to be provided to them at home or to reside in an assisted living facility, while for others long-term care expenditures are akin to other health care expenditures. Paying for long-term care is a problem not because the financial resources of the elderly are small compared to the financial resources of other age groups, but rather because long-term care is expensive and can quickly consume much or all of an elderly person's income and assets. In fact, Medicaid has become the safety net for the middle class as well as the poor. It finances some portion of nursing home care for nearly 70 percent of nursing home residents. As figure 13.6 shows, nursing home care ac-

Fig. 13.6.    Medicaid expenditures for elderly beneficiaries

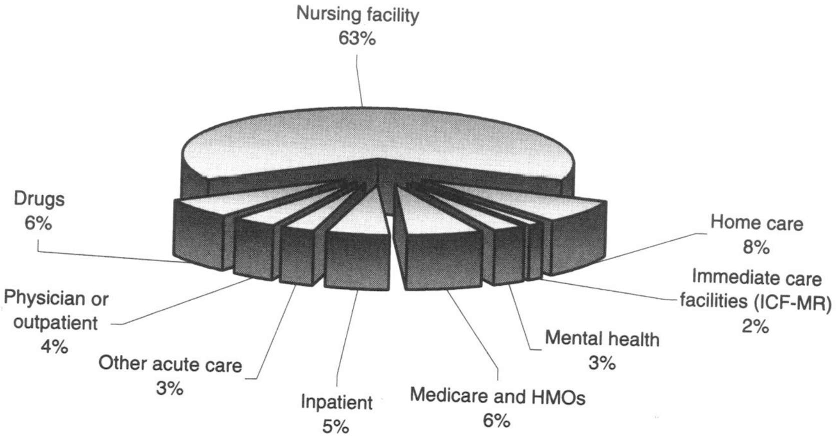

Nursing facility
63%

Drugs
6%

Home care
8%

Immediate care
facilities (ICF-MR)
2%

Physician or
outpatient
4%

Mental health
3%

Other acute care
3%

Medicare and HMOs
6%

Inpatient
5%

(*Source:* Joshua M. Weiner and David G. Stevenson, The Urban Institute, *Long-Term Care for the Elderly: Profiles of Thirteen States,* fig. 1. Calculations based on 1995 HCFA data.)

counts for almost two-thirds of all Medicaid expenditures for the elderly. When home health care is taken into account, the proportion rises to nearly three-quarters.

While some elderly persons will require enormous long-term care expenditures, others will need little. For example, at age sixty-five about one-third of all men and half of all women can expect to spend some time in a nursing home. About a quarter of these will spend less than three months there, about half will require at least a one-year stay, and about one-fifth will spend five or more years in a nursing home.[27] Nursing home expenditures for each elderly resident averaged nearly $8,000 in 1995, ranging from a low of about $4,300 in California to $15,400 in Minnesota. Spreading these costs across all elderly persons in each state lowers the average to less than $1,000, a low of less than $500 in Florida to a high of $2,400 in New York.[28] Long-term care, therefore, is a good candidate for pooling risks through insurance. Indeed, the financing of long-term care through public and private insurance has been growing rapidly. Medicare expenditures on home health care, for example, rose from just under $4 billion in 1990 to more than $18 billion in 1996—an annual growth rate of 29 percent—nearly triple the 11 percent growth rate for all Medicare spending. More than half of current expenditures for long-term care of the elderly have been financed in recent years through Medicare

Fig. 13.7.    Growth in sales of private long-term care insurance

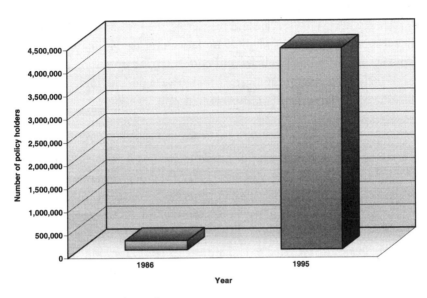

*(Source: 1998 Green Book, 1063.)*

and Medicaid. As the earlier numbers suggest, there is substantial variation across states. Although private insurance now pays for only a tiny
portion of all spending by the elderly on nursing home and home health
care, sales of private long-term care policies are growing rapidly (fig. 13.7).

Despite the growth in commercial sales of long-term care insurance, insurance companies are cautious about their ability to insure long-term
care. First, insurers are worried about adverse selection, where only those
persons most likely to need care actually purchase insurance. And both
public and private insurers are concerned about moral hazard problems,
where individuals use services that they otherwise would not have, simply
because they have insurance. If insured, a large number of people may
shift away from unpaid support services from friends or family members
in the home to paid care or assisted living arrangements. Insurance companies are also concerned that their liability under a long-term care policy
may be open-ended because much long-term care of the elderly is for
chronic conditions that will not be cured in their lifetimes.

Public insurance programs with responsibility for long-term care—
Medicare and Medicaid—have responded to fears of runaway costs by a
combination of traditional cost-cutting techniques: limiting the supply of

nursing homes, and cutting reimbursement rates. Insurance companies are responding to these risks by limiting their liability to fixed amounts for each day of covered service and restricting the number of days covered. They also are engaging in medical underwriting to eliminate risky cases before issuing individual policies and concentrating on selling group policies, principally to large employers. Most private policies include inflation adjustments, but these inflation-protected policies require substantial increases in premiums.

The cost of commercial long-term care insurance varies dramatically with the age of the purchaser. For example, in 1995 a policy paying $100 a day for nursing home care and $50 a day for home health care (with a twenty-day deductible period and an inflation adjustment) sold for an average of $798 to people age fifty, $1,881 to people age sixty-five, and $5,889 to people age seventy-nine.[29]

Private insurers have tried to expand their market for long-term care insurance by concentrating their marketing efforts on employers as a way to attract younger workers with low levels of risks into the risk pool. Congress helped facilitate these sales in 1996 when it extended the favorable income and payroll tax treatment applicable to health insurance and health care expenditures to commercial long-term care insurance policies.[30] Congress also extended the favorable income tax treatment previously accorded to private life insurance to accelerated death benefits received by people eligible for long-term care insurance exclusions and to terminally ill persons.

We are skeptical, however, that this expanded voluntary tax-subsidized program encouraging employers to insure long-term care—or indeed any voluntary program—will prove to be an effective policy response. Coverage will inevitably be spotty and will tilt toward those with high incomes. If employer-based, it also will favor those who work for large employers. Moreover, in the long-term care context, younger people are understandably short-sighted about their potential need for such care during their eighties. Even with a tax subsidy, very few young people are likely to want to purchase long-term care policies. Moreover, many people mistakenly believe that Medicare or their Medigap insurance policies will cover their future long-term care costs.

Our current long-term care social insurance package can be pictured as a four-legged stool, with Medicaid paying the expenses for poor people and many middle-class elderly who quickly become poor as a result of a nursing home stay. Medicare contributes principally to short-term nursing home stays but increasingly also to home health care for chronically ill patients. Voluntary tax-subsidized private insurance provides long-term care for a small number of people, and private savings finances home health care and nursing home care for higher-income and wealthier retirees. This is neither an adequate nor a prudent social insurance program.

Medicaid generally does not cover nursing home care for single people who have more than $2,000 in countable assets, but it still provides most public payments for nursing home care.[31] A medical care program for the poor has taken on this role in part because many of the elderly now using Medicaid coverage of nursing home care were middle class, at least prior to entering a nursing home. In addition, Medicaid's assets and income tests have encouraged creative "estate planning"—early transfers of assets to family members in order that long-term care spending not consume assets that had been intended to be used for gifts or bequests.[32]

A handful of states have attempted to protect their Medicaid programs by enhancing the appeal of commercial long-term care insurance. Elderly people are encouraged to purchase insurance based on the level of assets that they wish to protect rather than buying an open-ended long-term care policy.[33] For example, in California individuals may decide that they wish to protect $75,000 of assets and purchase a long-term care policy with a ceiling of $75,000 of coverage for actual long-term care expenses. In New York, residents can protect an unlimited amount of assets by purchasing three years of long-term care coverage. Eight states now extend Medicaid long-term care protections to persons buying such insurance coverage and increase their allowances of assets for Medicaid eligibility by a dollar for each dollar of private long-term care insurance payouts. In these states, Medicaid coverage for long-term care kicks in after private policies have been exhausted.

Although these programs have so far enjoyed very limited success—of the more than six million elderly residents of New York and California, only 17,000 have purchased private long-term care policies—we won't know for some time what effect this approach will have on the market for commercial long-term care insurance or on Medicaid financing requirements. To date, their prices have been high, and these Medicaid linkage programs have been targeted to persons in their early years of retirement, who typically will not require long-term care services until they are age eighty or older.[34]

The relatively benign demography we have experienced to date has made long-term care expenditures (barely) manageable within the contours of existing programs. But the forthcoming increases in the elderly population, particularly of the "old" elderly (over age eighty), threatens to produce a very large financing burden. One study estimates that long-term care expenditures will nearly double as a share of GDP and triple as a percentage of payroll in the next fifty years, rising from less than 2.5 per cent of payroll today to 7.75 percent in the year 2048.[35] Clearly, imposing a payroll tax this high on workers to finance long-term care expenditures of the elderly is neither wise nor sustainable public policy.

The challenge is to design a method of prefunding and insuring long-term care expenditures. There are two basic approaches: requiring universal purchases of a specified level of private long-term care insurance, or instituting a prefunded public long-term care insurance program. If private insurance coverage to protect a specific amount of assets from exhaustion by long-term care expenditures were made mandatory for the entire adult population, it would be relatively inexpensive, even for the population currently between age fifty-five and sixty-five. Indeed, for the under fifty-five population, coverage would be cheap. Universalizing long-term care insurance would enable people to cover the risk of long-term care expenditures without experiencing a major shock to their standard of living or impoverishing themselves.

To implement universal coverage of long-term care insurance, our first choice would be to add long-term coverage to the basic health insurance program for all persons under age sixty-five that we outlined in Chapter 9. Enforcement would piggyback on enforcement of the health insurance mandate, and long-term care premiums would be subsidized out of general revenues in a manner similar to the basic health care premiums.

We are not confident, however, that our health care insurance program will be embraced by Congress, and if not, enforcing mandatory purchases of long-term care insurance alone would be difficult and costly. As an alternative, adding prefunded long-term care insurance protection to Social Security could be financed by very small addition to payroll taxes, no more than 0.5 percent.[36] This method of financing future long-term care expenditures for all of the nonelderly population would be simpler and require fewer administrative expenses than mandating purchases of commercial long-term care insurance. The worry in this case is that, even when such amounts are put into trust funds and annual statements of benefits are provided to beneficiaries, the prefunding will become an illusion, simply another way to finance increased government expenditures. Prefunding in government accounts always carries this risk. On balance, however, we believe that the best approach would be to finance long-term care by an almost invisible addition to FICA taxes for the current population under age sixty-five and have the government use the funds to purchase long-term care insurance for individuals through private insurance companies.

In any event, failing to put in place now a mandatory universal prefunded long-term care insurance program guarantees that future long-term care expenditures will become a huge element of federal and state budgets. The nation will not abandon lightly the social insurance protection that Medicaid now offers to those who find themselves impoverished by long-term care expenditures. In fact, as the over-eighty population increases, pressures will build to fund more widespread and generous long-term care coverage. Funding that care on a pay-as-you-go basis from the then-working population will be expensive and unfair. Only by putting a mandatory program in place today can we avoid major financial stress in the future.[37]

### SUMMARY

We cannot be sure today exactly how much the elderly population or individual life expectancies will increase. We can, however, be relatively certain that our population will be older in the future and that we can expect to live longer than we do today. We must prepare for the forthcoming demographic shifts by firming up social insurance protections for the elderly. The one thing we cannot afford to do is to wait until the aged population finds itself in dire need of cash infusions from the then-working population. By acting promptly, we can, with relatively small adjustments, protect Social Security benefits into the indefinite future. We can also put in place a mechanism for funding individual savings accounts that over time will create large aggregate resources to finance the necessary expenditures of a future elderly population.

Protections against the costs of health care and long-term care for seniors are inadequate, and without major changes they will be even less adequate in the future. We have proposed here major revisions to these policies that will offer greater security against large health or long-term care expenditures that otherwise would threaten retirees' standards of living. We also would put these protections on a sounder and fairer financial footing. The kinds of changes that we have advanced may seem dramatic, but a failure to move now in these directions will greatly increase the risks of either significantly underinsuring the elderly population in the future or putting unwarranted (and, perhaps, politically unacceptable) burdens on subsequent generations of American workers.

Part Four **Institutions and Politics**

# Chapter 14  Institutional Commitments

Social Security pensions are America's largest and most popular instance of social insurance. The pension program's structure—a tax on wages, put in a federal trust fund, to finance current and future benefits based on levels of prior wages—is one way of providing social insurance. But that structure neither accurately describes the existing techniques for providing social insurance to American families, nor properly dictates those available to us. As we have shown, existing programs reveal a complex set of social insurance arrangements, including both "public" and "private" provision, as well as a variety of methods of finance and administration by states and the federal government.

Our criticisms of existing arrangements and our proposals to improve them also belie the notion that effective reform lies in the direction of some universally applicable fix for family economic security. While we have had much to criticize in existing programs, those criticisms have been driven by two considerations: first, our insistence that the unitary goal of social insurance is protection against income loss upon the occurrence of specific risks; and second, functional concerns of adequacy, fairness, and afford-ability, not a distaste for heterogeneity.

But this is not to say that in social insurance design, anything goes. Our reform proposals have been guided by a set of principles for the design of an effective system of social insurance. Many of these principles were enunciated earlier in rather abstract form. We return to that topic now, using more concrete illustrations and sometimes different labels as a way of highlighting some important lessons that we believe should be drawn from the whole of our discussion.

### PURPOSES FIRST, TECHNIQUES SECOND

That you should know what you're trying to do before deciding how to do it is hardly a startling proposition. Our quarrel with what we have termed the "conventional conception" of social insurance could be characterized as a criticism of defining social insurance as a set of common techniques (universal coverage, contributory finance, income-related benefits, and so on) rather than as a set of common purposes.

We have approached social insurance by trying to understand its essen-tial social purpose—the provision of a degree of income security due to risks common in a dynamic market economy. Moreover, it seems clear that income security has two elements: the protection of income against absolute inadequacy, and the protection of income streams from sudden termination or massive diminution because of risks that are commonly shared but uniquely distributed.

Looked at in this way, and in the context of a modern market economy, social insurance is directed to a relatively small category of risks that de-tach workers or their families from their income-producing activity. Age (either youth or old age), death, illness, injury, and involuntary unem-ployment thus describe the major categories of risks that are relevant to the design of a social insurance system. This vision of social insurance has a number of advantages as one moves on to consider the ways in which such insurance might be provided to protect against the relevant risks.

One of the principal advantages is the ability to paint a clearer picture of what is needed in order to provide true security. In our discussion, this has been particularly evident with respect to the treatment of children. For once it is understood that age limits labor market participation both at the beginning and at the end of life, it is easy to understand why the protection of children is as much a task of social insurance as is the protection of the elderly. The techniques necessary to provide these protections will clearly differ across these two groups. But that techniques necessarily vary does not justify the view that social insurance should be designed to deal with age-related income insecurities at one end of the life cycle but not at the other. Indeed, we are convinced that the walling off of "social assistance" from "social insurance," and the consignment of most children's programs to the former category have contributed to the appalling statistics on childhood poverty in the United States.

Second, looking first at purposes permits a clearer focus on what the necessary function of social insurance should be. In the case of children, for example, it is the protection of those who are too young to work from the potentially negative impacts of their dependency. The design problem then becomes how to accomplish that purpose without severe adverse consequences on other social goals—in particular, how to maintain the personal responsibility, work effort, and self-respect of the child's parents. These latter considerations clearly place constraints on the techniques by which one would support the income of children. But these constraints should not be confused with the basic purposes of the relevant programs.

The benefits of greater clarity about purposes is obviously not limited to programs dealing with childhood poverty; it has also been important to our discussions of health insurance, unemployment insurance, and workers' compensation. Because we view these programs, like all social insurance programs, as directed at income security, we treat the provision of health care, the improvement of managerial capacities to maintain a stable workforce, or the suppression of work-based accidents as independent social purposes. It is possible, maybe even sometimes necessary, to pursue these purposes in part through the design of social insurance regimes. But whenever their pursuit undermines the adequacy and effectiveness of social insurance, we would divorce these purposes from social insurance provision.

Third, putting purposes first provides a more complete understanding of what is currently being done. This nation's social insurance programs protect family income through a remarkable array of governmental interventions that augment individual or family income. Some of these have traditionally been excluded from social insurance analyses because they involve testing of income or means. Others have simply been ignored because the transfers are implicit and occur through provisions in the tax code.

Once one views all these efforts as a part of a general social insurance regime, it becomes possible to ask a crucial question about each of our current programs: How successful is it in providing income security for American families? The answer is that many of our current efforts fail miserably in terms of basic criteria, such as universal availability, protecting those who need it most, stability and reliability over time for individuals and families, and fairness in financing benefits.

Fourth, a focus on purposes and an evaluation of techniques in terms of those purposes produces a much richer kit bag of means by which we can reach our true security ends. Providing income security against massive health care costs does not have to be accomplished by providing insurance—mandates with subsidies can work as well. Insuring decent shelter for children does not require either poorly targeted tax deductions or nonuniversal voucher programs; a universal tax credit approach may work better.

Finally, a unified look at the purposes of social insurance makes clear that social insurance is not just about maintenance or protection of the status quo, as private insurance is, but also about the assurance of adequacy in an economic system where the returns to a common enterprise (productive activity) end up in individual pockets for a host of relatively arbitrary, as well as nonarbitrary, reasons. Put another way, social insurance allows us to accept having only some members of society succeed financially in an environment where both luck and effort make a difference. The fact that social insurance redistributes across families, rather than just across time within families, is not a dirty secret to be hidden in the details of taxing and benefit formulas. Social insurance planners should not conceal what they are doing, but should address what level of redistribution and what form is necessary and fair in the economy of today and tomorrow.

## INCOME SUPPORT DOMINATES
## MARKET REGULATION

Although we may chafe at the restrictions that collective arrangements require, there are more and less restrictive ways to design them. As we suggested much earlier, we believe that income security arrangements of the sort that we have analyzed and proposed in this book are superior to other techniques of market intervention—techniques that would leave the economy as a whole less flexible and resilient. For example, regulating wage levels directly, or through minimum wage requirements, is one way to attempt to raise low lifetime wages. Similarly, threatened domestic industries and labor organizations often urge erecting barriers to international trade to protect employee job security and perhaps also to maintain wage levels.

Certainly the easy movement of goods and capital across international borders can threaten the job security and wage levels of some American workers. But we believe that the benefits of international trade outweigh its costs. International trade lowers the prices of goods and services, thereby making every dollar of an American family's income go further. Moreover, holding back the tide of cheaper goods from elsewhere, while occasionally successful in the short-run, ultimately requires dikes that are too high to be maintained. Robust economic growth—which is fostered by flexible markets—offers the best protection against stagnant wages and unemployment.

Employers will also frequently shift the costs of employer mandates—such as minimum wages and trade barriers—to workers, either by keeping the other parts of wage packets lower than they otherwise would be, by hiring fewer new workers, or both. Benefiting one low-wage employee at the expense of another provides true security to neither; it is a zero-sum game, an arbitrary and regressive way to finance social insurance.[1] To the extent possible, we have avoided interfering directly with factor prices or factor mobility as a method of providing family income protections. For example, we have urged increasing the Earned Income Tax Credit rather than the minimum wage and providing broader unemployment insurance coverage rather than restricting employers' ability to terminate employment. Inflexible labor market protections and restrictions will ultimately undermine rather than contribute to Americans' security.

## COUPLING UNIVERSALITY AND CONTRIBUTORY FINANCE WITH REDISTRIBUTION

In his effort to enact Social Security and to secure its future, Franklin Roosevelt insisted that the payroll taxes imposed on virtually all employees and their employers to fund benefits to retirees and survivors be called "contributions." Individuals were supposed to view their payroll reductions as contributing to their own retirement, not as transferring money to someone else. The same approach was employed by Congress in the 1950s and 1960s when it enacted disability insurance coverage and financed hospital coverage (Medicare, Part A) through additional taxes on wages.

The characterization of these wage taxes as "contributions" has had two salient political consequences. First, it has produced in every retiree (whether by reason of age or disability) a genuine sense of entitlement. Until now retirees at every income level have received far more in Social Security benefits than they paid in taxes, but this has in no way shaken their confidence that they have "earned" whatever they are receiving. As long as benefits were going up, Roosevelt's rhetoric succeeded remarkably well in masking Social Security's redistribution of income to retirees who had experienced low lifetime wages.

But today that very success threatens the political stability of Social Security. High-wage workers are asking whether they will get their "money's worth" from their Social Security contributions, whether they might do better by withdrawing their "contributions" from this social insurance program and placing the same money in the stock market. As we have shown, this is the wrong question, but calling taxes contributions makes it a natural one to ask.

Medicare payroll taxes have never quite fallen into the same trap. Given escalating health care costs, it is impossible to know how much money one needs to put aside today to fund hospital insurance during retirement. Perhaps more importantly, until the cap on wages subject to the Medicare tax was raised in 1990 and removed completely in 1993, this was a relatively small tax for all workers. Now, however, some high-wage earners are paying Medicare taxes greater than their Social Security taxes. So far this has not inspired a tax revolt by the rich, but we would not be surprised at such a turn.

Because wage taxes have grown so rapidly in recent decades—so that they now constitute a greater burden than income taxes for many middle-income individuals and families—and because we see no reason that growth in and earnings from capital should be exempt from financing social insurance, we have generally resisted increasing wage taxes to finance better social insurance protections. On the rare occasions when we have recommended doing so—such as to finance short-term disability insurance and long-term care for workers now under age sixty-five—the increases have been very small. And in the latter case we also have insisted that benefits be prefunded.

Limiting taxes on wages necessarily increases reliance on general revenues as a source of social insurance benefits. Using general revenues is nothing new. The large government contributions to Medicare physicians' insurance (Part B) have always been funded from general revenues, and Earned Income Tax Credits reduce general revenues, even when their explicit purpose is to offset Social Security and Medicare taxes on low-wage workers. Income taxes imposed on Social Security beneficiaries have been transferred from general revenue accounts to the Social Security or Medicare Trust Funds, and the use of general tax surpluses to bolster the Social Security Trust Fund seems overnight to have achieved the status of bipartisan consensus. Equally important, a large proportion of American social insurance spending has been financed out of general tax subsidies for pensions and health, disability, and life insurance.

Because capital income tends to be concentrated among higher-income people, general revenue financing at the federal level, which involves income, capital gains, and estate taxes, tends to be more progressive than financing through taxes on wages. Greater progressivity does not, however, flow inevitably from using general revenues. As we have seen, current general tax subsidies to "private" social insurance are regressive. Our proposals for health insurance, housing, and child care subsidies use general revenues in a more progressive fashion. For us the critical point is to combine individual or family responsibility with the socialization of risks in ways that maintain a sense of universal participation, avoid we versus they politics, and fulfill the redistributional purposes of social insurance. These objectives can be accomplished in part by recognizing that "contributions" are made in a number of ways, not just by payroll taxes.

For example, to obtain physicians' coverage under Part B of Medicare, people over age sixty-five must pay a portion of the cost of their insurance premiums—currently about 25 percent—with the remainder financed from general revenues. Having made such contributions, the elderly feel every bit as entitled to their Medicare physicians' coverage as to their hospital coverage, even though they must know they are paying only a fraction of its cost. When health services are needed, additional payments are sometimes also required. To be sure, Medicare's Part B financing raises serious questions about the appropriate distribution of financial burdens. By providing a subsidy this large while avoiding any link between a person's income or wealth and the premiums required, middle-income workers sometimes pay to insure rich retirees. Perhaps this distribution of burdens and benefits is offset somewhere else in the system, but we are skeptical.

As our proposals demonstrate, we believe that social insurance, including health insurance for the elderly, should be financed progressively. But each person should be required to contribute to his or her package of protections. When cash transfers are involved—as with Social Security for retirees, disabled persons, and survivors; temporary assistance to needy families; and unemployment insurance—contributions necessarily occur through past and future tax payments. In the cases of retirement and unemployment, we would bolster individual responsibility by also requiring individuals to fund social insurance savings accounts.

When social insurance protections are provided in-kind—as we have recommended for health insurance, child care, and housing—individuals should generally be required to contribute commensurate with their ability to pay. Progressive financing of the subsidies provided to these goods and services is itself a mechanism for sharing economic risks. Those who avoid such risks—those whom the market rewards with high levels of income, or wealth—pay more; those who do less well are required to pay less. In addition, there are substantial copayments connected to our consumption subsidy proposals. We require some contribution from everyone, with the contribution required rising gradually as the family becomes financially stronger.

Varying social insurance subsidies according to income or wealth can be administratively challenging, and can produce high implicit tax rates on earned income. A flat per capita subsidy of the Medicare Part B variety is considerably easier to implement and avoids these work disincentive effects. These multiple considerations have driven us to propose a very mixed system of "contributions" that combines proportional payroll taxes, progressive income taxes, income-tested subsidies, and flat percentage-of-cost subsidies along with substantial copayments. Overall we believe that this produces an appropriate balance between responsibility and redistribution.

Critics of means-tested programs have long argued that a sense of universality—of everyone in the same boat—is critical to the political legitimacy of social insurance provision, and that means-tested programs are not universal in this important sense. This is a conceptual error, but it may also be a political truth. If means-tested benefits are designed as entitlements, everyone is in principle eligible to participate if their incomes are low enough. And, if we view society from an *ex ante* perspective (before we know who we are and what our family and life circumstances will be), each of us has the same probability of making use of such programs as anyone else.

Nevertheless, we clearly do agree in part with those who oppose conditioning benefits on income or wealth: means tests are difficult to implement, create significant suspicion of fraud, are likely to result in high implicit tax rates, and lend themselves to a we-they form of politics. However much we may ground arguments of principle in terms of a hypothetical social contract that makes actual economic positions morally arbitrary, it is hard to maintain that detached spirit of common fate and common purpose in day-to-day political life. Any social insurance program should, therefore, limit the use of explicitly means-tested interventions.

Better targeting of benefits to assure adequacy is at the heart of social insurance provision in all programs. The trick is to design programs that achieve the broadest possible participation in receiving benefits and that "means test" or "income test" in nonintrusive ways. Social Security and many of our existing disability insurance programs do just that. But in our view, many supporters and analysts of Social Security protest too much that these programs provided everyone with an "equitable return on their investments." When people discover that redistribution is actually going on, they may regard themselves as having been subjected to some elaborate governmental fraud. We must face up to the redistributional purposes of social insurance and engage in a more illuminating debate about how best to organize those transfers.

When judged by the criteria of universality and distributional fairness, many current programs do a very bad job. Subsidies for health care, housing, and child care are embedded in the tax code in ways that produce, and simultaneously conceal, regressive distributional consequences. Meanwhile programs for the poor in these same areas, such as Medicaid, draw arbitrary income or asset lines above which they provide no assistance. In addition, when such programs are structured as discretionary grants (for example, housing and child care subsidies) they leave many of the poor and all of the middle class without assistance.

By contrast, our proposals are universal entitlements and provide progressive benefits that include the struggling middle class. As might be expected, this approach yields major benefits for those poor families who are now excluded from discretionary housing and child care programs and for all working families who are now receiving little or no support for their medical, housing, or child care expenses. The "lucky poor," those who currently receive nonuniversal discretionary subsidies, may do less well under our proposals, as will the affluent who benefit most from current tax expenditures. But that is to be expected in programs designed to broaden coverage without spending a lot more money.

### DEVOLVING THE RIGHT FUNCTIONS

When the Republicans captured a majority of both houses of Congress in 1994, they started a devolution—a transfer of responsibilities from the federal to state governments, and from collective governmental arrangements to individuals or families. While this devolution has occurred in a variety of contexts, it has been especially vigorous with regard to social insurance protections for the poor. Congress capped federal financial responsibility for both welfare and Medicaid and gave state governments greater discretion over who is covered and how. It also insisted that states shift responsibilities to individuals through time limits on supports and enhanced work requirements.

Increasing state responsibility was driven both by ideology and by federal budgetary politics. Some key politicians seem to believe that state governments always function better than the national government, and that even if they do not, the Constitution commits us to a national government of quite limited power and functions. This, after all, was the constitutional vision that originally located responsibility for unemployment insurance at the state level. An opportunity to shift additional responsibility to the states arose when Congress and the president agreed to make balancing the federal budget their highest domestic policy priority. Assuring balance between the revenues and expenditures of the federal budget remained elusive as long as open-ended federal commitments to fund welfare and Medicaid remained in place. But it was politically impossible to cap the federal contributions to these programs without giving the states far more control over how to spend the money.

Locating financial responsibility for basic social insurance protections at the state level is a mistake. Not only does it have the potential for inducing destructive competition—a "race to the bottom"—but it also often makes a family's economic security depend on which bank of the river they call home.[2]

In contrast, creating a national risk pool spreads economic risks across the entire country. Originalist constitutional scruples notwithstanding, we have long since committed both the power and responsibility for our economic well-being to the federal government. When things go well, we (perhaps erroneously) credit the president, the Congress, and the Federal Reserve. When economic misfortune strikes, these same actors are blamed because we understand ourselves to be participants in a national economy over which the national government exercises the most important controls. Large state-by-state variations in social insurance protections are difficult to justify given that reality.

Financing basic social insurance coverage should be done at the federal level. If particular states wish to top off social insurance coverages for their residents, fine, but we do not believe that relying on the states as the first line of social insurance finance is wise. Entities that are constitutionally barred from printing currency, regulating interstate commerce, or controlling immigration are simply incapable of bearing that burden.

Allocating the principal financial responsibility to the federal government does not mean that the states are relegated to playing an unimportant role in providing social insurance protections to American families. The states should be centrally involved in administering certain social insurance programs to avoid bloating the federal bureaucracy and to take advantage of state offices and personnel who have vital local knowledge about the circumstances of the insured and their community. This also promotes integration of income supports with state-administered social services that demand individual assessments and flexible responses to individual circumstances.

For example, assisting displaced workers in finding a new job or helping injured and ill workers access appropriate rehabilitation and training opportunities requires detailed local knowledge. These services have historically been provided at the state and local levels and appropriately so. They are closely related, and sometimes statutorily required to be connected, to the provision of disability or unemployment benefits. It makes perfect sense for the federal government to contract with state agencies for the adjudication of unemployment and disability benefit claims—even if those benefits are paid entirely from the federal Treasury. Our argument is not with devolving functions to the states, it is with devolving the wrong ones.

Devolution of responsibility to individuals has had similar ideological and political roots. And we believe that devolution from collective to individual responsibility should be evaluated by the same criterion: Does it put responsibility where it can be exercised effectively?

Thus, for example, we believe that time limits on the receipt of means-tested assistance to needy families and unemployment insurance make perfect sense, as do substantial copayments for major medical, housing, or child care expenditures. But demanding personal responsibility must not be the equivalent of making individuals or families into one-member risk pools. And insisting that people be self-supporting, even at low wages, makes sense only if society is prepared to engage in the sorts of wage and consumption subsidies that we have proposed to assure that families reach minimum levels of adequacy. The sensible demand that families support themselves by working becomes self-defeating where wages are demonstrably inadequate to provide a decent level of family income.

We also support some use of mandatory personal savings accounts for particular social insurance purposes. Personal savings accounts can limit some of the moral hazard in unemployment insurance and diversify risk with respect to retirement income by tying returns to the performance of the capital market rather than only the labor market. But our support for individual accounts does not lead us to want to substitute them for the basic collective security arrangements now provided by Social Security pensions or unemployment insurance.

Nor do we believe that ideological enthusiasm for individual control over retirement account investments should ignore either the potential for mismanagement of these accounts by unsophisticated investors or the potential for allowing large administrative costs to gobble up the earnings of small accounts. Indeed, notwithstanding a plethora of recent proposals that presuppose a role for individual retirement accounts in the reform of the Social Security pension system, relatively little attention has been given to the problems of implementing and administering such accounts. These issues make clear that notions of individual responsibility, or individual liberty, which are often associated with IRA proposals, must be tempered by a realistic vision of how these vehicles can be made to contribute effectively to the retirement security of all American families.[3]

First, there inevitably will be a large number of quite small accounts. If, for example, an amount equal to 3 percent of wages covered by Social Security were added to such accounts annually, amounts going into accounts for the 46 million workers earning less than $10,000 in 1996 would have been $300 or less. Without collective arrangements for pooling administrative costs and limits on choices about investment alternatives in small accounts, the simple collection, allocation, and record-keeping functions necessary to administer the scheme could virtually eliminate the investment earnings of these small accounts. Personal accounts must also be set up to minimize burdens on employers. This means that the current wage-reporting, payroll, and income tax systems must be used to deposit amounts into these accounts and that a limited number of investment options should be provided, at least until accounts reach a certain minimum size. Individuals could choose among investment options either on their W-2 forms currently filed with employers, or on their individual income tax returns filed with the IRS.

While these personal savings accounts can be managed by the private sector, it is essential that marketing costs be kept to a minimum. It will also be necessary to limit investment options and to ensure the solvency of private fund managers. Government insurance like that provided for bank accounts or pensions will almost certainly be necessary. Finally, withdrawals from such accounts must be limited to specific social insurance uses, and if account balances are required to be annuitized upon retirement, rules will be essential to minimize adverse selection and annuitization costs.

We believe that, subject to the constraints we have outlined here, such accounts can be a feasible and useful addition to social insurance provision. The crucial point, however, is that these constraints are substantial. The "shared luck" principle that informs all true economic security arrangements demands restrictions on individual responsibility and liberty that cannot be ignored without destroying the capacity of the system to perform its basic income security function. Unless these realities are kept constantly in view, "privatizing" social insurance provision is either a vacuous buzzword, or worse, an oxymoron.

## THE LIMITS OF
## EMPLOYER-FINANCED BENEFITS

Employers' contributions to social insurance on behalf of their workers will continue to serve as an important source of financing, as they have in the past, but we should be aware that when employers make such payments, they adjust downward the wages that they would otherwise be willing to pay. To an employer a dollar of labor cost is a dollar, whether paid directly to a worker or to a social insurance fund on the worker's behalf. Thus when taxes are levied or payments otherwise required from employers, individual workers usually bear the burden of these payments, even if the workers don't see it that way. Politicians often also ignore this basic economic truth in an effort to reap political gain from masking the tax burdens of employees. To a politician confronted with the necessity to raise revenue, the best tax is one that everyone thinks someone else is paying.

If employers are required to provide social insurance coverage for their employees, rather than mandating that individuals obtain that coverage, a variety of disadvantages will follow. Employers who wish to minimize the costs of mandates will game the system, as they have in the past, by using part-time workers and temporary help; substituting overtime for additional hiring; engaging in cash, off-the-books transactions; and classifying workers as independent contractors rather than as employees. Moreover, because employer mandates tend to raise the costs of hiring and retaining workers the most for small businesses, there are great pressures for exceptions and subsidies. For example, the Family Leave Act of 1993, which required only a relatively short period of unpaid leave, completely exempted small businesses and covered only employees who were employed by the same employer for at least twelve months and worked at least 1,250 hours in the twelve-month period.

These accommodations lead to unfairness as well as tricks and dodges. Subsidies to small businesses or other employers will not be well targeted. If they turn on the business's size—whether in terms of number of employees, assets, or receipts—they do not distinguish those well able to afford the mandate's costs from those less able. Basing subsidies on average wages is somewhat better, but because it is based on averages is still inefficient and inequitable. Adjusting subsidies based on each worker's income is really just a way of transforming an employer-based requirement into an individual mandate.

In our view, responsibility for and receipt of social insurance must reside with individuals, not with employers. We have attempted therefore to link individual responsibility with social insurance protections by providing social insurance directly to individuals and families and, to the extent feasible, have divorced the provision of social insurance from employment with any particular employer.

The separation of social insurance provision from a specific site of employment bears special emphasis. Employer mandates are second-best techniques by comparison with individual mandates; subsidizing non-mandatory employer-sponsored benefits—which constitute a very substantial part of current American social insurance expenditures—is often a distant third-best solution.

True security for individuals and families requires that benefits be durable over time, portable through changes in residence and occupation, and progressive to ensure that long-term low wages do not translate into limited protections from common risks to economic security. The subsidizing of employer-sponsored benefit plans has had a poor track record with respect to each of these criteria. Durability cannot be assured when employers go bankrupt, mergers and acquisitions are rampant, and changes in markets cause employers to reevaluate both the levels and the mix of the labor costs that they can bear. Portability under current arrangements varies enormously with the type of risk insured and with the particular arrangements that are built into particular employers' employee-benefit packages.

The fairness of employer-sponsored benefit plans is also very problematic. Notwithstanding Internal Revenue Code nondiscrimination provisions, the coverage of employee benefit plans tends to favor higher-income workers both within the confines of the same employer and quite dramatically across employers. Although there are other factors at work, such as the size of the employer and the nature of the industry, a simple rule is pretty close to the truth: the higher the wage, the better the employer-sponsored benefit package.

This fact does not lead us to the proposition that employer-sponsored benefits should be avoided in all circumstances. But such benefits should be a means for implementing mandatory insurance participation by individuals, not an alternative to universal coverage. For example, it may well be that some employers can organize disability programs or health insurance programs that protect their employees at lower costs than the level of universally mandated contributions, or that provide greater benefits for the same cost. We see no reason to eschew the superior benefits to some employees that such arrangements might provide. But we also see no reason to continue the profligate subsidization of employer-sponsored plans that are nonuniversal and nonportable, of uncertain durability, and target their benefits to higher-income people.

### INCENTIVES ARE NOT BEHAVIORS,
### BUT BEHAVIOR MATTERS

The problem of moral hazard—of people changing their behavior with re-spect to risks that are insured—is endemic to any insurance program, pri-vate or social. To be sure, incentives to incur a risk because it is insured do not translate directly into behaviors. People do not abandon all work be-cause of the existence of a subsistence level of public assistance payments, nor do they destroy their health to collect disability benefits. But faking disability—or at least accentuating one's impairments—is not unknown, nor is hiding or transferring assets in order to receive means-tested old-age benefits, particularly Medicaid. The degree to which insurance will change people's behavior depends on a host of factors that might be cap-tured generically as the extent of the benefit conferred balanced against the personal cost of incurring (or fabricating) the occurrence of the risk. The design of social insurance provision must be attentive to these prob-lems without being obsessed by them.

There are surely examples of benefits arrangements whose effects sur-prised their designers. In 1909, when the British Old Age Pensions Act started paying pensions of five shillings a week to any low-income person over age seventy, Ireland's population instantly aged. Taking advantage of poor birth records, many elderly Irish recalled their parents remarking that they had been born in "the year of the big wind," coincidentally 1839.[4]

Although the work disincentives of welfare have received the greatest public attention recently in the United States, the low-income require-ments to qualify for Medicaid's health and long-term care coverage im-pose the largest financial costs on earning extra income or amassing assets. Disabled persons and single parents are properly fearful about losing health insurance coverage under Medicaid when they take a job, particu-larly a job with an employer that offers no health insurance coverage. Likewise, when a family accumulates a relatively small amount of assets, food stamps will be cut off. The EITC also imposes high costs on earning extra income as it phases out, and sometimes the cutbacks of TANF can have similar consequences, at least on a temporary basis.

The current system may thus impose high burdens on earning extra in-come, especially as a family struggles to leave poverty and settle in the middle class. Assessing these burdens generally, or for the "average family," is either impossible or incomplete because the loss of benefits as income increases often turns on family characteristics (such as the age and number of the children), because income is not measured consistently across the programs, and because state-based financing means that benefits and their claw-backs vary depending on where one lives. This problem has been exacerbated by designing and operating each program separately, rather than thinking them through as a package of protections as we have urged here. Within the closed and often crisis-ridden worlds of particular programs, interactions with other social insurance programs tend to be ignored.

The largest problems occur when programs terminate completely at some level linked to the poverty line. The current structure of Medicaid, for example, sometimes means that earning an extra dollar of income can cost a family a couple of thousand dollars worth of health insurance coverage. One analyst has shown that it is theoretically possible under current arrangements for a family to be better off earning $9,000 than $25,000.[5] And as we have argued, the so-called negative income tax (which was embraced by both liberals and conservatives) is rife with moral hazard problems. Conditioning income transfers simply on low income, rather than looking to identifiable events such as becoming disabled or unemployed, is not the kind of social insurance protection we regard as wise, save on a temporary basis.

Disincentives of some sort may be impossible to avoid. For example, Social Security pensions and Part A of Medicare try to address these problems by providing some benefit to almost everyone, and by imposing costs at a time very different from the occasion (retirement or hospitalization, respectively) that initiates benefits. Even so, many economists believe that the protections offered by these programs have created disincentives to save.[6]

We have attempted to design social insurance protections to minimize the disincentives that many aspects of today's U.S. social insurance policies embody. By insuring a large pool of people and multiple risks, social insurance can offer protections that minimize, and in some cases avoid altogether, the adverse selection and moral hazard problems that routinely confront private insurance. We have tried to reduce the work and savings disincentives of social insurance by eliminating the largest "cliffs" in current programs—for example, by replacing Medicaid with a universal system of government subsidies for catastrophic health costs. And we combine current tax incentives and direct expenditures for child care and housing into a unified system of consumption subsidies that are proportional to child care and housing costs, but in effect taper gradually as income rises. This not only improves incentives, but also offers greater social insurance protection for the middle class.

Critics of existing programs have often pointed to the extremely high implicit tax rates that result from the combined withdrawal of multiple means-tested programs as incomes increase. Because under current law these "tax" rates are often over 100 percent, it is surely plausible to believe that they will have real behavioral effects. Increasing effort in order to make your family worse off is a game that few are likely to want to play, unless there is some realistic prospect that the losses will be short-lived and followed by real gains. But few low-income families go catapulting into the solid middle class. Instead they tend to make slow progress at wage rates that remain modest.

Our proposals never produce 100 percent or greater implicit tax rates as income increases. Net of positive taxes and subsidy withdrawals, a family is always better off earning more rather than less. And unlike current programs, there are no "cliffs" that impose large losses on the earning of a marginal dollar. Table 14.1 compares implicit tax rates under existing law with those under our proposals.[7] Implicit tax rates, nevertheless, remain higher than we would prefer. This is the necessary effect of providing baseline subsidies that approach adequacy and phasing subsidies out fast enough that total transfer expenditures remain within our overall budget limits.

Table 14.1    Current and Proposed Implicit Tax Rates

| Annual Income Range | Current Implicit Marginal Tax Rates | Implicit Marginal Tax Rates under Proposals |
|---|---|---|
| $10,300–$12,849 | 89.6% | 19.5% |
| $12,850–$14,349 | 109.2% | 38.4% |
| At $14,350 | Cliff loss of $1,800 | No cliff loss |
| $14,350–$14,699 | 78.0% | 55.4% |
| At $14,700 | Cliff loss of $1,800 | No cliff loss |
| $14,700–$15,049 | 61.3% | 52% |
| $15,050–$19,449 | 78.5% | 54.7% |
| At $19,550 | Cliff loss of $1,000 | No cliff loss |
| $19,550–$25,000 | 78.5% | 57.9% |

*Source:* "Current Marginal Tax Rates" from Daniel N. Shaviro, "Effective Marginal Tax Rates on Low-Income Households," 1998 manuscript on file with authors; "Implicit Marginal Tax Rates Under Proposals" are based on authors' calculations.

We are uncertain how big an impact these implicit tax rates will have on work effort. The existing literature suggests that the effects will be negligible for primary workers, but larger for secondary workers. For our purposes, however, the question is not what the absolute level of behavioral response will be, but how it compares to current arrangements. And on a comparative basis, our proposals have incentive effects that are vastly superior to the income support programs now in place.

We have also attempted to control disincentives in relation to our proposed health care, housing, and child care subsidies by requiring copayments as more is spent. We believe that these design features will reduce unwanted behavioral effects, but not eliminate them. Good design is not a panacea for moral hazard. And many attempts to combat that "disease" may produce "cures" that are both offensive and unadministerable. Designing programs with a proper respect for their effects on behavior matters, but we cannot allow the inability to avoid all such effects to paralyze efforts at providing income security through social insurance.

## REMEMBERING THE TAX CODE AND ITS LIMITS

As we argued much earlier, there has been a tendency for social insurance planners to forget about the tax code and the social insurance subsidies that it contains. This has resulted in large implicit public expenditures that are not evaluated systematically in terms of their capacity to effectuate social insurance goals. In addition, as we argued with respect to employer-sponsored and tax-subsidized employee health and pension plans, this incomplete approach can result in substantial expenditures for programs that have spotty coverage, limited durability, and little or no progressivity in their financing.

Lack of progressivity often has been exacerbated by the form of tax subsidies chosen. The use of deductions or exclusions from income rather than credits means that the tax break is more valuable the more money a family makes. Moreover, even when credits are used, they often are not "refundable." Hence those with little or no tax liability get little or no benefit.

We have generally urged that social insurance be paid in cash, relying on individual recipients to take responsibility for putting the money to good use. In such cases, the principal administrative challenge is determining eligibility to receive the money. Knowing a person's age is no longer challenging, but evaluating eligibility for disability or unemploy-ment benefits and monitoring compliance with TANF can be difficult tasks. As we have said, we would contract out such judgments to state administrators.

On the other hand, as the low administrative expenses of Social Secu-rity and Medicare attest, the federal government is quite efficient at writ-ing checks.[8] And the IRS has risen to the challenge of administering means-tested, cash benefits under the EITC—at least as long as the ac-counting period (a year) and reporting method (self-reporting backed by audits) remain consistent with the rest of the tax system's administrative routines.

There are some circumstances, however, where we have recommended providing social insurance in the form of income-based subsidies for spe-cific kinds of expenditures. In the case of health insurance, this is because the diversion of cash to a different use would undermine the very basis for providing the insurance: to protect families from shocks to their standards of living due to catastrophic medical expenses. In the other two instances where we have proposed social insurance in-kind—to insure against exces-sive expenditures for child care and housing by families with children—we have done so in part to make sure that a few irresponsible parents cannot easily shift the social insurance protection away from their chil-dren, its intended beneficiaries. Moreover, consumption subsidies are a much better targeted device than wage subsidies because these relatively large expenses vary with location and family composition, not with wage rates. We have advanced two alternative mechanisms for implementing consumption subsidies of this sort: refundable or transferable income tax credits, and vouchers. Each has advantages and disadvantages.

There are at least six arguments for using the tax system. First, the tax law already requires a determination of annual income, and although that measure is far from ideal, it does offer a ready basis for linking the calcula-tion of an income-based subsidy to income information otherwise being provided.[9] Second, by locating subsidies in the tax law, coordination among them and with the tax rates applicable to income provides an op-portunity to integrate policy in a way to minimize disincentives to work and savings.[10] Third, although the lack of subject matter expertise is often claimed to be a drawback of using tax expenditures rather than direct ex-penditures, in this case, putting new social insurance payments under the jurisdiction of the House Ways and Means and Senate Finance committees locates them in the legislative bodies with jurisdiction over the bulk of other social insurance programs (including Social Security; old age, disability, and survivors' insurance; unemployment insurance; Medicare; and employer-based health insurance and pensions). It thereby offers an opportunity for coordinated social insurance legislation. Reform of transfer programs can be evaluated simultaneously with reform of tax subsidies for employer-sponsored benefits. If our analysis is correct, these subsidies must be reconfigured to produce a more rational and comprehensive program of social insurance.

Fourth, reconfiguring current tax subsidies from employer or individual deductions to individual tax credits keeps the government's budgetary accounting within the same framework. Cutting out deductions to fund vouchers could be characterized as a large tax increase. Shifting from tax deductions to tax credits will change individual tax liabilities, but in aggregate will not increase, and may even reduce, overall tax receipts—it represents a "tax cut," not a "spending increase."

Fifth, tax credits—even when refundable or transferable—enjoy a more benign political status than vouchers or other forms of direct spending. Much of this is political mythology: at the very least it is a mystery why tax credits for specified purposes reduce the size of government while direct spending for the same purposes increases it. Nevertheless, in his first appearance before the House Ways and Means Committee after becoming Speaker of the House in 1995, Newt Gingrich, who had been urging cutting the federal government down to size, recommended a tax credit to fund laptop computers for poor children to help them become more effective in the new "third wave" information age. Gingrich soon realized that tax-based government incentives to purchase particular goods or services were not so different from direct spending or regulatory requirements and withdrew this idea, calling it "nutsy."

Nevertheless, despite the similarities between tax incentives and equivalent direct spending programs, tax cuts—no matter how directed—are still widely regarded as reducing the size of government rather than increasing it. Indeed, the standard practice of omitting our tax-based social insurance provisions in international comparisons of social insurance arrangements is one reason that the United States is regarded as spending so much less than other countries on social insurance.[11] As we have pointed out, when one counts both tax and direct spending, the United States spends considerably more money on social insurance than is gener-

Fig. 14.1. Comparative social insurance transfers and tax expenditures

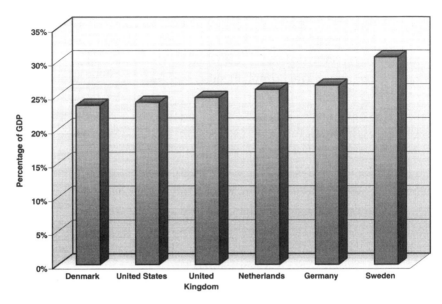

(*Source*: Calculations by Jacob Hacker, based on 1993 OECD data.)

ally realized, and as figure 14.1 shows, U.S. social insurance expenditures are relatively close to those of many other nations.

Finally, tax credits carry no stigma. Tax breaks have been provided to so many successful people for so long that anyone who benefits from them simply feels good—perhaps even entitled. As a result, tax incentives also enjoy great stability. Many prove impossible to remove even long after they are widely recognized to serve little or no useful purpose. Such longevity can be a serious drawback, but for social insurance, it may ensure a stable long-term source of financing. The major risk becomes some radical structural change in the tax system, such as replacing the income tax with a value-added or sales tax.

Vouchers in many respects reverse the advantages and disadvantages of tax credits. Politically, they often are subject to the whims of annual appropriations and restricted by budget caps. Congress tends to universalize tax benefits and to treat all with similar income as equally eligible. No such universalistic ethic attends means-tested vouchers, as we have seen in the case of current housing subsidies under Section 8.

The greatest advantage of vouchers over tax credits is that they are able to deliver subsidies on a monthly basis, which is a more timely pattern for funding health insurance, housing, and child care spending. Although in principle tax credits can do the same through transferability to providers of the subsidized goods or services, or by reduced employer withholding of payroll and income taxes, experience with the advance-funding provisions of the EITC is not encouraging.

Administration of vouchers also permits assessing income on a more frequent basis than annual tax reports and can more readily take levels of wealth into account. In addition, a program of vouchers can determine income and assets on a household basis, as the Food Stamp Program now does, rather than having to rely on the filing status of income tax returns. This offers the potential to vary benefits to households of different size and composition. If benefits are extended up the income scale, as we have proposed here, vouchers may avoid stigma, although it is far more likely that effective criticism can be mounted against providing vouchers to middle- and upper-income families than against tax allowances. It is obviously easier to characterize a housing voucher to Bill Gates as public policy run amuck than to challenge a tax allowance for his housing costs, an allowance that he surely now enjoys through deductions for property taxes and home mortgage interest. (Bill Gates may not have a mortgage, but the tax code encourages him to have one.)

On balance, we favor using refundable or transferable tax credits for providing the social insurance benefits we have recommended here, but we have no principled objection to vouchers. Such tax credits probably will have to be backward-looking (based on the previous year's income) and transferable to providers of health insurance, housing, and child care, who can use them immediately to reduce their own estimated tax or required withholding deposits. As a technical matter, either vouchers or tax credits can do the job.

## REMEMBER THE STRUGGLING MIDDLE CLASS

The large group of Americans who in the current vernacular "play by the rules" but fail to really get ahead face the most poignant problems of both affordability and adequacy in the operation of existing social insurance protections. We are thinking here of families that have escaped poverty but have not achieved affluence—those families earning roughly $20,000 to $50,000 per year. This group now bears the burdens of wage and other taxes, but gets less than adequate social insurance protections.

Social Security's retirement income and disability programs are reasonably well targeted to this group. But Social Security, Medicare, and disability insurance emphasize the income and health needs of persons in or near retirement. Unemployment insurance, workers' compensation, and public and private short-term disability insurance are "workers' programs," but their spotty coverage limits their effectiveness. The same is true for employer-based pensions and health care and disability programs. Employees are more likely to get substantial benefits from these programs if their incomes are in the solidly middle-class to affluent range and if they work for large employers.

Wage and income subsidies are normally limited to the poor and near-poor and therefore miss those who are not poor but struggling. Consumption subsidies for medical care and housing have similarly been limited to the poor or near-poor, as have food stamps. And whenever subsidies are provided through the tax code, they tend to favor the more affluent, who have larger mortgages, better health insurance, and get a bigger benefit from the tax deductibility of expenditures for these purposes.

Many of our proposals would shore up those programs that are of the greatest importance to what we have called the "struggling middle class." Some shift support from the affluent to the less affluent. For example, we have shifted consumption subsidies by replacing income tax exclusions and deductions with a system of explicit guarantees so that assistance for health care costs, housing, and child care will go more in the direction of those who need it the most—and currently have it the least.

For example, in the case of a family with two children earning $2,500–$4,200 a month ($30,000–50,000 a year), our proposals for child care and housing subsidies would provide an additional $227 each month for a family in Omaha and $413 a month for a family in New York City, assuming the families rent their homes. For families who own a home, the net additional benefit from our proposals would be less, depending on exactly what changes were made in the home-mortgage interest deduction. But generally even homeowners would be better off. For example, that deduction now saves from $100 to about $187 a month in taxes for families with this level of income that have a mortgage of $100,000 at an 8 percent interest rate.

Assessing the value of our universal health insurance protection to particular families is more difficult because its value depends both on whether the family is now insured and on what its health costs are. As we have pointed out, workers in this income group are among the most likely to be uninsured today. Of course, being uninsured is now costless for families who incur no health care costs. Our proposed health insurance coverage would cost the families about $152 a month (at the $30,000 income level), $305 (at the $40,000 level) or $404 (at the $50,000 level). In return, they would have the security of knowing that large unexpected medical expenses would not threaten their standard of living. For workers at these income levels who are insured, their current costs are hidden because coverage is provided by their employers, but, as we have explained, it is reasonable to believe that about two-thirds of such costs are now, in effect, being paid by workers in the form of reduced wages. Our proposals would generally not increase those costs, only their visibility.

Our proposals to broaden short-term disability insurance and unemployment insurance are similarly targeted to increase the protections for less affluent workers. Long-term care insurance likewise provides security with respect to a risk that is now affordable for the rich and provided to the poor through Medicaid. Finally, mandating capital-market participation by the group that is now least represented by requiring personal savings accounts will increasingly permit this segment of workers to share in the returns to capital, not just in the returns to wage growth.

Because of the standard arc of life-cycle earnings, these shifts in emphasis also tend to produce gains for younger workers and their families. We believe this trend is also appropriate because it dampens the excessive skew in existing American social insurance programs toward middle-aged and elderly workers or retirees.

In sum, we have attempted here to craft a set of more comprehensive social insurance protections that will provide economic security at all levels of income and throughout the life cycle. In so doing, we have endeavored to strike an appropriate balance between social and personal responsibility—to describe a program of social insurance that will provide protection against the risks of working and living in a vibrant dynamic market economy. If we are on the right track, social insurance as we envision it can pave the path to true security for all Americans.

## Chapter 15 The Politics of Institutional Design

We cannot now embark on a study of the politics of American social insurance programs and develop a detailed political strategy for implementing our proposed reforms. Yet to say nothing about politics would be irresponsible. We fully anticipate, for example, that some readers will dismiss our analysis and proposals with the knowing, but facile, pronouncement that however desirable our approach to social insurance reform may be, it is a political "nonstarter." Indeed, our own observations of national politics suggest that most proposed changes are immediately characterized by certain policy and political communities as either impossible or inevitable. The middle ground between these polar positions is seldom glimpsed. If seen, it is usually treated as too uninteresting to bear mention. Yet whether a proposal will succeed may not have much to do with initial reactions; in American politics, much that is labeled impossible occurs, and the "inevitable" often disappears without a trace.

We know that many of the specific proposals we have advanced in Chapters 9–13 would encounter rough political sledding, at least in the short-term. For example, our criticisms of relying so heavily on voluntary tax incentives to provide economic security fly in the face of the current congressional practice of treating the tax code as the chicken soup of public policy, an elixir that can solve all of the nation's political, social, or economic ills. Likewise, our insistence that national financing of social insurance is a bedrock for true security runs counter to the current devolution craze. Even some of our more limited suggestions—for example, raising the retirement age to conform to enhanced life expectancies—would confront stiff resistance in the political arena.

But relying on tax incentives is usually a distributionally perverse and fiscally inefficient way to provide social insurance, and placing financial responsibility with the states, rather than the national government, is a formula for inadequate income security for many Americans. Likewise the notion that fewer and fewer workers should be prepared to fund growing periods of retirement for more and more retirees seems unfair. We do not believe that insuring true security for the elderly should be abandoned. But endless expansion of entitlements for the elderly is inconsistent with an appropriate balance of our intergenerational social contract.

Rather than being stymied by obvious short-term political obstacles, we have attempted to look at social insurance whole and have tried to understand how the underlying aspiration for economic security can be worked out in relation to particular risks across the life cycle of individuals. We have let the logic of that aspiration, and its complex relationship to the maintenance of a durable capitalist economic order, lead us where it would. This is an approach to program design deeply at odds with a more politically opportunistic style of reform effort. But it is also a stance that need not be politically naive.

## STRUCTURAL POLITICS

Although we have ignored short-term "strategic politics," we have been attentive to what we call "structural politics." Structural politics includes at its core considerations of constitutional allocations of political power, limitations on governmental jurisdiction, and the deep ideological commitments of the polity. Strategic politics, by contrast, involves the framing and marketing of issues in light of the current alignment of political forces and the creation of winning coalitions by deft distributions of benefits and burdens. Because we are reformers, not revolutionaries, core structural commitments do not limit our options. Because we are policy analysts rather than politicians, we cannot create detailed strategies for an ever-changing political context.

Somewhere between these domains, however, lie stable but nonconstitutional institutional rules and relationships, the inertial weight of existing arrangements and ideological commitments that are malleable, but not in the short run. We have been particularly attentive to these lower-level structural constraints in fashioning our reform proposals. Intermediate structural politics has not only informed our design of reforms that we believe are "doable" over time but has played an equally important role in our consideration of how to make our proposed policy changes durable and resilient. In many instances, we have avoided direct confrontation with structural political constraints by proposing changes that can fairly be called incremental. On other occasions, however, we have had to admit candidly that our goals cannot be accomplished without major realignment of existing social insurance arrangements.

To fix ideas more concretely, reconsider the discussion of unemployment insurance in Chapters 4 and 10. The original designers of the unemployment insurance system clearly took constitutional politics into account. They considered the peculiar structure of unemployment insurance—federal tax forgiveness for the enactment of state unemployment insurance regimes—to be a constitutional necessity. The basic shape of this program has been determined to this day by a design decision driven by now-defunct constitutional politics. And, of course, the fact that the early 1930s understanding of constitutional allocations of national and state power *is* defunct means that our proposals for "federalization" of social insurance violate no constitutionally based political constraints.

The understanding in the 1930s of how the Constitution divided federal-state powers and responsibilities was, of course, not wholly disconnected from long-term, ideological understandings of the appropriate roles of the states and the federal government in carrying out domestic policies. But those understandings have shifted. Today virtually any problem that simply occurs in all localities in the country (street crime and public education are two favorites) tends to be defined as a "national problem" requiring national solutions. Much of this type of talk is simply political opportunism. But this is not the case with unemployment insurance. There are persuasive macroeconomic, fiscal capacity, and interstate competition reasons to treat unemployment insurance as a national rather than a state problem. No entrenched "states' rights" ideology is likely to demand retention of the current structure.

The intermediate structural politics of unemployment insurance poses more relevant concerns. The long history of state administration of unemployment insurance benefits, combined with state provision of job search services and retraining and rehabilitation programs, integrates these benefits into a broader set of social policies. Many may believe that these linkages are sensible and should continue. In any event, their existence means that a durable and intensely interested group of state officials and private-service providers will regard federalization of unemployment insurance as a major threat.

Federal budget accounting rules are of similar structural importance. Although the Federal Unemployment Tax Act (FUTA) in effect coerces states to levy taxes to finance unemployment insurance, those taxes and unemployment insurance expenditures show up in state budgets rather than the federal budget. This not only makes the federal budget look smaller, but it also insulates that budget (at least partially) from deficit spending in economic downturns. Moreover, under current congressional rules, a proposal to move unemployment insurance benefits into the federal budget would require an equal and offsetting reduction to expenditures elsewhere or a tax increase.

Political dynamics also help explain the difficulty in raising the tax base for funding unemployment insurance benefits. In 1937 wages subject to Social Security (FICA) taxes were capped at \$3,000, as was the unemployment tax (FUTA), an amount that then included 92 percent of the nation's total wages. By 1999, the FICA tax had risen to apply to \$72,600 of a worker's wages, but FUTA taxed only \$7,000 of wages. Why has Congress been so slow to raise the wage level on a tax that it doesn't intend to collect? Because it would have to take the political heat of a "tax increase" without the offsetting political rewards of increasing workers' unemployment insurance benefits. The benefit checks come from the states.

These longstanding structural commitments to state administration and federal budget accounting cannot be ignored. But our proposals for expanding the real coverage of unemployment insurance and for putting it on a sounder financial footing do not necessarily entail overcoming these constraints directly. Like the original designers of the unemployment insurance system, we can continue to work around them. Coverage expansion and national unification of benefit levels does not require federal administration or even complete federal financing of unemployment insurance. It demands only that the federal government impose different and more uniform rules for eligibility, require a shift from firm-specific to industry-wide experience rating, and change the way it backs up financially strapped states. The Congressional Budget Office might view the last of these as increasing federal outlays, but it would be a very small increase compared with the complete federalization of the unemployment insurance program.

At the level of strategic politics, we have less to contribute. We do not believe that the changes we suggest to unemployment insurance create any big "losers." But by the same token, the "winners" are an amorphous group of middle- to lower-middle-income Americans who are difficult to organize around this issue. Their principal proxy representative, organized labor, is not likely to put unemployment insurance reform at the head of its reform agenda. In some sense the strategic battle is one that must be won with ideas and entrepreneurship. We have tried to supply some of the ideas.

## PROPOSALS AND POLITICS: A BRIEF REVIEW OF THE BIDDING

None of the proposals we offer in the preceding pages faces serious problems with what we have called the core of structural politics—considerations of governmental structure and of constitutional limitations or fundamental ideological beliefs. Our vision of social insurance poses no threat to democratic governance, to the basic economic system of market allocation, or to deeply held social norms concerning individual and social responsibility. Indeed, as we have sought to explain, cushioning the risks of shocks to labor market income is a crucial underpinning for a vibrant economy. And our approach to providing and funding social insurance is much more consistent with efficient markets and high productivity than with alternative interventions that might otherwise be necessary to provide an appropriate measure of income security for American workers and their families. High tariffs, guaranteed employment, "stakeholder democracy" in firm governance, and "living wage" mandates might do some of the income security work that is the goal of social insurance. But these types of interventions have a poor record from the standpoint of maintaining a flexible and highly productive economy in a world of rapid change.

We have little to offer concerning the strategic politics of agenda setting and coalition building that might bring any of our proposals to prompt passage in the Congress. We will focus this discussion, therefore, on how our reform ideas can respond to mid-level structural features of the political landscape. By this, again, we mean regularities in the way people think about certain issues, the way power is arrayed in relation to them, and the way political institutions are organized to deal with them. This is a category of important constraints on what is doable—not just now, but for the foreseeable future.

### Health Insurance

In some ways our health insurance proposals are politically sophisticated. Having witnessed past failures, we do not propose a government takeover of health care, a single-payer health insurance system, or even a set of broad employer mandates. Our subsidized voucher system does not attack the health insurance industry or regulate the manner in which doctors or other health care providers are organized or remunerated. In short, we have sidestepped some of the serious ideological opposition, entrenched interests, and institutional commitments that have defeated all previous American attempts to universalize health insurance. Nor can we be charged with fiscal folly in a polity currently committed to living within its means. We arc proposing to cover the whole population for the price we now pay for leaving 43 million Americans uninsured.

But our plan surely will encounter significant political difficulties. By sidestepping the traditional enemies of health insurance reform, we may well have left reform's friends behind as well. The long-standing desire of most Americans to realize the goal of universal health *insurance* probably is better understood as a desire for universal health *care*. Most proponents of universal health insurance tend to be egalitarians with respect to health care. They regard health care as a good (or service) that they believe to be a fundamental human right. They want comprehensive and uniform health care coverage. And their egalitarian impulse will be offended by any scheme, such as ours, that permits opportunities for risk segmentation that might lead to broader (or less expensive) coverage for populations having lower health risks.

In short, the usual sentiments that have rallied supporters of universal health insurance do not have a nice fit with our plan. As an economist friend said to us, "Of course yours is the kind of insurance people *ought* to want, but its not the kind they *do* want. They want everything covered, no questions asked—and hold the copayments, thank you very much."

Additional political obstacles occur because we are funding our in-come-security health insurance program in part from tax subsidies that now disproportionately benefit politically potent upper-income groups. But this may not prove as big a problem as it seems. There are genuine economies in group plans, and under our proposals the healthy-wealthy are unlikely to see much change in the health insurance that their employ-ers provide. Moreover, we propose subsidizing health insurance coverage through transferable (or refundable) tax credits. We thereby retain the po-litical insulation and durability that stuffing social policies into the tax code generally provides.

The major political obstacle to our health insurance proposals, there-fore, seems ideational. We have to persuade ordinary people (as well as the elite proponents of universal health insurance) that they *do* want what they *ought* to want—true income security in the face of substantial health care costs. Costless annual physical examinations, which include mammo-grams and PSA prostate cancer screening, are nice. But we believe that real protection from the staggering costs of treatment should those tests prove positive is nicer.

Convincing people of that view is sure to be an uphill battle. But we have offered a coherent explanation for why social insurance protection against the costs of health care should be structured to protect income se-curity, rather than equality of access to health care. Fighting a political war of ideas on these grounds may prove unsuccessful. But it cannot be said to be more politically naive than those previously fought, and lost, against the material interests of strong, institutionally entrenched adversaries.

### Children

Our proposals for the protection of children's income security, like our health care proposals, require people to reorder their ideas. Here too, we attempt to reshape the terms of political engagement. In one sense our job here is easier: Most people view children as economically vulnerable through no fault of their own. The political problem with providing ade-quate security to children has been a conceptualization of childhood poverty (or near poverty) as fundamentally a problem of social control. Politicians have tended to believe that the problem would disappear if only programs would reform poor children's parents' behavior to reinforce personal and family responsibility.

Rather than attempting to contradict that understanding of the "welfare" problem, we have tried to build on it. The behaviorist vision of welfare reform has already been enacted. The job now is to respond to the reality that many working families are poor too. The material deprivation of children is not solved by a simple transfer of their parents from the status of "welfare recipient" to "working poor." In short, children's risks parallel the risks of the aged: the significant likelihood of having inadequate current or accumulated (saved) labor income.

To be sure, collective approaches to providing for the aged must be structured differently than those for the young. In conventional economic terms, the task with respect to the aged is to assure individual and collective accumulation of sufficient wealth to support a dignified retirement. The task with respect to children is to organize sufficient levels of individual and collective borrowing against their future productivity to avoid material deprivation prior to entering the workforce.

Because people have long understood these tasks largely by analogy to private, individual economic behavior, the first task seems doable, the second not. Social insurance can mandate individual savings and/or contributions to a social insurance retirement fund by workers and allow them to draw down the accumulations later to fund their retirement. But how can we be sure that youthful "borrowers" will pay back their loans in their prime working years?

The answer lies in recognizing that the individual saver analogy misdescribes how old age pensions actually work. Social Security is not a bank account, but rather a contract across generations to do two things: assure appropriate spreading of consumption across a lifetime that includes working and then nonworking years, and transfer some income from high lifetime earners to low lifetime earners—that is, to redistribute resources across families, as well as across time.

Because Social Security redistributes more resources across time within families than across families, and because it is financed from wage taxes (often called "contributions"), many people have tended to think of it in "bank account" terms. Indeed, Social Security's defenders have often emphasized this view in countering the hyperbole of libertarian critics. The latter often have tried to reconceptualize Social Security as "welfare" and have derided as fraudulent the notion of "contributions" and of a "trust fund" from which benefits are paid.

But whatever the purpose of such derogatory labels, they capture a partial truth about the way social insurance works. Social Security is a collective and redistributional system in which the capacity of the pension program to pay reasonable benefits depends upon the productivity of today's workers, not the accumulated savings of today's retirees. The ongoing political viability of this system depends upon the degree to which the American public believes that this intergenerational contract both provides true security and fairly allocates benefits and burdens.

If this description is true—and we believe that it undeniably is true—then social insurance protections for children can have a similar structure and similar economic and political durability. For the question is not whether any particular child beneficiary of social insurance will be able to pay up in his or her working years. The question is instead whether the age cohort of which they are a part will be required to shoulder its productive and redistributional responsibilities, as did the generation that preceded it.

From this perspective, the feasibility of consumption smoothing across time and among individuals or families is no greater or lesser a problem when providing income support for children than when providing social insurance for retirees. In both cases, social insurance can work where private insurance cannot. And in both cases beneficiaries "earn" their entitlements in exactly the same sense, by their participation in a cohort of citizens that has borne or will bear its age-appropriate productive burden. This is the social contract across generations that social insurance creates. Understood in this way, income security for children is no more a "welfare handout" than Social Security. Rather it is the responsible execution of an intergenerational compact among Americans.

Efforts at organizing effective income security for children have faced other political burdens as well. Worries about reinforcing an anti-work ethic or a culture of poverty, about rewarding sloth and profligacy, about losing productivity from perverse economic incentives, and about achieving fairness for near-poor and middle-class workers, not to mention about fraud, have always been a prominent part of "welfare" politics. The question then is whether social insurance supports for children, which of necessity must be provided through support for their families, can be designed to mitigate these problems.

We will not repeat here the arguments of Chapter 12. Remember, how-ever, that our proposals are radically different from historic American wel-fare schemes and from the negative income tax proposal. Our income security package supports work by supplementing earned income. It avoids entitlement cliffs and the confiscatory implicit tax rates that pro-duce perverse economic incentives. And, perhaps most important, it pro-vides help for children in families that are above the poverty line, but still struggling to maintain a secure middle-class life in the face of inadequate wages and lumpy demands for high-priced goods—particularly health care, housing, and child care.

Virtually all of our proposals extend and generalize programs that al-ready exist. Their administrability, including their capacities to avoid fraudulent manipulation, should parallel existing efforts. And because our programs universalize current discretionary expenditures and reallocate tax advantages to those who need them most, our approach increases enormously the fairness of existing efforts. Whether that proves a political asset or a political liability remains to be seen. Our goal has been to clarify the nation's understanding of social insurance and thereby to reorient the policy and political debates.

## THE POLITICS OF INCREMENTALISM

Our package of proposals for children's income security is incremental. It expands and builds on existing structures rather than starting anew. The same can be said of most of our proposals concerning disability income security, retirement security, and unemployment insurance.

Universalizing temporary disability insurance, for example, builds on programs with a forty-year history in five states and on widespread prac-tices among large employers. Our "big" innovation concerns substituting temporary disability insurance for most of workers' compensation cover-age. But even there, private employers and insurers have begun a similar shift to what is labeled "twenty-four-hour coverage"—a combination of workers' compensation and disability coverage. Many in the private sector agree that this is a more desirable approach than separate insurance pro-grams for disability and workers' compensation. But unifying coverage is often limited by existing workers' compensation legislation.

Likewise, our retirement security proposals fall in the mid-range of sta-tus quo versus radical privatization debates that have been swirling around the nation's capital. Our major difference with most proponents of personal accounts is that we do not see them as a solution to a looming financial crisis in Social Security. Instead, following modern portfolio theory, we regard maintaining the current defined-benefit system, along with a new universal defined-contribution addition, as a way of providing greater security for America's retirees through diversification of their holdings.

In short, if incrementalism is the only realistic political game in town because of the numerous mid-level structural constraints that attend all U.S. democratic politics, our proposals should be in no greater trouble than anyone else's.

### A CODA ON SHORT-TERM ELECTORAL POLITICS AND IDEAS

Ultimately, the major political strengths and weaknesses of our reform suggestions will turn on a competition between short-term electoral politics and the politics of ideas. As an illustration, consider the differences between our proposals for insuring that the costs of long-term care do not drive those who need it into poverty and the proposed tax credit for long-term care offered by President Clinton in his budget for fiscal year 2000. In brief, the president offered a tax credit of up to $1,000 a year to defray some of the costs of people needing long-term care or of relatives taking care of them. This tax credit would be made available only for those who are severely disabled and would be phased out for high-income people. That such an idea enjoys widespread political appeal is confirmed by the fact that House Republicans offered a similar $500 tax credit in their 1994 Contract with America. In the short-term at least, this bipartisan proposal seems far more likely to be enacted than our recommendation for instituting a prefunded long-term care insurance program.

The long-term-care tax credit proposed by Clinton and the Contract with America, however, is merely a fig leaf. It covers less than $3.00 a day of expenses. It has very limited applicability. It does not even begin to address the potential long-term care costs of the baby-boom generation, nor does it confront the anticipated continuing increases in the elderly population and their attendant need for long-term care insurance. As we pointed out in Chapter 13, these challenges can really be addressed in only one of two ways: requiring everyone to purchase a specified level of private long-term care insurance, or instituting a prefunded public insurance program along the lines of Social Security. And as we detailed, tackling this problem sooner rather than later means that security can be purchased at a relatively small cost. To be sure, offering a program like ours carries political risks. It requires either an individual mandate or a small tax increase. Because of its prefunding feature, its costs are immediate, and its payoff is long-term. These costs cannot be concealed.

Tax credits, by contrast, are comparatively easy to enact because they feed into the wishes of politicians to take credit and avoid blame. And they sometimes make programs more durable. Most Americans hold a relatively undifferentiated belief that any provision that reduces taxes restores the natural order of things and should be supported. With tax credits, the failures of voluntary tax-subsidized programs to provide true security for all Americans can easily be ignored, while the politicians congratulate themselves on "making a start" on the long-term care problem.

Hence the issue is joined. We all must choose between short-term electoral politics and the politics of ideas. For social insurance design, we have chosen the latter. Social insurance is, on our view, a long-term intergenerational compact. And where social insurance is concerned, if not elsewhere, we believe that focusing on the short-term political advantage will ultimately make programs dysfunctional (state-based unemployment insurance and voluntary, tax-subsidized health insurance are major examples) or tend to delegitimate them (as the "bank account" representation of Social Security pensions now threatens). Our preference for the politics of ideas is not, therefore, just some academic notion of where the moral high ground lies. We believe, in the long run at least, that it is the only successful strategy for a regime as important, long-lived, and contestable as the attempt to create true security through social insurance.

## Epilogue  Revising Old Fables

Craig Pleasants turns the story of the Three Little Pigs on its head.[1] He describes his version as "an English folktale which began to be told in the early 17th century," based on a "Powhatan" legend, and "attributed to Captain John Smith, who had recently returned from the settlement of Jamestown in the New World." In Pleasants' tale, like the original, no one is giving anything away. The pigs are out in the world fending for themselves because their mother is not able to take care of them. Knowing that wolves live in the nearby forest, the three pigs set out to build themselves houses, but this time, the first two pigs claim the moral high ground. Ecological conditions drive their choices to build houses from straw and sticks: they use the materials at hand. The third pig—contrary to Walt Disney's version—is not practical and is far from heroic. This third pig craves a house finer and stronger than the other two pigs can manage, but he spends much of his time making fun of the flimsiness and crudeness of the other pigs' houses. He moves very slowly to build his elaborate structure, and by the time the wolf arrives at the door of the first pig, the third pig has managed to build only his foundation.

When the huffing and puffing wolf arrives at the first pig's house, the wind he blows courses "mostly through the spaces between the straw," and the wolf "could not make the house fall down." After all the huffing and puffing, the first pig invites the exhausted wolf to dinner, where he partakes of a meal of corn and potatoes. When the wolf arrives at the second pig's house, he is able to rattle and shake it, but because the sticks have been properly notched together, the house remains standing. The wolf leaves, greatly frustrated. He then comes to the uncompleted house of the third pig, leaps over the unfinished brick wall, and gobbles him up. The moral of the classic tale of the Three Little Pigs, it seems, is all in the way the story is told. Which pig turns out to be prudent depends on the character and timing of events that no pig can control.

Like Pleasants, we believe that the Bob and Betsy Pigs of the world tend to get the short end of the stick. As a result, we are most concerned in this book with providing true security to those many Americans who strive hard, but still struggle to stay firmly in the middle class—people who simply do not have sufficient assets to protect themselves against financial adversity. Americans often feel reasonably secure, but their security can collapse in the face of any severe setback such as losing a job, becoming sick or disabled, or losing a loved one. We also are especially concerned here with those who work hard, but whose skills, training, and diligence are not valued by the market at a sufficiently high wage to house, feed, clothe, and care for their children at a level that gives them a good start in life.

The aging of the population, the dislocations of the transition from a manufacturing to a service economy, the globalization of production, the gyrations of instantly mobile capital, the felt necessities of businesses to trim down to compete—all of these changes have heightened anxieties about our individual economic fortunes, notwithstanding our strong economy. People are rightly concerned about how they can provide for their children and about how they will be cared for when they are old. They struggle to keep their homes—whether made of sticks, straw, or bricks—together and functioning.

We have attempted in this book to develop a coherent set of aspirations for a social insurance system that will guarantee all Americans true security without breaking the bank. And we have sketched the institutional re-

forms that we believe would make this vision a reality. But if we are to accomplish that task, we must be clear about our income protection goals,
and we must design social insurance programs that respond effectively
when risks become reality. In many instances, the foundations for such a
system are already in place. But, as the third little pig discovered, a foundation without the house provides limited protection. Despite our
nation's affluence, we have yet to adequately protect Americans from the
many wolves that come to call—both inevitably and unannounced. In
our view, too many little pigs are still being gobbled up.

# Budgetary Appendix

Life-Cycle Breakdown of Social Insurance Transfers and Tax Expenditures,
Fiscal Year 1996

| | $ (millions) | % of GDP | % of Federal direct expenditures | % of Federal direct & tax expenditures |
|---|---|---|---|---|
| **Total Transfers and Tax Expenditures** | **1,205,690** | **15.9** | **76.6** | **59.3** |
| *Total Transfers* | *917,341* | *12.1* | *58.3* | *45.1* |
| *Total Tax Expenditures* | *288,349* | *3.8* | *18.3* | *14.2* |
| **Retirement** | **674,879** | **8.9** | **42.9** | **33.2** |
| *Transfers* | *554,846* | *7.4* | *35.2* | *27.2* |
| Social Security: old-age survivors' insurance | 303,900 | 4.0 | 19.3 | 14.9 |
| Medicare: hospital insurance | 126,500 | 1.7 | 8.0 | 6.2 |
| Medicare: supplementary medical insurance | 67,200 | 0.9 | 4.3 | 3.3 |
| Medicaid | 49,401 | 0.7 | 3.1 | 2.4 |
| SSI | 6,499 | 0.1 | 0.4 | 0.3 |
| Housing | 1,346 | 0.0 | 0.1 | 0.1 |
| *Tax Expenditures* | *120,034* | *1.6* | *7.6* | *5.9* |
| Net exclusion of pension contributions and earnings | 69,600 | 0.9 | 4.4 | 3.4 |
| Nontaxation of 85% of Social Security benefits | 19,365 | 0.3 | 1.2 | 1.0 |
| Exclusion of Medicare Part A benefits | 9,000 | 0.1 | 0.6 | 0.4 |
| Exclusion of Medicare Part B benefits | 5,884 | 0.1 | 0.4 | 0.3 |
| Individual retirement plans | 8,800 | 0.1 | 0.6 | 0.4 |
| Keogh plans | 3,500 | 0.0 | 0.2 | 0.2 |
| Housing | 3,885 | 0.1 | 0.2 | 0.2 |

*(continued on next page)*

Life-Cycle Breakdown of Social Insurance Transfers and Tax Expenditures, Fiscal Year 1996 *(continued)*

| | $ (millions) | % of GDP | % of Federal direct expenditures | % of Federal direct & tax expenditures |
|---|---|---|---|---|
| **Working Years** | **334,992** | **4.4** | **21.3** | **16.5** |
| *Transfers* | *255,898* | *3.4* | *16.3* | *12.6* |
| Medicaid | 84,459 | 1.1 | 5.4 | 4.2 |
| Social Security: disability insurance | 43,500 | 0.6 | 2.8 | 2.1 |
| Unemployment compensation (includes state) | 43,252 | 0.6 | 2.8 | 2.1 |
| Workers' compensation | 47,048 | 0.6 | 3.0 | 2.3 |
| SSI | 19,192 | 0.3 | 1.2 | 0.9 |
| State temporary disability | 3,597 | 0.0 | 0.2 | 0.2 |
| General assistance (medical care component)—state dollars | 5,429 | 0.1 | 0.3 | 0.3 |
| Housing | 9,421 | 0.1 | 0.6 | 0.5 |
| *Tax Expenditures* | *79,095* | *1.0* | *5.0* | *3.9* |
| Exclusions of employer contributions for medical insurance premiums and medical care | 48,400 | 0.6 | 3.1 | 2.4 |
| Housing | 27,195 | 0.4 | 1.7 | 1.3 |
| Deductibility of medical expenses | 3,500 | 0.0 | 0.2 | 0.2 |
| **Families with Children** | **195,819** | **2.6** | **12.5** | **9.6** |
| *Transfers* | *105,644* | *1.4* | *6.6* | *5.2* |
| Food stamps | 27,344 | 0.4 | 1.7 | 1.3 |
| Medicaid | 25,497 | 0.3 | 1.6 | 1.3 |
| AFDC | 23,677 | 0.3 | 1.5 | 1.2 |
| Social services block grant (Title XX) | 6,095 | 0.1 | 0.4 | 0.3 |
| SSI | 4,677 | 0.1 | 0.3 | 0.2 |
| Housing | 16,150 | 0.2 | 1.0 | 0.8 |
| Child care for recipients (and ex-recipients of AFDC) | 1,737 | 0.0 | 0.1 | 0.1 |
| At-risk child care (to avert eligibility for AFDC) | 487 | 0.0 | 0.0 | 0.0 |
| *Tax expenditures* | *89,220* | *1.1* | *5.6* | *4.4* |
| Housing | 46,620 | 0.6 | 3.0 | 2.3 |
| EITC—nonrefundable portion (effect on receipts) | 3,600 | 0.0 | 0.2 | 0.2 |
| EITC—refundable portion (increase in outlays) | 19,900 | 0.3 | 1.3 | 1.0 |

| | $ (millions) | % of GDP | % of Federal direct expenditures | % of Federal direct & tax expenditures |
|---|---|---|---|---|
| Child tax credit (nonrefundable portion) (effect on receipts) | 17,933 | 0.2 | 1.1 | 0.9 |
| Child tax credit (refundable portion) (effect on outlays) | 467 | 0.0 | 0.0 | 0.0 |
| Exclusion of employer-provided dependent care | 700 | 0.0 | 0.0 | 0.0 |

*Note:* Having neither the computers nor the staff of the Congressional Budget Office or the President's Office of Management and Budget, we have been able to present only rough estimates of the costs of or proposals as compared with current law. The table above sets forth the FY 1996 expenditures relating to the social expenditure programs we have considered. These data have served as our baseline for existing expenditures. In a number of instances, we have been forced to make our own estimates of how much a particular category of expenditures benefits a particular age group. Some other estimates have also been required. The basic sources we used were *The Budget of the United States,* FY 1997; the *1998 Green Book; Statistical Abstract of the United States, 1997* (115th ed.); Joint Committee on Taxation, *Estimates of Federal Tax Expenditures for Fiscal Years 1996–2000* (JCS-21-98); U.S. Department of Health and Human Services, Health Care Finance Review, *Medicare and Medicaid Statistical Supplement, 1996; State and Metropolitan Data Book, 1997–98; Annual Statistical Supplement to the Social Security Bulletin, 1997;* and Congressional Budget Office, *The Economic and Budget Outlook: An Update* (August 1998). Because our claim is merely to have proposed reforms that are roughly within current overall spending limits, pages of tedious methodological notes have not been included here to explain how each data problem was resolved.

# Notes

**PROLOGUE: OF FABLES, FEARS, AND FUNDAMENTALS**

1. Josh Jacobs, ed., "The Story of the Three Little Pigs," in *English Fairy Tales* (New York: G. P. Putnam's Sons, 1892), 69.
2. "The Unrevised True History Concerning the Three Little Pigs and the Big Bad Wolf" at http://www.clandjop.com/mlindste/3pigs.html.
3. James Finn Garner, *Politically Correct Bedtime Stories* (New York: Macmillan, 1994), 11.
4. "Three Little Pigs" at http://www.jps.net/xephyr/rich/dzone/hoozoo/3pigs.html.
5. Roald Dahl, "The Three Little Pigs," in *Revolting Rhymes,* available at http://www.xs4all.nl/ace/Literaria/Txt-Dahl2.html.
6. Humphrey Carpenter and Mari Pritchard, *The Oxford Companion to Children's Literature* (New York: Oxford University Press, 1984).
7. National Conference on Social Welfare, *The Report of the Committee on Economic Security of 1935,* 50th anniversary ed. (Washington, D.C.: National Conference on Social Welfare, 1985).
8. P. J. Ferrara, *Social Security: Averting the Crisis* (Washington, D.C.: Cato Institute, 1982).
9. Lawrence R. Jacobs and Robert Y. Shapiro, "Myths and Misunderstandings about Public Opinion toward Social Security," in R. Douglas Arnold, Michael

J. Graetz, and Alicia H. Munnell, eds., *Framing the Social Security Debate* (Washington, D.C.: National Academy of Social Insurance/Brookings Institution, 1998).

10. Robert Kuttner, *Revolt of the Haves: Tax Rebellions and Hard Times* (New York: Simon and Schuster, 1980).

11. See generally Abraham Epstein, *Insecurity, a Challenge to America: A Study of Social Insurance in the United States and Abroad* (1938; New York: Agathon, 1968); Isaac Max Rubinow, *Social Insurance* (New York: Holt, 1916); and H. H. Wolfenden, *The Real Meaning of Social Insurance: Its Present Status and Tendencies* (Toronto: MacMillan, 1932). See also George E. Rejda, *Social Insurance and Economic Security* (Englewood Cliffs, N.J.: Prentice-Hall, 1988); W. Beveridge, *Social Insurance and Allied Services* (New York: MacMillan, 1942); and J. L. Cohen, *Social Insurance Unified, and Other Essays* (London: P. S. King and Son, 1924). For a study focusing on collective action to reform social insurance, see D. S. Sanders, *The Impact of Reform Movements on Social Policy Change: The Case of Social Insurance* (Fair Lawn, N.J.: R. E. Burdick, 1973).

### CHAPTER 1: THE FOUNDATIONS OF SOCIAL INSURANCE

1. For general literature on theories of development and critiques of insurance systems, see H. S. Denenberg et al., *Risk and Insurance* (Englewood Cliffs, N.J.: Prentice-Hall, 1964); G. E. Rejda, *Social Insurance and Economic Security* (Englewood Cliffs, N.J.: Prentice-Hall, 1988); and A. H. Willett, *The Economic Theory of Risk and Insurance* (Philadelphia: University of Pennsylvania Press, 1951).

2. See C. A. Heimer, *Reactive Risk and Rational Action: Managing Moral Hazard in Insurance Contracts* (Berkeley: University of California Press, 1985).

### CHAPTER 2: THE SOCIAL INSURANCE CONTRACT

1. There are many sources for numbers similar to those in the text, although they vary somewhat depending upon the data source, the way that income is aggregated in a family, and the way that inflation is taken into account. The numbers we have used here are from Benjamin M. Friedman, "The New Dream," *New York Review of Books,* Oct. 8, 1998, p. 52.

2. U.S. Bureau of the Census, *Statistical Abstract of the United States: 1997,* 117th ed. (Washington, D.C., 1997), tables 730 and 752. (Hereinafter *Statistical Abstract.*)

3. For example, in 1940 about 6% of all families were in extended families; in 1990 that number was only 3%. U.S. Department of Commerce, *Historical Statistics of the United States* (Washington, D.C., 1971), ser. A288–312; *1997 Statistical Abstract,* sec. 1, table 66.

4. For an analysis of some of these issues and a compendium of the relevant literature, see Katherine Baicker, "Fiscal Federalism and Social Insurance," Ph.D. diss., Harvard University, 1998.

## CHAPTER 3: PROVIDING SOCIAL INSURANCE

1. See generally W. A. Klein, "The Definition of 'Income' under a Negative Income Tax," *Florida State University Law Review* 2 (1974): 2; Organization for Economic Cooperation and Development, Directorate for Financial and Fiscal Affairs, Taxation Division, *Negative Income Tax: an Approach to the Coordination of Taxation and Social Welfare Policies* (Paris: OECD, 1974); H. Parker, *Instead of the Dole: An Enquiry into Integration of the Tax and Benefit Systems* (London: Routledge, 1989); P. H. Rossi and K. Lyall, *Reforming Public Welfare: A Critique of the Negative Income Tax Experiment* (New York: Russell Sage Foundation, 1976); A. Tella et al., *The Hours of Work and Family Income Response to Negative Income Tax Plans: The Impact on the Working Poor* (Kalamazoo, Mich.: W. E. Upjohn Institute for Employment Research, 1971); J. Tobin et al., *Is a Negative Income Tax Practical?* (Washington, D.C.: Brookings Institution, 1967); W. Williams, *The Struggle for a Negative Income Tax: A Case Study, 1965–70* (Seattle: Institute of Governmental Research, University of Washington, 1972).

2. See, e.g., Budgetary Appendix.

3. For an extended argument in favor of wage subsidies, see Edmund S. Phelps, *Rewarding Work* (Cambridge: Harvard University Press, 1997).

4. Joint Committee on Taxation, "Estimates of Federal Tax Expenditures," *Tax Notes* 82 (Jan. 4, 1999): 95.

5. U.S. Congress, Committee on Ways and Means, U.S. House of Representatives, *1998 Green Book* (Washington, D.C., May 19, 1998), 870.

6. W. Andrew Achenbaum, *Social Security: Visions and Revisions* (New York: Cambridge University Press, 1986).

7. Ibid.

## CHAPTER 4: INSURING A WORKING LIFE

1. Paul Samuelson, quoted in Geoffrey Moore and John Cullity, "Does the Rally Signal Recession's End?" *New York Times,* Feb. 17, 1991, sec. 3, p. 13.

2. See generally Saul Blaustein, *Unemployment Insurance in the United States: The First Half Century* (Kalamazoo, Mich.: W. E. Upjohn Institute for Employment Research, 1993); Saul Blaustein, *Job and Income Security for Unemployed Workers: New Directions* (Kalamazoo, Mich.: W. E. Upjohn Institute for Employment Research, 1981); Jonathan Gruber, "The Consumption Smoothing Benefits of Unemployment Insurance," *American Economic Review* 87 (1997): 192; W. Haber and G. M. Merrill, *Unemployment Insurance in the American Economy* (Homewood, Ill.: Richard D. Irwin, 1966); Philip Harvey, *Joblessness and the Law before the New Deal* (forthcoming, 1999); Robert Hutchens, "Distributional Equity in the Unemployment Insurance System," *Industrial and Labor Relations Review* 34 (1981): 377; Interstate Commission on Unemployment Insurance, Report to the Governors of Connecticut, Massachusetts, New Jersey, New York, Ohio, Pennsylvania, and Rhode Island (Washington, D.C., March 1932); Richard McHugh and Ingrid Kock, "Unemployment Insurance: Responding to the Expanding Role of Women in the Work Force," *Clearing House Review* 27 (1994):

1422; Daniel Nelson, *Unemployment Insurance: The American Experience, 1915–1935* (Madison: University of Wisconsin Press, 1969); and Daniel Price, "Unemployment Insurance Then and Now, 1935–1985," *Social Security Bulletin* 48 (1985): 22.

3. Nelson, *Unemployment Insurance*.

4. The race to the bottom in benefits provision has been studied most extensively with respect to welfare. For a recent review of the empirical literature, see Jan K. Brueckner, "Welfare Reform and Interstate Competition: Theory and Evidence," occasional paper no. 21 in The Urban Institute, *Assessing the New Federalism* (Washington, D.C.: Urban Institute, 1998).

5. See Patricia M. Anderson and Bruce D. Meyer, "The Effects of Firm-Specific Taxes and Government Mandates with an Application to the U.S. Unemployment Insurance Program," *Journal of Public Economics* 65 (1997): 119.

6. See, e.g., Marc Baldwin and Richard McHugh, "Unprepared for Recession: The Erosion of State Unemployment Insurance Coverage Fostered by Public Policy in the 1980s," briefing paper, Economic Policy Institute (Washington, D.C., February 1992); Rebecca M. Blank and David Card, "Recent Trends in Insured and Uninsured Unemployment: Is There an Explanation?" *Quarterly Journal of Economics* 106 (1991): 1157; Walter Corson and Walter Nicholson, "An Examination of Declining UI Claims during the 1980s," U.S. Department of Labor, Unemployment Insurance occasional paper 88-3 (Washington, D.C., 1988); Wayne Vroman, "The Decline in Unemployment Insurance Claims Activity in the 1980s," U.S. Department of Labor, Unemployment Insurance occasional paper 91-2 (Washington, D.C., 1991); Marc Baldwin, "Benefit Recipiency Rates under the Federal/State Unemployment Insurance Program: Explaining and Reversing Decline," Ph.D. diss., Massachusetts Institute of Technology, 1993; see also Brian P. McCall, "The Impact of Unemployment Insurance Benefit Levels on Recipiency," *Journal of Business and Economic Statistics* 13 (1995): 189; Patricia M. Anderson and Bruce D. Meyer, "Unemployment Insurance Takeup Rates and the After-Tax Value of Benefits," *Quarterly Journal of Economics* 112 (1997): 913. For a summary of the literature, see Daniel P. McMurrer and Amy Chasanov, "Trends in Unemployment Insurance Benefits," *Monthly Labor Review* 35 (September 1995).

7. See Blank and Card, "Recent Trends in Insured and Uninsured Unemployment," 1168–71; Corson and Nicholson, "An Examination of Declining UI Claims during the 1980s," 123; Vroman, "Decline in Unemployment Insurance Claims Activity in the 1980s," 13; and McMurrer and Chasanov, "Trends in Unemployment Insurance Benefits," 36.

8. See John W. Budd and Brian P. McCall, "The Effect of Unions on the Receipt of Unemployment Insurance Benefits," *Industrial and Labor Relations Review* 50 (1997): 478; see also Baldwin and McHugh, "Unprepared for Recession," 17; Blank and Card, "Recent Trends in Insured and Uninsured Unemployment," 1178.

9. See Baldwin and McHugh, "Unprepared for Recession," 18; Corson and Nicholson, "An Examination of Declining UI Claims during the 1980s," 119–20.

10. See, e.g., Lonnie Golden and Eileen Appelbaum, "What Was Driving the 1982–88 Boom in Temporary Employment? Preferences of Workers or Decisions and Power of Employers," *American Journal of Economics and Society* 51 (1992): 473 (attributing

boom to intensified competition in product markets, volatility in product demand, and decline in relative bargaining power of unions); Karylee Laird and Nicolas Williams, "Employment Growth in the Temporary Help Supply Industry," *Journal of Labor Research* 17 (1996): 663 (attributing growth in temporary help supply industry in part to firms' efforts to reduce costs while maintaining a flexible workforce in the face of increases in aggregate output and heightened foreign competition); see also Lewis M. Segal and Daniel G. Sullivan, "The Growth of Temporary Services Work," *Journal of Economic Perspectives* 11 (1997): 117. But compare Laird and Williams, "Employment Growth" (which also attributes part of growth in temporary help supply industry to continued growth in married females in the labor force) with Golden and Appelbaum, "What Was Driving the 1982–88 Boom in Temporary Employment?" 485–87 (which finds no effect of increases in married women, younger workers, and older workers in the labor force). See generally Steven Hipple, "Contingent Work: Results from the Second Survey," *Monthly Labor Review* 22 (November 1998) (which reports results of the February 1997 supplement to *Current Population Survey*).

11. For rules about the period for which leaving one's job disqualifies one for UI, see Baldwin and McHugh, "Unprepared for Recession," 18–19; Corson and Nicholson, "An Examination of Declining UI Claims during the 1980s," 131–35; and McMurrer and Chasanov, "Trends in Unemployment Insurance Benefits," 35–36. On the effects of the job search requirement, compare Paul L. Burgess, "Compliance with Unemployment-Insurance Job-Search Regulations," *Journal of Law and Economics* 35 (1992): 371; and Walter Corson et al., "Work Search among Unemployment Insurance Claimants: An Investigation of Some Effects of State Rules and Enforcement," U.S. Department of Labor, Unemployment Insurance occasional paper 88-1 (Washington, D.C., 1988) with Orley Ashenfelter et al., "Do Unemployment Insurance Recipients Actively Seek Work? Randomized Trials in Four U.S. States," working paper no. 6982, National Bureau of Economic Research (Cambridge, Mass., 1999).

12. See Laurence E. Norton and Marc Linder, "Down and Out in Weslaco, Texas, and Washington, D.C.: Race-Based Discrimination Against Farm Workers under Federal Unemployment Insurance," *University of Michigan Journal of Law Reform* 29 (1996): 177.

13. *Florida v. Mellon,* 273 U.S. 12 (1927).

14. See Amy B. Chasanov, "Clarifying Conditions for Nonmonetary Eligibility in the Unemployment Insurance System," *University of Michigan Journal of Law Reform* 29 (1996): 89; 106, table 4 (finding, based on 1994 survey of UI agencies in all fifty states, District of Columbia, Puerto Rico, and the Virgin Islands, that such a reason does not constitute "good cause" in at least thirty-eight jurisdictions).

15. See generally National Institute on Disability and Rehabilitation Research, *Chartbook on Work and Disability in the United States* (Washington, D.C.: National Institute on Disability and Rehabilitation Research, 1998).

16. See generally Jerry L. Mashaw and Virginia P. Reno, eds., *Balancing Security and Opportunity: The Challenge of Disability Income Policy,* report of the Disability Policy Panel (Washington, D.C.: National Academy of Social Insurance, 1996); Jerry L. Mashaw and Virginia P. Reno, *The Environment of Disability Income Policy: Programs,*

*People, History and Context,* Disability Policy Panel interim report (Washington, D.C.: National Academy of Social Insurance, 1996).

17. Deborah A. Stone, *The Disabled State* (Philadelphia: Temple University Press, 1984).

18. Leo J. M. Aarts, Richard Burkhauser, and Philip R. DeJong, *Curing the Dutch Disease: An International Perspective on Disability Policy Reform* (Brookfield, Vt.: Avebury, 1996).

19. On the early history, see Abraham Epstein, *Insecurity: A Challenge to America* (New York: Agathon, 1968), 577–617.

20. See, e.g., Randolph E. Bergstrom, *Courting Danger: Injury and Law in New York City, 1870–1910* (Ithaca, N.Y.: Cornell University Press, 1992), showing tort law accounting for 1% of the caseload in 1870, 11.3% in 1910. For contested cases, these numbers are 4.2% and 40.9%, respectively (see Epstein, *Insecurity,* 16–18, tables 1–2).

21. Orin Kramer and Richard Briffault, *Workers' Compensation: Strengthening the Social Compact* (New York: Insurance Information Institute Press, 1991), 2.

22. For a general discussion, see Emily A. Spieler and John F. Burton, Jr., "Compensation for Disabled Workers: Workers' Compensation," in Terry Thomason et al., eds., *New Approaches to Disability in the Workplace* (Ithaca, N.Y.: ILR Press, 1998).

23. Robert J. Longman and Robert M. Hutchens, "The Future of Workers' Compensation," in John F. Burton, ed., *New Perspectives in Workers' Compensation* (Ithaca, N.Y.: ILR Press, 1998), 113.

24. Ibid., 116.

25. John F. Burton, "Workers' Compensation Benefits, Costs, and Profits: An Overview of Dollars in the 1990s," *John Burton's Workers' Compensation Review* (November–December 1996).

26. William Safire, *Safire's New Political Dictionary* (New York: Random House, 1993), 672.

27. See Kramer and Briffault, *Workers' Compensation,* 1991.

28. Burton, "Workers' Compensation Benefits, Costs, and Profits." These system-level statistics can be very misleading, for workers' compensation programs are very dynamic across both space and time. Total costs of workers' compensation programs were very flat in the 1960s at about 1% of payroll. These costs escalated rapidly in the 1970s and 1980s, peaking at 1.66% of payroll in 1992, but have declined in every subsequent year for which data are available. Virtually no workers' compensation insurers made money in the early 1980s, but virtually all have in the 1990s.

   The picture across space is even more heterogeneous than across time. Total benefits paid per 100,000 covered workers as a percentage of the national average ranged from 176% in Hawaii to 38% in Indiana. And while individual states show fairly strong within-state patterns of high, low, or middling costs, changes can be fairly abrupt. Between 1985 and 1995 some states increased or decreased their payments for major permanent partial disabilities by 25% to as much as 40%. For an overview of developments in the late 1980s and 1990s, see generally *John Burton's Workers' Compensation Monitor*—vol. 9, no. 6; vol. 10, no. 3; and vol. 10, no. 4 (1996–97).

29. See Longman and Hutchens, "Future of Workers' Compensation," 130–31; and Emily A. Spieler, "Perpetuating Risk? Workers' Compensation and the Persistence of Occupational Injuries," *Houston Law Review* 31, no. 1 (symposium, 1994): 119–264.

30. See Kramer and Briffault, *Workers' Compensation,* 1991.

31. David L. Durbin et al., "Workers' Compensation and Medical Expenditures: Price vs. Quantity," *Journal of Risk and Insurance* 63, no. 1 (1996): 13–33.

32. Emily A. Spieler and John F. Burton, Jr., "Compensation for Disabled Workers: Workers' Compensation," in Thomason et al., *New Approaches to Disability in the Workplace.*

33. See generally Edward D. Berkowitz, *Disabled Policy: America's Programs for the Handicapped* (Cambridge: Cambridge University Press, 1987).

34. See generally R. Prins, T. J. Veerman, and S. Andriessen, *Work Incapacity in a Cross-National Perspective* (The Hague: Netherlands Institute for the Working Environment, 1992).

35. Jerry L. Mashaw and Virginia P. Reno, eds., *Balancing Security and Opportunity: The Challenge of Disability Income Policy,* report of the Disability Policy Panel (Washington, D.C.: National Academy of Social Insurance, 1996).

36. See generally Jerry L. Mashaw, "Disability: Why Does the Search for Good Programs Continue?" in Eric Kingson and James Schulz, eds., *Social Security in the Twenty-First Century* (New York: Oxford University Press, 1997).

## CHAPTER 5: INSURING THE POST-WORK YEARS

1. See generally H. J. Aaron and G. T. Burtless, *Retirement and Economic Behavior* (Washington, D.C.: Brookings Institution, 1984); V. L. Bergston and W. A. Achenbaum, *The Changing Contract across Generations* (New York: Aldine de Gruyter, 1993); Library of Congress, Congressional Research Service, Congressional Budget Office, et al., *Retirement Income for an Aging Population: A Report* (Washington, D.C., 1987); and President's Commission on Pension Policy, *Coming of Age: Toward a National Retirement Income Policy* (Washington, D.C., 1981).

2. Recent works discussing Social Security generally include S. J. Schieber and J. B. Shoven, *Public Policy toward Pensions* (Cambridge: MIT Press, 1997); Henry J. Aaron and Robert D. Reischauer, *Countdown to Reform: The Great Social Security Debate* (New York: Century Foundation Press, 1998); R. Douglas Arnold, Michael J. Graetz, and Alicia H. Munnell, *Framing the Social Security Debate: Values, Politics, and Economics* (Washington, D.C.: National Academy of Social Insurance, 1998); O. S. Mitchell et al., *Prospects for Social Security Reform* (Philadelphia: University of Pennsylvania Press, 1998); Eric R. Kingson and James H. Schulz, *Social Security in the Twenty-First Century* (New York: Oxford University Press, 1997); Peter A. Diamond, David C. Lindeman, and Howard Young, *Social Security: What Role for the Future?* (Washington, D.C.: National Academy of Social Insurance, 1997); E. M. Gramlich, *Is It Time to Reform Social Security?* (Ann Arbor: University of Michigan Press, 1998); H. J. Aaron et al., *Can America Afford to Grow Old? Paying for Social Security* (Washington, D.C.: Brookings Institution, 1989); H. J. Aaron and R. D. Reischauer, *There When You Need It: Saving Social Security for Future Generations of Americans* (New York: Century Foundation, 1998); M. J. Boskin, *Too Many Promises: The Uncertain Future of Social Security* (Homewood, Ill.: Dow Jones-Irwin, 1986); M. J. Boskin and G. F. Break, *The Crisis in Social Security: Problems and Prospects* (San Francisco: Institute for Contemporary Studies, 1977); P. G. Peterson, *Will America Grow Up before It*

*Grows Old? How the Coming Social Security Crisis Threatens You, Your Family, and Your Country* (New York: Random House, 1996).

3. Gary Burtless of the Brookings Institution has produced data showing that since 1910, while the average returns to equity investments have been 7.18%, average market returns to particular age cohorts (assuming a forty-year working life) have ranged from 1.69% to 9.93%. Sylvester Schieber and John Shoven have found substantially less variation by recalculating these returns on a variety of different assumptions, including an earlier starting date and that people invest in patterns similar to the way workers allocate 401(k) money—roughly 60/40 stocks to bonds from age twenty to fifty-five and 40/60 stocks to bonds in their fifties and sixties. See Sylvester J. Schieber and John Shoven, *The Real Deal: The History and Future of Social Security* (New Haven and London: Yale University Press, 1999), chap. 23.

4. James Banks, Richard Blindell, and Sarah Tanner, "Is There a Retirement Savings Puzzle?" *American Economic Review* 88 (1998): 769–88.

5. In 1900, for example, retirees who had worked with the Pennsylvania Railroad for twenty to thirty years, until age seventy, without disobeying or provoking management, received at retirement 1% of their final ten-year average salary times the number of years spent with the company—a "defined benefit" pension (Steven A. Sass, *The Promise of Private Pensions: The First Hundred Years* [Cambridge: Harvard University Press, 1997], 54). The company did so not as a legal right, mind you, but as a means of labor force management, or as an act of charity (see Carole Haber, *Beyond Sixty-Five: The Dilemma of Old Age in America's Past* [Cambridge: Cambridge University Press, 1983], 114–16). International Harvester led the move toward compulsory retirement by including such a requirement in its 1908 pension plan. See Sass, *Promise of Private Pensions*, 54; and Dora L. Costa, *The Evolution of Retirement: An American Economic History, 1880–1990* (Chicago: University of Chicago Press, 1998).

6. Murray W. Latimer, *Industrial Pension Systems in the U.S. and Canada* (New York: Industrial Relations Counselors, 1932), 852.

7. Sass, *Promise of Private Pensions*, 56–57.

8. Ibid.

9. Ibid., 183–85. For a careful evaluation of the Studebaker episode, see John H. Langbein and Bruce A. Wolk, *Pension and Employee Benefit Law*, 2d ed. (New York: Foundation Press, 1995), 62–67.

10. A. Epstein, *Insecurity, a Challenge to America: A Study of Social Insurance in the United States and Abroad* (New York: Agathon, 1968), 500.

11. David M. Cutler and Lawrence F. Katz, "Rising Inequality? Changes in the Distribution of Income and Consumption in the 1980s," *American Economic Review* 82 (May 1992): 546.

12. For more detail, see Employee Benefits Research Institute, *Databook on Employee Benefits*, Deborah Holmes et al., eds., 4th ed. (Washington, D.C.: EBRI, 1998), table 7.4.

13. EBRI, *Databook on Employee Benefits*, 5.

14. U.S. Social Security Administration, 1997, *Annual Report of the Board of Trustees of the Federal Old-Age and Survivors Insurance and Disability Insurance Trust Funds* (Balti-

more, Md.: U.S. Social Security Administration, 1997); see also EBRI, *Databook on Employee Benefits.*

15. Committee on Ways and Means, U.S. House of Representatives, 102d Congress, 1st sess., "Overview of the Federal Tax System," Apr. 10, 1991.

16. In addition to the other sources cited in this chapter, see generally Richard A. Ippolito, *Pension Plans and Employee Performance* (Chicago: University of Chicago Press, 1997); and Dow Jones-Irwin, *Pensions and Public Policy* (Homewood, Ill.: Dow Jones-Irwin, 1986); G. S. Fields and O. S. Mitchell, *Retirement, Pensions, and Social Security* (Cambridge: MIT Press, 1984); M. S. Gordon, O. S. Mitchell, and M. M. Twinney, *Positioning Pensions for the Twenty-First Century* (Philadelphia: University of Pennsylvania Press, 1997); S. J. Schieber and J. B. Shoven, *Public Policy toward Pensions* (Cambridge: MIT Press, 1997); and Z. Bodie, O. S. Mitchell, and J. A. Turner, *Securing Employer-Based Pensions: An International Perspective* (Philadelphia: University of Pennsylvania Press).

17. EBRI, *Databook on Employee Benefits,* 5.

18. Staff of the Joint Committee on Taxation, *Estimates of Federal Tax Expenditures for Fiscal Years 1999–2003* (JCS7-98) (Washington, D.C., Dec. 14, 1998). The two next largest tax expenditure items, exclusions from taxable wages of employer-provided health benefits and the home mortgage interest deduction, were of roughly similar magnitudes. The tax expenditures may be overstated for two reasons. First, they are described in terms of cash flow, not present value (see A. H. Munnell, *The Economics of Private Pensions* [Washington, D.C.: Brookings Institution, 1982]). Second, they include more than the exemption of investment income (see Daniel I. Halperin, "Interest in Disguise: Taxing the 'Time Value of Money,' " 95 *Yale Law Journal* 506 [January 1986]). Even if the tax expenditure estimates somewhat overstate the size of the government subsidy, the tax incentive to employer-provided pensions undoubtedly constitutes an extremely important feature of this nation's retirement security program.

19. Report of the 1994–96 Advisory Council on Social Security, vol. 2: *Reports of the Technical Panel on Trends and Issues in Retirement Savings, Technical Panel on Assumptions and Methods, and Presentations to the Council* (Washington, D.C., 1997), 30.

20. Dallas L. Salisbury, "Employers and Individuals Must Do More to Allow Retirement Tomorrow," in R. Douglas Arnold, Michael J. Graetz and Alicia H. Munnell, eds., *Framing the Social Security Debate: Values, Politics and Economics* (Washington, D.C.: National Academy of Social Insurance, 1998).

21. The tendency of many workers to take their pension benefits in a lump sum when they change jobs exacerbates this problem (see ibid.).

## CHAPTER 6: SOCIAL INSURANCE PRIOR TO WORK

1. See generally R. M. Blank, *It Takes a Nation: A New Agenda for Fighting Poverty* (New York: Russell Sage Foundation, 1997); P. L. Chase-Lansdale and J. Brooks-Gunn, *Escape from Poverty: What Makes a Difference for Children?* (New York: Cambridge University Press, 1995); S. Danzier and P. Gottschalk, *How Have Families with Children Been Faring?* (Madison: University of Wisconsin, Institute for Research on Poverty,

1986); D. Del Boca, *Children as Public Goods: An Economic Approach to Child Support Payments in Relation to the Custody Decision* (Madison: University of Wisconsin, Institute for Research on Poverty, 1986); I. B. Harris, *Children in Jeopardy: Can We Break the Cycle of Poverty?* (New York: Cambridge University Press, 1991); S. E. Mayer, *What Money Can't Buy: Family Income and Children's Life Chances* (Cambridge: Harvard University Press, 1997).

2. U.S. Congress, Committee on Ways and Means, U.S. House of Representatives, *1998 Green Book* (Washington, D.C., May 19, 1998), 870; Joseph Dalaker and Mary Naifeh, U.S. Department of Commerce, Bureau of the Census, *Poverty in the United States: 1997* (Washington, D.C., 1998), p. vi.

3. Of the single-parent families with children under age 18 in 1996, 38% of the mothers had never been married, 58% were divorced or separated from their spouse, and 4% were widows.

4. *1998 Green Book,* 870. Nearly one-fourth of the 69 million children under age eighteen now live in a one-parent family; see *1998 Green Book,* 542.

5. Congressional Budget Office, Long Term Budgetary Pressures and Policy Options (Washington, D.C., May 1998), 6.

6. See, e.g., Katherine McFate, Timothy Smeedling, and Lee Rainwater, "Markets and States: Poverty Trends and Transfer System Effectiveness in the 1980s"; Greg J. Duncan et al., "Poverty and Social Assistance Dynamics in the United States, Canada and Europe"; and Susan Mayer, "A Comparison of Poverty and Living Conditions in the United States, Canada, Sweden and Germany," all in Katherine McFate, Roger Lawson, and William Julius Wilson, eds., *Poverty, Inequality and the Future of Social Policy* (New York: Russell Sage Foundation, 1995).

7. Center for the Future of Children, *The Future of Children: Children and Poverty* 7, no. 2 (1997): 58.

8. See, e.g., John M. Broder, "Keeping Score: Big Social Changes Revive the False God of Numbers," *New York Times,* Aug. 17, 1991, sec. 4, p. 1.

9. National Conference on Social Welfare, *The Report of the Committee on Economic Security of 1935,* 50th anniversary ed. (Washington, D.C., 1985), 56.

10. Abraham Epstein, *Insecurity, a Challenge to America: A Study of Social Insurance in the United States and Abroad* (1938; New York: Agathon, 1968), 624.

**CHAPTER 7: THE SPECIAL CASE OF MEDICAL INSURANCE**

1. Jacob Hacker, *The Road to Nowhere: The Genesis of President Clinton's Plan for Health Security* (Princeton, N.J.: Princeton University Press, 1997); H. J. Aaron, *The Problems That Won't Go Away: Reforming U.S. Health Care Financing* (Washington, D.C.: Brookings Institution, 1996); F. P. Albritton, *Health Care Insurance Reform in the United States: A Market Approach with Application from the Federal Republic of Germany* (Lanham, Md.: University Press of America, 1993); F. J. Angell, *Health Insurance* (New York: Ronald Press, 1963); K. J. Arrow, *Theoretical Issues in Health Insurance* (Colchester, Eng.: University of Essex, 1973); J. M. Feder et al., *National Health Insur-*

*ance: Conflicting Goals and Policy Choices* (Washington, D.C.: Urban Institute, 1980); R. Fein, *Medical Care, Medical Costs: The Search for a Health Insurance Policy* (Cambridge: Harvard University Press, 1986); D. S. Hirshfield, *The Lost Reform: The Campaign for Compulsory Health Insurance in the United States from 1932 to 1943* (Cambridge: Harvard University Press, 1970); M. P. LaPlante et al., *Disability, Health Insurance Coverage, and Utilization of Acute Health Services in the United States* (Washington, D.C.: U.S. Department of Health and Human Services, 1993); J. P. Newhouse and Rand Corporation, *Free for All? Lessons from the Rand Health Insurance Experiment* (Cambridge: Harvard University Press, 1993); and U.S. Social Security Administration, *History of the Provisions of Old-Age, Survivors, Disability, and Health Insurance, 1935–1996* (Washington, D.C.: Social Security Administration Office of the Chief Actuary, 1997).

2. Theodore R. Marmor, *The Politics of Medicare* (Chicago: Aldine, 1973), 8.

3. Hacker, *Road to Nowhere.* For background on the proposal, critiques, and politics of the failed Clinton health-care plan, see generally M. A. Hall, *Reforming Private Health Insurance* (Washington, D.C.: American Enterprise Institute Press, 1994); R. B. Helms, *American Health Policy: Critical Issues for Reform* (Washington, D.C.: American Enterprise Institute, 1993); T. R. Marmor, *Understanding Health Care Reform* (New Haven and London: Yale University Press, 1994); and T. Skockpol, *Boomerang: Clinton's Health Security Effort and the Turn Against Government in U.S. Politics* (New York: Norton, 1996).

4. See T. R. Marmor, "Doctors, Politics, and Health Insurance for the Aged: The Enactment of Medicare," discussion paper 86-803 (Madison: University of Wisconsin, Institute for Research on Poverty, 1968), 116–28.

5. Congressional Budget Office, *Long Term Budgetary Pressures and Policy Options* (Washington, D.C., May 1998), 54.

6. Ibid., 48–49.

7. See Marilyn Moon, *Restructuring Medicare's Cost Sharing* (New York: Commonwealth Fund, 1991).

8. Health Care Financing Agency, Health Care Financing Review, *Medicare and Medicaid Statistical Supplement, 1997* (Washington, D.C., 1997).

9. Sources vary as to whether eighty or eighty-five is "old elderly." For the one-fifth figure, see P. Kemper and C. M. Murtaugh, "Lifetime Use of Nursing Home Care," *New England Journal of Medicine* 324, no. 9 (1991).

10. Sheila R. Zedlewski and Timothy D. McBride, "The Changing Profile of the Elderly: Effects on Future Long-Term Care," *Milbank Quarterly* 70, no. 2 (1992): 247–75.

11. Employee Benefit Research Institute, *Databook on Employee Benefits* (Washington, D.C.: EBRI, 1995), 389.

12. See generally L. Burman and the U.S. Congressional Budget Office, *The Tax Treatment of Employment-Based Health Insurance* (Washington, D.C.: U.S. Congressional Budget Office, 1994); and M. V. Pauly, *Health Benefits at Work: An Economical and Political Analysis of Employment-Based Health Insurance* (Ann Arbor: University of Michigan Press, 1997).

CHAPTER 9: SOCIAL INSURANCE AND HEALTH CARE

1. See figure 7.3.
2. In the United States, various public policies surely helped. Wartime price controls got employers into the health benefits business. Tax incentives kept them there. ERISA's prohibition of state regulation of the self-insured turned employers into insurers. See generally Michael J. Graetz, "Universal Health Insurance without an Employer Mandate," *Domestic Affairs* 2 (1994): 79–104.
3. American Academy of Actuaries, *Medical Savings Accounts: Cost Implications and Design Issues* (Washington, D.C.: American Academy of Actuaries, May 1995), 2–8.
4. The following table provides an example of how these subsidies might phase-down as family income rises, limiting a family's total health expenditures to no more than 0 to 15% of income. The table assumes a $4,850 annual premium and $4,000 out-of-pocket expenses.

| Income | Percent of Income | Annual subsidy | Monthly subsidy | Annual cost to family | Monthly cost to family |
|---|---|---|---|---|---|
| $10,000 | 0 | $8,850 | $738 | $  — | $ — |
| $12,000 | 1 | 8,787 | 732 | 63 | 5 |
| $14,000 | 1 | 8,690 | 724 | 160 | 13 |
| $16,000 | 2 | 8,569 | 714 | 281 | 23 |
| $18,000 | 2 | 8,423 | 702 | 427 | 36 |
| $20,000 | 3 | 8,252 | 688 | 598 | 50 |
| $22,000 | 4 | 8,057 | 671 | 793 | 66 |
| $24,000 | 4 | 7,837 | 653 | 1,013 | 84 |
| $26,000 | 5 | 7,593 | 633 | 1,257 | 105 |
| $28,000 | 5 | 7,324 | 610 | 1,526 | 127 |
| $30,000 | 6 | 7,030 | 586 | 1,820 | 152 |
| $32,000 | 7 | 6,711 | 559 | 2,139 | 178 |
| $34,000 | 7 | 6,368 | 531 | 2,482 | 207 |
| $36,000 | 8 | 6,000 | 500 | 2,850 | 237 |
| $38,000 | 9 | 5,608 | 467 | 3,242 | 270 |
| $40,000 | 9 | 5,191 | 433 | 3,659 | 305 |
| $42,000 | 10 | 4,749 | 396 | 4,101 | 342 |
| $44,000 | 10 | 4,283 | 357 | 4,567 | 381 |
| $46,000 | 11 | 3,792 | 316 | 5,058 | 422 |
| $48,000 | 12 | 3,276 | 273 | 5,574 | 464 |
| $50,000 | 12 | 2,736 | 228 | 6,114 | 509 |
| $52,000 | 13 | 2,171 | 181 | 6,679 | 557 |
| $54,000 | 13 | 1,582 | 132 | 7,268 | 606 |
| $56,000 | 14 | 967 | 81 | 7,883 | 657 |

| Income | Percent of Income | Annual subsidy | Monthly subsidy | Annual cost to family | Monthly cost to family |
|--------|-------------------|----------------|-----------------|-----------------------|------------------------|
| $58,000 | 15 | 329 | 27 | 8,521 | 710 |
| $60,000 | 15 | — | — | 8,850 | 738 |
| $62,000 | 15 | — | — | 8,850 | 738 |
| $64,000 | 15 | — | — | 8,850 | 738 |
| $66,000 | 15 | — | — | 8,850 | 738 |
| $68,000 | 15 | — | — | 8,850 | 738 |
| $70,000 | 15 | — | — | 8,850 | 738 |

5. Eric Patashnik, *Taxes and Trust Funds: The Evolution of Long-Term Commitments in the U.S. Budget* (Cambridge: Cambridge University Press, forthcoming).

6. We have no objection in principle to age-adjusted premium rates, but do not recommend such adjustments here.

7. For the "no change" result, see American Academy of Actuaries, *Medical Savings Accounts*; for the 4–6% result, see Marilyn Moon, Len M. Nichols, and Susan Wall, "Winners and Losers under Medical Savings Accounts," The Urban Institute, *Policy and Research Report* (summer–fall 1996). And for the 50% prediction, see Martin Feldstein and Jonathan Gruber, "A Major Risk Approach to Health Insurance Reform," working paper 4852 (Cambridge, Mass: National Board of Economic Research, August 1997).

8. American Academy of Actuaries, *Medical Savings Accounts*. For individuals, the policy chosen has a $1,500 deductible, a 20% copayment requirement thereafter, and a $2,500 stop-loss limit on out-of-pocket costs. The annual premium price of this policy was estimated at approximately $2,000 (1998 dollars) by the American Academy of Actuaries. For families, the policy has a $3,000 deductible, a 20% copayment requirement, and a $4,000 stop loss limit. The premium that the Actuaries estimated for this policy was about $4,850 ($4,848). It should be noted that lower premium estimates exist but were not used. For example, an Urban Institute study estimates a similar catastrophic policy for individuals to cost only $1,110. See Len M. Nichols, Marilyn Moon, and Susan Wall, *Tax-Preferred Medical Savings Accounts and Catastrophic Health Insurance Plans: A Numerical Analysis of Winners and Losers* (Washington, D.C.: The Urban Institute, April 1996), 6; http://www.urban.org/pubs/hinsure/winlose.htm. The Urban Institute has also estimated a $1,000 premium for a $2,000 deductible, $2,000 stop-loss policy. See Moon, Nichols, and Wall, "Winners and Losers under Medicaid Savings Accounts," 2.

9. We estimate that coverage of the entire population under age sixty-five would require purchase of 58 million family policies and 51 million individual policies for an aggregate policy cost of about $385 billion, using the Actuaries' policy cost estimates. This breaks down to approximately $282 billion for families and $102.5 billion for individuals. Based on average family size, these estimates cover a population of 238 million people rather than the actual 231 million total population under age sixty-five, so this may be a slight overestimate, but there could be some offset in the allocation between

individual and family policies. The Urban Institute estimates of policy costs would lower these amounts substantially.

10. The cost assessments fall into three categories: (1) the aggregate costs to the government and to individuals of purchasing high-deductible policies for all persons covered under the terms of the proposal, (2) the cost to the government of covering the out-of-pocket non-catastrophic costs of the under-sixty-five Medicaid population, and (3) the cost to the government of subsidizing premium payments and out-of-pocket costs for the near poor who are not eligible for Medicaid.

11. For example, given the estimated costs for the catastrophic policies, individuals with incomes of about $13,000 (175% of the poverty level) and families with incomes of about $32,000 (roughly 200% of the poverty level for a family of four, nearly 267% for a family of three) can pay their insurance premium costs without exceeding 15% of their incomes. At income levels of $60,000 (400% or more of the poverty level for most families), the combined costs of their insurance policies and out-of-pocket expenditures will never exceed 15% of their incomes, even if they incur the maximum in annual out-of-pocket health care costs not covered by insurance. Thus, the government's social insurance obligation to subsidize health insurance costs is limited to individuals with annual incomes below $30,000 and families with incomes of less than $60,000.

12. We estimate that 15 million to 25 million (of the 51.2 million) individuals and 25 million to 30 million (of the 58.2 million) families will be eligible for some partial subsidy. Eligibility does not equal receipt of funds, however, because some will have low out-of-pocket costs in a given year. Thus, it was estimated that $70 billion would have to be provided to low-income members of the currently uninsured and privately insured populations.

## Estimated Costs of Partial Subsidization for Persons under Age 65

| Policyholders | Number in group (in thousands) | Average annual out-of-pocket expenditure |
|---|---|---|
| Individuals | 51,000 | $1,000 |
| With money income above $30,000, needing no subsidization | 20,000–30,000 | |
| Covered by Medicaid | 7,000 | |
| Remainder, needing some subsidy | 15,000–25,000 | |
| Families | 58,000 | $1,600 |
| With money income above $60,000, needing no subsidization | 20,000–25,000 | |
| Covered by Medicaid | 10,000 | |
| Remainder, needing some subsidy | 25,000–30,000 | |

*Source:* Out-of-pocket expenditure data, American Academy of Actuaries.

With these figures in mind, we estimate that roughly $30 billion would be needed to subsidize fully the out-of-pocket costs of the Medicaid population. Further, as the following table shows, an additional $70 billion would be needed to cover the subsidy costs of those needing only a partial subsidy.

Aggregate Catastrophic Insurance System Costs

| Population group | Number of people (in thousands) | High deductible premium costs (in billions) | Out-of-pocket subsidy (in billions) | Total out-of pocket (in billions) |
|---|---|---|---|---|
| Covered by Medicaid | 30,000 | $ 50 | $ 30 | $ 30 |
| Uninsured | 41,000 | 70 | 20 | 40 |
| Private policyholders | 160,000 | 270 | 50 | 120 |
| Total | 231,000 | $390 | $100 | $190 |

*Source:* Authors.

Using average family size (3.2) from the Statistical Abstract, 7.8 million family policies would be required to cover the 25 million Medicaid recipients living in single-family and married-family households. The 5 million not living in such families would possess individual policies. Providing for the entire $4,000 (family) and $2,500 (individual) out-of-pocket limits under each of these policies would cost $43.7 billion. This represents an estimated maximum limit on costs, not an estimate of expected actual costs. A more realistic estimate of costs is in the range of $30 billion.

13. David Routh, "Catastrophic Health Insurance: A Different Approach to 'Universal Coverage,'" spring 1998, manuscript on file with authors.

14. Urban Institute researchers predict similar effects. See Moon, Nichols, and Wall, "Winners and Losers under Medical Savings Accounts"; Nichols, Moon, and Wall, *Tax-Preferred Medical Savings Accounts and Catastrophic Health Insurance Plans,* 6; http://www.urban.org/pubs/hinsure/winlose.html.

15. Anne Beeson Royalty, "Tax Preferences for Fringe Benefits and the Health Insurance Offered by Employers," Stanford University, August 1998, manuscript on file with authors.

**CHAPTER 10: UNEMPLOYMENT INSURANCE**

1. These events are described in the brochure prepared by the W. E. Upjohn, Jr., Institute for Employment Research that provides a sketch of the institute's history and purposes (on file with authors).

2. See generally Phillip Harvey, *Joblessness and the Law before the New Deal* (forthcoming 1999).

3. Craig R. Whitney, "Euro-Ready France Pleases a Guide with Vision," *New York Times,* Apr. 19, 1998, sec. 1, p. 3.

4. Without unemployment insurance, losses would have been $121.9 billion in consumer spending; $134.6 billion in real personal income; and unemployment, in thousands, of

5,049.4. With unemployment insurance, the losses equaled $112.7 billion in consumer spending; $115.9 billion in real personal income; and unemployment, in thousands, of 4,934.2.

Unemployment insurance thus prevented the loss of $9.2 billion in consumer spending (7.5%), $18.8 billion in real personal income (14.0%), and 2,300 jobs. See U.S. Department of Labor, Employment and Training Administration, *The Cyclical Effects of UI: Final Report,* UI occasional paper 91-3 (Washington, D.C., 1991).

5. Advisory Council on Unemployment Compensation, *Unemployment Insurance in the United States: Benefits, Financing, Coverage: A Report to the President and Congress* (Washington, D.C., February 1995). tables 3-1 and 3-2. Figure 10.2 shows replacement rates of average gross wage except for Germany, whose rate is 63% of average net wage. Canada has a maximum benefit of $353/week. France's replacement rate is technically $6.91/day plus 30% of average gross wage. The rate used here is calculated using most recent manufacturing hourly wage (1993) and converting it using the average exchange rate for 1993. Based on an eight-hour day, the French flat rate comes to approximately 10.4% of the daily wage. Thus, the French rate used here is 40% of the average gross wage. Italy has a flat rate of $0.87 per day plus 66% of average gross wage for workers in manufacturing and construction. Japan actually has two rates, 80% for low wages, and 60% for high wages. We have used 70% for this chart. The United Kingdom has a flat rate of $64.91 a day. Using 1995 hourly manufacturing wages, the 1995 average exchange rate, and an eight-hour workday, $64.91/day comes to about 66% of average gross wages. Finally, the rate in the United States is 50% of average gross wages in most states, with a median maximum of $212/week. In addition, the unemployment insurance benefit formula varies according to age in Japan and the United Kingdom, work history in France and the United Kingdom, region in the United States, and dependents in Germany, the United Kingdom, and some states in the United States.

6. Ibid.

7. Congressional Budget Office, *Family Incomes of Unemployment Insurance Recipients and the Implications for Extending Benefits* (Washington, D.C., 1990).

8. That comparison also highlights the critical role of necessary expense assumptions in assuring the adequacy of current payments. Based on the low estimates, most states have adequate replacement rates. In relation to the high estimates, however, most states have inadequate payment levels.

9. Advisory Council on Unemployment Compensation, *Unemployment Insurance in the United States,* table 10-2.

10. See Amy B. Chasanov, "Clarifying Conditions for Nonmonetary Eligibility in the Unemployment Insurance System," *University of Michigan Journal of Law Reform* 29 (1996): 116, table 6 (finding that an individual seeking part-time work "due to domestic circumstances [e.g., care giving]" was ineligible in 44 jurisdictions); see generally National Employment Law Project, *Women, Low-Wage Workers, and the Unemployment Compensation System: State Legislative Models for Change* (Washington, D.C.: National Employment Law Project, 1997); Deborah Maranville, "Changing Economy, Changing Lives: Unemployment Insurance and the Contingent Workforce," *Boston University Public Interest Law Journal* 4 (1995): 241, 319–27.

11. See Chasanov, "Clarifying Conditions," 106, table 4 (finding ineligibility in 38 jurisdictions if an individual voluntarily left the job "due to new personal circumstances").

12. See Patricia M. Anderson and Bruce D. Meyer, "The Effects of Firm-Specific Taxes and Government Mandates with an Application to the U.S. Unemployment Insurance Program," *Journal of Public Economics* 65 (1997): 119.

13. Although this financing mechanism cries out for reform, most states strongly resist raising their caps or further federal coercion through raising the federal minimum. Federal budgetary politics, however, are the real culprit in this story. Although FUTA taxes go into a "trust fund," they are a part of the unified federal budget. Thus, while these taxes are meant to support the administration of the unemployment compensation system (and state borrowing from federal funds during periods of extended high unemployment), deficit-fixated Congresses have refused to release large portions of the fund back to the states. States that tax their employers more by increasing the covered wage base, or supported an increase in the federal minimum, would be making gifts to the federal Treasury.

14. See, e.g., Patricia M. Anderson, "Linear Adjustment Costs and Seasonal Labor Demand: Evidence from the Retail Trade Firms," *Quarterly Journal of Economics* 108 (1993): 1015 (finding that UI experience rating stabilizes employment in retail trade industry); David Card and Phillip B. Levine, "Unemployment Insurance Taxes and the Cyclical and Seasonal Properties of Unemployment," *Journal of Public Economics* 53 (1994): 1 (finding that during cyclical and seasonal slumps, imperfect experience rating positively correlates with increases in temporary layoffs); see also Donald R. Deere, "Unemployment Insurance and Employment," *Journal of Labor Economics* 9 (1991): 307, 324 (finding—based on 1962–69 data from 31 states using reserve ratio experience rating—that imperfect experience rating accounted for increased hiring in construction; a 1.7% increase in share of employment; and decreased hiring in services sector—representing almost a 1% decrease in employment share).

15. For further discussion of the experience-rating controversy, see Joseph M. Becker, *Experience Rating in Unemployment Insurance: Virtue or Vice* (Kalamazoo, Mich.: W. E. Upjohn Institute for Employment Research, 1972); Joseph M. Becker, *The Problem of Abuse in Unemployment Benefits: A Study in Limits* (New York: Columbia University Press, 1953); Herman Feldman, *The Case for Experience Rating in Unemployment Compensation and A Proposed Method* (New York: Industrial Relations Counselors, Inc., 1939); Robert H. Topel, "Experience Rating of Unemployment Insurance and the Incidence of Unemployment," 27 *Journal of Law and Economics* 61 (1984).

16. Several states currently consider more than base-period earnings. Washington, New York, New Jersey, and Michigan are the major examples. U.S. Department of Labor, Employment and Training Administration, *Comparison of Unemployment Insurance Laws* (Washington, D.C., 1997), 3–27, table 301; U.S. Department of Labor, Employment and Training Administration, supplement to *Comparison of Unemployment Insurance Laws* (Washington, D.C., 1998), 3–28, table 301.

17. For discussions of the "alternative base period" that counts more recent work experience, see Planmatics, Inc., "Implementing ABP: Impact on State Agencies, Employ-

ers, and the Trust Fund," Unemployment Insurance occasional paper 98-4, U.S. Department of Labor; Washington, D.C., 1998; Wayne Vroman, "The Alternative Base Period in Unemployment Insurance: Final Report," Unemployment Insurance occasional paper 95-3, U.S. Department of Labor; Washington, D.C., 1995.

18. Complications of pregnancy are "good cause" for quitting in most states, but if the complications continue, the worker will not be considered "available for work" and will therefore usually be disqualified from receiving unemployment insurance benefits. See Amy B. Chasanov, "Nonmonetary Eligibility: State Variations and Effects," in *Advisory Council on Unemployment Compensation: Background Papers* 1 (1995): A3.

19. As with the current system, self-employed persons would not be covered by unemployment insurance. Whether a person is an employee or self-employed is sometimes a difficult judgment to make. But the unemployment insurance system is designed to insure workers against the risk of unemployment, not small businesses against the risks of failure. Nor does it seem feasible to insure workers against involuntary unemployment who can render themselves redundant by their own choice. To be sure, this leaves some earners without significant income protections related to risks that they cannot control. But this gap may have to remain unfilled. We have been unable to see how it can be remedied by unemployment insurance without making the moral hazard unbearable.

Temporary, part-time, and seasonal workers also pose difficult issues under current unemployment insurance rules. We would cover all agricultural workers, as is done in the major agricultural states today, but without the "small farm" loophole that permits easy avoidance of coverage by subcontracting to "crew chiefs." In addition, we believe that our more flexible requirements for workforce attachment would permit qualification of many temporary and part-time workers who are currently excluded. And, as with the current system, we believe that special rules are necessary to insure that seasonal workers are not viewed as unemployed when out of work because of the usual rhythms of their seasonal work, if they have every expectation of reemployment when their customary seasonal activity resumes.

20. For a similar suggestion, see Saul J. Blaustein, *Job and Income Security for Unemployed Workers: New Directions* (Kalamazoo, Mich.: W. E. Upjohn Institute for Employment Research, 1981). Because the unemployment assistance program is a "safety net" program, we propose to "income test" it by family income. Hence income from other sources, whether savings or the earnings of a spouse, would be subtracted dollar for dollar from the amounts payable under the unemployment assistance program. But because the program provides only temporary assistance—limited to one year—we would not "means-test" payments and, thereby, we avoid requiring recipients to spend down assets (if they have any) in order to qualify.

21. See Robert F. Cook et al., *The Effects of Increasing the Federal Taxable Wage Base for Unemployment Insurance,* Unemployment Insurance occasional paper 95-1, U.S. Department of Labor, Washington, D.C., 1995.

## CHAPTER 11: THE RISK OF WORK DISABILITY

1. For a comprehensive treatment of early laws, see International Labour Office, *Sickness Insurance: Comparative Analyses of National Laws, Studies and Reports on Social Insurance,* ser. M, no. 4 (Geneva: International Labour Office, 1925).

2. Leo J. M. Aarts, Richard V. Burkhauser, and Philip de Jong, *Curing the Dutch Disease: An International Perspective on Disability Policy Reform* (Aldershot, Eng.: Avebury, 1996); Deborah Stone, *The Disabled State* (Philadelphia: Temple University Press, 1984); and Edward Berkowitz, *Disabled Policy: America's Programs for the Handicapped* (Cambridge: Cambridge University Press, 1987).

3. For a more extended discussion of these matters, see Jerry L. Mashaw, "Disability: Why Does the Search for Good Programs Continue?" in Eric Kingson and James Schulz, eds., *Social Security in the Twenty-First Century* (New York: Oxford University Press, 1997), 105–26.

4. U.S. Department of Labor, *Employee Benefits in Medium and Large Establishments,* bulletin 2422 (Washington, D.C., 1991), and U.S. Department of Labor, *Employee Benefits in Small Private Establishments,* bulletin 2388 (Washington, D.C., 1990).

5. Of all clerical and sales workers, 59% have sick-leave benefits, 33% have short-term disability coverage, and only 28% have long-term disability benefits through private group policies. Blue-collar workers do worse than clerical and sales personnel with respect to sick leave and long-term disability coverage—33% and 13% have coverage, respectively—but they have slightly greater coverage for short-term disabilities.

6. Low levels of coverage are also attributable to the serious moral hazard and covariance of risks that afflict private disability insurance providers. While private insurers have worked hard to identify groups with low risks and a strong work ethic, they have failed spectacularly in a number of instances—most recently with respect to physicians. Moreover, the tendency of courts to construe insurance contracts against insurers produces an incremental "rewriting" of policies to favor policyholders who have medical difficulties and who have decided to take "early retirement." Finally, decisions to file a disability claim are often motivated by some difficulty that is common to a large number of workers, e.g., general unemployment, a decline in a particular industry, or a decline in market returns to particular occupations. In short, the risk that particular injureds will decide to apply for disability benefits are not independent; they "covary" with labor market conditions and certain other factors (e.g., epidemics). See generally Leo J. M. Aarts and Philip R. de Jong, *Economic Aspects of Disability Behavior* (Amsterdam, N.Y.: North-Holland, 1992); R. Prins, T. J. Veerman, and S. Andriessen, *Work Incapacity in a Cross-National Perspective* (The Hague: VUGA, 1992).

7. Lance Liebman, "The Definition of Disability in Social Security: Drawing the Boundaries of Social Insurance," 89 *Harvard Law Review* 883 (1976).

8. Jerry L. Mashaw, *Bureaucratic Justice: Managing Social Security Disability Claims* (New Haven and London: Yale University Press, 1983).

9. Orin Kramer and Richard Briffault, *Workers' Compensation: Strengthening the Social Compact* (New York: Insurance Information Press, 1991), 37.

10. See generally Aarts et al., *Curing the Dutch Disease.*

11. For general information on state temporary disability provisions, see Charles D. Spencer and Associates, *Spencer's Research on Employee Benefits* 359 (May 1, 1998), and All Digital Insurance Agency at http://www.alldigins.com. Specific information on the California system is at http://www.edd.cahwnet.gov.

12. U.S. Congress, Committee on Ways and Means, U.S. House of Representatives, *1998 Green Book* (Washington, D.C., May 19, 1998), table 13.1.

13. Whereas the average age of an SSDI worker beneficiary is fifty, 63% of all adult SSI disability beneficiaries are below that age.

14. See Grant M. Osborn, *Compulsory Temporary Disability Insurance in the United States* (Homewood, Ill.: R. D. Irwin, 1958).

### CHAPTER 12: FAMILIES WITH CHILDREN

1. See, e.g., Trudi J. Renwick and Barbara R. Bergman, "A Budget-Based Definition of Poverty," *Journal of Human Resources* 28 (1993): 1–24; B. R. Bergman, *Saving Our Children from Poverty* (New York: Russell Sage, 1996); Kathryn Edin and Laura Lein, *Making Ends Meet: How Single Mothers Survive Welfare and Low-Wage Work* (New York: Russell Sage Foundation, 1997); Zoë Neuberger, "Lessons from Families Leaving Welfare to Work," spring 1998, manuscript on file with authors. See also David T. Ellwood, "Working Off of Welfare: Prospects and Policies for Self-Sufficiency of Women Heading Families," discussion paper 18-68 (Madison: University of Wisconsin, Institute for Research on Poverty, 1968); S. B. Kamerman, "Gender Role and Family Structure Changes in the Advanced Industrialized West: Implications for Social Policy," in Katherine McFate, Roger Lawson, and William J. Wilson, eds., *Poverty, Inequality, and the Future of Social Policy* (New York: Russell Sage Foundation, 1995); T. J. Renwick, *Poverty and Single Parent Families: A Study of Minimal Subsistence in Household Budgets* (New York: Garland, 1998); Harrell R. Rodgers, Jr., *Poor Women, Poor Children: American Poverty in the 1990s* (Armonk, N.Y.: M. E. Sharpe, 1996).

2. Likewise, in 1997 the poverty guideline for a family of two was $10,610, and for a family of four, $16,050, regardless of the division of the family between adults and children.

3. Sara McLanahan and Karen Booth, "Mother Only Families: Problems, Prospects, and Politics," 51 *Journal of Marriage and Family* 557 (1989); Sara McLanahan, "Family Structure and the Reproduction of Poverty," *American Journal of Sociology* 90 (1985): 873–901; Irwin Garfinkel and Sara S. McLanahan, *Single Mothers and Their Children* 12–14 (Washington, D.C.: Urban Institute Press, 1986).

4. *1998 Green Book,* 870, table G-71, at 1256. Children find themselves in single parent families in the United States both because of the growth in out-of-wedlock births and the high divorce rate. The United States leads the industrial world in marriage rates, divorce rates, and out-of-wedlock birthrates. See Kamerman, "Gender Role and Family Structure Changes."

5. *1996 Green Book,* 461, table 7-26.

6. We do not discuss the adequacy of such efforts here. We regard them as relating to economic opportunity rather than economic security; see Chapter 2.

7. Families with one child and maximum earnings of less than about $12,000 (in 1997) received a maximum annual credit of about $2,200; families with two or more children received a maximum annual credit of nearly $3,700. The EITC amount is phased-down as earnings exceed $12,000, disappearing altogether when earnings reach $25,750 for a family with one child, about $30,000 for families with two or more children. The phase-out rate is at 16% for a family with one child and about 21% of earnings in excess of $12,000 for families with more than one child.

8. The law provides that no qualifying family need spend more than 30% of its income on food, but when expenses are taken into account the number is really 20–25% of income.

9. U.S. Congress, Committee on Ways and Means, U.S. House of Representatives, *1998 Green Book* (Washington, D.C., May 19, 1998), 870, table 15-11, at 949. To be eligible for food stamps, a three-person family must earn a gross income of less than $1,445 a month and generally cannot have liquid assets of more than $2,000. (For this purpose, along with virtually all types of savings, including IRAs, the value of an automobile in excess of $4,650 counts as a "liquid asset.")

The Food Stamp Program assumes that participating households can spend 30% of their monthly cash income on food purchases with food stamp benefits intended to make up the difference between this amount and an amount deemed to be sufficient to purchase an adequate low-cost diet (based on the Department of Agriculture's Thrifty Food Plan, its lowest-cost food plan). Thus the maximum amount of food stamp benefits per month is reduced by 30 cents for each dollar of a household's income. See *1998 Green Book,* 923; and James C. Ohls and Harold Baebout, *The Food Stamp Program* (Washington, D.C.: Urban Institute, 1993). But in fact, because benefits are calculated by reducing gross income by certain deductions for other necessary expenses, including child care, and because not all forms of household income are counted in determining income for food stamp purposes, food stamps make up the difference between 20–25% of a household's income and the cost of the Thrifty Food Plan (*1998 Green Book,* 923, n. 2, and 934). No household with a gross monthly income in excess of 130% of the federal poverty level, however, is eligible for food stamps. In 1998, this meant that a family of three with a gross monthly income in excess of $1,445 was not eligible; for a family of four, the monthly income ceiling was $1,739 (*1998 Green Book,* 931, table 15-5). The number of persons receiving food stamps peaked in spring 1994 at about 28 million people, more than 10% of the U.S. population (*1998 Green Book,* 941, table 15-8).

One special feature of the Food Stamp Program is that benefits and eligibility are determined on a "household" rather than family or individual basis. Thus, although there are exceptions for the elderly and disabled, the income and assets of people living together who customarily purchase food and prepare meals together is generally aggregated to determine both whether a household is eligible for food stamps and the amount they receive. While this sometimes creates disputes and raises privacy concerns, it does have the advantages of attempting to measure the income (and assets) of the relevant economic unit, avoids disincentives for marriage for people living together, and generally reflects a proper indifference regarding people's decisions about their living arrangements (see *1998 Green Book,* 928). We return to this issue in Chapter 14, where we discuss institutional alternatives for determining income in assessing eligibility and benefits of our social insurance programs for catastrophic expenditures.

10. For more on food stamps, see generally American Enterprise Institute, *Food Stamp Reform* (Washington, D.C.: American Enterprise Institute, 1977); J. M. Berry, *Feeding Hungry People: Rulemaking in the Food Stamp Program* (New Brunswick, N.J.: Rutgers University Press, 1984); J. D. Gilbert, *United States Food Stamp Program: The Changing Picture* (Monticello, Ill.: Vance Bibliographies, 1982); F. K. Hines and U.S. Department of Agriculture, Economic Service, *Factors Related to Participation in the Food Stamp Program* (Washington, D.C.: U.S. Department of Agriculture, 1975); M. Macdonald, *Food, Stamps, and Income Maintenance* (New York: Academic Press, 1977); R. Moffitt, *Has State Redistribution Policy Grown More Conservative? AFDC, Food Stamps, and Medicaid, 1960–1984* (Madison: University of Wisconsin Press, 1988); J. C. Ohls and H. Baebout, *The Food Stamp Program: Design Tradeoffs, Policy, and Impacts* (Washington, D.C.: Urban Institute Press, 1993); and P. H. Rossi, *Feeding the Poor: Assessing Federal Food Aid* (Washington, D.C.: American Enterprise Institute Press, 1997).

11. See Edin and Lein, *Making Ends Meet.*

12. See U.S. Department of Health and Human Services, Administration for Children and Families, *Child Care and Development Block Grant Report of State Plans, October 1, 1997–September 20, 1999* (Mar. 16, 1998), http://www.acf.dhhs.gov/programs/ccb/programs/plan/part3.htm.

13. CRS estimates based on March 1997 Current Population Survey, reprinted in *Tax Notes Today,* Apr. 29, 1998.

14. The Census Bureau found that child care costs for preschool age children averaged $79 a week in 1993 for all preschool age children, a more than 20% increase in constant dollars from 1986. Despite the longstanding provision of public education for children beginning at age six, public preschool education or child care for younger children is rare in the United States. The Head Start Program is the major exception, but in 1996 it served only 752,000 children from low-income families at an annual cost of $4,500 per child. As in so many areas of U.S. public policy, this contrasts sharply with the experiences of European nations. France, for example, makes government-operated child care facilities available to all working parents whose children are at least age three. But if history is a guide, the direct provision of child care (or preschool education) by federal, state, or local governments is not likely to be a major aspect of future U.S. policy.

15. The average weekly child care expenditures and percentage of income spent on care vary by poverty status and family income. Those families in poverty spend on average $49.56 a week on child care (17.7% of income); those with incomes above the poverty level spend on average $76.03 a week on child care (7.3% of income). In particular, families with monthly incomes of less than $1,200 spend on average 25.1% of their income on child care ($47.29); families with monthly incomes of $1,200–$2,999 spend an average of 12% ($69.16) on child care; those with monthly incomes of

$3,000–$4,499 spend an average of 8.5% ($73.10) on child care; and those families with monthly incomes of $4,500 or more spend an average of 5.7% ($91.93) on child care. See *1998 Green Book,* 870, table 9-9 (data are from 1993).

16. See "Congressional Budget for the United States Government for Fiscal Years 1999, 2000, 2001, 2002, and 2003," *Congressional Record,* 105th Congress, 2d sess., Mar. 30, 1998, vol. 144, S2803 (statement by Sen. Murray); Gina C. Adams and Nicole Oxendine Poersch, *Key Facts about Child Care and Early Education; A Briefing Book* (Washington, D.C.: Children's Defense Fund, 1997), table 7 (listing the unmet need for child care assistance by state in 1994).

17. *Congressional Record,* 105th Cong., 2d sess., Mar. 30, 1998, vol. 144, J 2700–701.

18. Louise Stoney and Mark H. Greenburg, "The Financing of Child Care: Current and Emerging Trends," *Future of Children: Financing Child Care* 6, no. 2 (summer/fall 1996): 84.

19. Stoney and Greenburg, "Financing of Child Care," 85. Cf. $23.6 billion from the Census Bureau in 1991.

20. *Congressional Record,* 105th Cong., 2d. sess., Mar. 30, 1998, vol. 144, J 2797–802; see also statement of Sen. Pete Domenici at J 2807.

21. The following list, from Karol Brown, "Who Cares Most for America's Children" (1998, manuscript on file with authors), illustrates the major federal sources of child care support from the federal government. Child care and development block grants, Head Start, the child and adult care food program, and social services block grants are direct outlays; the child and dependent care tax credit, child tax credit, and the exclusion of employee-provided child care are tax expenditures.

- Child care and development block grant. In this initiative, grants are given to states for child care assistance and quality improvement. The states determine their own eligibility criteria, but federal law limits them to assisting families with incomes below 85% of the state's median income. FY 1998 federal funding: $3.07 billion.
- Head Start. This is a discretionary program providing a range of services for young children. Children from birth to age five are eligible; primarily low-income children are served. FY 1998 federal funding: $4.36 billion.
- Child and adult care food program. This entitlement program provides subsidies for meals served to children in licensed child care. Children under age twelve (migrant children under age fifteen) are eligible. FY 1998 federal funding: $1.51 billion.
- Social services block grant (Title 20). Given to states, these entitlement grants may be used for child care subsidies. The states determine the eligibility of participants. FY 1998 federal funding: $2.30 billion.
- Child and dependent care tax credit. This is a nonrefundable tax credit. Taxpayers with qualifying employment-related child care expenses are eligible. FY 1998 federal funding: $2.80 billion.
- Child tax credit. All families with children under age 17 are eligible for this credit. FY 1998 federal funding: $12.20 billion.
- Exclusion of employee-provided child care. This program excludes child care benefits provided by employers. Taxpayers with qualifying child care benefits provided by

their employers are affected. Qualifying child care benefits include employer-provided child care purchased through dependent care flexible spending accounts. FY 1998 federal funding: $0.90 billion.

22. *1998 Green Book*, 500.
23. Lynn M. Casper, "What Does It Cost to Mind Our Preschoolers?" *Current Population Survey* (September 1995).
24. Department of Health and Human Services, *Child Care and Development Block Grant, Report of State Plans, October 1, 1997–September 30, 1999* (Washington, D.C., 1999), pt. 3.
25. Ann Dryden Witte et al., "Unintended Consequences: Welfare Reform and the Working Poor," August 1998, manuscript on file with authors.
26. The amount that we have set for the tax credit is by its very nature arbitrary. Having no better rationale than continuity, we have simply chosen the amount currently made available through the tax code. The difference, and it is not a small one, is that our scheme pays tax credits to families who pay no income tax.
27. The first effort by the federal government to intervene directly to attempt to improve the housing stock of the nation's major cities was inspired by a 1908 report by President Theodore Roosevelt's Housing Commission. After a decade of debate, Congress created the U.S. Housing Corporation, which built and managed more than 5,000 single family homes and numerous multi-family housing units. As with most social insurance legislation, the period 1932–37 was a watershed. In 1932, Congress created the Reconstruction Finance Corporation to make loans and to fund directly low-income housing for the poor. The Federal Home Loan Bank Act of 1932 and the Homeowners' Loan Act of 1933 reorganized the nation's system for providing for housing loans, establishing both the Federal Home Loan Bank Board and creating the savings and loan industry. The National Industrial Recovery Act of 1933 began a program of public housing as part of a broader system of Depression-era public employment. The National Housing Act of 1934 created the Federal Housing Administration and originated federal government insurance for mortgages made by private lenders for low-interest loans to farmers, and the Housing Act of 1937 assisted the development, acquisition, and administration of housing for low-income families. During the 1940s and 1950s, federal housing and development programs were extended, reorganized, and liberalized, and new programs for housing the low-income elderly were added. World War II produced temporary rent controls as well as legislation intended to create substantial numbers of new housing units. The urban renewal program began with the Housing Act of 1949, which added more than 800,000 public housing units. This act also created the Farmers' Home Administration to provide direct loans for housing in rural and farm areas.

During the 1960s, other major housing initiatives were launched. Less than two months after his inauguration, President Kennedy declared the provision of decent housing for all Americans to be a national objective, proposed a variety of new housing programs, and sought the creation of a new cabinet-level Department of Housing and Urban Affairs (HUD). Beginning with the Housing Act of 1961, Congress throughout the 1960s broadened existing federal housing programs, created new federal rent and loan subsidies, and established HUD as a cabinet-level department in 1965.

28. Between 1994 and 1997, Congress authorized between $2.5 billion and nearly $4 billion for such expenditures. Per-unit operating and modernization subsidies quadrupled between 1980 and 1997.

29. John C. Weicher, *Privatizing Subsidized Housing* (Washington, D.C.: American Enterprise Press, 1997), 15, 45.

30. In 1997, these tax benefits were estimated to total about $1.8 billion.

31. There are some differences between the certificate program, which was enacted in 1974, and the voucher program, added in 1983, but these are not generally relevant here. For example, the voucher program gives the family wider options for housing than does the certificate program and allows the family to keep any savings from finding housing at less than the fair market rent.

32. *1998 Green Book,* tables 15-28 and 15-29. In recent years, Congress has curtailed project-based support in favor of Section 8 vouchers and certificates subsidizing low-income families' rentals of existing housing, which it has found to be more cost effective. In 1995 and 1996, however, funds were appropriated to replace public housing units that were to be demolished. Even though HUD had proposed to demolish and replace 84,000 units (at a cost of $100,000 a unit, totaling $8.4 billion), it received funding to demolish only 19,000 units, to be replaced by 11,000 new units and 4,000 tenant-based certificates. See Weicher, *Privatizing Subsidized Housing,* 34.

33. Weicher, *Privatizing Subsidized Housing,* 33.

34. In 1997, the total number of assisted renters was 5,120,000; the total number of assisted homeowners was 631,000. Of those assisted (both renters and homeowners), 1,465,000 were in household-based homes (existing housing); 586,000 were in project-based homes (existing housing); and 3,305,000 were in newly constructed homes. See *1998 Green Book,* table 15 26.

35. Joint Center for Housing Studies of Harvard University, *The State of the Nation's Housing* (Cambridge: Joint Center for Housing Studies of Harvard University, 1998), 3; http://www.gsd.harvard.edu/jcenter/sonh1998/index.htm.

36. *1998 Green Book,* table 1-22; National Association of Home Builders, www.nahb.com/gap.html.

37. National Association of Home Builders, www.nahb.com/gap.html. Younger families in particular struggle to achieve home ownership. For example, in 1996 about 65% of families owned their own homes, but for families where the head of household is between thirty and thirty-five years of age, just over half of households owned their own homes, and for households where the head was between age twenty-five and thirty only about one-third lived in owner-occupied homes (see U.S. Census Bureau, www.nahb.com/ownership.html).

The pattern of higher-income families owning their homes, with low- and moderate-income families renting, has continued for some time. During the period 1985–95, the number of renter households with incomes above 120% of the area's median income declined by more than 5%, while, in contrast, the number of very-low-income renter households (households where members earn less than 50% of the area median) grew by 13.5% to a total of 14.4 million households in 1985. Within this group, there was a nearly 25% increase (774,000 households) in the number of very-low-income single-parent families (Joint Center for Housing Studies, *The State of the Nation's Housing* [Cambridge, Mass.: Joint Center for Housing Studies, 1997], table A-3).

While the standard vision of low-income renters is that they live in urban centers, this paints an incomplete picture. During the decade 1985–95, the number of very-low-income renters in the suburbs grew by nearly one-third, and such renters now account for one-tenth of suburban households. By comparison, very-low-income renters now account for one-fourth of households in center cities.

38. Joint Center for Housing Studies, *State of the Nation's Housing*, 35. Roughly 60% of renters with an annual income under $17,000 spent more than half their annual incomes on rent in 1995. Six million households—82%—spent more than 30% of their income on rent and utilities that year. Even among renter families with children with earnings of $12,000 or less but with earnings equal to at least the full-time year-round minimum wage, about one-third paid more than 50% of their income on housing (Joint Center for Housing Studies, *State of the Nation's Housing*, 28).

39. Joint Committee on Taxation Tax Expenditure Estimates, *Tax Notes Today*, Nov. 27, 1998. Deductions for interest to acquire a home are permitted for mortgages up to $1 million, and interest on home equity borrowing up to $100,000 is also deductible without regard to how the borrowed funds are used.

40. As other commentators—and five of the past six administrations—have suggested, we would also replace public housing and project-based subsidized private vouchers with tenant-based vouchers. By ensuring that low-income families can afford their housing, however, these units are currently performing an important social insurance function.

41. In 1996, nearly 200,000 children under age eighteen received monthly benefits averaging $441, and an additional 100,000 students under age twenty received survivors' benefits that averaged nearly $550 a month (*Social Security Bulletin, 1997 Annual Statistical Supplement,* table 6D-5). In addition, nearly 45,000 widowed mothers and fathers received an average monthly survivor's benefit of $486 in 1996. More than three-quarters of these widowed parents are under age forty-five. Thus, for dual-parent families eligible for survivors' insurance under Social Security, benefits averaging nearly $900 a month are paid to widows or widowers and their children.

42. McLanahan and Garfinkel, "Single Mother Families and Social Policy," 367.

43. M. A. Pirog, M. Klotz, and K. V. Beyers, *Interstate Comparisons of Child Support Awards Using State Guidelines* (Bloomington: Indiana University Press, 1997).

**CHAPTER 13: RETIREMENT SECURITY**

1. Couples with more than $3,000 in assets or $705 a month in income do not qualify for SSI; single persons cannot have more than $2,000 in assets and $500 in monthly income.

2. Data in the text, as most data about the elderly, are based on income levels, but a substantial number of retirees own homes with no mortgages and few have work or child-

related expenses. This is why many analysts prefer looking to the power to consume rather than income to assess the well-being of the elderly population.

3. See, e.g., Eric R. Kingson and James H. Schulz, eds., *Social Security in the Twenty-First Century* (New York: Oxford University Press, 1997).

4. Michael J. Boskin, "Toward a More Accurate Measure of the Cost of Living," Advisory Commission to Study the Consumer Price Index, U.S. Senate Finance Committee (Washington, D.C., Sept. 15, 1995).

5. Under current law, workers born before 1938 will have a normal retirement age of sixty-five, workers born during the period 1944–54 will have a normal retirement age of sixty-six, and workers born after 1960 will have a normal retirement age of sixty-seven.

6. See generally Scott Christofferson, "Why Sixty-Five? A Normative Case for Raising the Retirement Age," 1996, manuscript on file with authors. For example, life expectancy for males was about sixty years when Social Security was first enacted; today it is about seventy-three.

7. Congressional Budget Office, *Long-Term Budgetary Pressures and Policy Options* (Washington, D.C., May 1998), 39. In 1940 two-thirds of the men age sixty-five and over were still working. By 1960, when Social Security began to mature, labor force participation of men age sixty-five and over had dropped to about 33%. Throughout the nineties it has been about 17%. Labor force participation for men age 55–64 has also declined markedly.

8. The National Bureau of Economic Research has conducted a study comparing Social Security programs internationally. See Jonathan Gruber and David A. Wise, *Social Security and Retirement around the World* (Chicago: University of Chicago Press, 1999).

9. Ibid. At the turn of the century, Theodore Roosevelt recognized the link between disability and retirement in designing pensions for Civil War veterans. He issued a Presidential Order (which was enacted by Congress in 1907) providing that at age sixty-two, a veteran would be considered "disabled one-half in ability"; at sixty-five, two-thirds incapacitated; and after seventy, would be treated as totally disabled. Carol Haber, *Beyond Sixty-Five: The Dilemma of Old Age in America's Past* (Cambridge: Cambridge University Press, 1983), 112. Although we would increase the normal retirement age to age seventy, earlier retirement would be permitted at earlier ages—perhaps as early as age sixty-two—with actuarially appropriate reductions in retirement benefits.

10. While some proponents of funded individual accounts are principally interested in individual accounts as a mechanism for increasing national savings and potentially improving economic growth in the future, that is not our focus here—although we of course regard greater economic growth as a worthy and important goal.

11. See Theodore Angelis, presenter, and Warren L. Batts, discussant, "Public Investment in Private Markets," in *Framing the Social Security Debate* (Washington, D.C.: National Academy of Social Insurance, 1988).

12. Alan Greenspan, testimony before the Senate Banking Committee, July 21, 1998.

13. Congressional Budget Office, *The Economic and Budget Outlook 2000–2009* (Washington, D.C., January 1999). This estimate is up from a $1.5 trillion estimate in January

1998. Fully funding a mandatory individual retirement account at 2% of payroll up to the Social Security wage base could be accomplished using about half of the projected surpluses.

14. Only 8% of nonagricultural workers earning less than $10,000 a year are covered by employer-sponsored pension plans, compared to 60% of those earning between $20,000 and $50,000 annually and 80% of those earning $50,000 a year or more. For example, coverage was only 34% for workers ages twenty-one to thirty compared to more than 60% for those ages forty-one to sixty in 1994. Pension coverage is much higher for government employees, who enjoy 75–85% coverage compared to 50% for full-time employees of private enterprises. See Employee Benefit Research Institute, *Databook on Employee Benefits*, Deborah Holmes et al., eds., 4th ed. (Washington, D.C.: EBRI, 1998), ch. 10.

15. Ibid., table 4.7 and p. 81.

16. David I. Halperin, "Special Tax Treatment for Employer-Based Retirement Programs," *Tax Law Review* 49 (1993): 1.

17. Peter Diamond, "The Economics of Social Security Reform," in R. Douglas Arnold, Michael J. Graetz, and Alicia H. Munnell, eds., *Framing the Social Security Debate* (Washington, D.C.: National Academy of Social Insurance, 1988).

18. Fred T. Goldberg, Jr. and Michael J. Graetz, "Reforming Social Security: A Practical and Workable System of Personal Retirement Accounts," working paper no. 6970, National Bureau of Economic Research (Cambridge, Mass., 1999).

19. Most defined-benefit plans require a minimum of five years of service before the employee is eligible for any benefit. They also require that an employee reach a certain age—usually sixty-five—before receiving benefits pursuant to the plan formula, although some allow earlier retirement for workers with some specified combination of age and longevity of employment. Because private defined-benefit plans, unlike Social Security, do not follow workers from job to job, workers assume the risks of job turnover. In some cases, changing jobs will mean that a worker loses benefits entirely. Even when it does not, workers typically lose retirement benefits from changing jobs because the amount of benefits depend on the level of wages up to the time the worker leaves employment. Workers with multiple employers will tend to receive lower retirement benefits than those who stay with one employer, even if their earnings histories are identical. Workers also bear risks that their employers will go out of business, terminate their pension plans, inadequately fund them, or go bankrupt, although federal pension guarantee insurance protects workers somewhat from the risks of bankruptcy and underfunding. Workers in defined-benefit plans also bear the risk that the employer will change the benefit formula for future years and, by doing so, decrease the employee's retirement income.

Defined-contribution plans, by contrast, simply set aside an amount of funds in a retirement account for each employee. The fund available at retirement depends upon the amounts set aside, their rates of return, and the duration of the investment. In many defined-contribution plans, vesting is immediate. Workers tend to "own" their accounts and therefore suffer no loss upon changing jobs. But workers in defined-contribution plans generally bear greater financial risks than do workers covered by defined-benefit plans, where the investment risks and rewards tend to accrue to the employer. People with different investment experience may have significantly different retirement incomes. Short-term market corrections may also disadvantage participants in defined-contribution plans if the "correction" occurs near or during retirement.

Workers in both kinds of plans face some risks of inflation, particularly of inflation during the retirement years. For participants in defined-contribution plans, the decisions in 1997 and 1998 by the U.S. Treasury to offer inflation-indexed bonds offer retirees some opportunity to reduce or eliminate the inflation risk.

20. See EBRI, *Databook on Employee Benefits,* table 17.2.

21. Congressional Budget Office, *Long-Term Budgetary Pressures and Policy Options* (Washington, D.C., May 1998), 11.

22. See Chapter 9. In 1997 Congress introduced into Medicare "medical savings accounts" (MSAs), which allow retirees to capture a portion of their Medicare benefits in tax-free savings accounts, which are combined with high-deductible insurance policies that provide coverage against catastrophic medical expenditures. The deductible is expected to be paid out of savings built up in the medical savings account. Such an account permits both tax-free accumulations of investment income and tax-free withdrawals to pay medical expenses. There is one critical difference between medical savings accounts and our plan. On a voluntary basis, medical savings accounts, like managed care, are most attractive for the lowest-risk part of the eligible population. In Medicare, this tends to be the youngest group and those without chronic or acute illnesses. As presently constituted, both MSAs and managed care seem likely to segment the Medicare population into the kinds of risk pools that differ according to health risks. This kind of risk segmentation has been common in private health insurance and has often been prohibited through federal and state regulation. But if a sufficiently large number of relatively healthy Medicare enrollees establish MSAs so that a mandatory move in this direction for all beneficiaries becomes an incremental change, the MSA experiment may point the way to the kind of policy shift that we are urging here.

23. We do not have actuarial estimates of the costs of catastrophic health insurance for the over-sixty-five population as we do for the population under age sixty-five, so it is not possible for us to make estimates as detailed as we did in Chapter 9 of the relationship of the costs of the program we are advocating here for the over-sixty-five population relative to existing Medicare and Medicaid coverage. The costs of existing programs are so large and the current out-of-pocket health care expenditures so great, however, that we can be reasonably confident that our program can be funded without increasing the burdens on the elderly population beyond what will inevitably occur under Medicare and Medicaid.

In 1995, for example, Medicare spent an average of more than $4,800 per enrollee (approximately 33 million persons), and this amounted to only 55% of the health care expenditures of the over-sixty-five population (*1998 Green Book,* 105–6, 1056). Medicaid contributed an additional 14 percent of total health care expenditures of this population, nearly $8,900 apiece for the 4,100,000 Medicaid recipients over age sixty-five (*1998 Green Book,* 970–71, 979). The beneficiaries financed 20% of these costs out-of-pocket and 10 percent through private supplemental—"Medigap"—insurance (*1998*

*Green Book,* 1056). Beneficiaries are estimated to spend on average more than $2,500 each out-of-pocket for their health care. See *1998 Green Book,* 1056; and Marilyn Moon, C. Kuntz, and L. Pounder, *Protecting Low-Income Medicare Beneficiaries* (New York: Commonwealth Fund, December 1996). Moreover, out-of-pocket spending in 1996 represented an average of 21% of household income, with a very regressive distribution: 11% for high-income elderly, 18% for the middle-income, 26% for the low-income, and 31% for the near-poor elderly (Moon et al., *Protecting Low-Income Medicare Beneficiaries; 1998 Green Book,* 1056–57). To qualify for Medicaid's more extensive coverage, you have to be poor.

24. In 1988 Congress enacted the Medicare Catastrophic Coverage Act to substantially expand prescription drug and catastrophic health benefits provided to the elderly under Medicare. To avoid having these new Medicare benefits significantly increase federal deficits, Congress insisted that the elderly pay for them, principally through an additional tax calculated as a percentage of each elderly person's income tax liability. Because this was a progressive tax, most elderly people would have come out ahead, paying relatively little for the additional health coverage, but others—a very vocal minority, as it turned out—would have had to pay considerably more in taxes than the value of the benefits they would get. The net additional tax was as high as $1,000 a year for some people.

   Many higher-income elderly people already had private insurance coverage for drugs and catastrophic medical expenses through their former employers or private Medigap insurance coverage. They saw only pain and no gain from this legislation. In addition, the calculations required to determine the additional tax due were so complex that they made filing an elderly person's health insurance claims look like a walk in the park.

   The Medicare Catastrophic Coverage Act quickly became a political catastrophe. One Thursday morning, August 17, 1989, an angry group of elderly constituents trapped Dan Rostenkowski, the Ways and Means Committee chairman, in his car in his hometown of Chicago, and wouldn't let him out. Many shouted "Liar," "Coward," "Recall," and "Impeach." One petite elderly woman, Leona Kozien, threw herself—and her sign reading "Seniors for Repeal of the Catastrophic Act"—on the hood of Rostenkowski's car. The six-foot, four-inch Rostenkowski managed to escape on foot, and his driver later picked him up at a nearby gas station. Ms. Kozien later admitted that she had been nervous about the protest, but insisted that Rostenkowski had been far more frightened than she. These events were recounted in numerous newspaper accounts, the best of which is William Rectenwald, "Insurance Forum Turns Catastrophic for Rostenkowski," *Chicago Tribune,* Aug. 18, 1989, p. 1. It was an incident that traumatized Rostenkowski, and one that all of his congressional colleagues feared might happen to them.

25. Managed care has recently served as the most frequent answer to both cost issues and coverage gaps in Medicare. Although some managed-care Medicare plans now provide prescription drugs and limits on catastrophic costs in addition to the basic Medicare coverage for Medicare payments, managed care has not penetrated the health market for the elderly nearly to extent that it has for workers. In fact, much Medicare enrollment in managed care seems to reflect an effort by managed care organizations to

"cream" the most favorable health insurance risks, and adverse experience in some managed care Medicare plans has forced their sponsors to cut back on the promised benefits or shut down the plans.

26. Joshua M. Weiner and David G. Stevenson, "State Policy on Long-Term Care for the Elderly," *Health Affairs* 17 (May–June 1998): 81–100.

27. P. Kemper and C. M. Murtaugh, "Lifetime Use of Nursing Home Care," *New England Journal of Medicine* 324, no. 9 (1991).

28. Joshua M. Weiner and David G. Stevenson, *Long-Term Care for the Elderly: Profiles of Thirteen States* (Washington, D.C.: Urban Institute, August 1998).

29. *1998 Green Book,* 1064.

30. This favorable treatment covers health and personal care services provided to a chronically ill person under a plan prescribed by a licensed health care professional. The tax law here piggybacks on other legal tests of disability for functional impairments and a requirement that eligible individuals be unable to perform at least two of the following "activities of daily living": bathing, dressing, transferring (such as from bed to a chair), toileting, eating, and continence.

31. *1998 Green Book,* 1059.

32. See, e.g., J. M. Weiner, C. M. Sullivan, and J. Skaggs, *Spending Down to Medicaid: New Data on the Role of Medicaid in Paying for Nursing Home Care* (Washington, D.C.: American Association of Retired Persons, June 1996). In 1993 and 1997, Congress enacted a series of provisions intended to close loopholes that allowed elderly people to shelter or divest assets in order to become eligible for Medicaid long-term care, but these rules are far from a complete solution; they generally apply only to asset transfers within three years of an application for Medicaid coverage.

33. *1998 Green Book,* 1067.

34. Ibid. For an excellent treatment of long-term care laws and policies, see Raymond C. O'Brien and Michael J. Flannery, *Long-Term Care: Federal, State, and Private Options for the Future* (New York: Hayworth Press, 1997).

35. Joshua M. Weiner, Laurel H. Illston, and Raymond J. Hawley, *Sharing the Burden: Strategies for Public and Private Long-Term Care Insurance* (Washington, D.C.: Brookings Institution, 1994), 41, 171.

36. This estimate is the authors' calculation based on the cost of long-term care protection offered to Yale University employees by UNUM Insurance Company and is based on coverage of either (1) $1,000 a month for six years of care in a nursing facility and total coverage of home health care, both after a ninety-day waiting period with a $72,000 lifetime maximum, or (2) $1,000 a month of facility care and 50% of home health care of unlimited duration and no lifetime ceiling. Both plans are inflation protected.

37. Defining exactly what is covered under long-term care insurance is an extremely difficult matter. The need to expand home health care services exacerbates these problems. There seem to be two basic approaches. One is to explicitly define services covered under the long-term care policy. To date, this has been done by requiring that services be provided by medical personnel, often only in nursing homes, but more and more covered services include care in homes as well. Requiring that services be provided by medical personnel has the effect of increasing the per-instance cost of providing ser-

vices that might be provided by lower-cost workers, but saves the costs of insuring most custodial services and companionship.

An alternative is to limit long-term care insurance to a specific dollar ceiling and require copayments as a means of limiting the moral hazard. This approach also has problems. Clearly the dollar amount must be higher for needed nursing home expenses than for home care expenses. It is difficult to set ceilings that are sufficiently high to provide true security without encouraging unnecessary expenditures. Because the social insurance goal of insuring income adequacy and protecting against large shocks to one's standard of living can be served by prefunding and spreading risks of long-term care expenditures up to a specified dollar ceiling, this is the course we tentatively recommend. A ceiling of about $500,000 (adjusted for future inflation) will cover up to eleven years in a nursing home at today's average costs, and a ceiling of $100,000 (20% of the nursing home amount) seems a reasonable limit on home care expenditures.

## CHAPTER 14: INSTITUTIONAL COMMITMENTS

1. See, e.g., Daniel Shaviro, "The Minimum Wage, the Earned Income Tax Credit, and Optimal Subsidy Policy," *University of Chicago Law Review* 64 (1997): 405.

2. Alvin K. Klevorick, "The Race to the Bottom in a Federal System: Lessons from the World of Trade Policy," *Yale Law and Policy Review* 14 (1996): 177.

3. On how individual accounts can be implemented, see Fred T. Goldberg, Jr. and Michael J. Graetz, "Reforming Social Security: A Practical and Workable System of Personal Retirement Accounts," working paper no. 6970, National Bureau of Economic Research (Cambridge, Mass., 1999).

4. Leslie Lenkowsky, *Politics, Economics and Welfare Reform* (Washington, D.C.: American Enterprise Institute, 1986), 35.

5. Daniel Shaviro has recently attempted a rather comprehensive analysis of existing programs, but as he recognizes, general calculations are virtually impossible. See, e.g., Daniel Shaviro, "Effective Marginal Rates on Low-Income Households," 1998, manuscript on file with authors; and Shaviro, "Minimum Wage."

6. Alan J. Auerbach and Laurence J. Kotlikoff, *Dynamic Fiscal Policy* (New York: Cambridge University Press, 1987).

7. Marginal tax rates are for a family headed by a single adult who works full-time year round and has two children. The rates take into account loss of benefits as well as payroll and income taxes. The income levels considered were chosen based on where implicit marginal tax rates change under current programs. Current marginal tax rates are for a family living in a state with relatively high TANF benefits and receiving a housing subsidy. If the same family were to be living in a low-TANF state, the first cliff loss would occur at $7,500 annual income, and the marginal tax rates for the annual income range of $10,300–$12,849 would be 58.4% and for $12,850–$14,350 would be 78.0%—lower than in a state with high TANF benefits, but higher than under our proposals.

There are no estimates of the current marginal tax rates for married couples with children. Under our proposals, however, if a single person were to marry someone who did not work but cared for the children full-time, or if a married couple had a combined annual income in the ranges shown but continued to require full-time child care, the marginal tax rates would be significantly lower (9–17%) than they would be for a single parent in the $14,700–$19,449 income range under our proposals. At the other income levels shown, the marginal tax rate would be nearly identical. If both parents were working, needed part-time child care, and had a combined annual income in the ranges shown, the marginal tax rates would be higher than for a single parent under our proposals, but the exact rates would depend on their specific work schedules and need for child care.

8. Although there has been some concern about an unacceptably high level of both overpayments and underpayments of the EITC, we believe the blame lies in Congress's willingness to tolerate a level of complexity more consonant with taxing financial or business transactions than delivering social insurance benefits.

9. Anne L. Alstott, "The Earned Income Tax Credit and the Limitations on Tax-Based Welfare Reform," *Harvard Law Review* 108 (1995): 533.

10. Shaviro, "Minimum Wage."

11. See, e.g., Christopher Howard, *The Hidden Welfare State: Tax Incentives and Social Policy in the United States* (Princeton, N.J.: Princeton University Press, 1997), 17.

## EPILOGUE: REVISING OLD FABLES

1. Craig Pleasants, *The "Three Little Pigs" as It Was Originally Passed into English Folklore in 1620* (Richmond, Va.: Gates of Heck, 1994).

# Index